DAYTIME SHOOTING STAR

Story & Art by
Mika Yamamori

12

DAYTIME SHOOTING STAR

Story & Art by
Mika Yamamori

CONTENTS

STORY THUS FAR

Suzume Yosano is a second-year in high school. Born in the country, she grew up living a free and easy life. Due to family circumstances, she was forced to transfer to a school in Tokyo. Lost on her first day in the city, she is found by a man who later turns out to be her homeroom teacher, Mr. Shishio. Suzume gradually develops feelings for him, but he ends up breaking her heart—twice.

Not long after Suzume decides to focus her attention solely on Mamura, Mr. Shishio declares his love for her. But before he can finish, Suzume interrupts him and scurries off to Mamura's side. However, Mamura isn't being his usual self...

Suzume invites Mamura to come with her on their summer trip to Okinawa, but he turns her down. Instead of giving up, she asks him again, and he finally agrees. Thanks to this, Suzume happily realizes that she can get things to go her way if she just remains resolute.

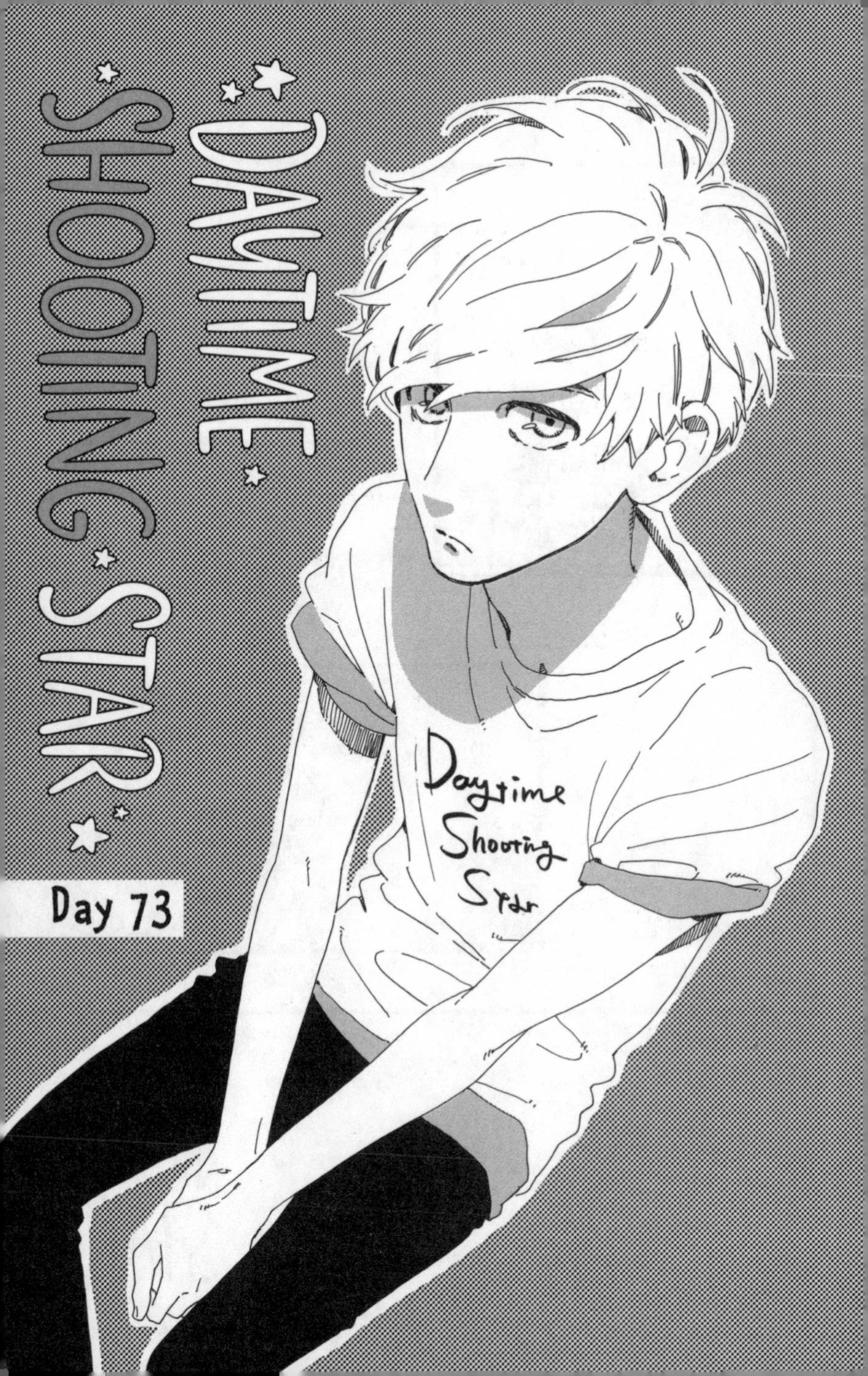
DAYTIME SHOOTING STAR
Day 73
Daytime Shooting Star

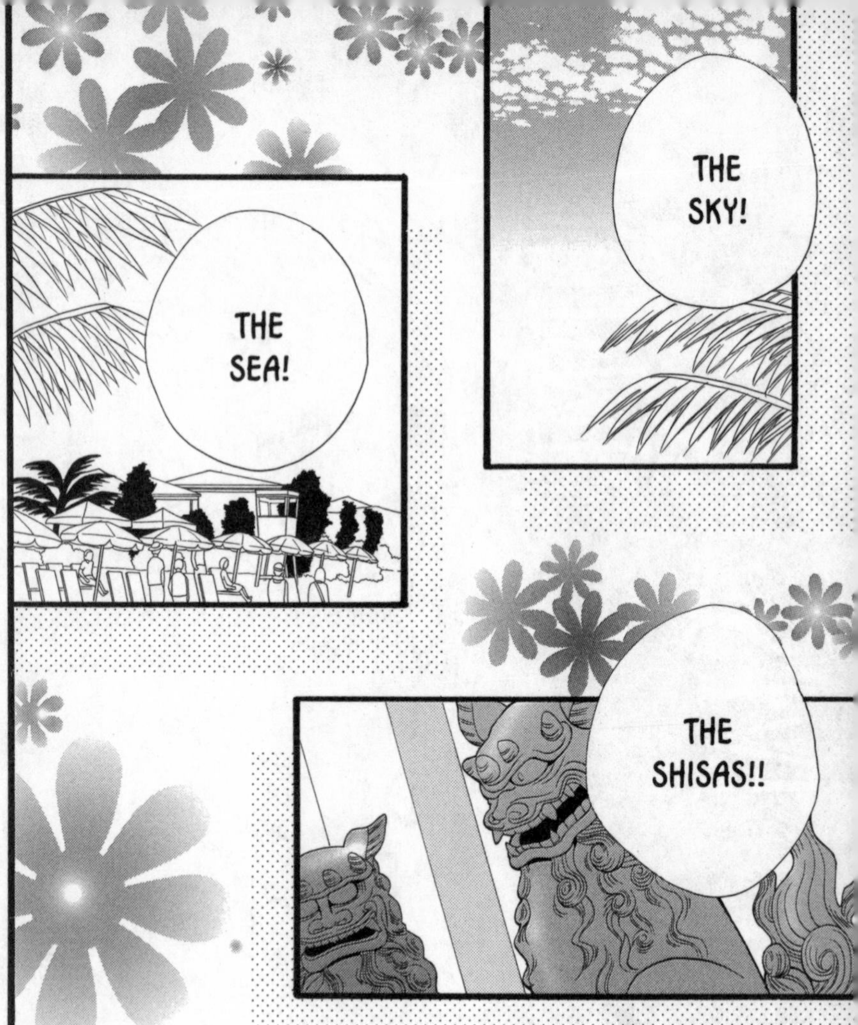
THE SKY!
THE SEA!
THE SHISAS!!

DAYTIME SHOOTING STAR

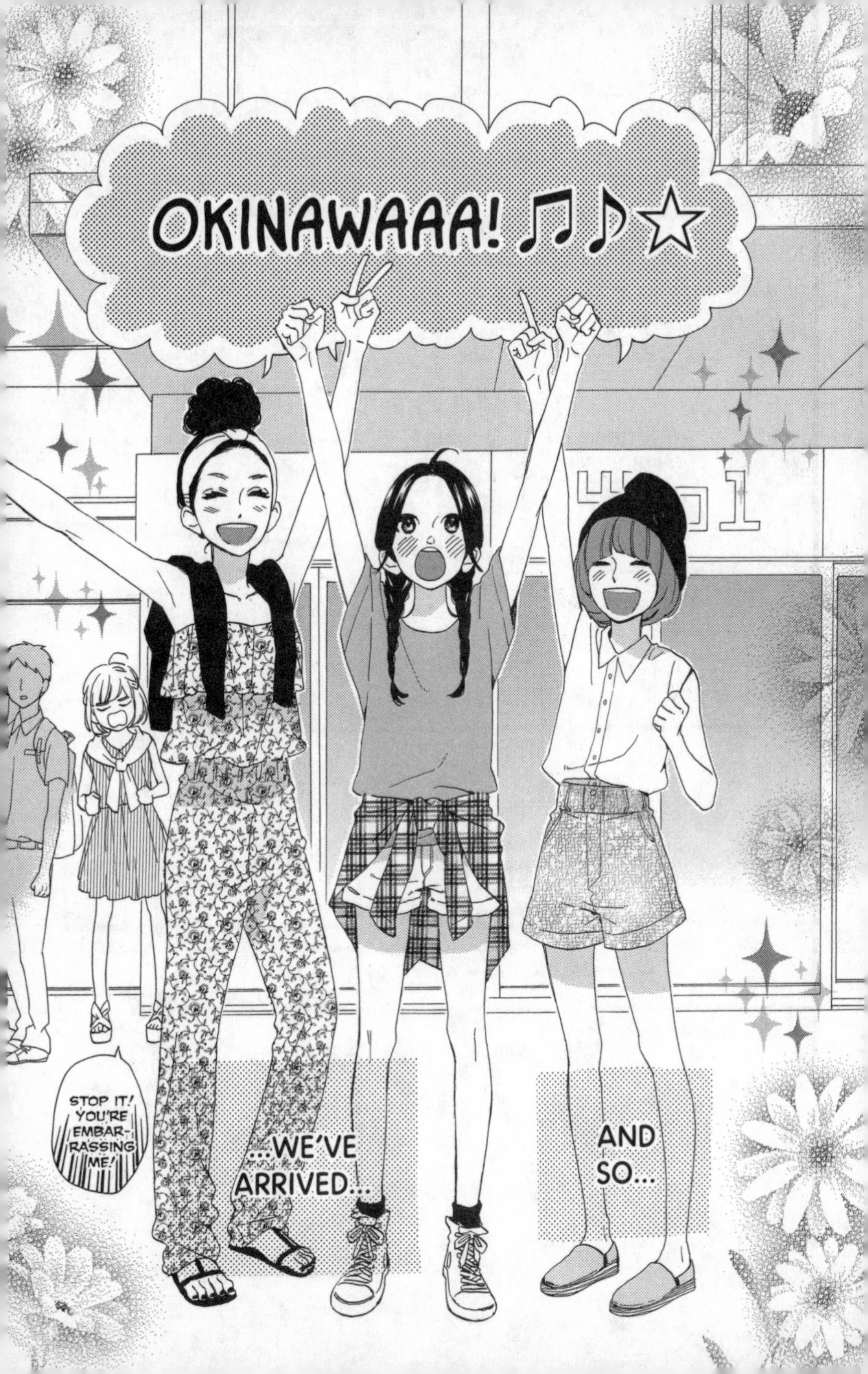
OKINAWAAA! ♫♪☆
AND SO...
...WE'VE ARRIVED...
STOP IT! YOU'RE EMBARRASSING ME!

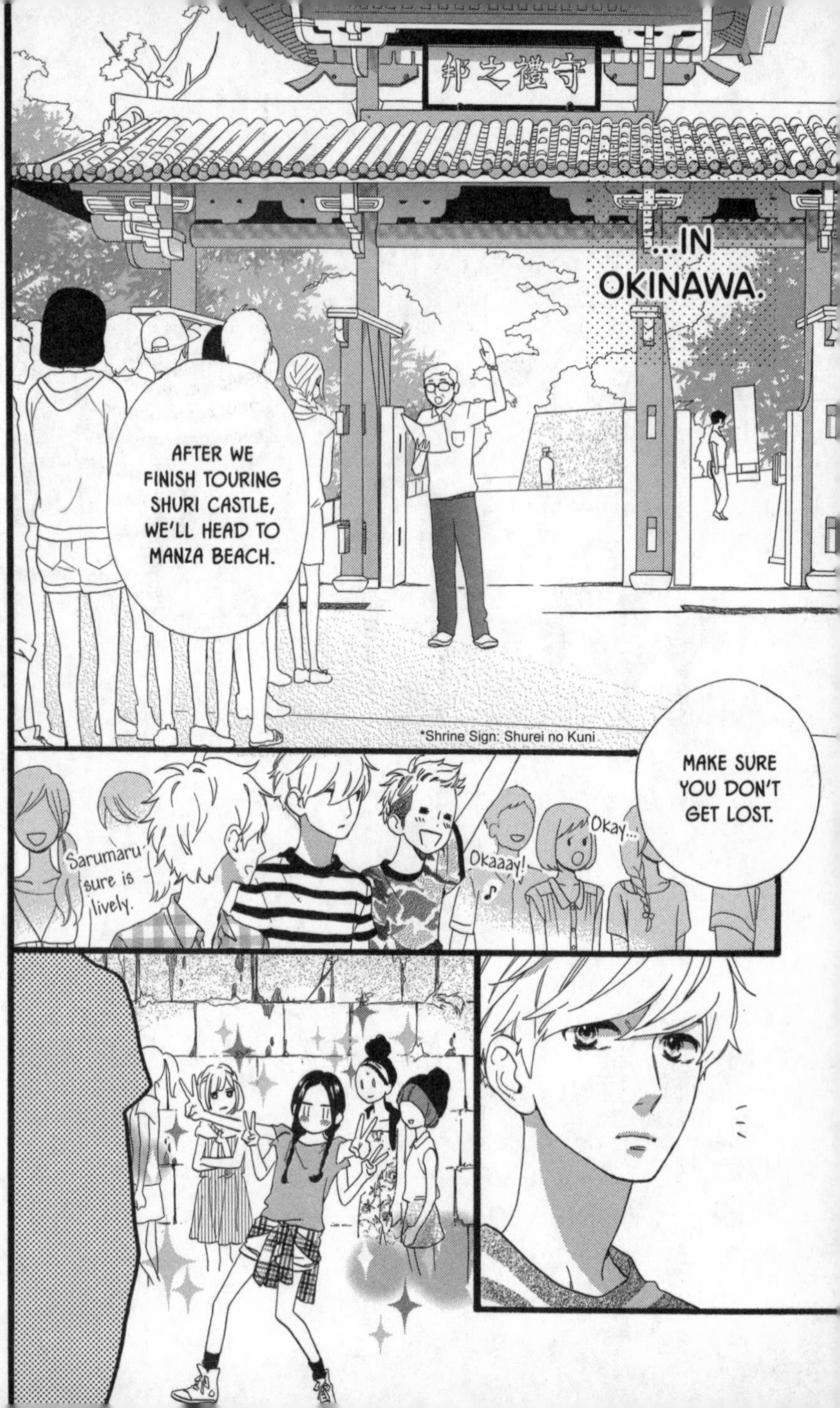
守禮之邦
...IN OKINAWA.
AFTER WE FINISH TOURING SHURI CASTLE, WE'LL HEAD TO MANZA BEACH.
*Shrine Sign: Shurei no Kuni
MAKE SURE YOU DON'T GET LOST.
Okay...
Okaaay! ♪
Sarumaru sure is lively.

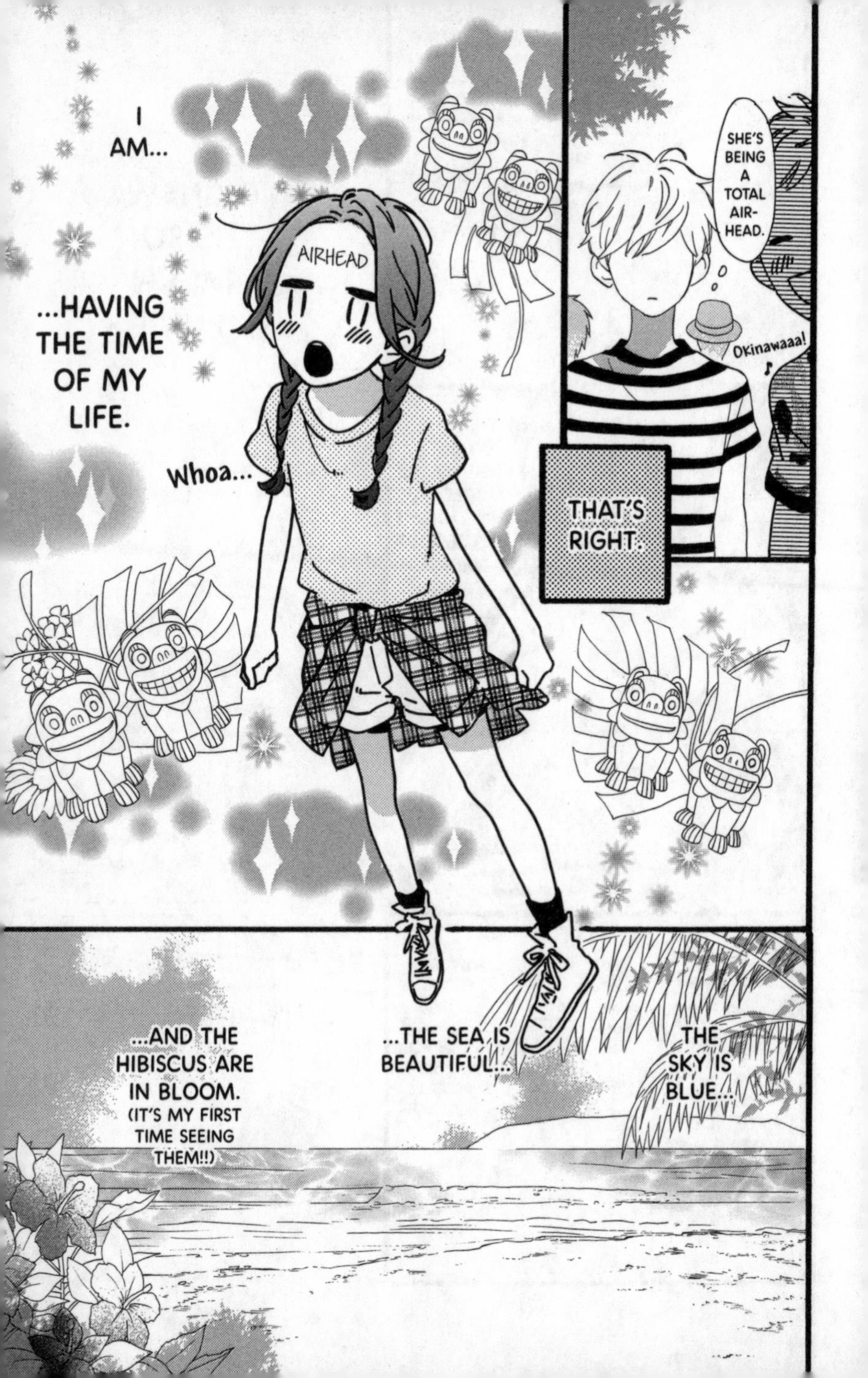
SHE'S BEING A TOTAL AIR-HEAD.
Okinawaaa!
THAT'S RIGHT.
I AM...
AIRHEAD
...HAVING THE TIME OF MY LIFE.
Whoa...
THE SKY IS BLUE...
...THE SEA IS BEAUTIFUL...
...AND THE HIBISCUS ARE IN BLOOM.
(IT'S MY FIRST TIME SEEING THEM!!)

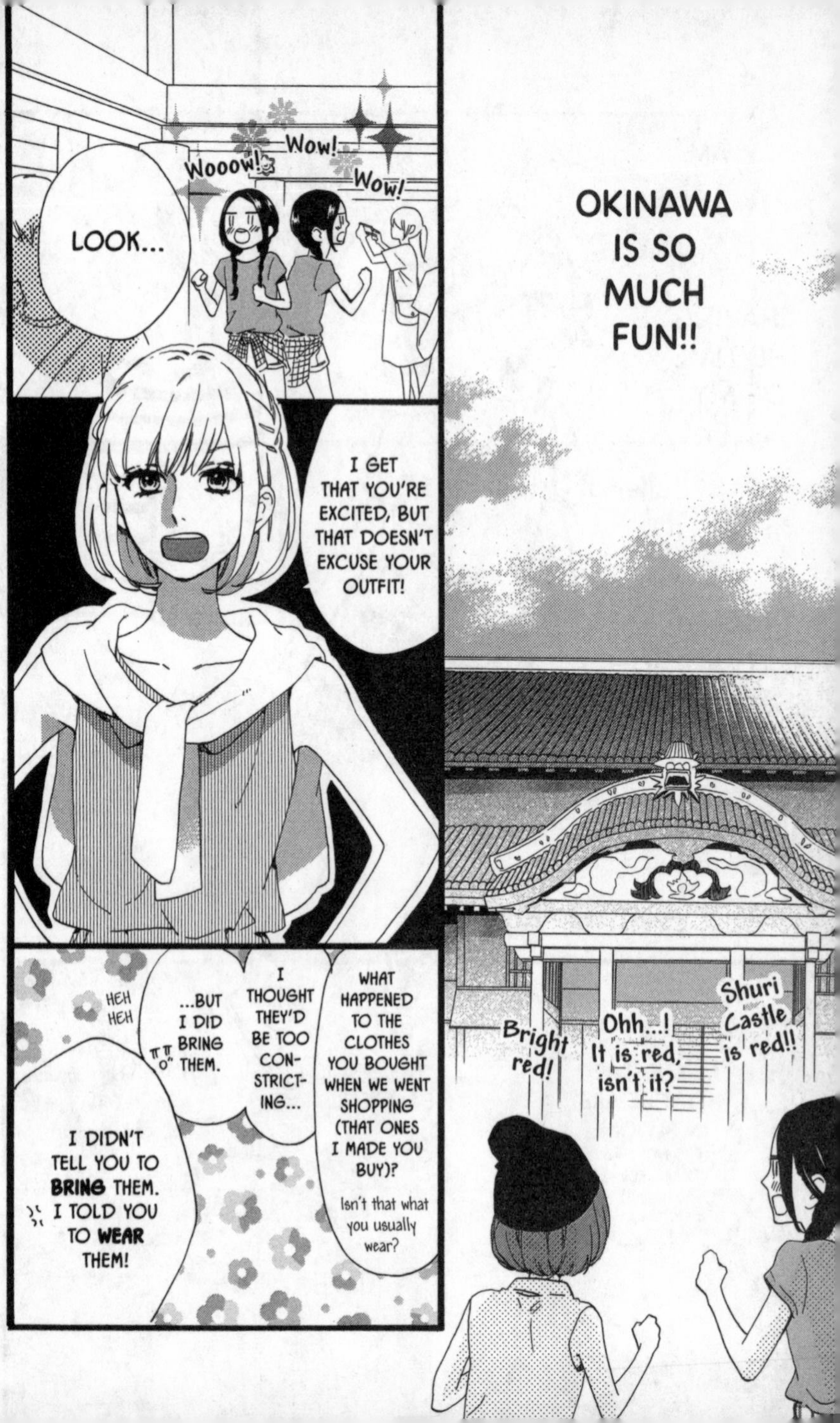
OKINAWA IS SO MUCH FUN!!
Shuri Castle is red!!
Ohh...! It is red, isn't it?
Bright red!
Wow!
Wow!
Wooow!
LOOK...
I GET THAT YOU'RE EXCITED, BUT THAT DOESN'T EXCUSE YOUR OUTFIT!
WHAT HAPPENED TO THE CLOTHES YOU BOUGHT WHEN WE WENT SHOPPING (THAT ONES I MADE YOU BUY)?
Isn't that what you usually wear?
I THOUGHT THEY'D BE TOO CON-STRICT-ING...
...BUT I DID BRING THEM.
HEH HEH
I DIDN'T TELL YOU TO BRING THEM. I TOLD YOU TO WEAR THEM!

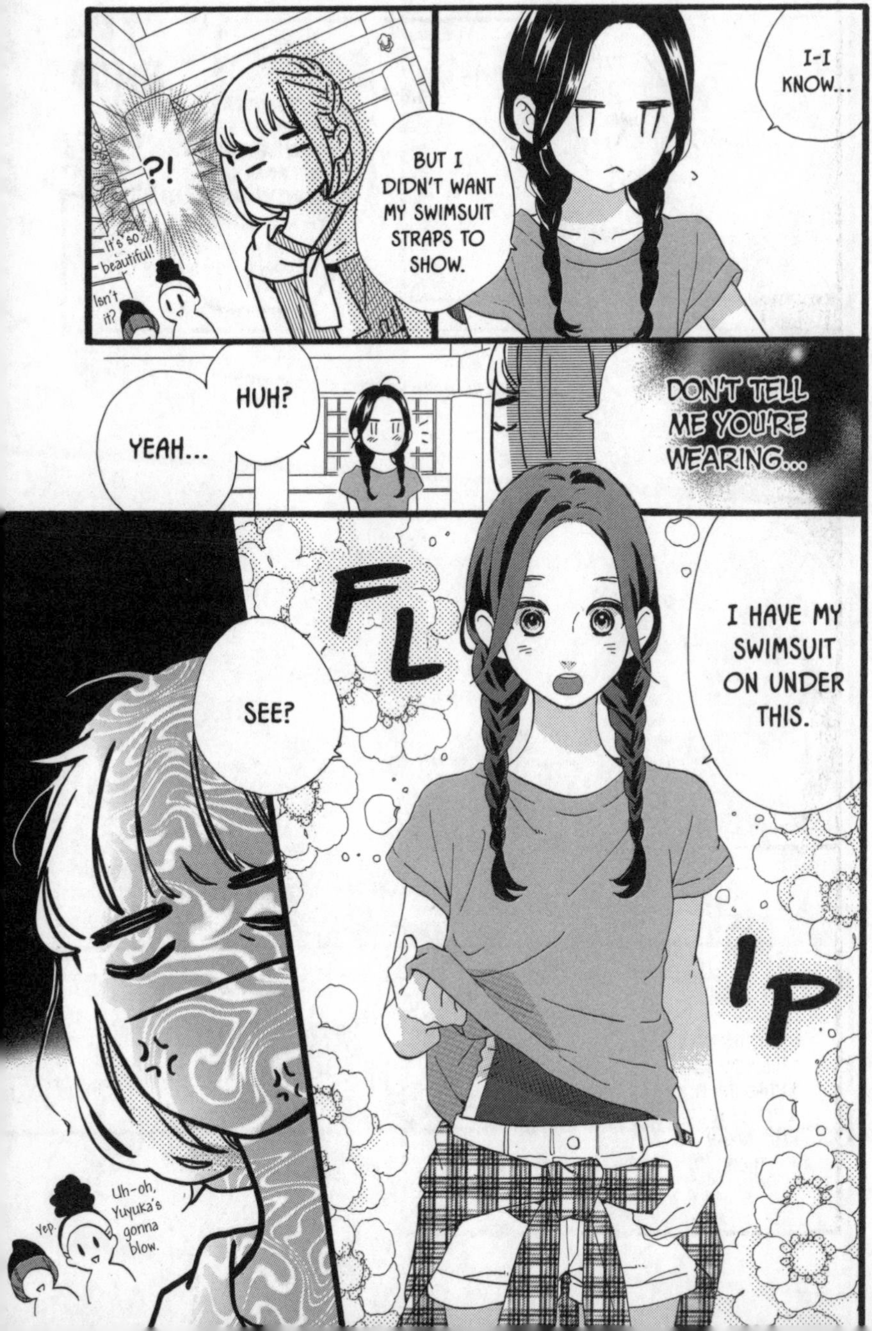
I-I KNOW...
BUT I DIDN'T WANT MY SWIMSUIT STRAPS TO SHOW.
?!
It's so beautiful!
Isn't it?
DON'T TELL ME YOU'RE WEARING...
HUH?
YEAH...
I HAVE MY SWIMSUIT ON UNDER THIS.
FL
IP
SEE?
Uh-oh, Yuyuka's gonna blow.
Yep.

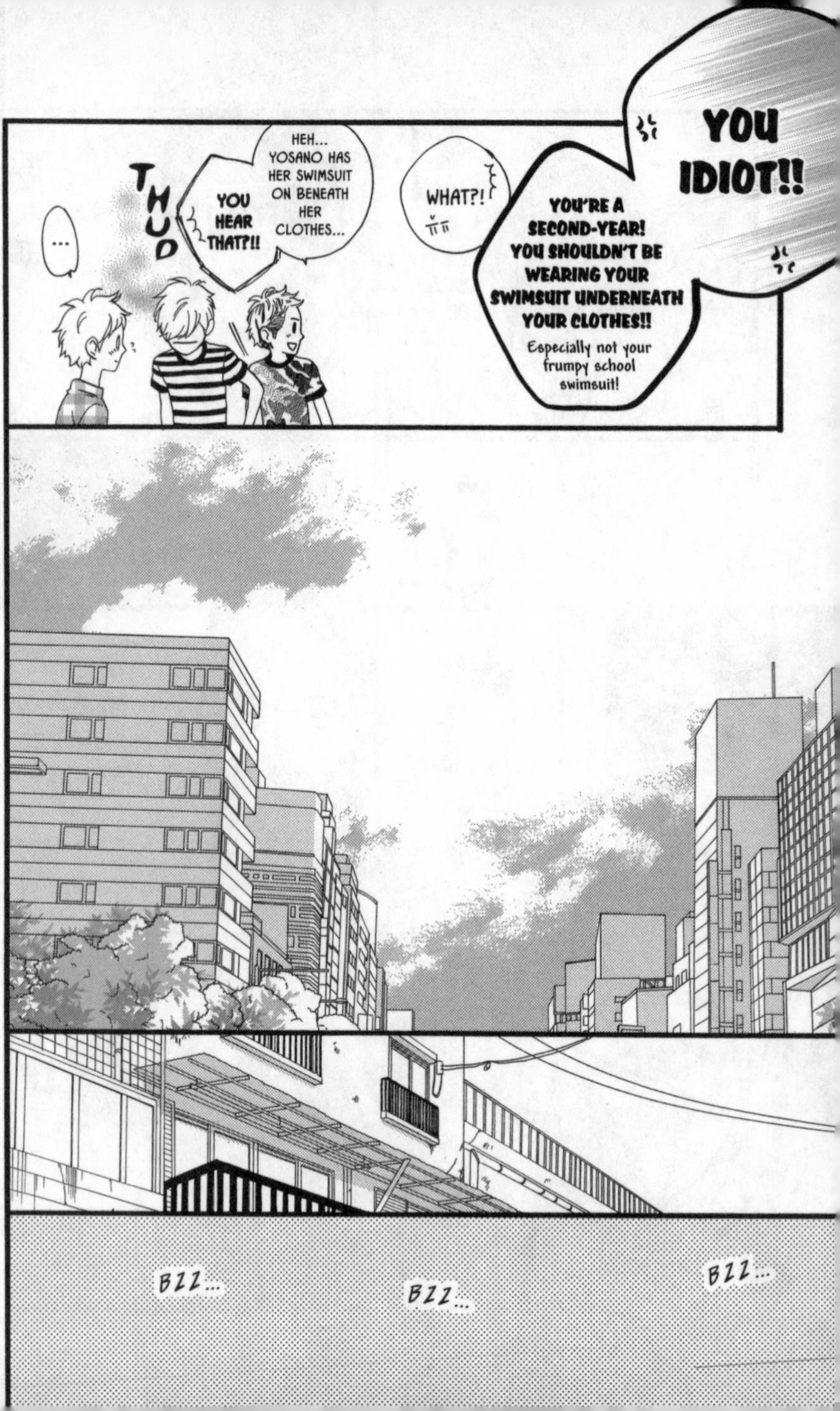
YOU IDIOT!!
YOU'RE A SECOND-YEAR! YOU SHOULDN'T BE WEARING YOUR SWIMSUIT UNDERNEATH YOUR CLOTHES!!
Especially not your frumpy school swimsuit!
WHAT?!
HEH... YOSANO HAS HER SWIMSUIT ON BENEATH HER CLOTHES...
YOU HEAR THAT?!!
THUD
...
BZZ...
BZZ...
BZZ...

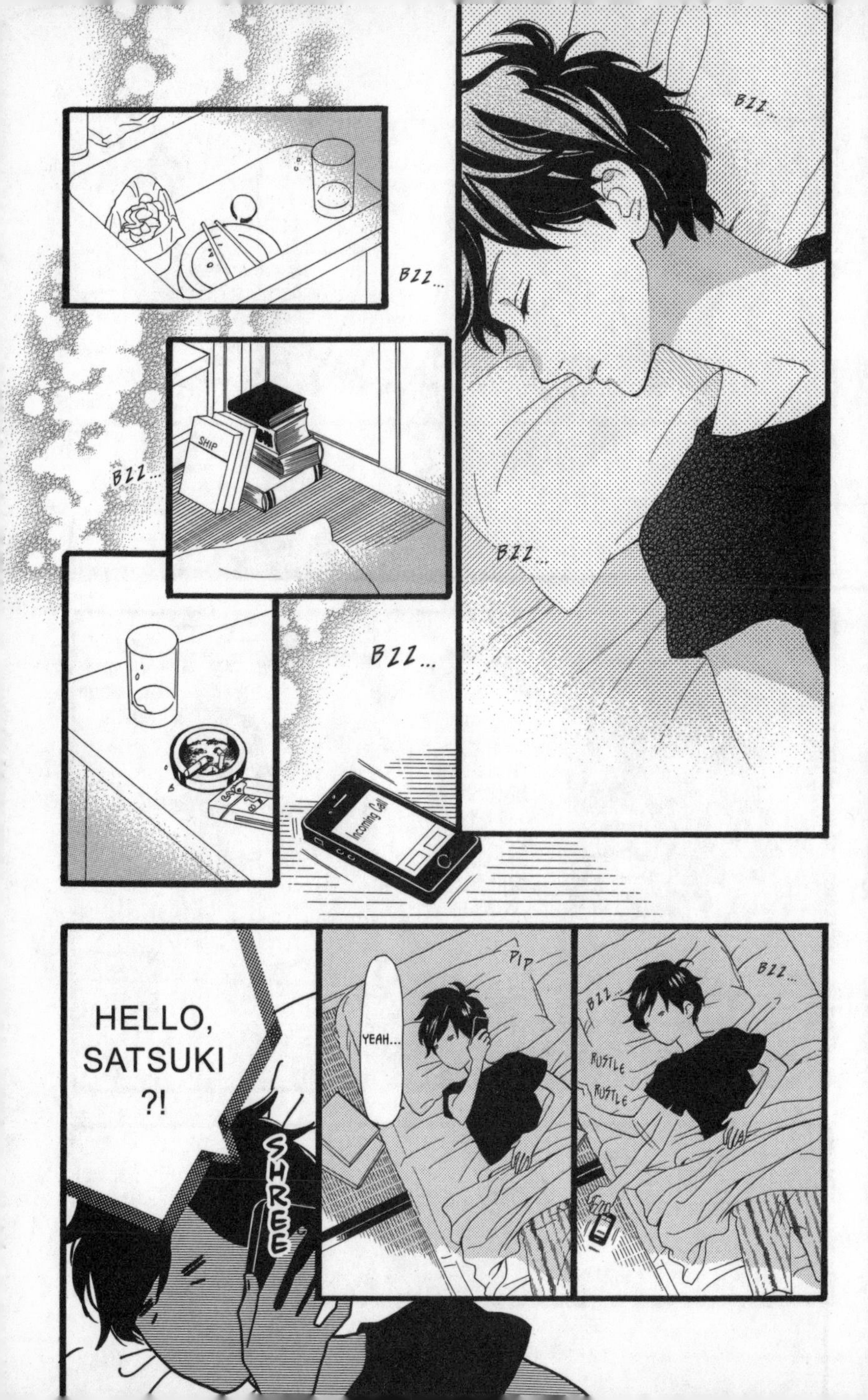
BZZ...
BZZ...
BZZ...
SHIP
BZZ...
BZZ...
Incoming Call
BZZ...
BZZ
RUSTLE
RUSTLE
PIP
YEAH...
HELLO, SATSUKI ?!
SHREE

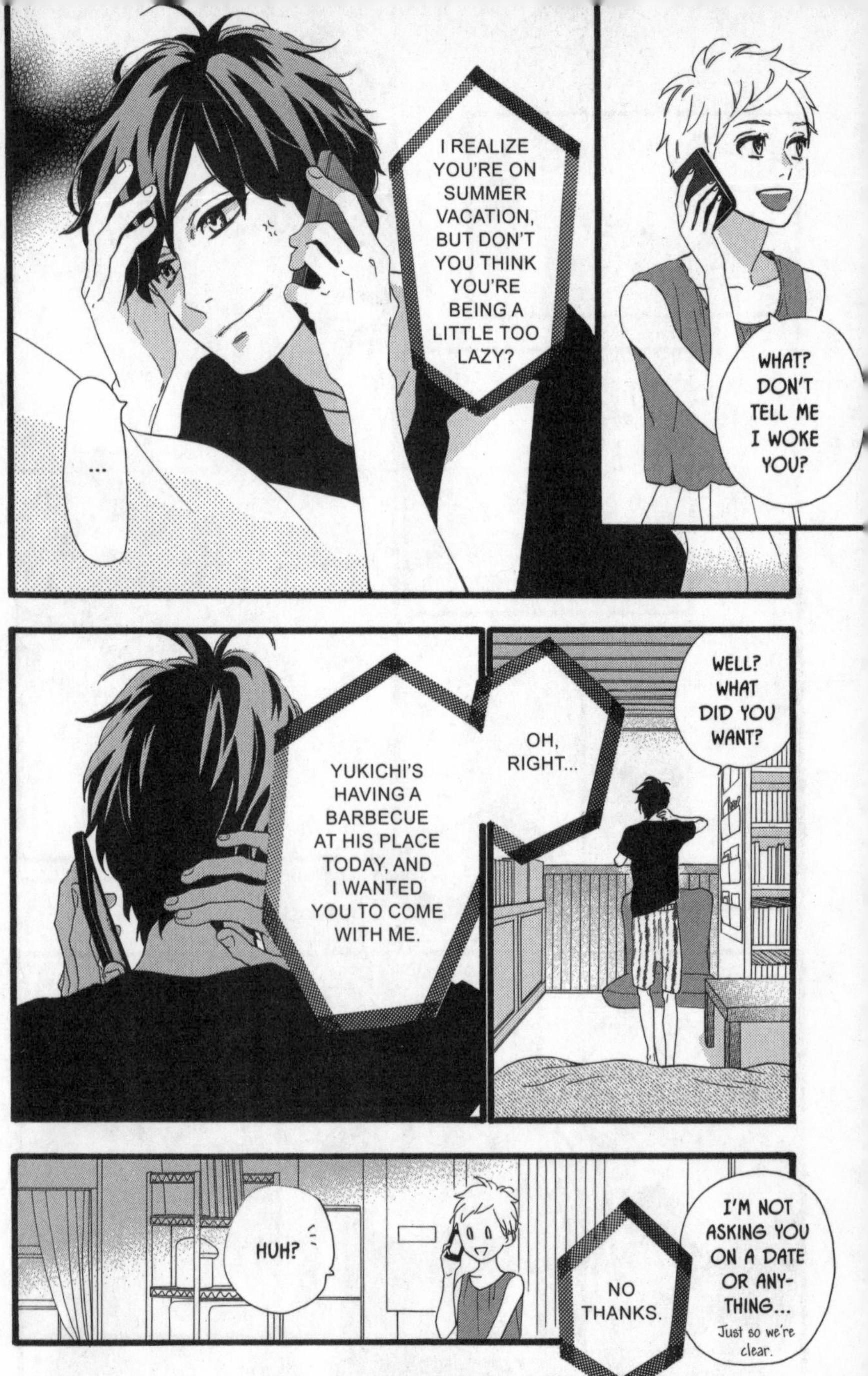
WHAT? DON'T TELL ME I WOKE YOU?
I REALIZE YOU'RE ON SUMMER VACATION, BUT DON'T YOU THINK YOU'RE BEING A LITTLE TOO LAZY?
...
WELL? WHAT DID YOU WANT?
OH, RIGHT...
YUKICHI'S HAVING A BARBECUE AT HIS PLACE TODAY, AND I WANTED YOU TO COME WITH ME.
I'M NOT ASKING YOU ON A DATE OR ANY-THING...
Just so we're clear.
NO THANKS.
HUH?

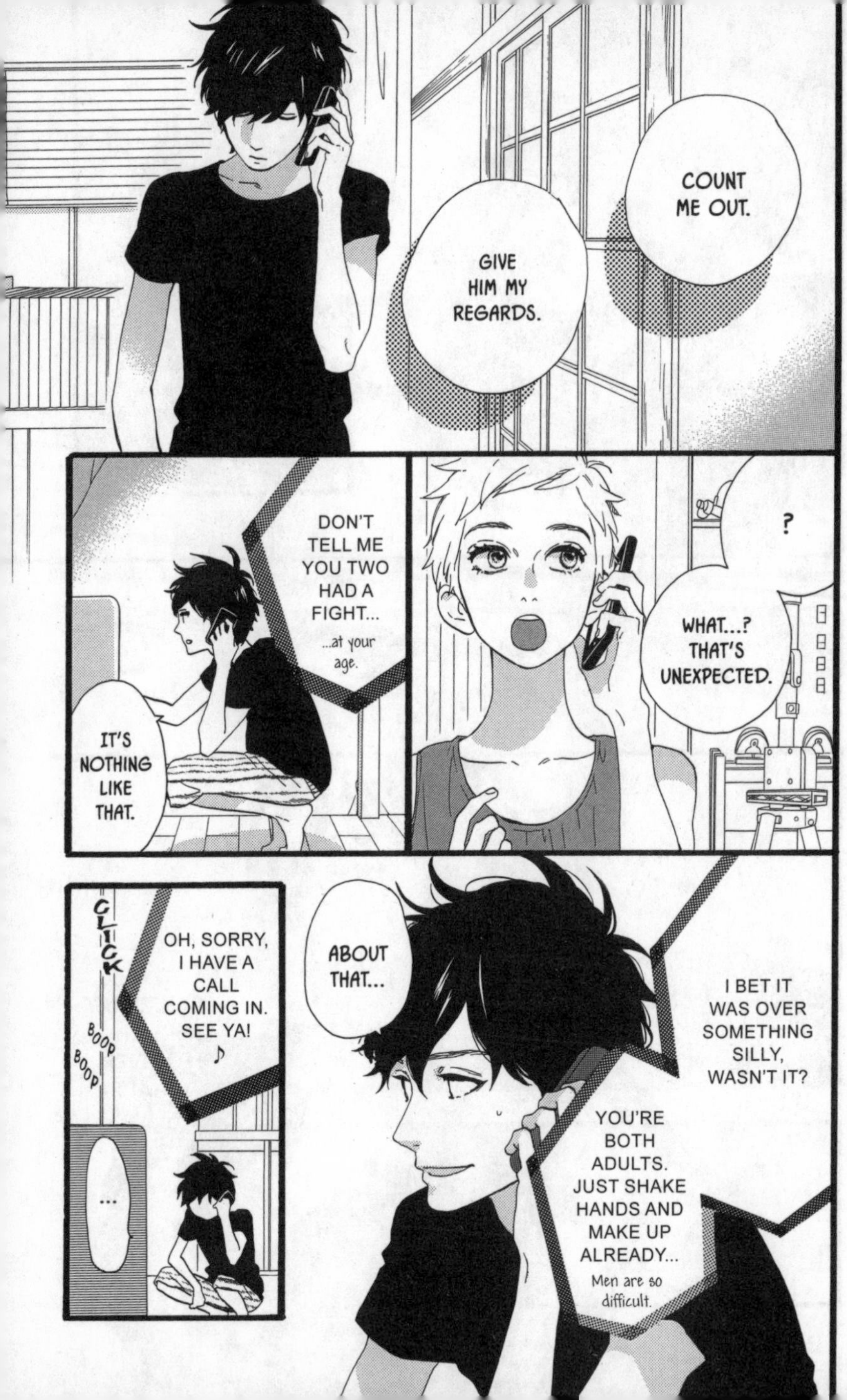
COUNT ME OUT.
GIVE HIM MY REGARDS.
?
WHAT...? THAT'S UNEXPECTED.
DON'T TELL ME YOU TWO HAD A FIGHT...
...at your age.
IT'S NOTHING LIKE THAT.
I BET IT WAS OVER SOMETHING SILLY, WASN'T IT?
ABOUT THAT...
YOU'RE BOTH ADULTS. JUST SHAKE HANDS AND MAKE UP ALREADY...
Men are so difficult.
OH, SORRY, I HAVE A CALL COMING IN. SEE YA! ♪
CLICK
BOOP BOOP
...

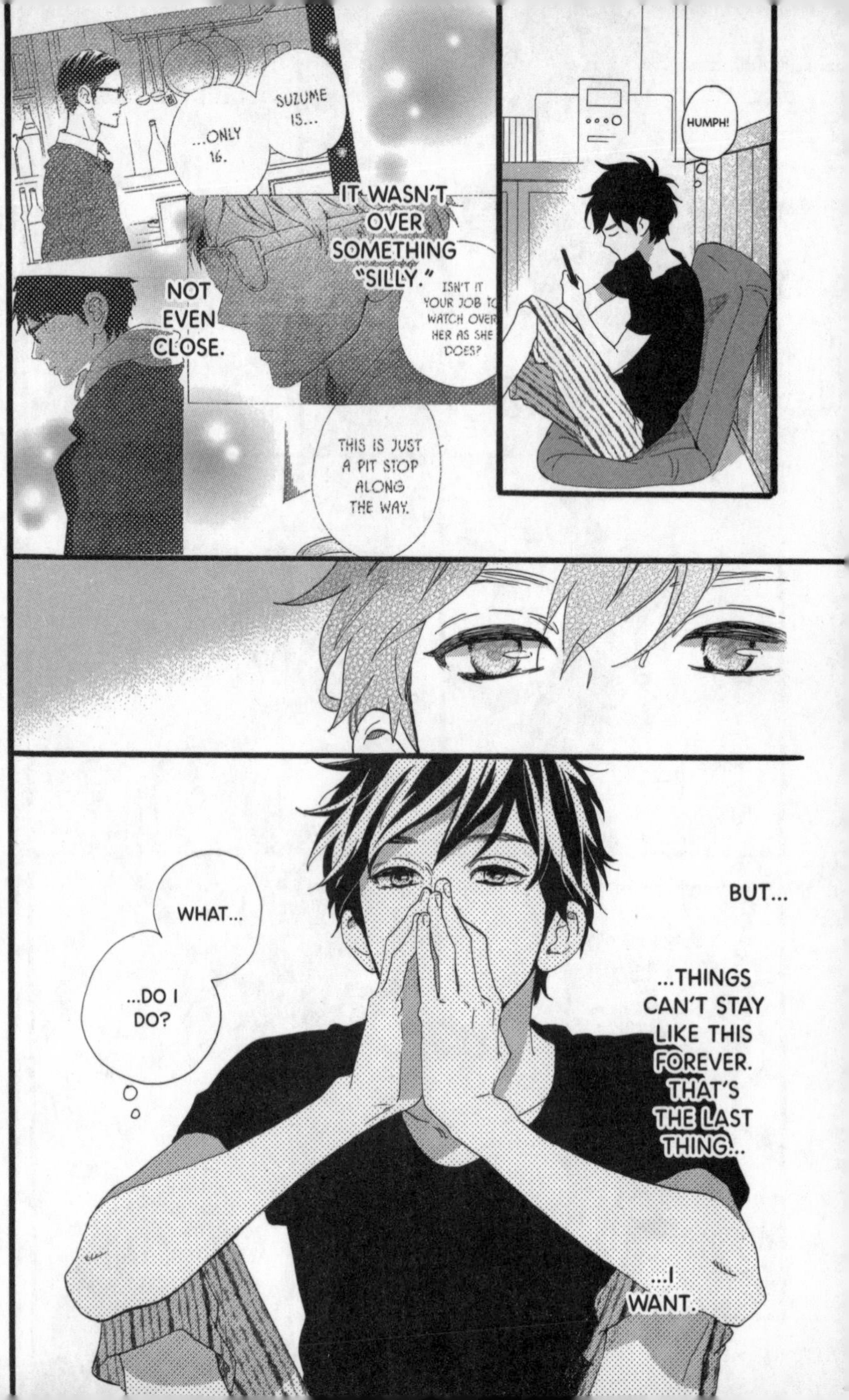
HUMPH!
SUZUME IS...
...ONLY 16.
IT WASN'T OVER SOMETHING "SILLY."
ISN'T IT YOUR JOB TO WATCH OVER HER AS SHE DOES?
NOT EVEN CLOSE.
THIS IS JUST A PIT STOP ALONG THE WAY.
BUT...
...THINGS CAN'T STAY LIKE THIS FOREVER. THAT'S THE LAST THING...
...I WANT.
WHAT...
...DO I DO?

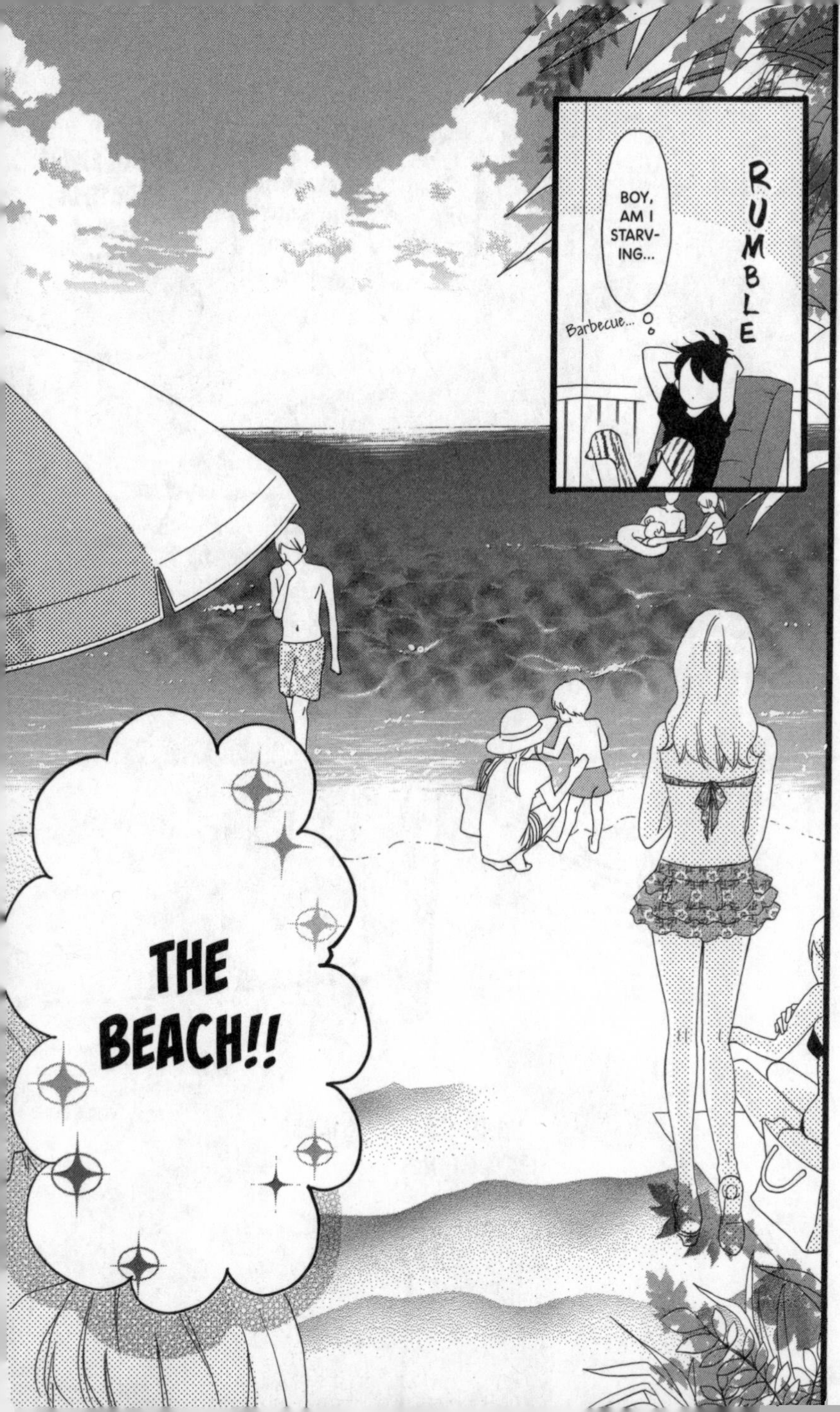
RUMBLE
BOY, AM I STARVING...
Barbecue...
THE BEACH!!

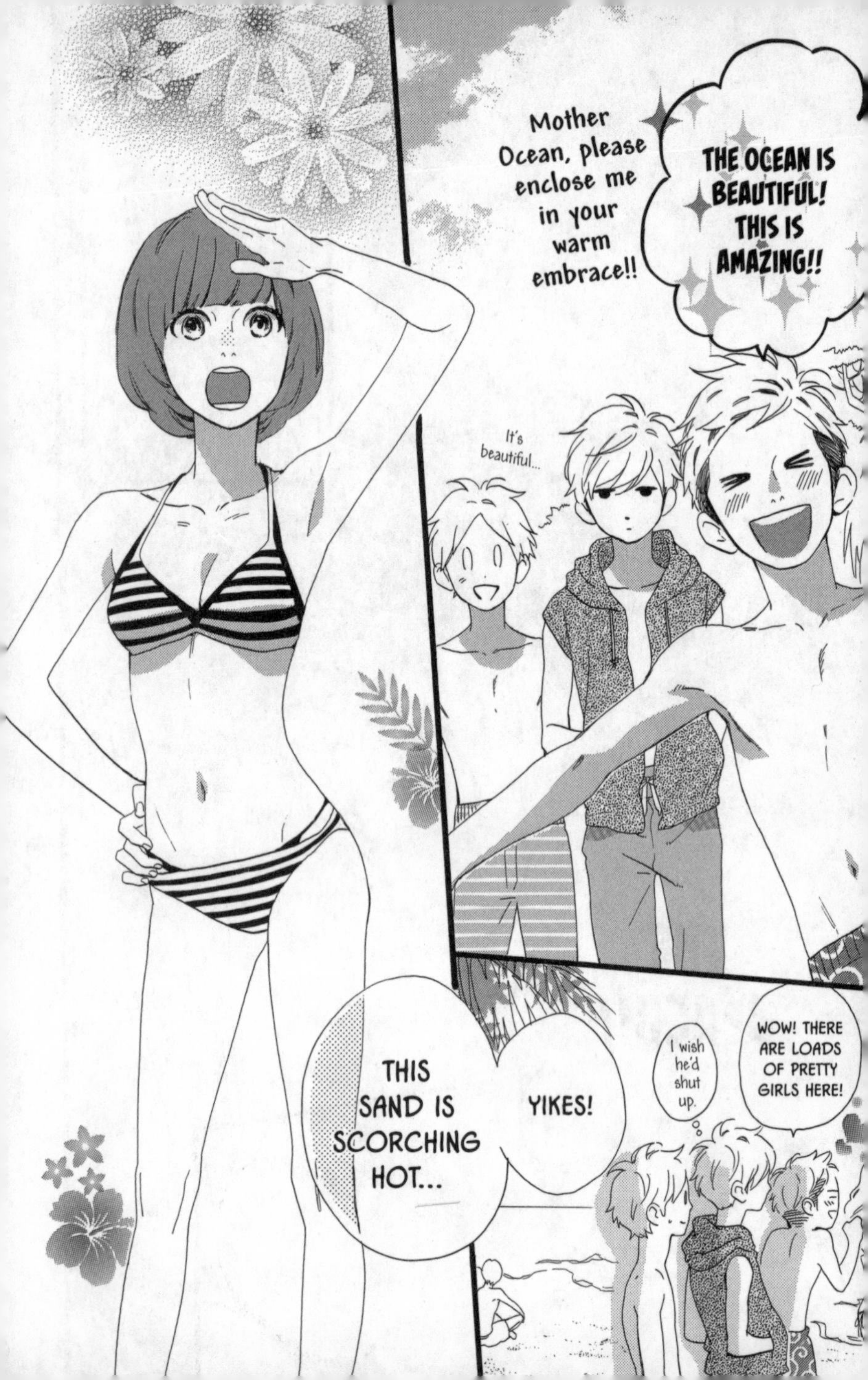
THE OCEAN IS BEAUTIFUL! THIS IS AMAZING!!
Mother Ocean, please enclose me in your warm embrace!!
It's beautiful...
WOW! THERE ARE LOADS OF PRETTY GIRLS HERE!
I wish he'd shut up.
YIKES!
THIS SAND IS SCORCHING HOT...

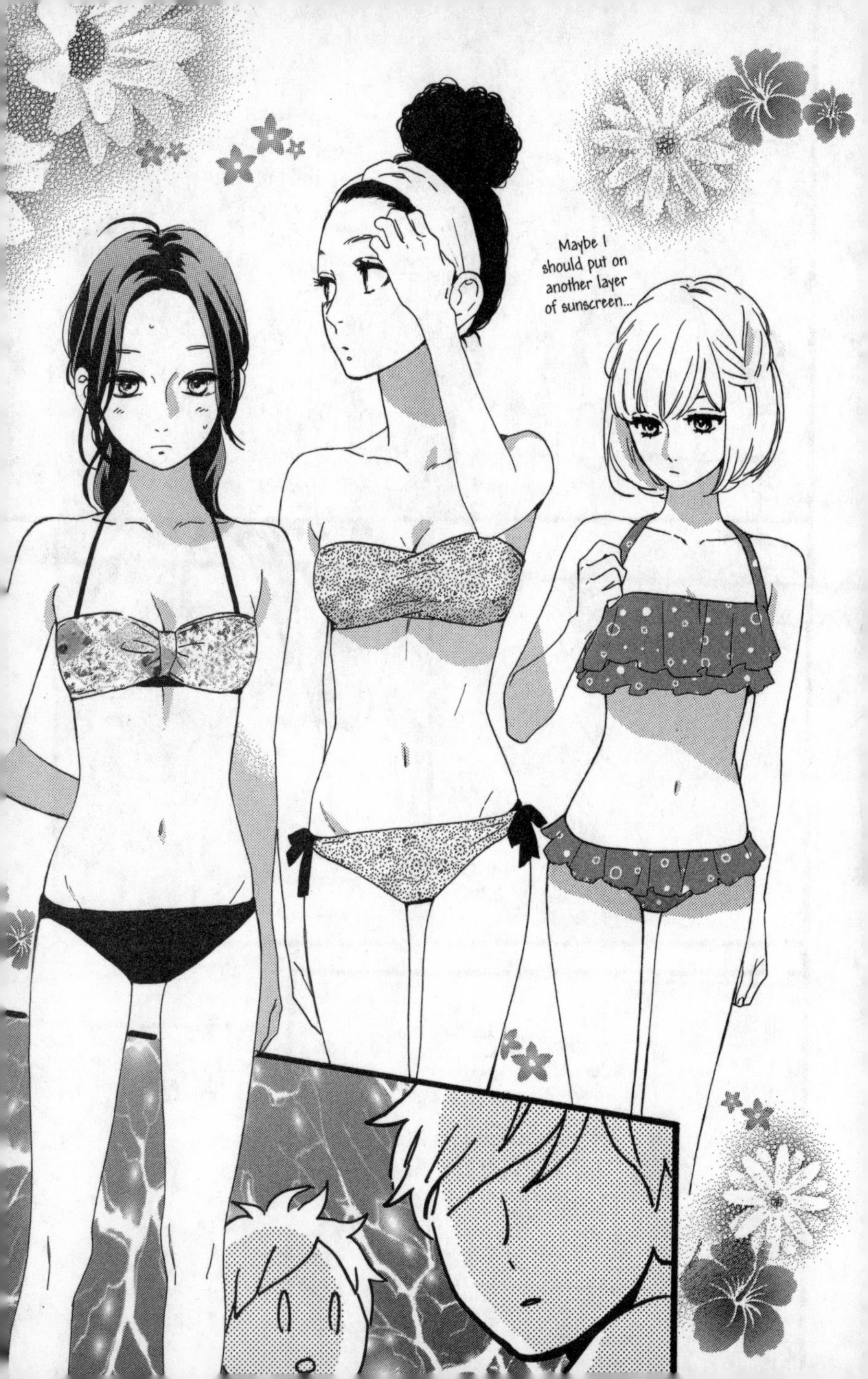
Maybe I should put on another layer of sunscreen...

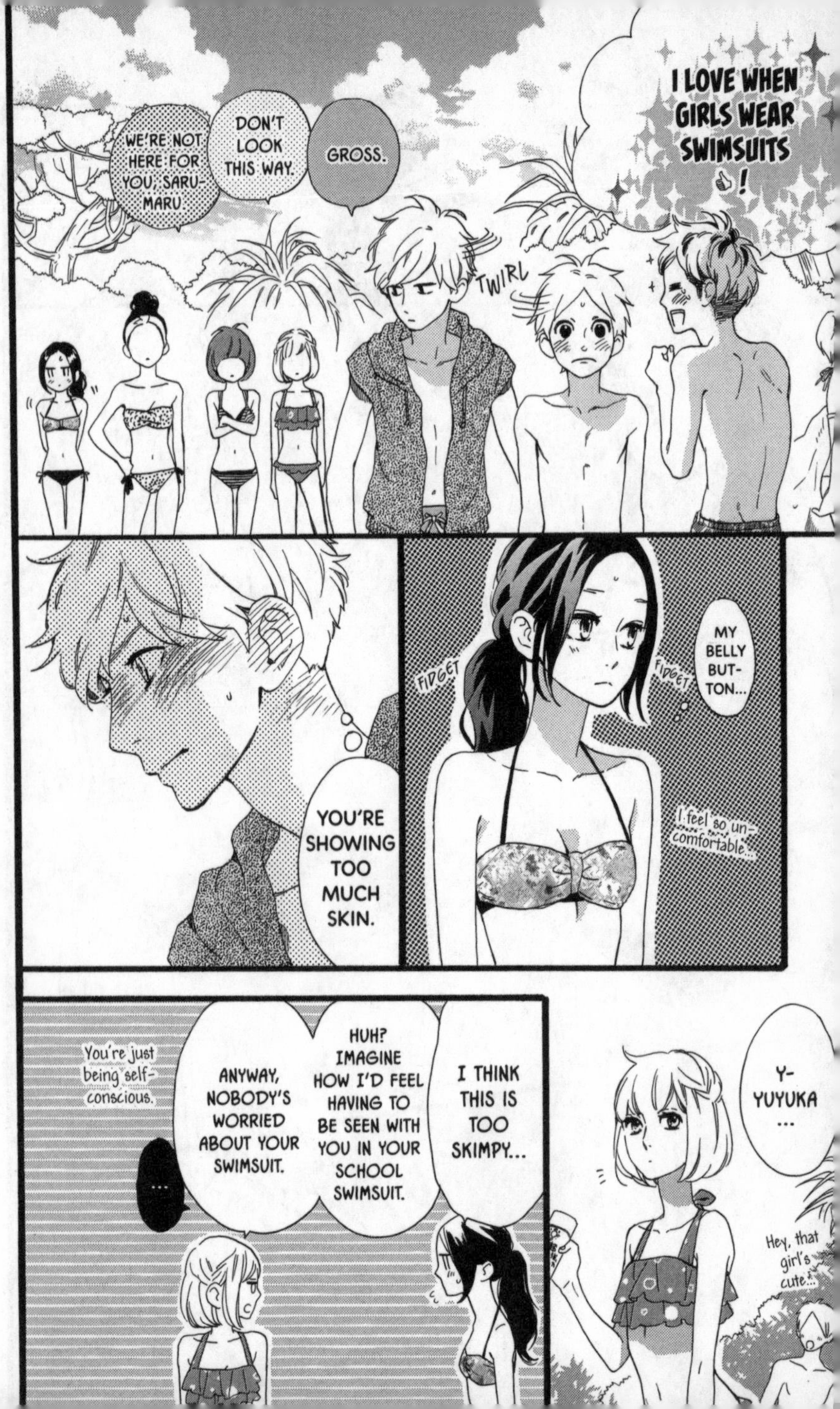
I LOVE WHEN GIRLS WEAR SWIMSUITS!
TWIRL
GROSS.
DON'T LOOK THIS WAY.
WE'RE NOT HERE FOR YOU, SARUMARU.
MY BELLY BUTTON...
FIDGET
FIDGET
I feel so uncomfortable...
YOU'RE SHOWING TOO MUCH SKIN.
Y-YUYUKA...
Hey, that girl's cute...
I THINK THIS IS TOO SKIMPY...
HUH? IMAGINE HOW I'D FEEL HAVING TO BE SEEN WITH YOU IN YOUR SCHOOL SWIMSUIT.
ANYWAY, NOBODY'S WORRIED ABOUT YOUR SWIMSUIT.
You're just being self-conscious.
...

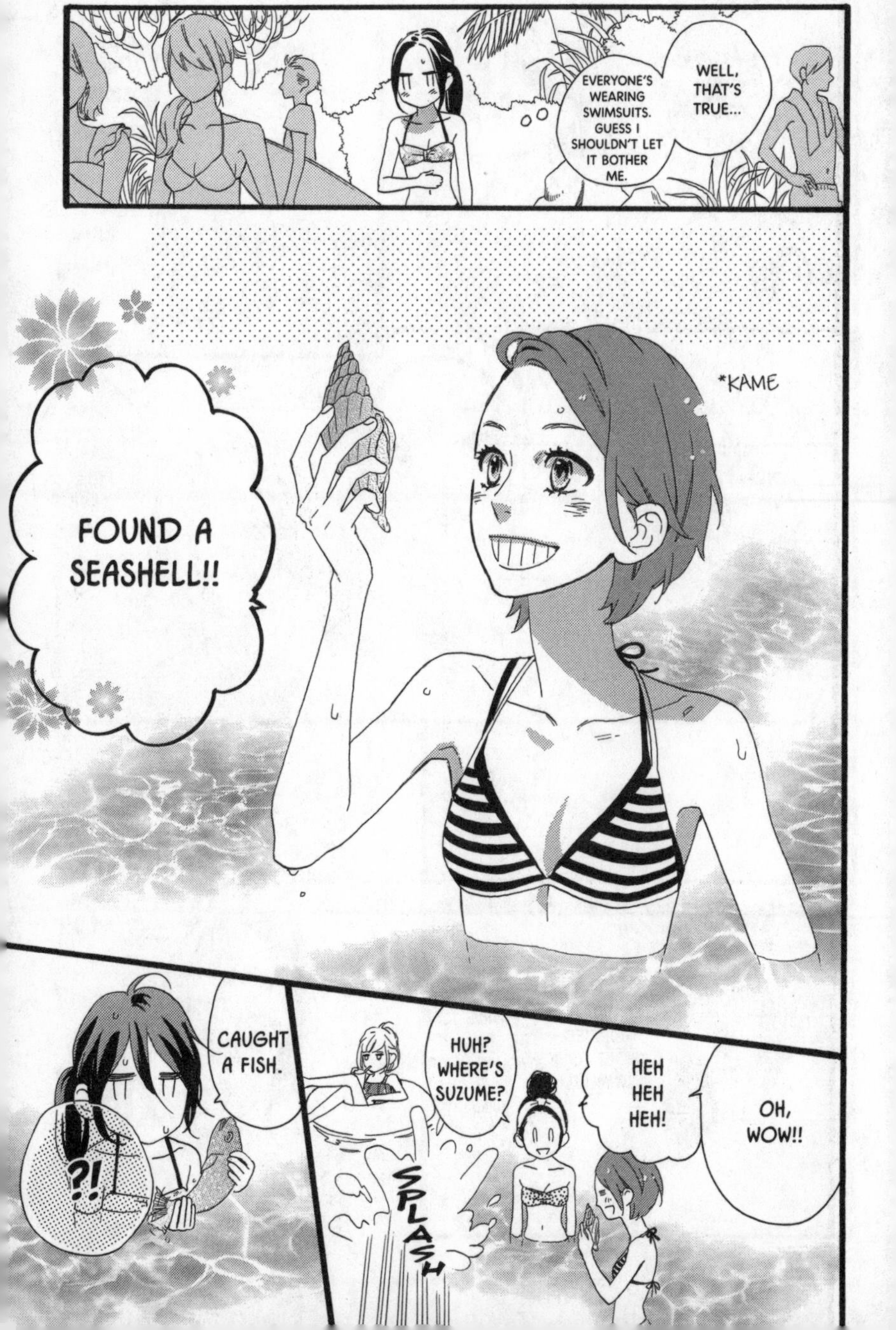
WELL, THAT'S TRUE...
EVERYONE'S WEARING SWIMSUITS. GUESS I SHOULDN'T LET IT BOTHER ME.
*KAME
FOUND A SEASHELL!!
OH, WOW!!
HEH HEH HEH!
HUH? WHERE'S SUZUME?
SPLASH
CAUGHT A FISH.
?!

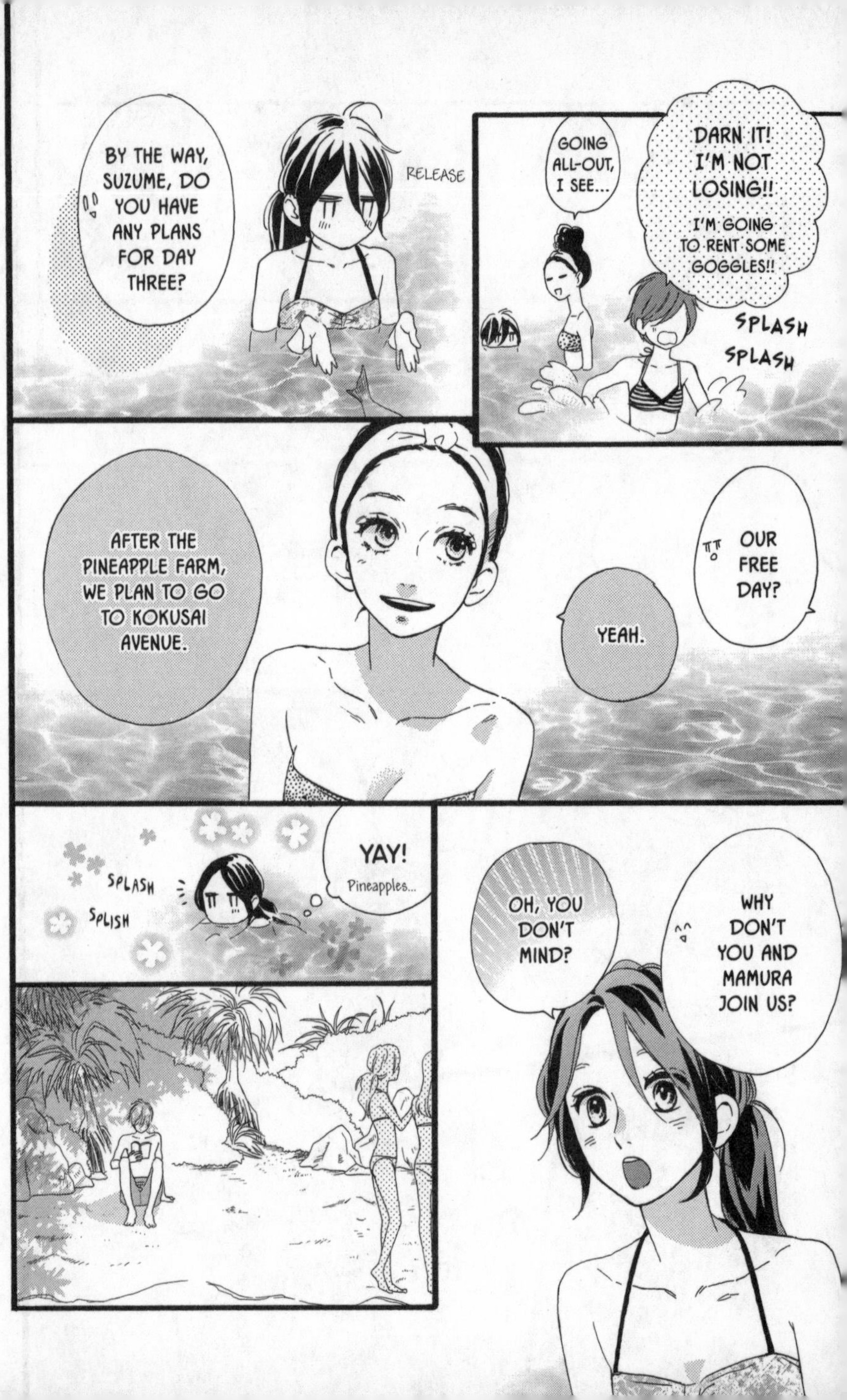
DARN IT! I'M NOT LOSING!! I'M GOING TO RENT SOME GOGGLES!!
GOING ALL-OUT, I SEE...
SPLASH
SPLASH
RELEASE
BY THE WAY, SUZUME, DO YOU HAVE ANY PLANS FOR DAY THREE?
OUR FREE DAY?
YEAH.
AFTER THE PINEAPPLE FARM, WE PLAN TO GO TO KOKUSAI AVENUE.
WHY DON'T YOU AND MAMURA JOIN US?
OH, YOU DON'T MIND?
YAY! Pineapples...
SPLASH
SPLISH

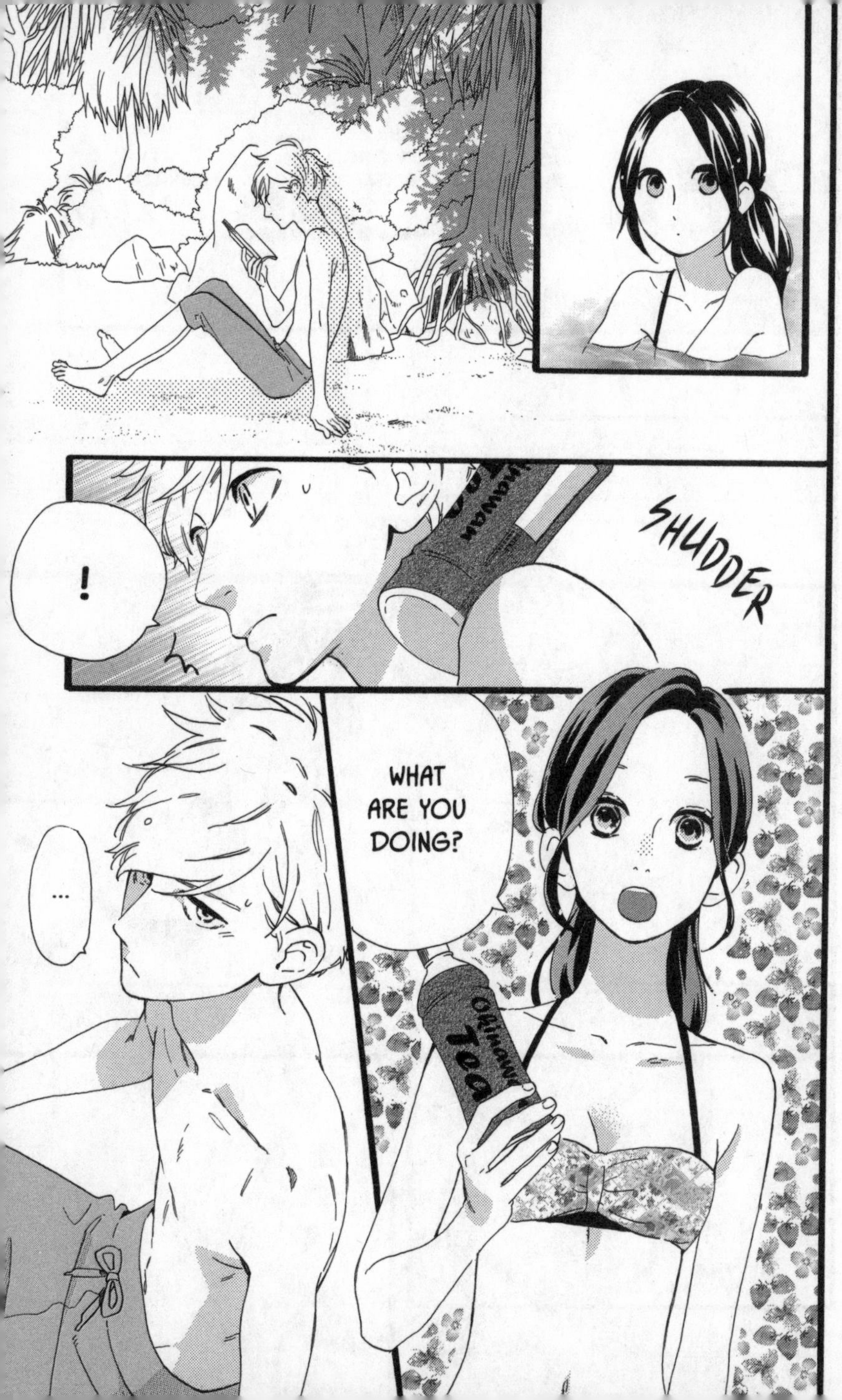
SHUDDER
!
WHAT ARE YOU DOING?
...
Tea

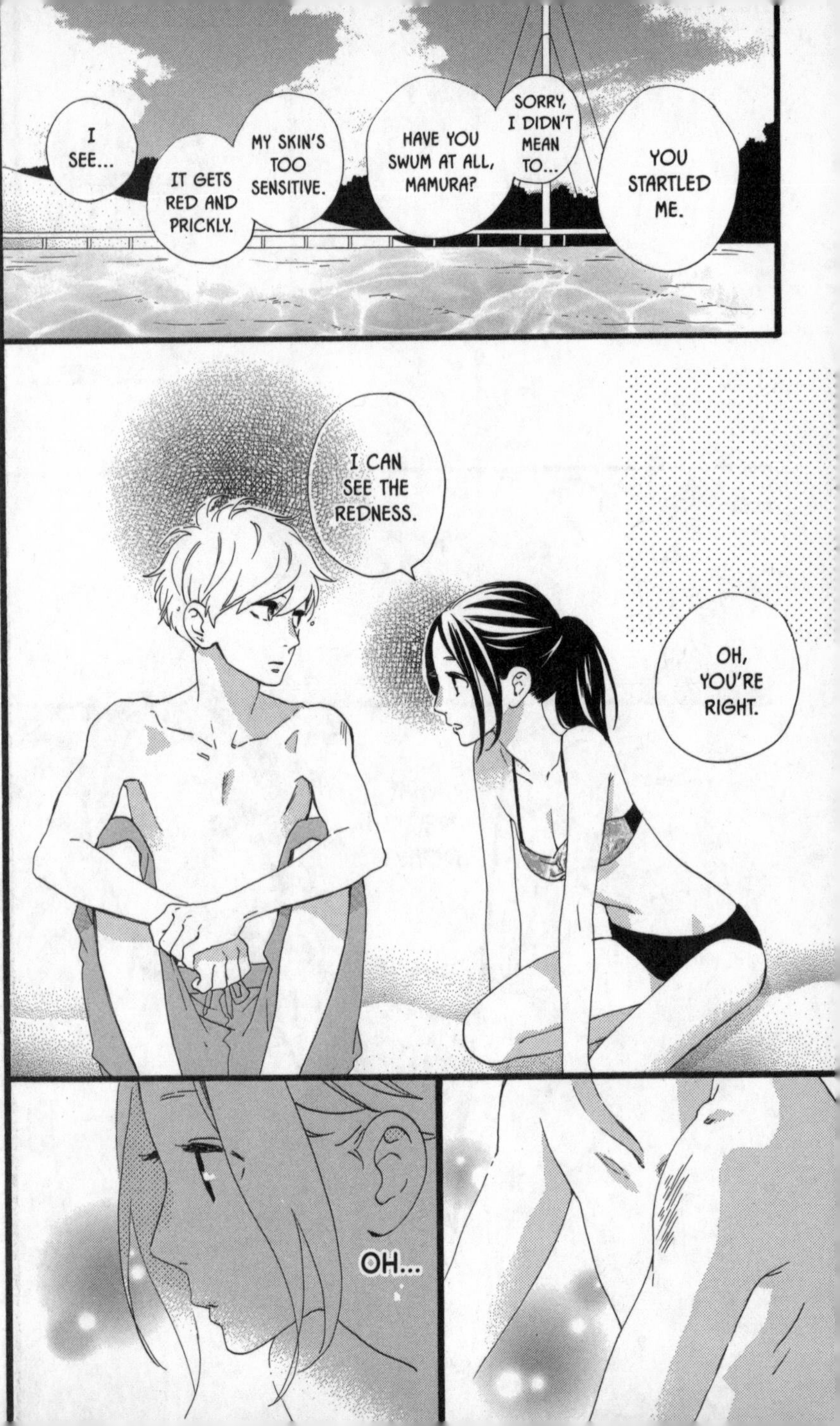
YOU STARTLED ME.
SORRY, I DIDN'T MEAN TO...
HAVE YOU SWUM AT ALL, MAMURA?
MY SKIN'S TOO SENSITIVE.
IT GETS RED AND PRICKLY.
I SEE...
I CAN SEE THE REDNESS.
OH, YOU'RE RIGHT.
OH...

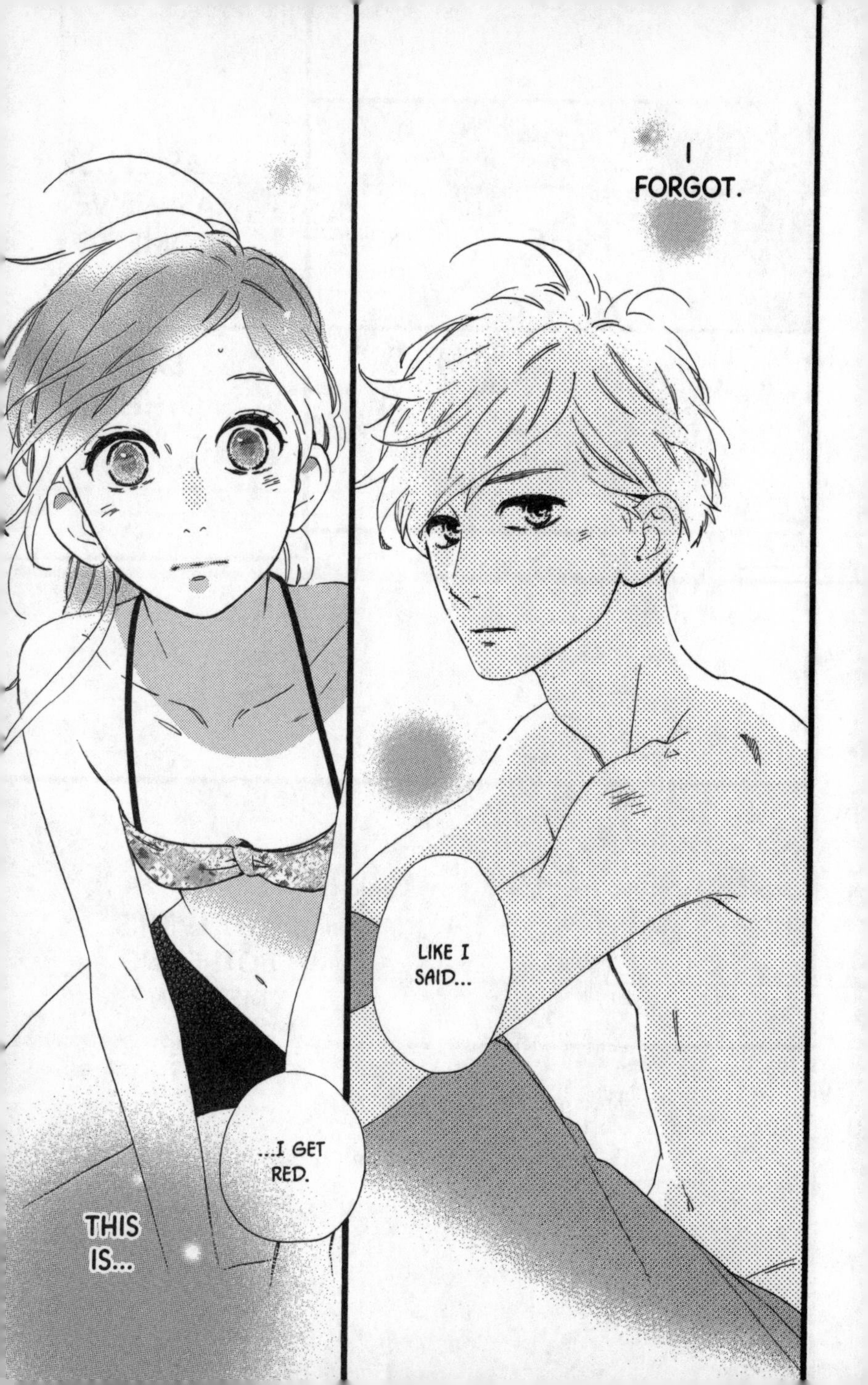
I FORGOT.
LIKE I SAID...
...I GET RED.
THIS IS...

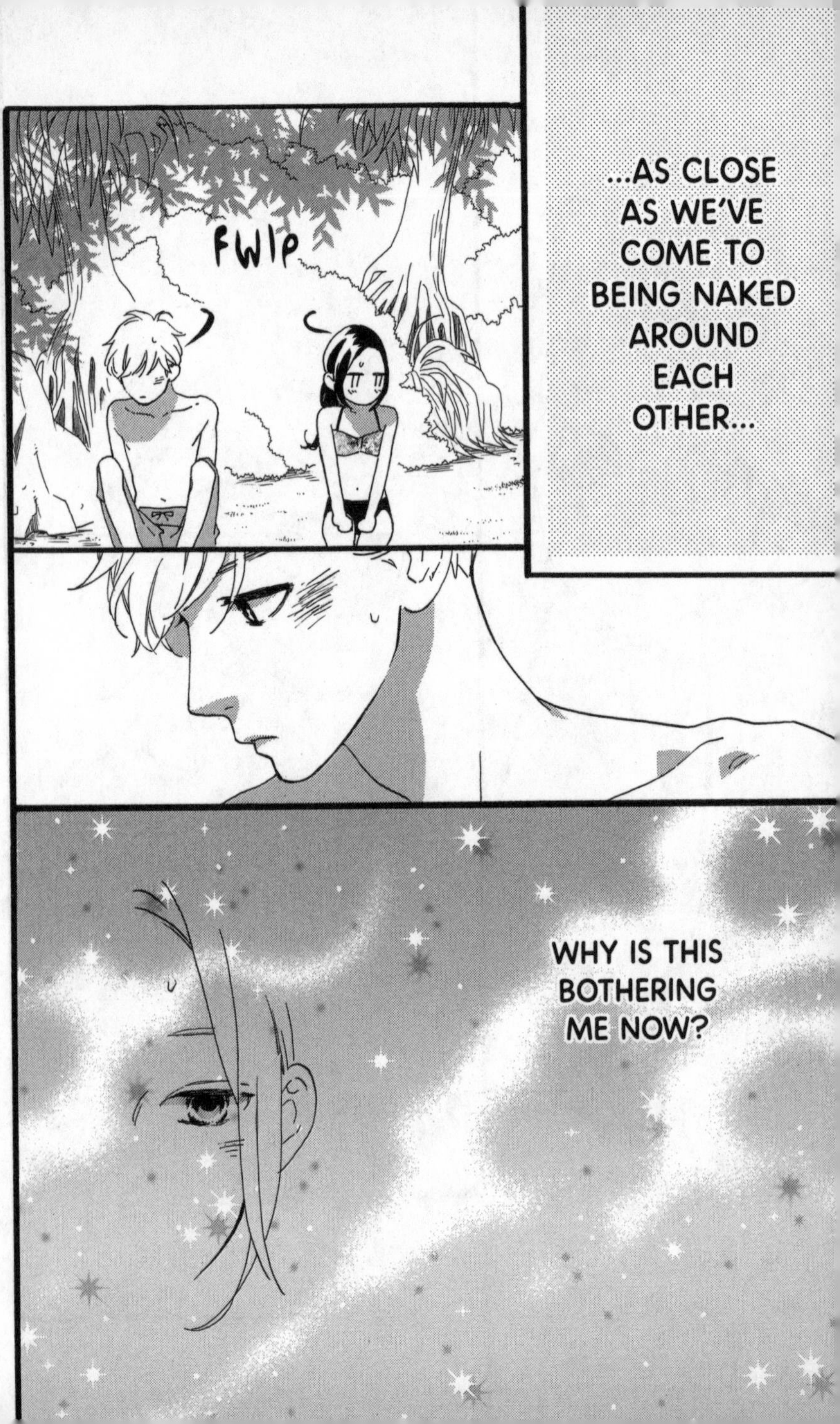

...AS CLOSE AS WE'VE COME TO BEING NAKED AROUND EACH OTHER...
FWIP
WHY IS THIS BOTHERING ME NOW?

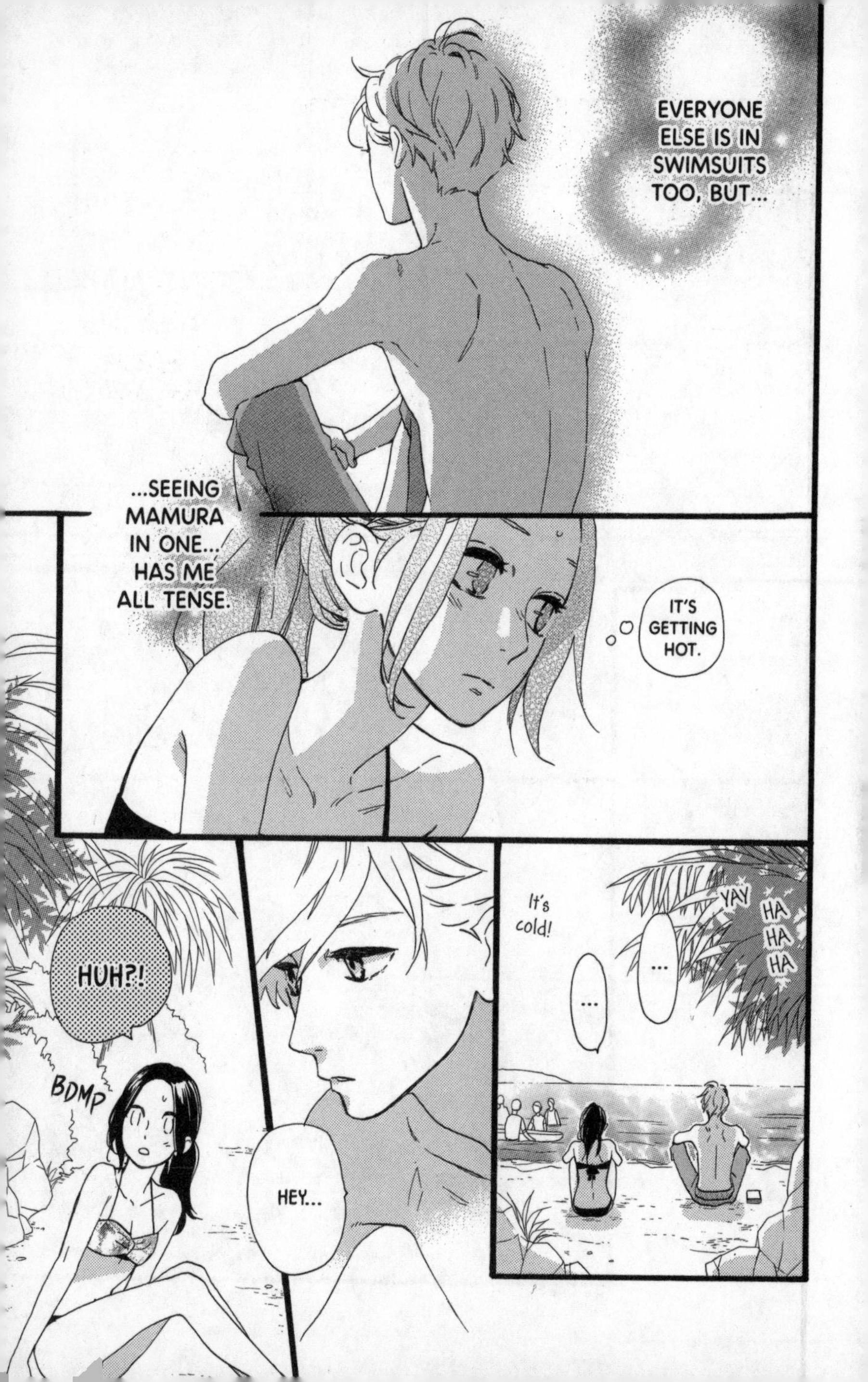
EVERYONE ELSE IS IN SWIMSUITS TOO, BUT...
...SEEING MAMURA IN ONE... HAS ME ALL TENSE.
IT'S GETTING HOT.
YAY
HA HA HA
It's cold!
...
...
HEY...
HUH?!
BDMP

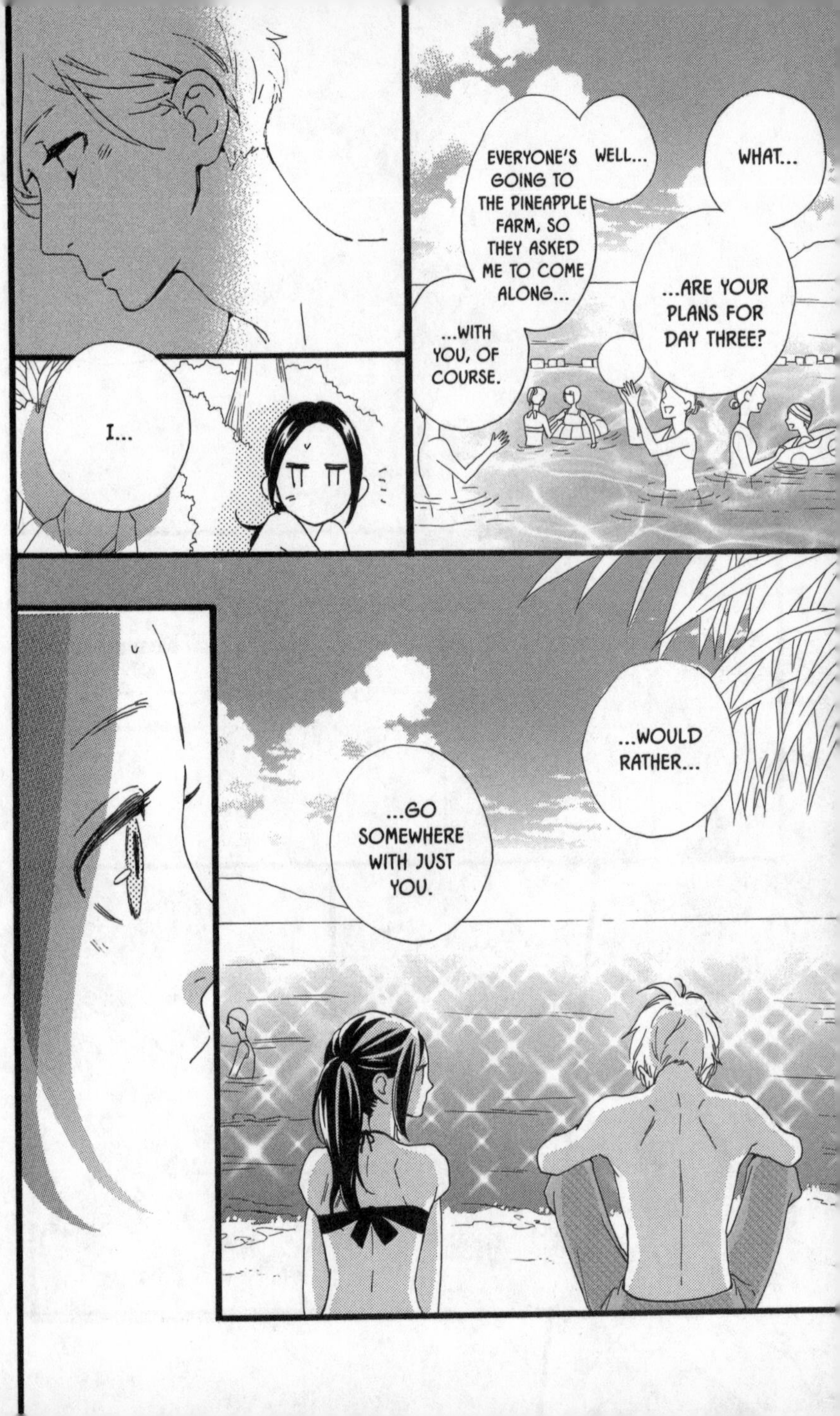
WHAT...
...ARE YOUR PLANS FOR DAY THREE?
WELL...
EVERYONE'S GOING TO THE PINEAPPLE FARM, SO THEY ASKED ME TO COME ALONG...
...WITH YOU, OF COURSE.
I...
...WOULD RATHER...
...GO SOMEWHERE WITH JUST YOU.

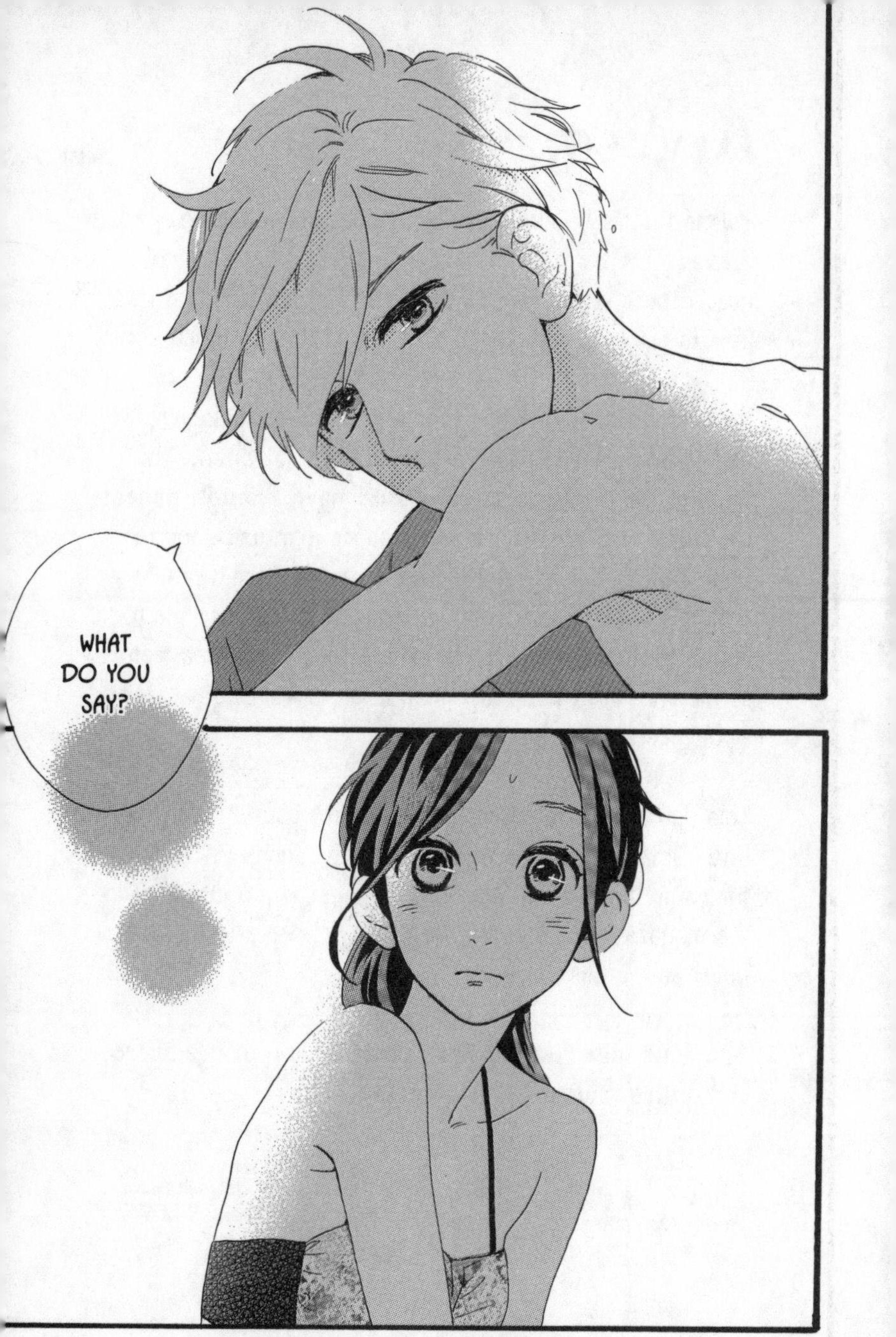
WHAT DO YOU SAY?

And so...

This is the final volume of *Daytime Shooting Star*!! Yay! *Clap clap clap*! ★ It's hard to believe this series has continued for nearly three years! And its thanks to you readers that I was able to see it to completion. Thank you all very much!!

However, there is one thing for which I must apologize. I've had to add a lot of pages to the end of this volume. The truth of the matter is, **I just didn't have enough pages!** My editor had allotted me more pages than usual for the final volume, but as I worked on the storyboard, I realized it simply wasn't enough! So we decided to increase the page count. (Actually, we were planning a special *Daytime* feature at the end, but had to give that space to the original story. Apologies to my editor.)

This was all due to poor planning on my part. And so, you'll find a lot of unexpected pages, but the conclusion remains the same. So I would appreciate it if you would just think of the magazine serial as the theatrical release and the graphic novel as the director's cut!

And don't miss Yuyuka's newly created mini-manga at the end of this volume. ♪ I hope you like it! ☆

MEANINGLESS POSE

WALKING DEAD

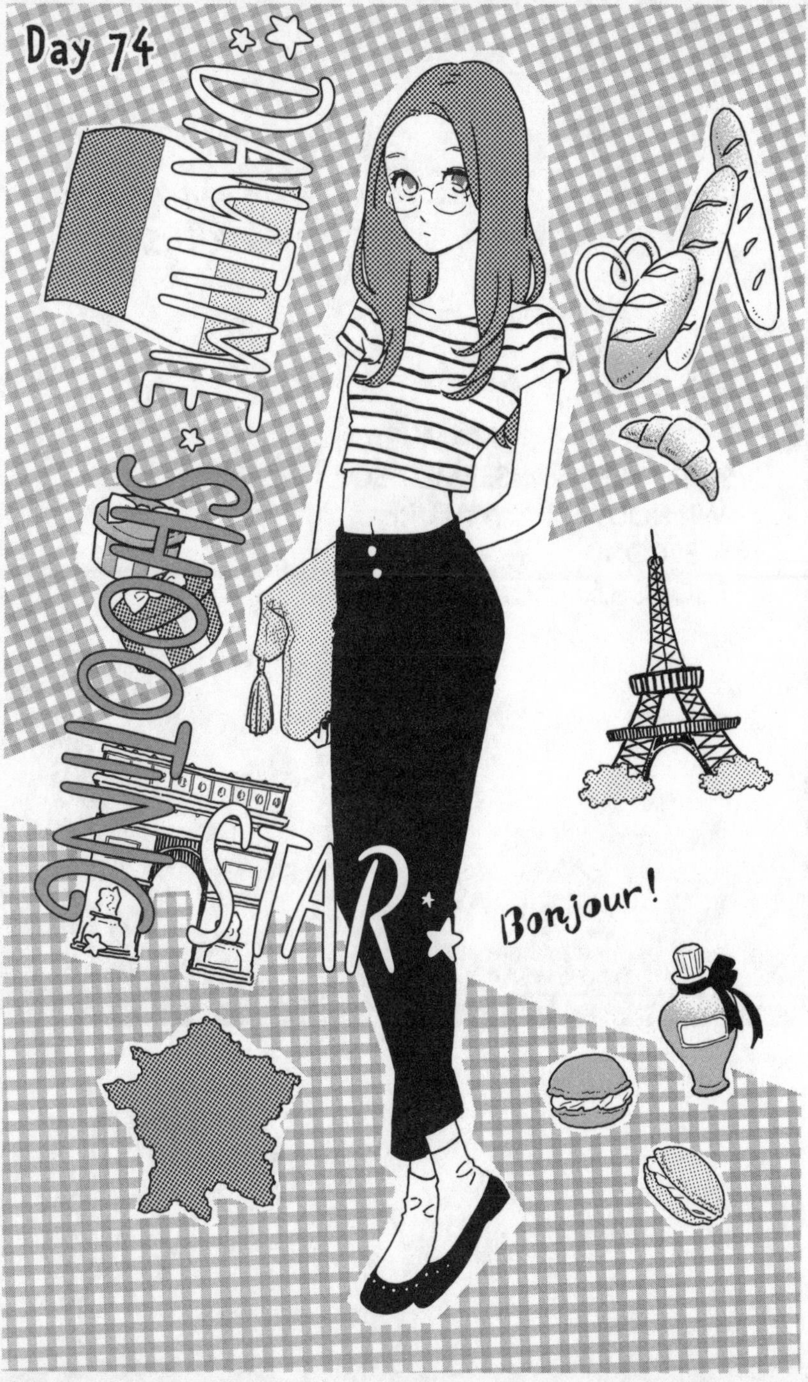
Day 74
DAYTIME SHOOTING STAR
Bonjour!

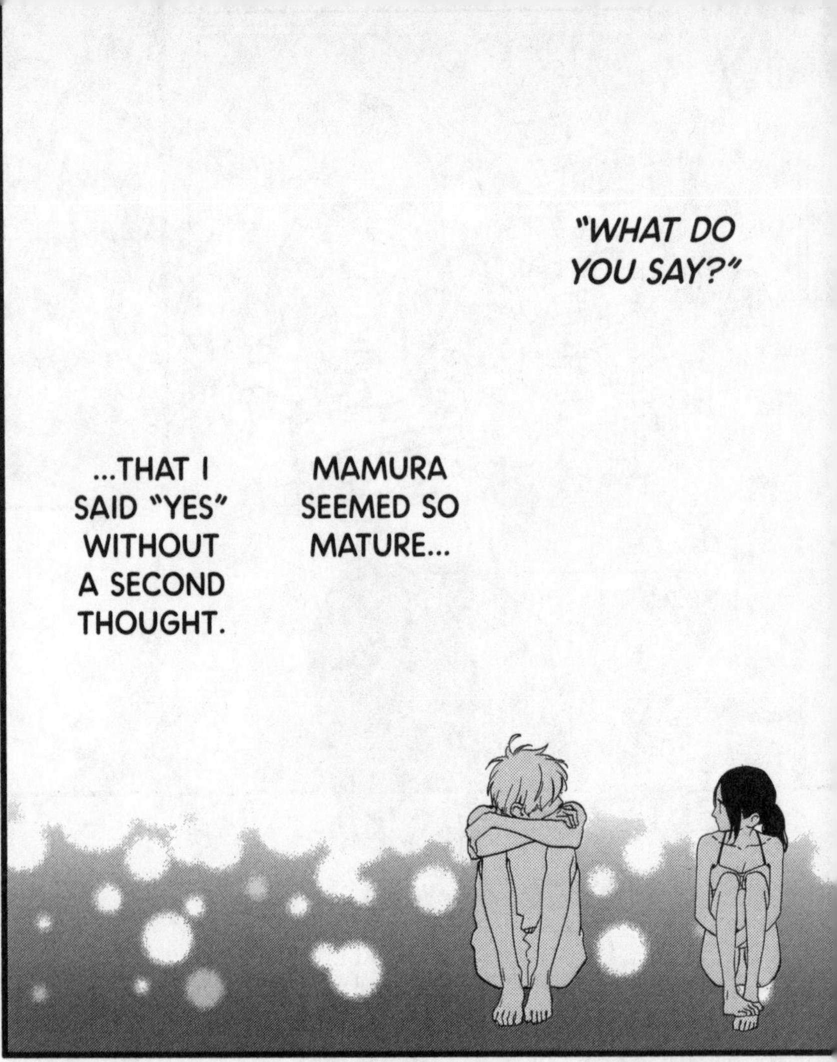
"WHAT DO YOU SAY?"
MAMURA SEEMED SO MATURE...
...THAT I SAID "YES" WITHOUT A SECOND THOUGHT.

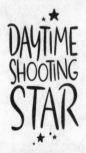

DAYTIME SHOOTING STAR

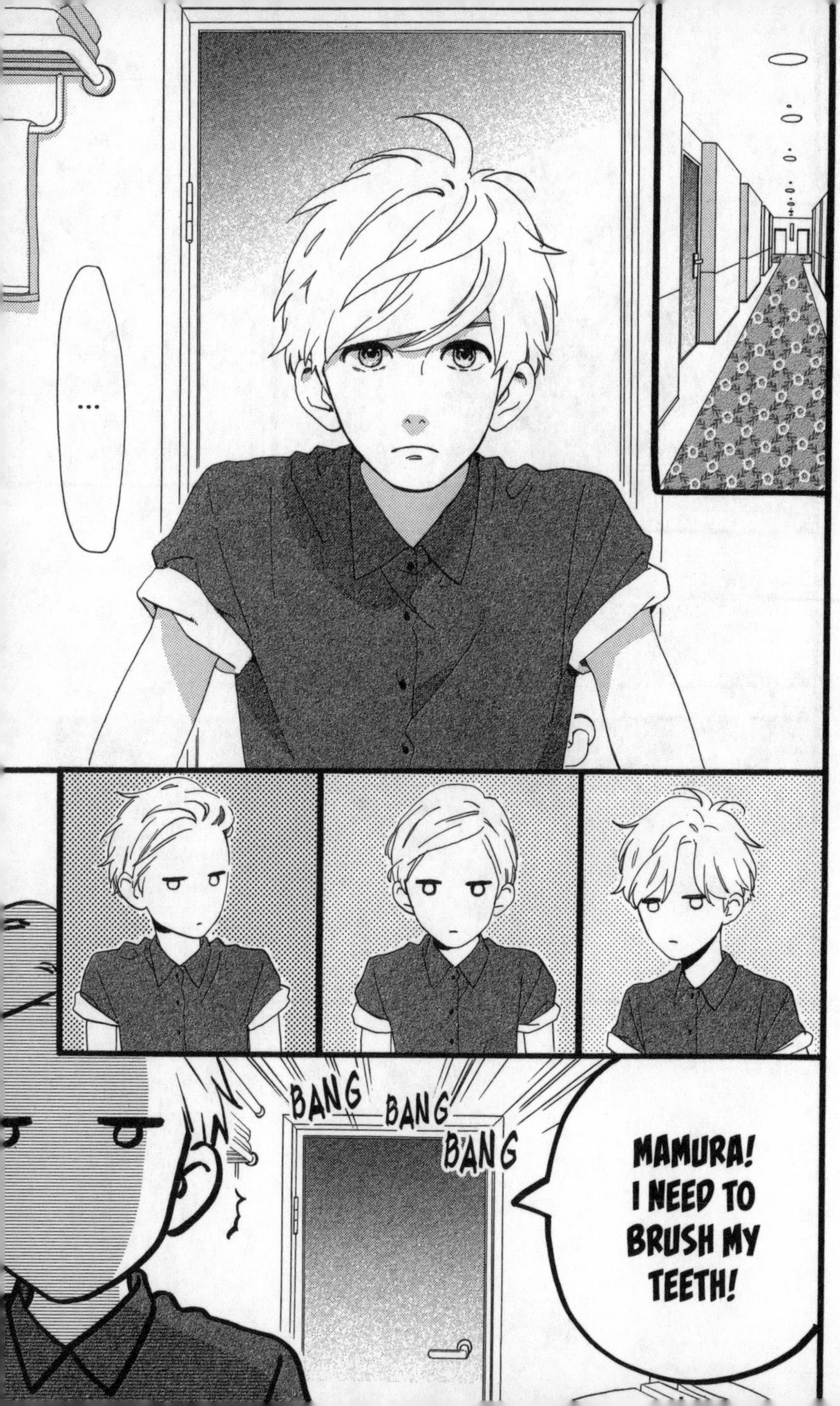
...
MAMURA! I NEED TO BRUSH MY TEETH!
BANG
BANG
BANG

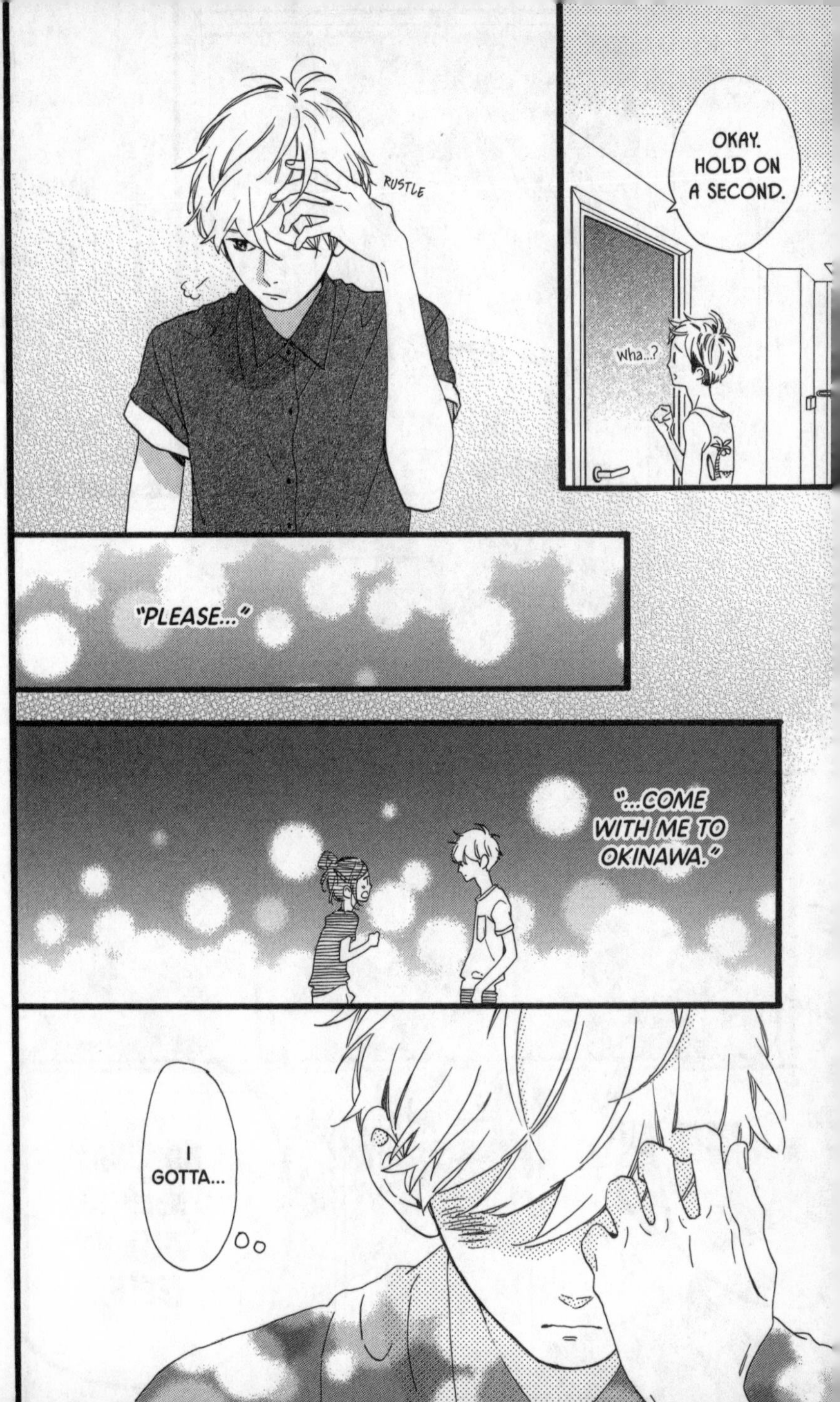
OKAY. HOLD ON A SECOND.
Wha...?
RUSTLE
"PLEASE..."
"...COME WITH ME TO OKINAWA."
I GOTTA...

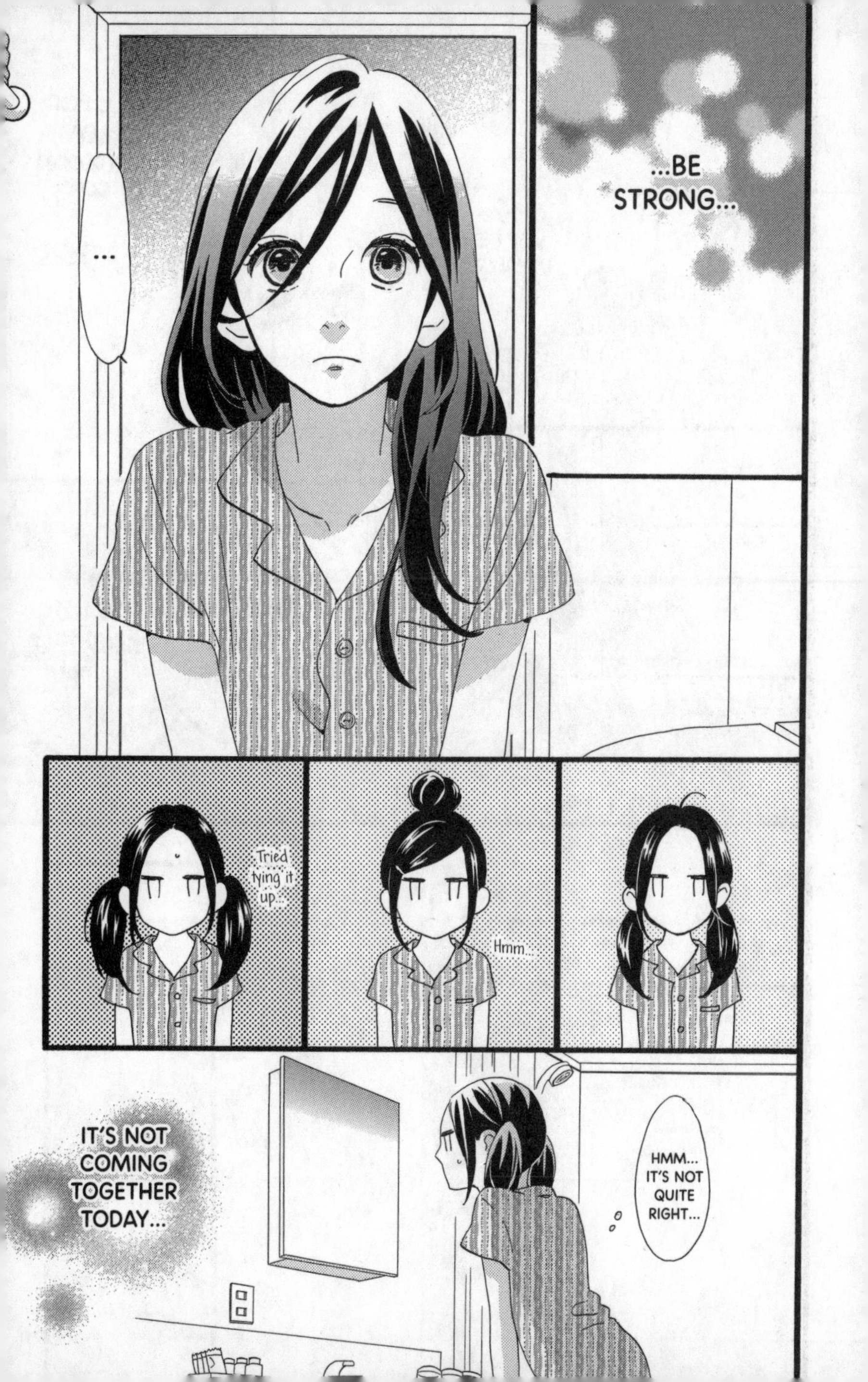
...BE STRONG...
...
Hmm...
Tried tying it up...
HMM... IT'S NOT QUITE RIGHT...
IT'S NOT COMING TOGETHER TODAY...

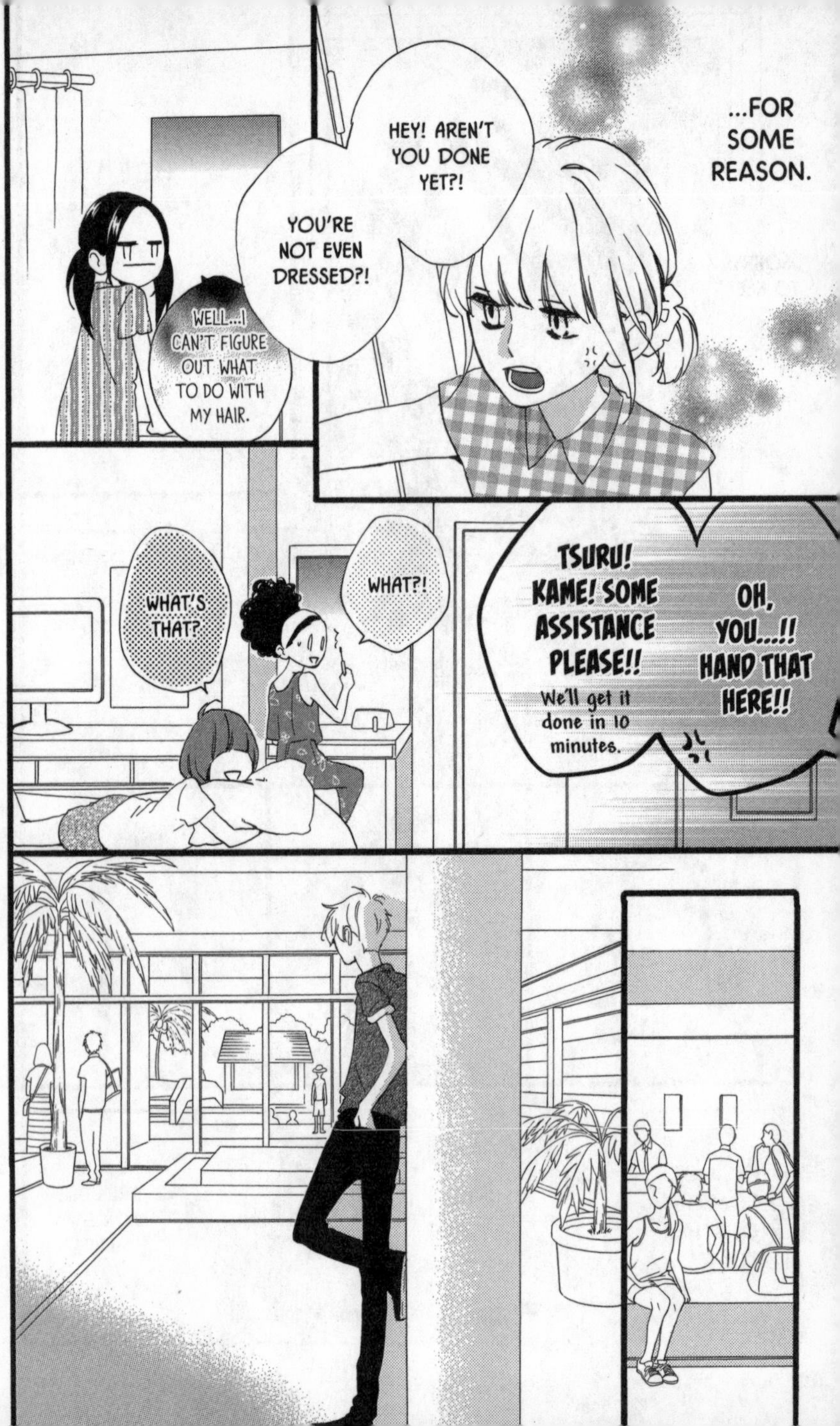
...FOR SOME REASON.
HEY! AREN'T YOU DONE YET?!
YOU'RE NOT EVEN DRESSED?!
WELL...I CAN'T FIGURE OUT WHAT TO DO WITH MY HAIR.
OH, YOU...!! HAND THAT HERE!!
TSURU! KAME! SOME ASSISTANCE PLEASE!!
We'll get it done in 10 minutes.
WHAT?!
WHAT'S THAT?

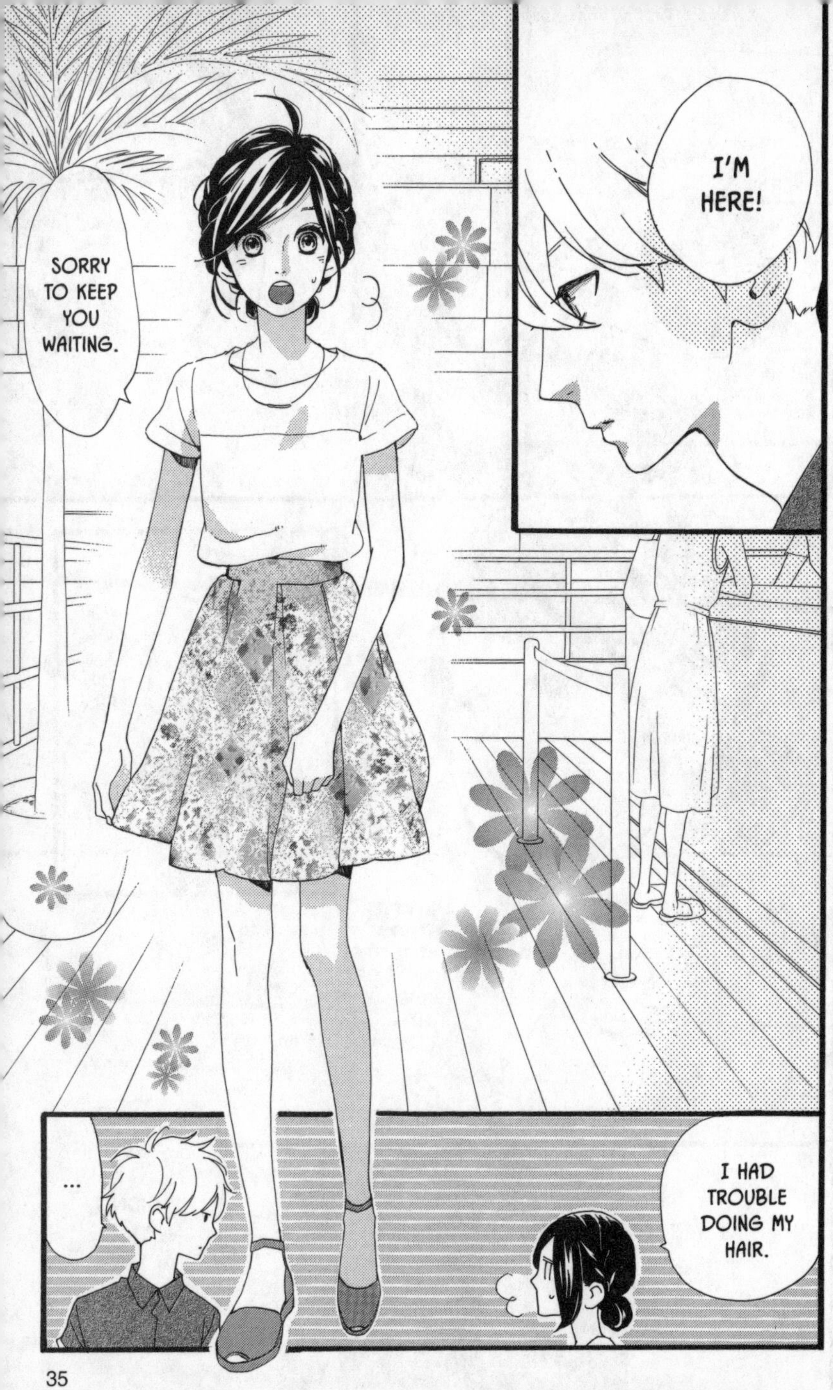
I'M HERE!
SORRY TO KEEP YOU WAITING.
I HAD TROUBLE DOING MY HAIR.
...

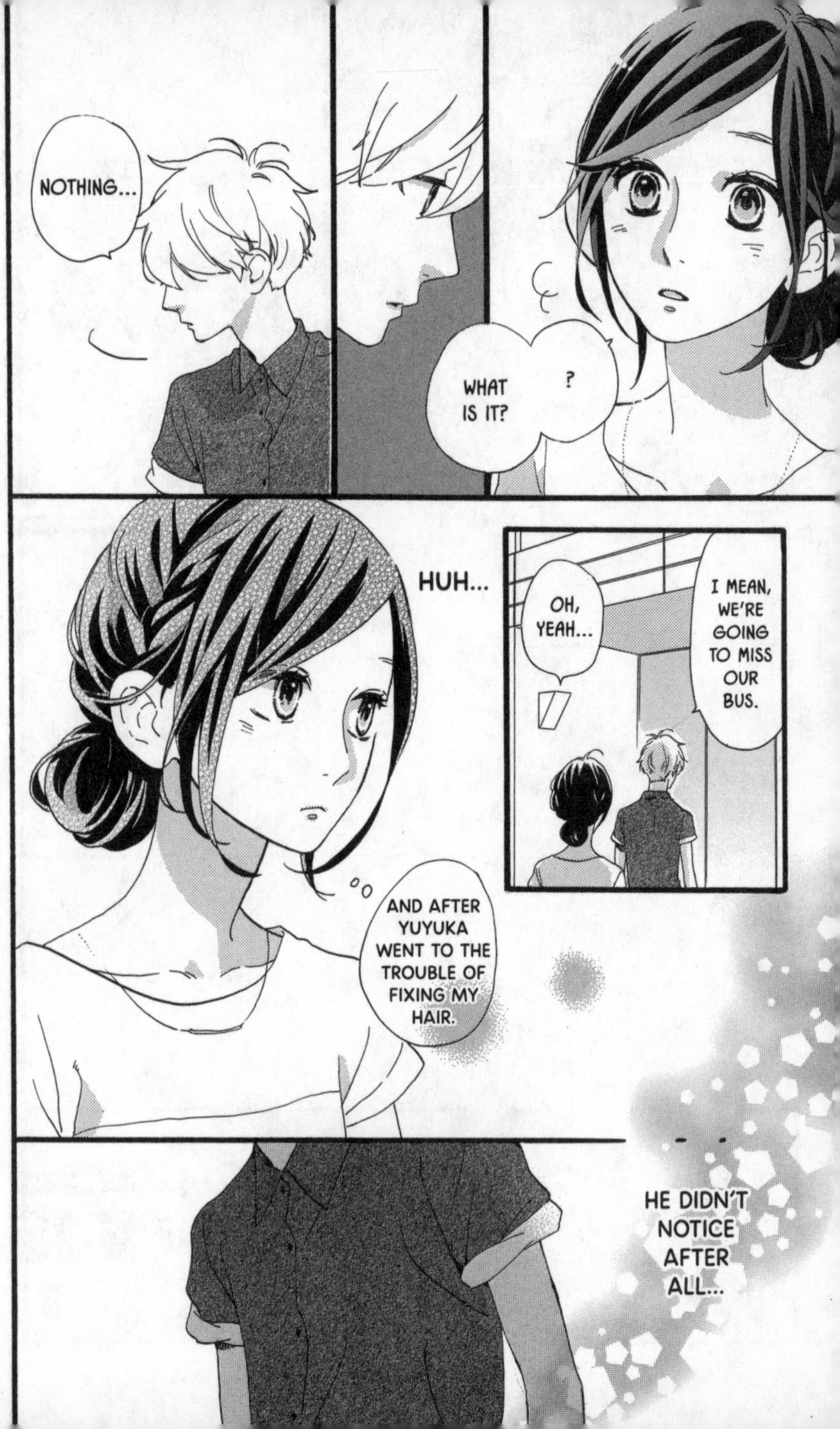
?
WHAT IS IT?
NOTHING...
I MEAN, WE'RE GOING TO MISS OUR BUS.
OH, YEAH...
HUH...
AND AFTER YUYUKA WENT TO THE TROUBLE OF FIXING MY HAIR.
HE DIDN'T NOTICE AFTER ALL...

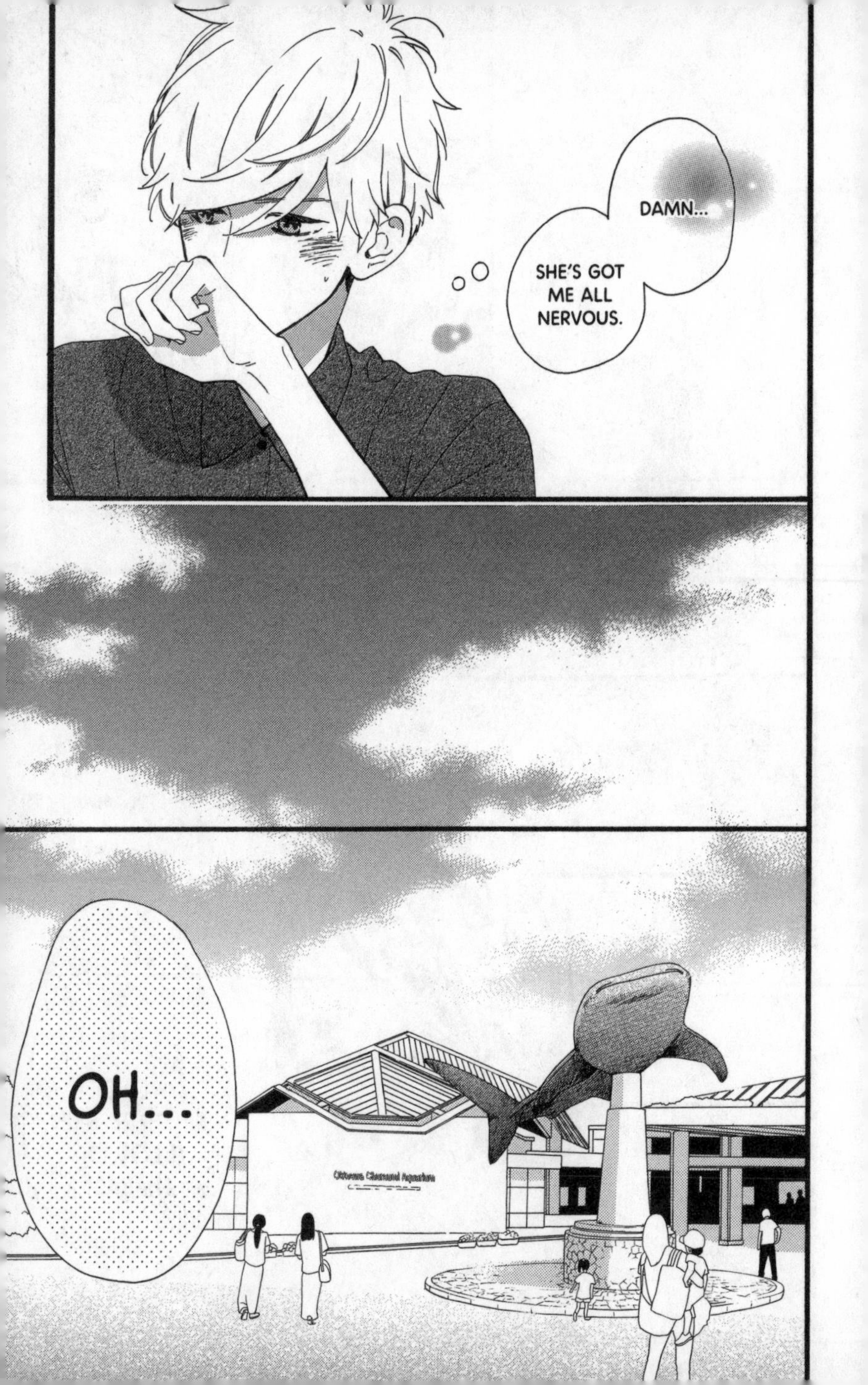
DAMN...
SHE'S GOT ME ALL NERVOUS.
OH...

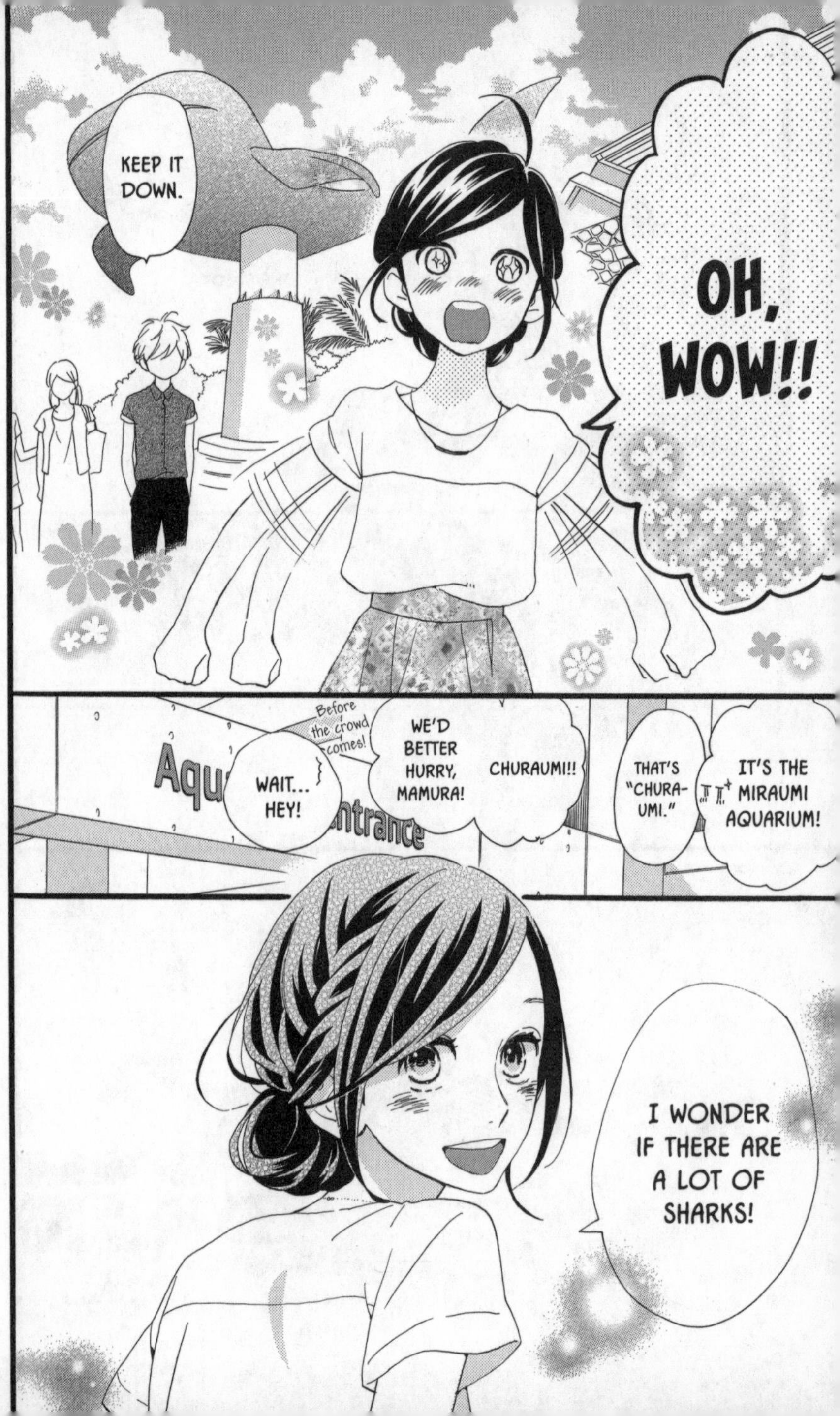
OH, WOW!!
KEEP IT DOWN.
IT'S THE MIRAUMI AQUARIUM!
THAT'S "CHURA-UMI."
CHURAUMI!!
WE'D BETTER HURRY, MAMURA!
Before the crowd comes!
WAIT... HEY!
I WONDER IF THERE ARE A LOT OF SHARKS!

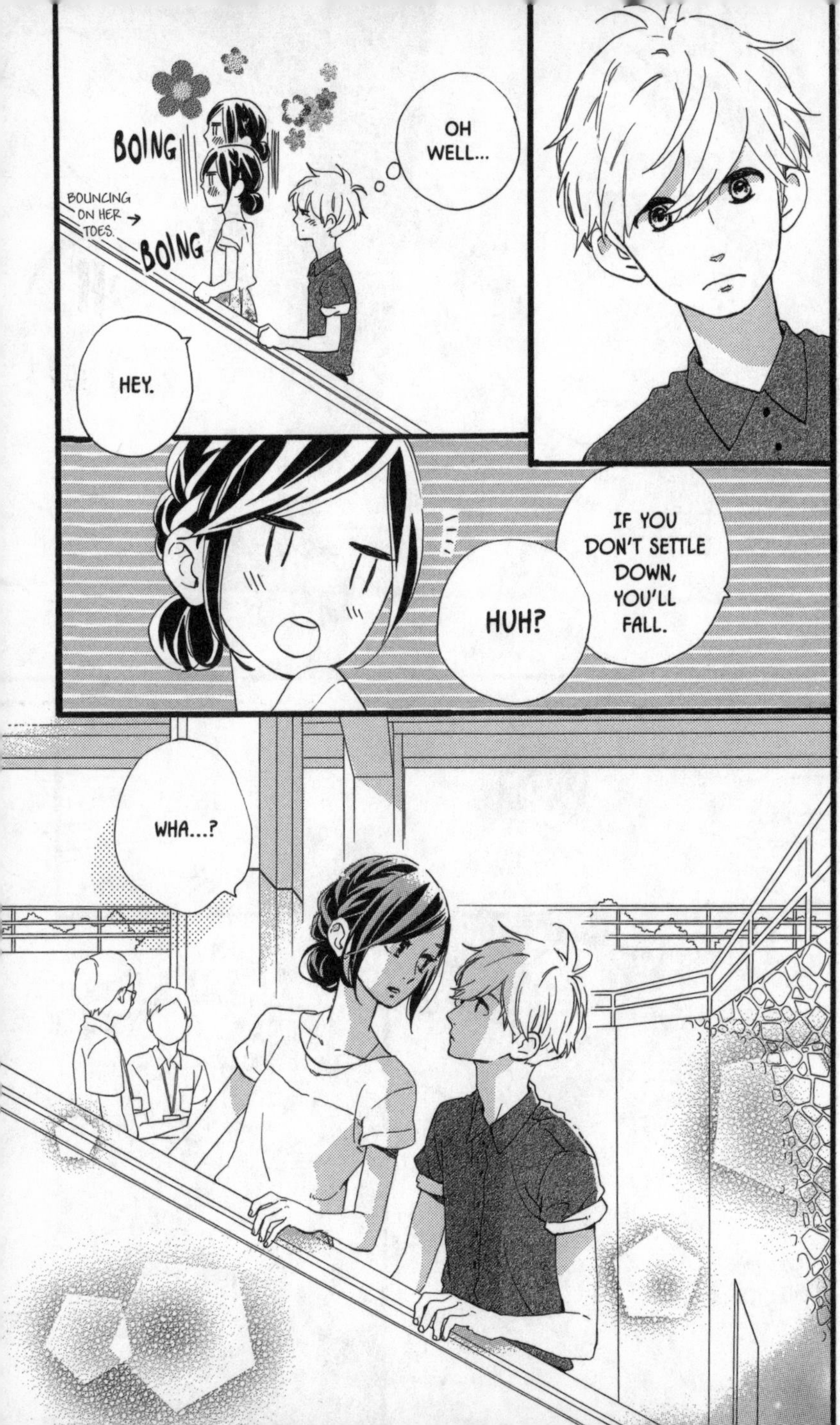
OH WELL...
BOING
BOUNCING ON HER TOES. →
BOING
HEY.
IF YOU DON'T SETTLE DOWN, YOU'LL FALL.
HUH?
WHA...?

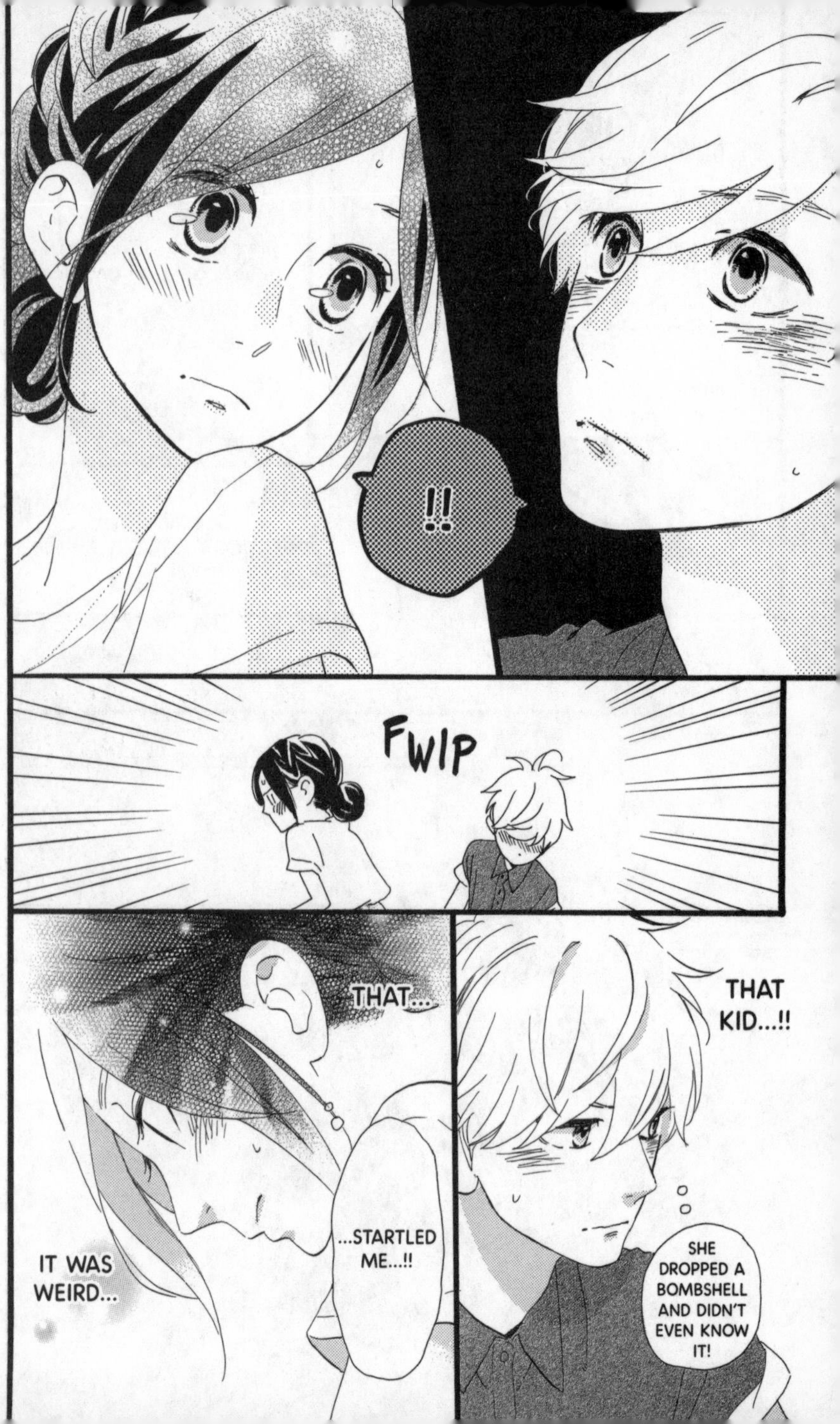
!!
FWIP
THAT KID...!!
SHE DROPPED A BOMBSHELL AND DIDN'T EVEN KNOW IT!
THAT...
...STARTLED ME...!!
IT WAS WEIRD...

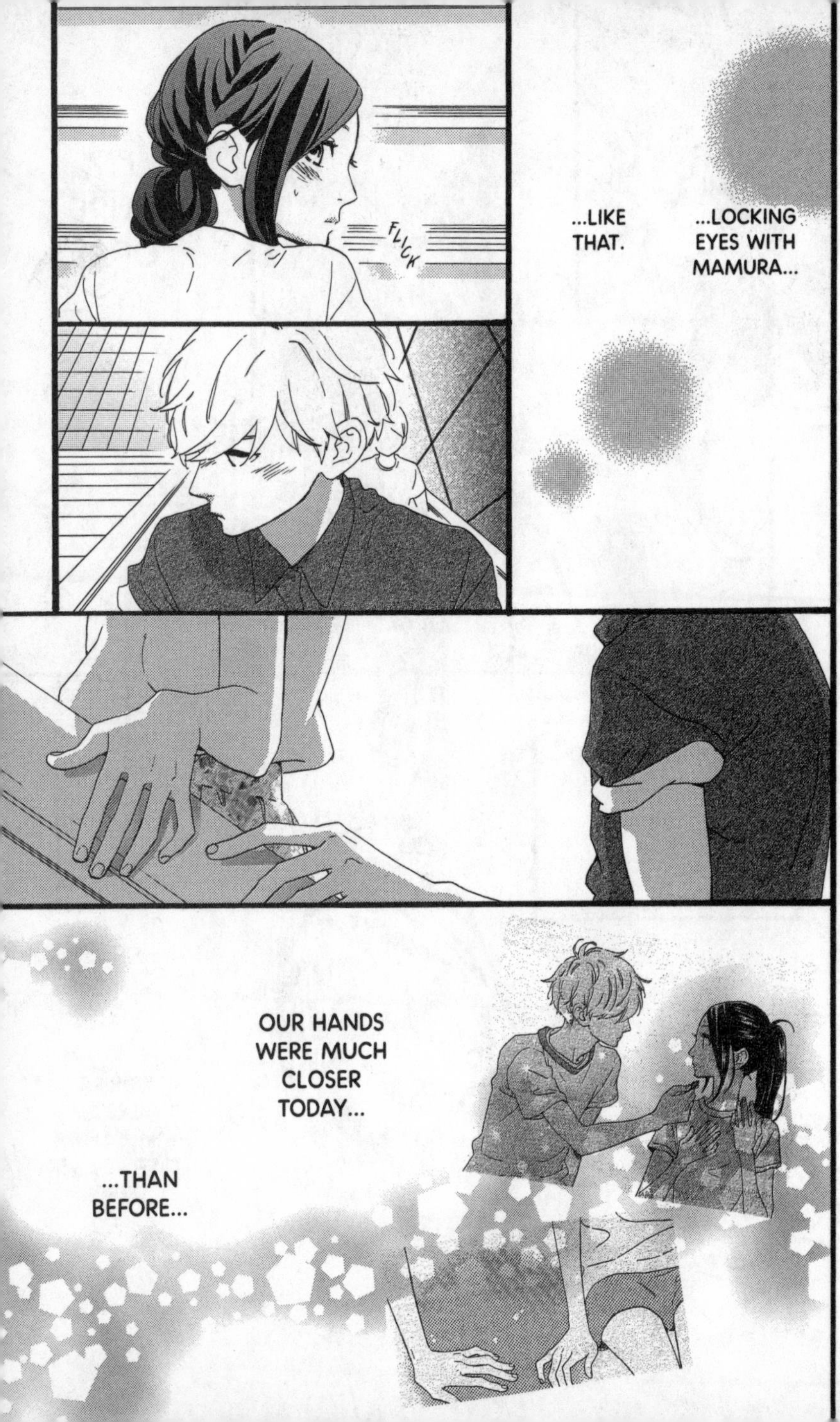
...LOCKING EYES WITH MAMURA...
...LIKE THAT.
FLICK
OUR HANDS WERE MUCH CLOSER TODAY...
...THAN BEFORE...

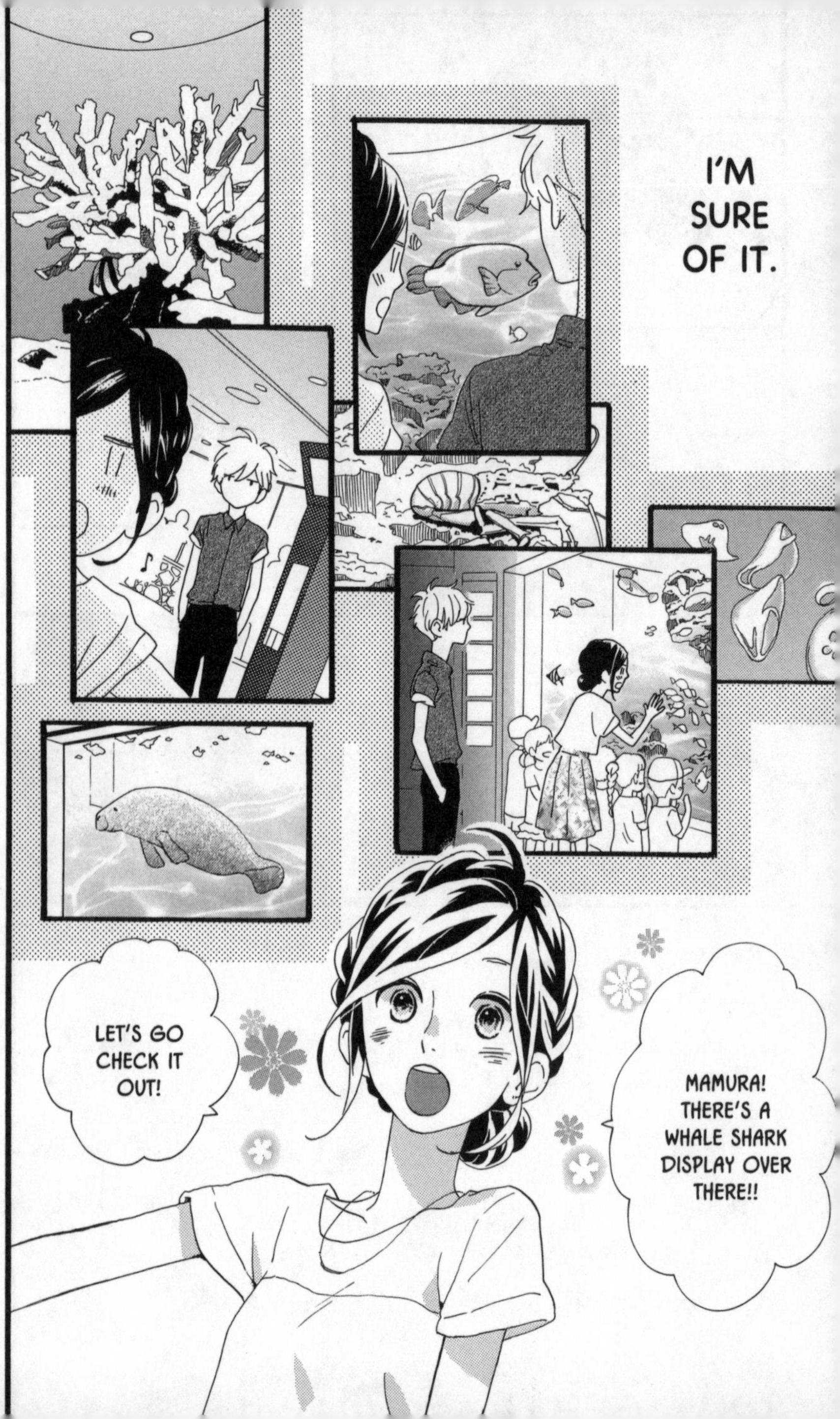
I'M SURE OF IT.
MAMURA! THERE'S A WHALE SHARK DISPLAY OVER THERE!!
LET'S GO CHECK IT OUT!

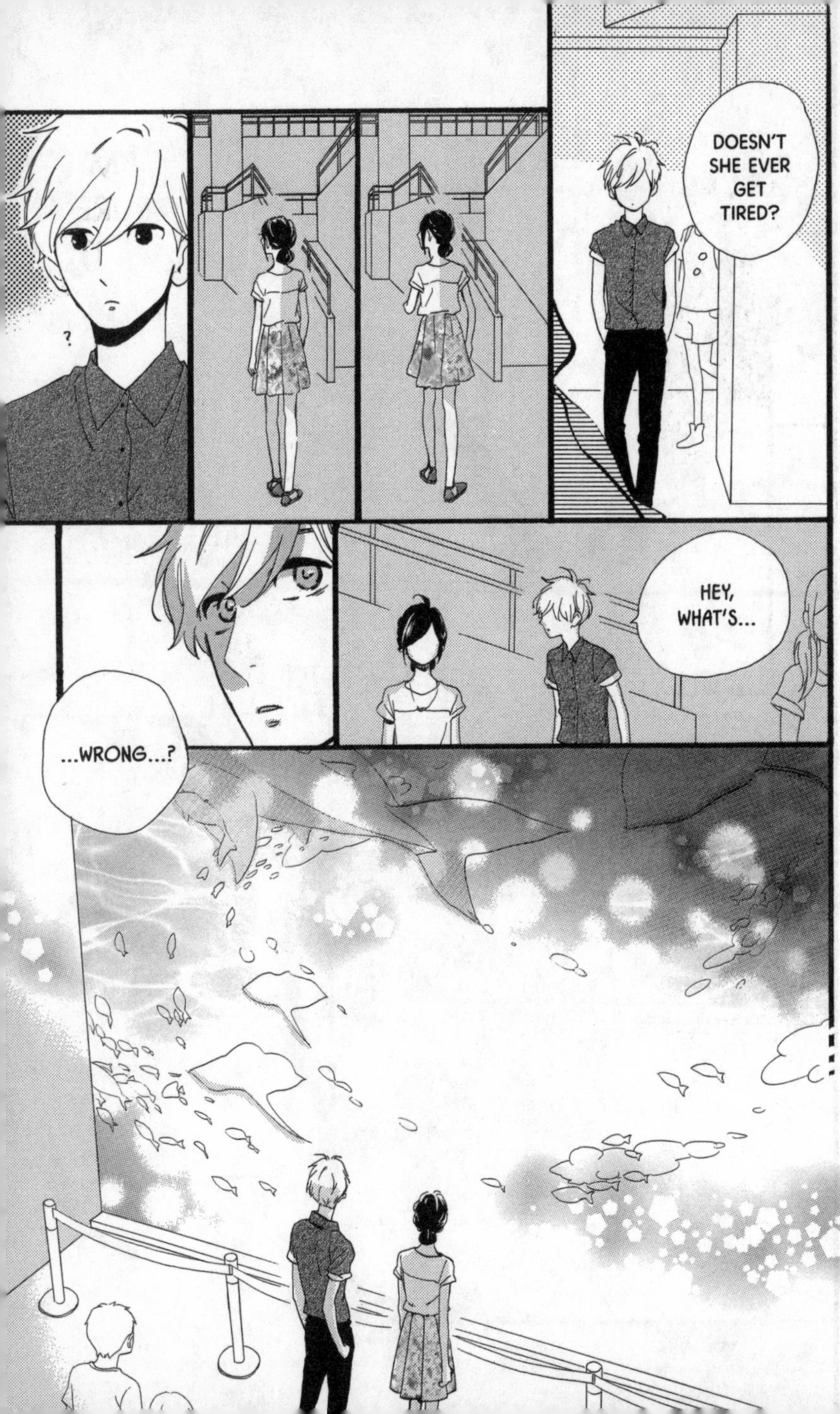
DOESN'T SHE EVER GET TIRED?
?
HEY, WHAT'S...
...WRONG...?

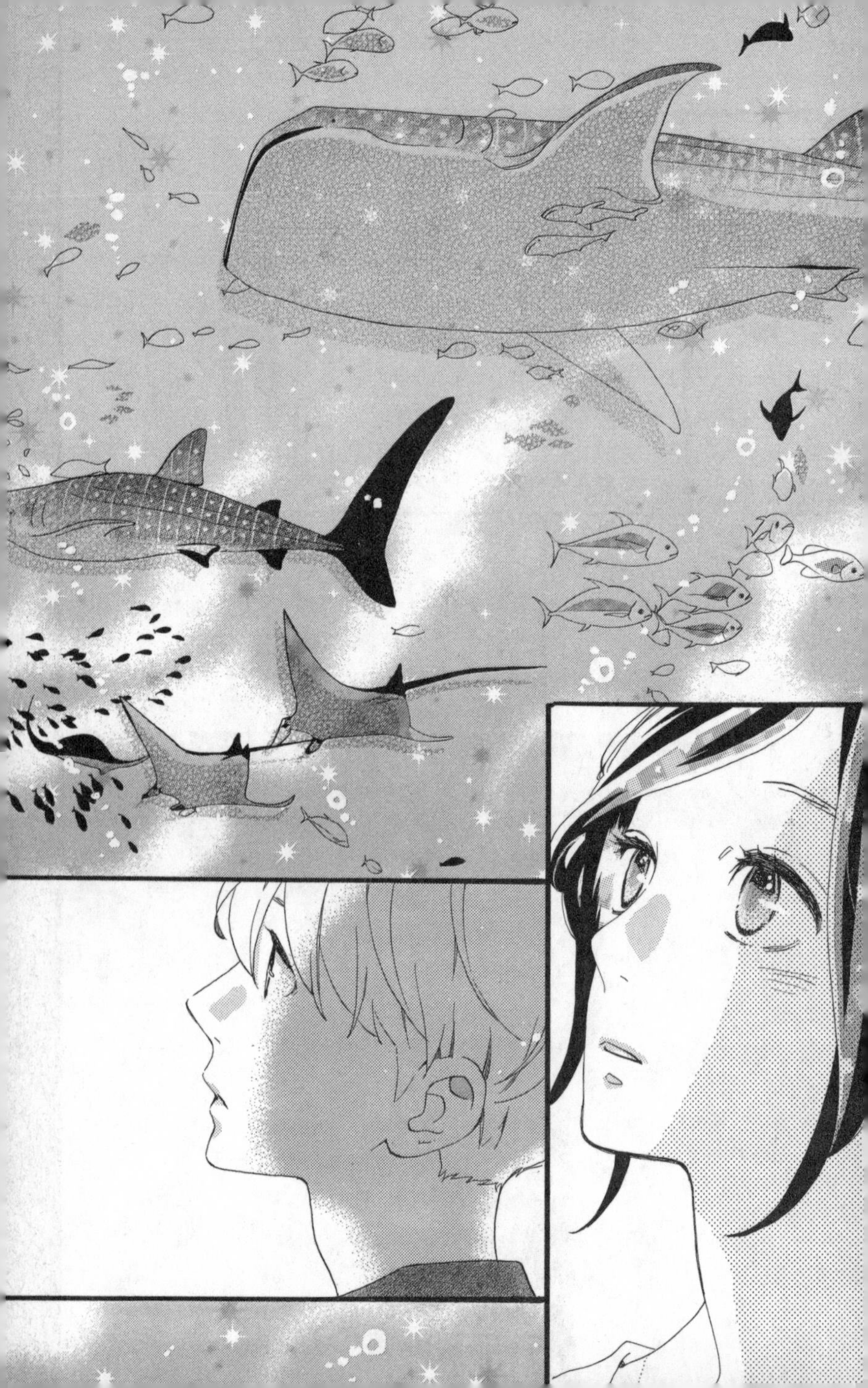

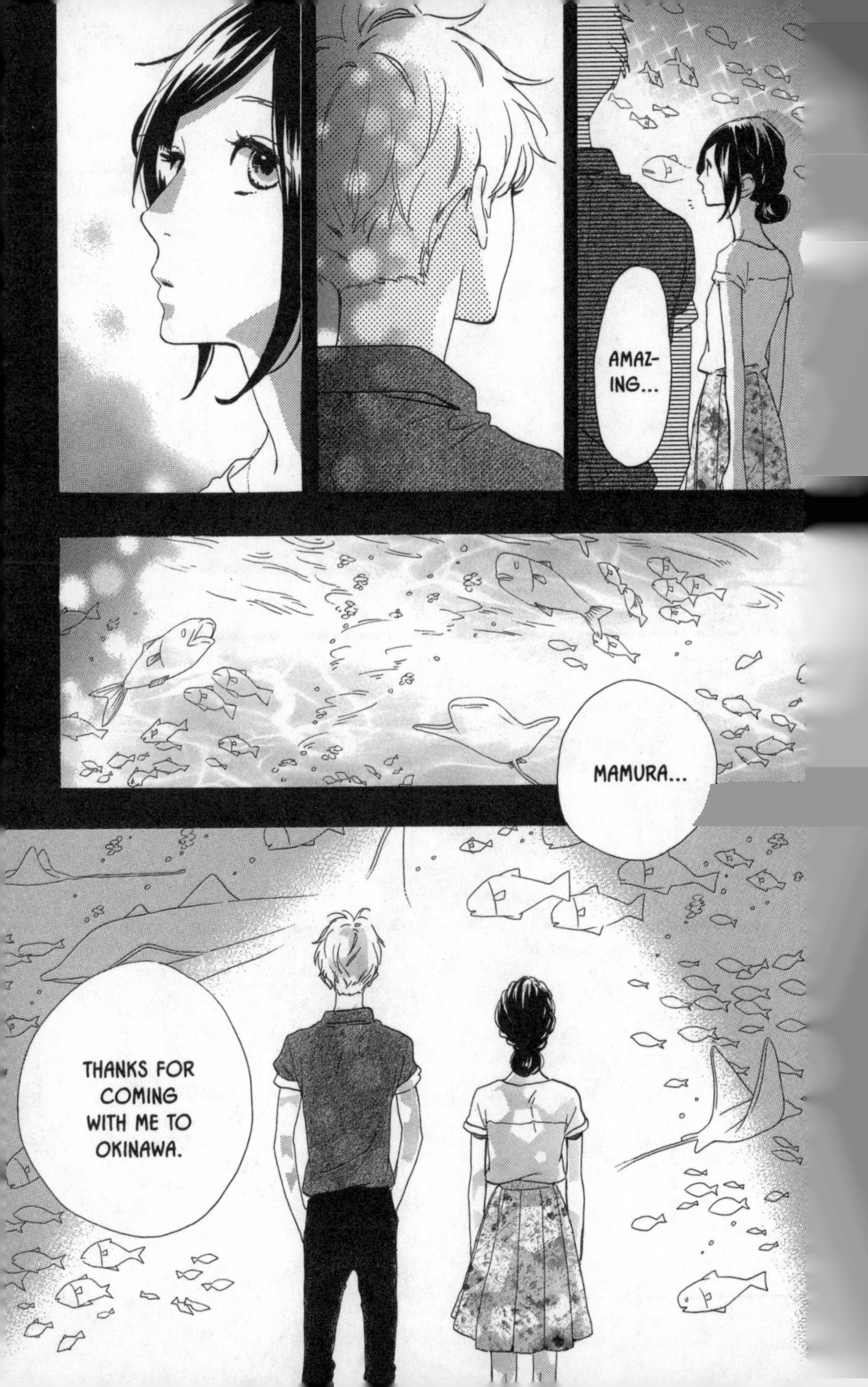
AMAZ-
ING...
MAMURA...
THANKS FOR
COMING
WITH ME TO
OKINAWA.

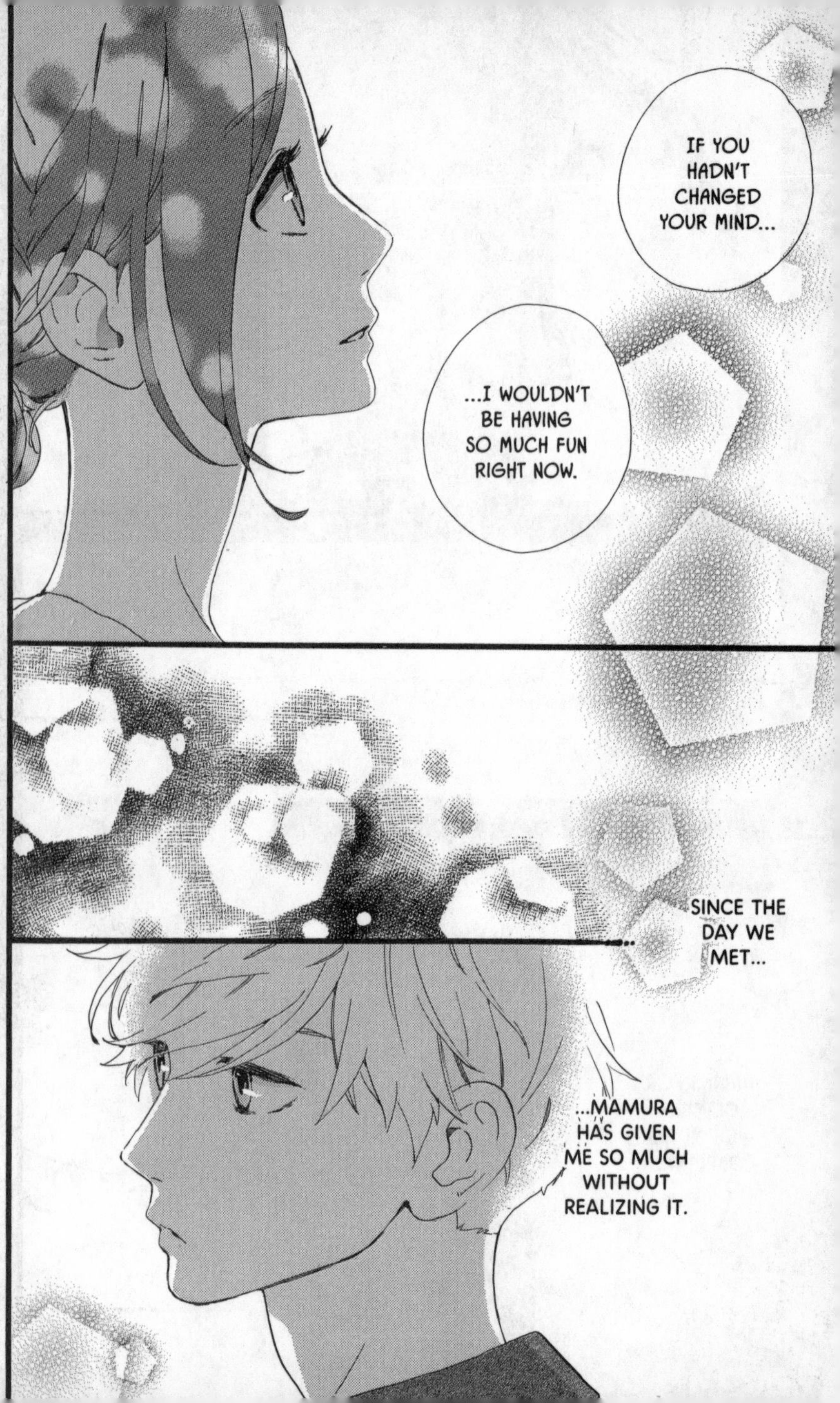
IF YOU HADN'T CHANGED YOUR MIND...
...I WOULDN'T BE HAVING SO MUCH FUN RIGHT NOW.
SINCE THE DAY WE MET...
...MAMURA HAS GIVEN ME SO MUCH WITHOUT REALIZING IT.

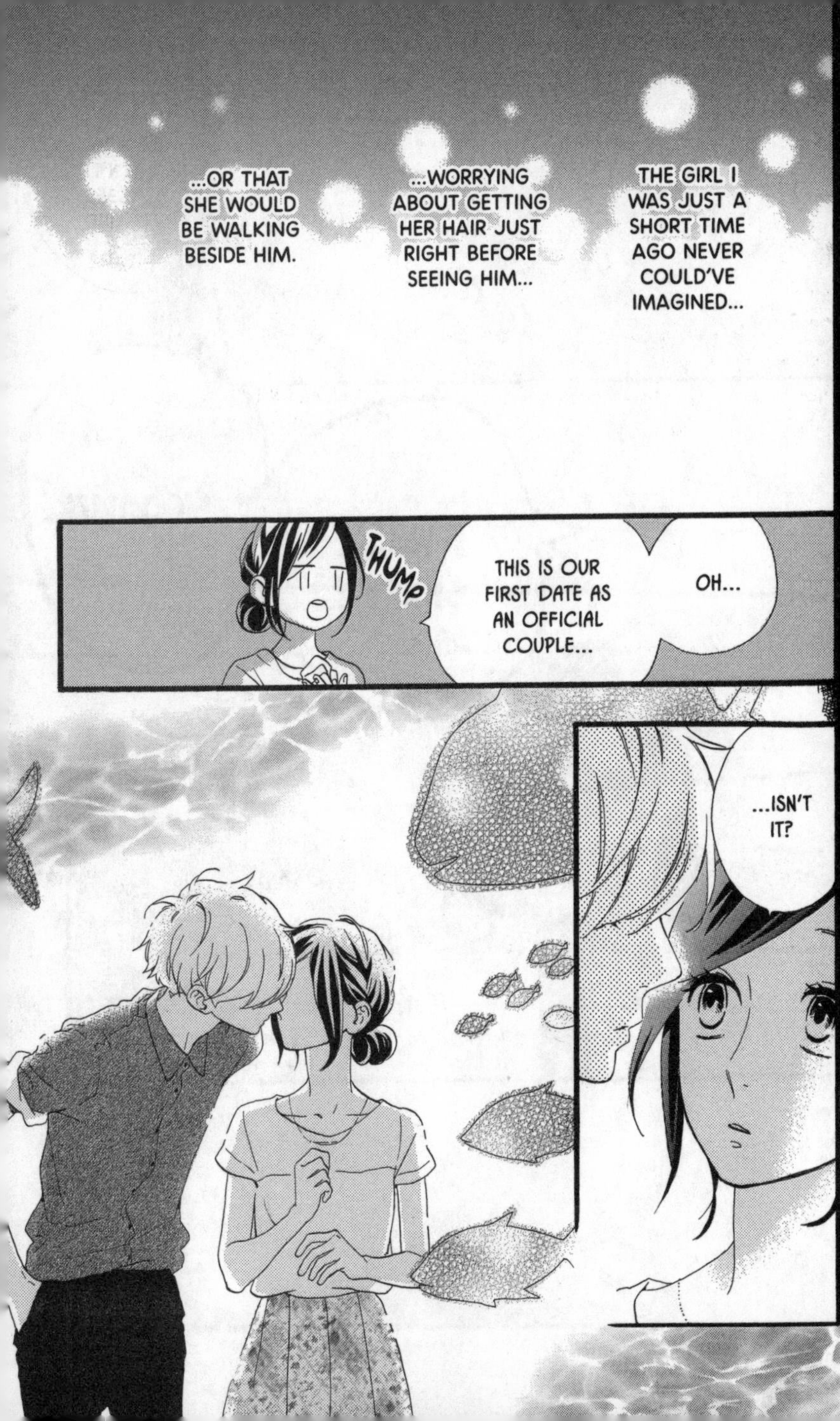
THE GIRL I WAS JUST A SHORT TIME AGO NEVER COULD'VE IMAGINED...
...WORRYING ABOUT GETTING HER HAIR JUST RIGHT BEFORE SEEING HIM...
...OR THAT SHE WOULD BE WALKING BESIDE HIM.
OH...
THIS IS OUR FIRST DATE AS AN OFFICIAL COUPLE...
THUMP
...ISN'T IT?

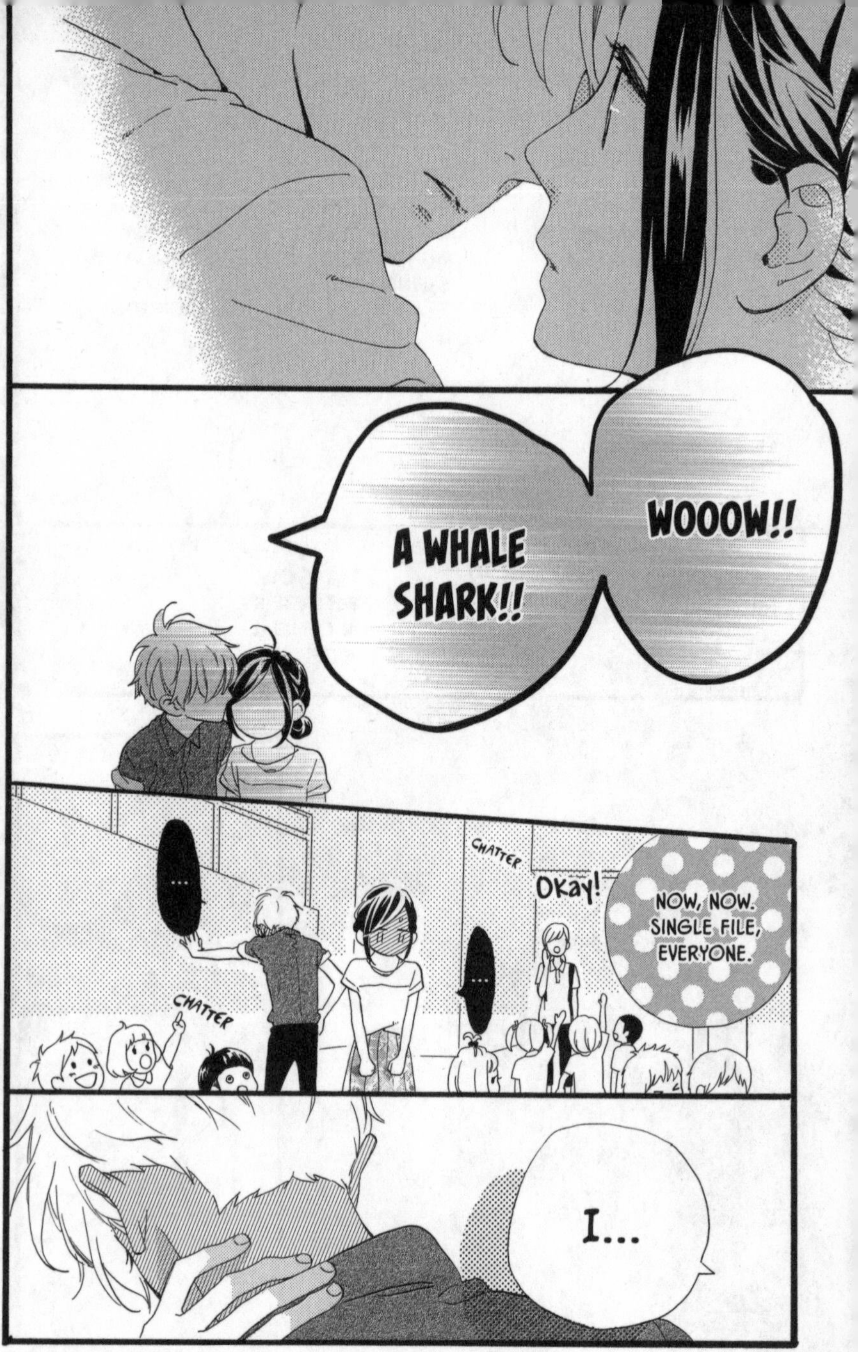
WOOOW!!
A WHALE SHARK!!
NOW, NOW. SINGLE FILE, EVERYONE.
Okay!
CHATTER
...
...
CHATTER
I...

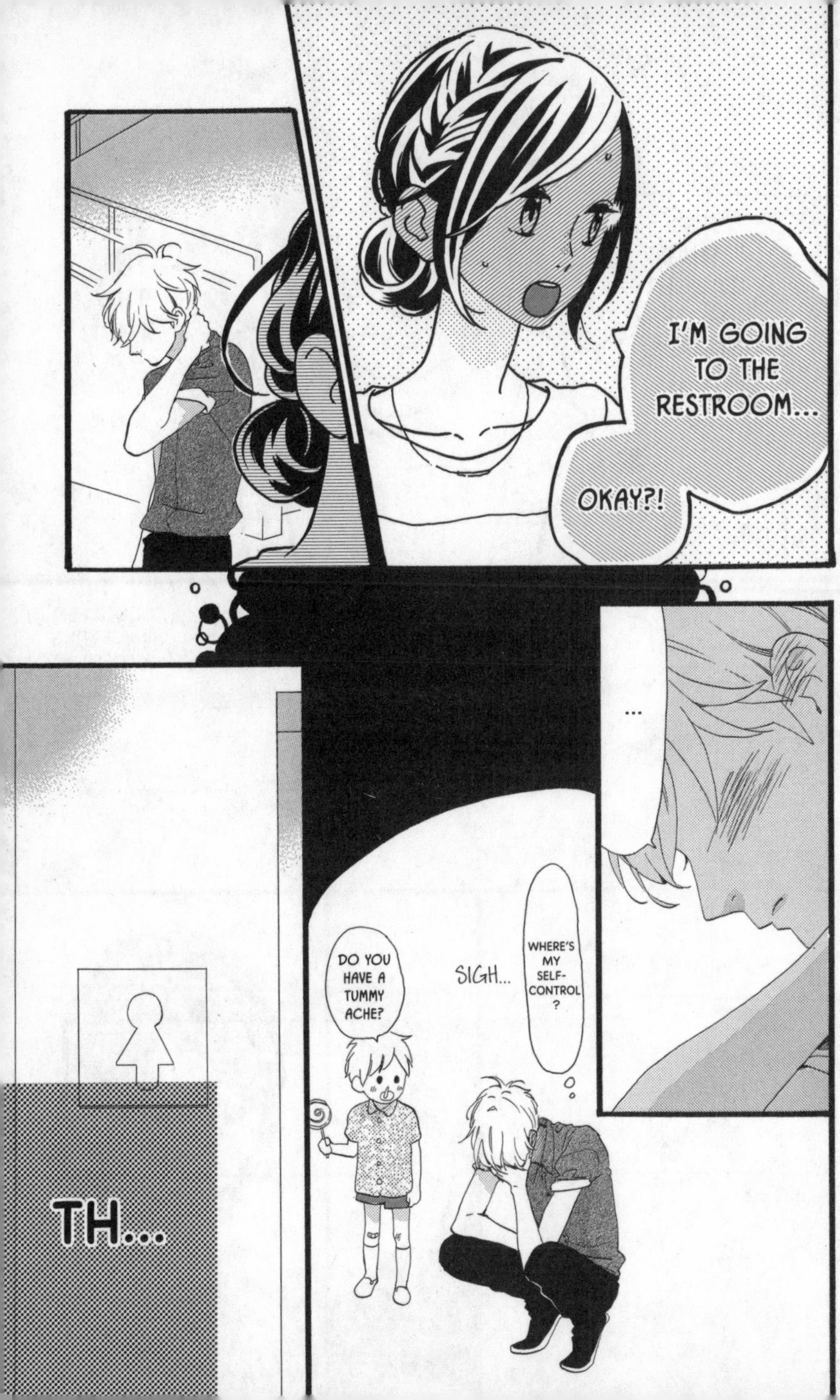
I'M GOING TO THE RESTROOM...
OKAY?!
...
WHERE'S MY SELF-CONTROL?
SIGH...
DO YOU HAVE A TUMMY ACHE?
TH...

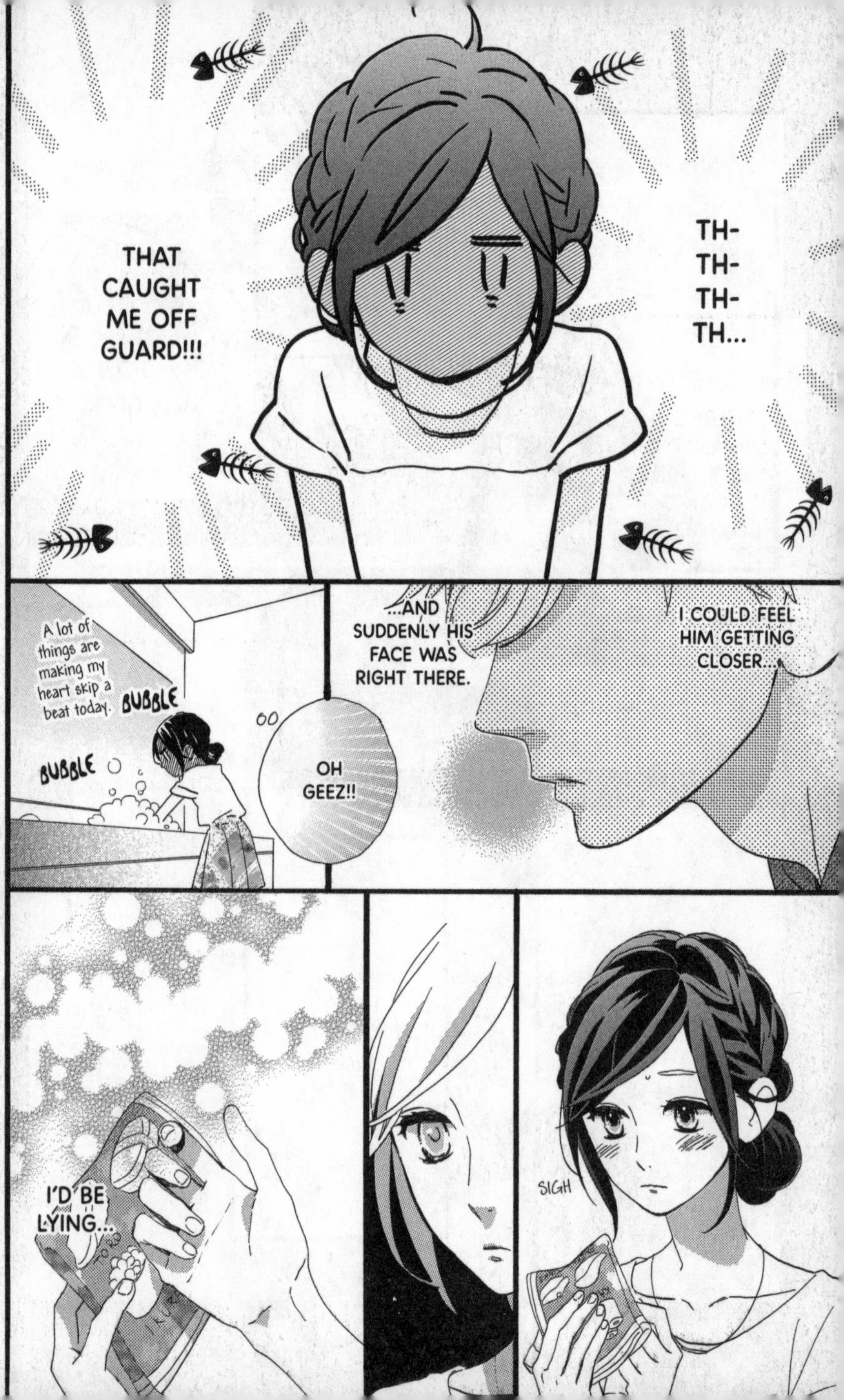
TH- TH- TH- TH...
THAT CAUGHT ME OFF GUARD!!!
I COULD FEEL HIM GETTING CLOSER...
...AND SUDDENLY HIS FACE WAS RIGHT THERE.
OH GEEZ!!
BUBBLE
A lot of things are making my heart skip a beat today.
BUBBLE
SIGH
I'D BE LYING...

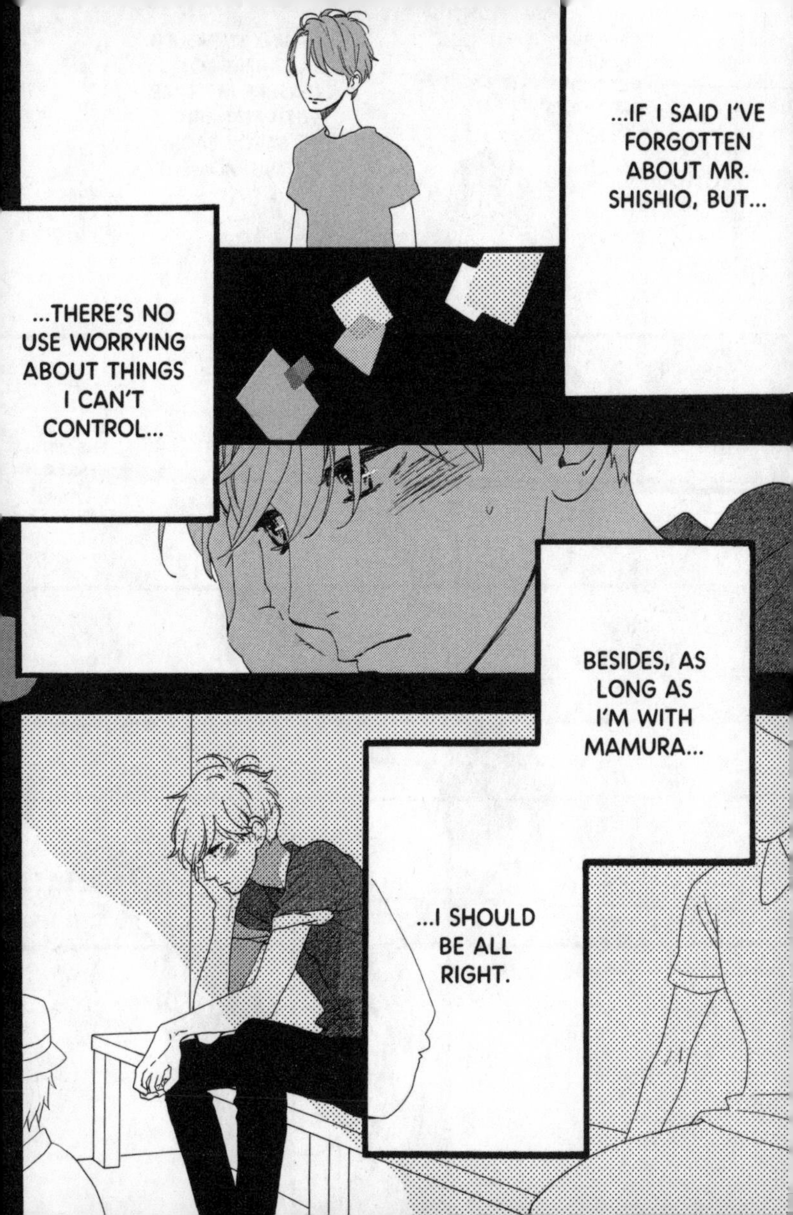
...IF I SAID I'VE FORGOTTEN ABOUT MR. SHISHIO, BUT...
...THERE'S NO USE WORRYING ABOUT THINGS I CAN'T CONTROL...
BESIDES, AS LONG AS I'M WITH MAMURA...
...I SHOULD BE ALL RIGHT.

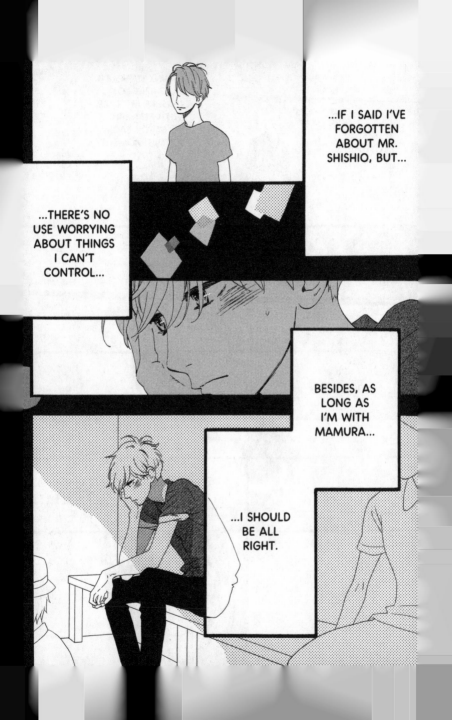

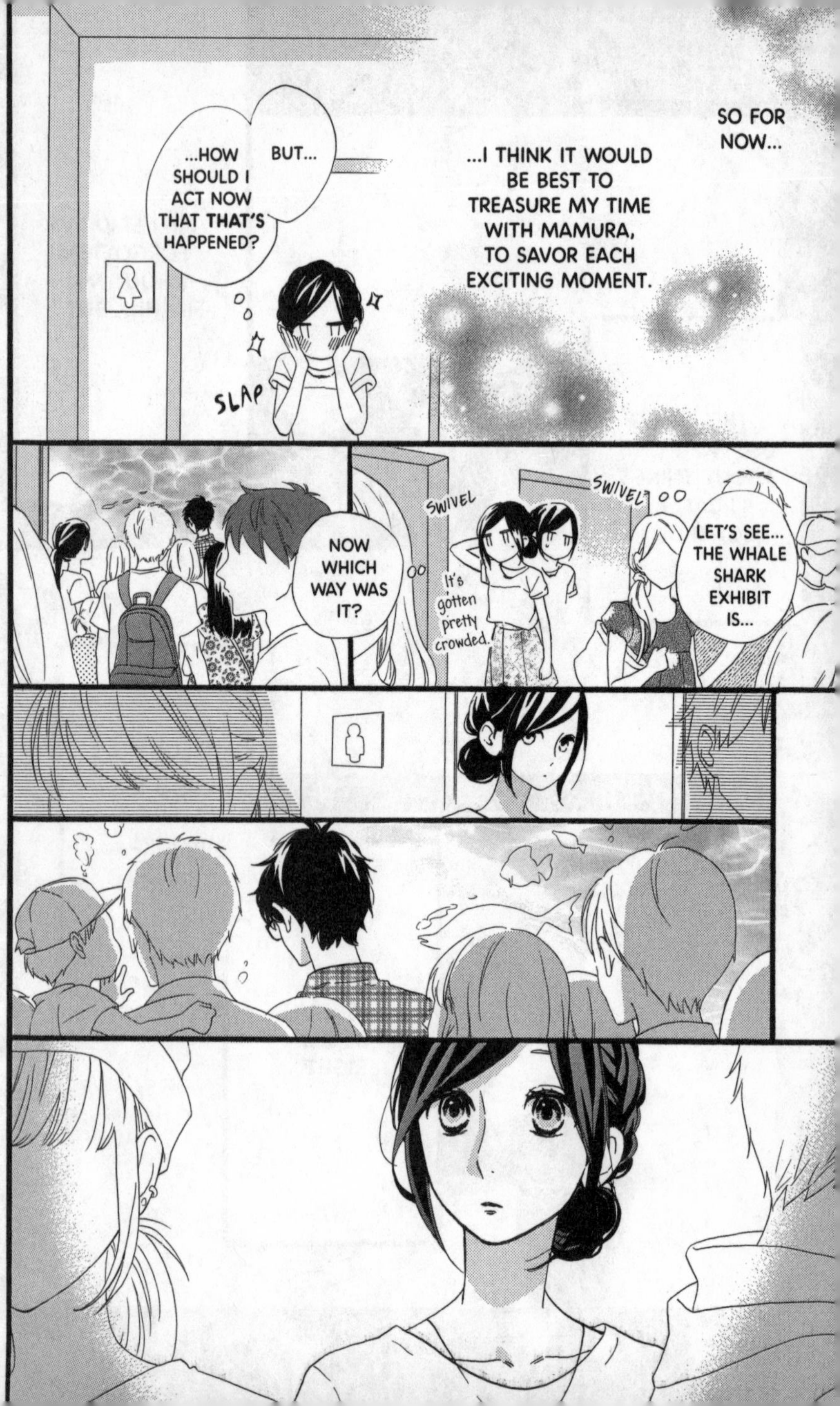
SO FOR NOW...
...I THINK IT WOULD BE BEST TO TREASURE MY TIME WITH MAMURA, TO SAVOR EACH EXCITING MOMENT.
BUT...
...HOW SHOULD I ACT NOW THAT THAT'S HAPPENED?
SLAP
LET'S SEE... THE WHALE SHARK EXHIBIT IS...
SWIVEL
SWIVEL
It's gotten pretty crowded.
NOW WHICH WAY WAS IT?

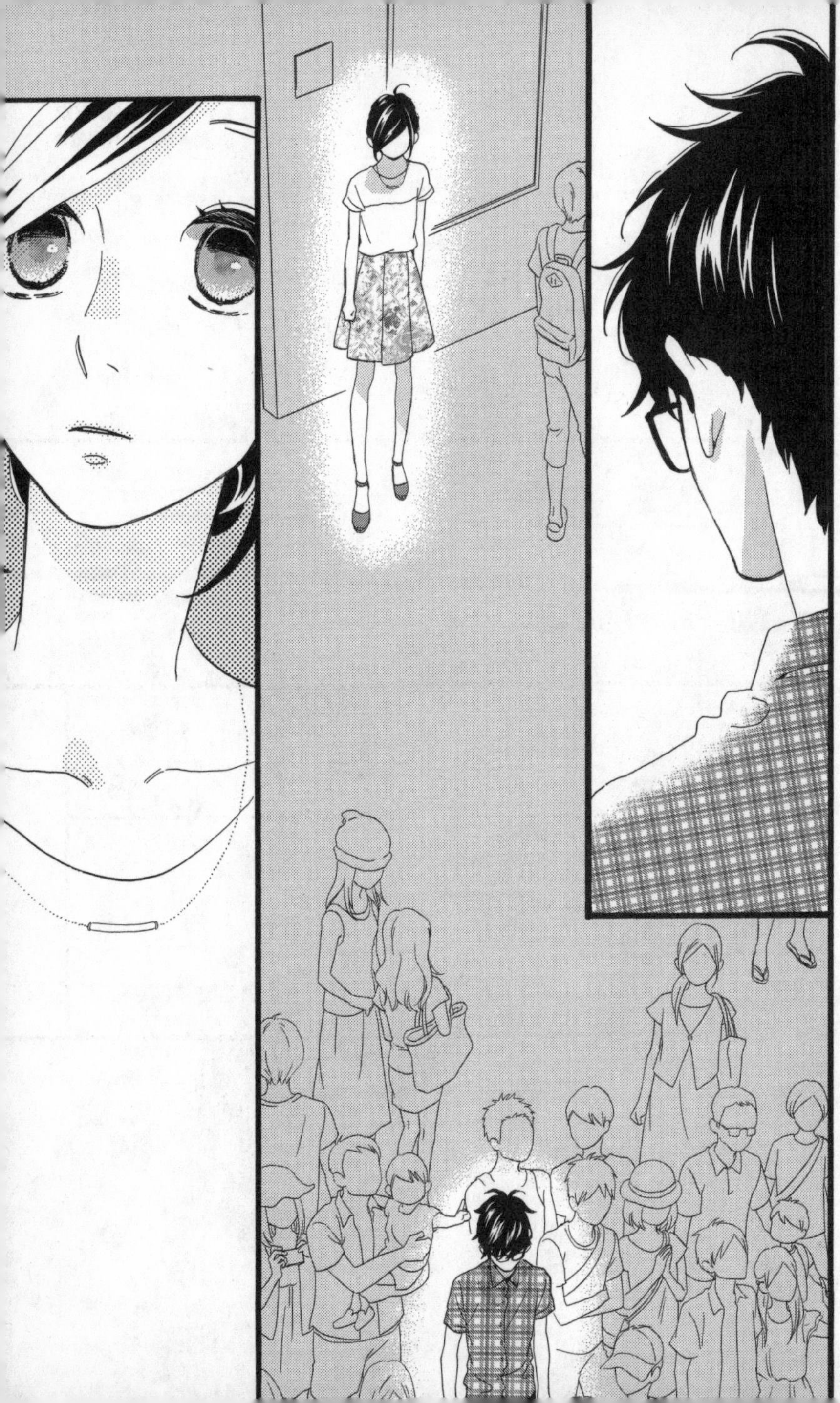

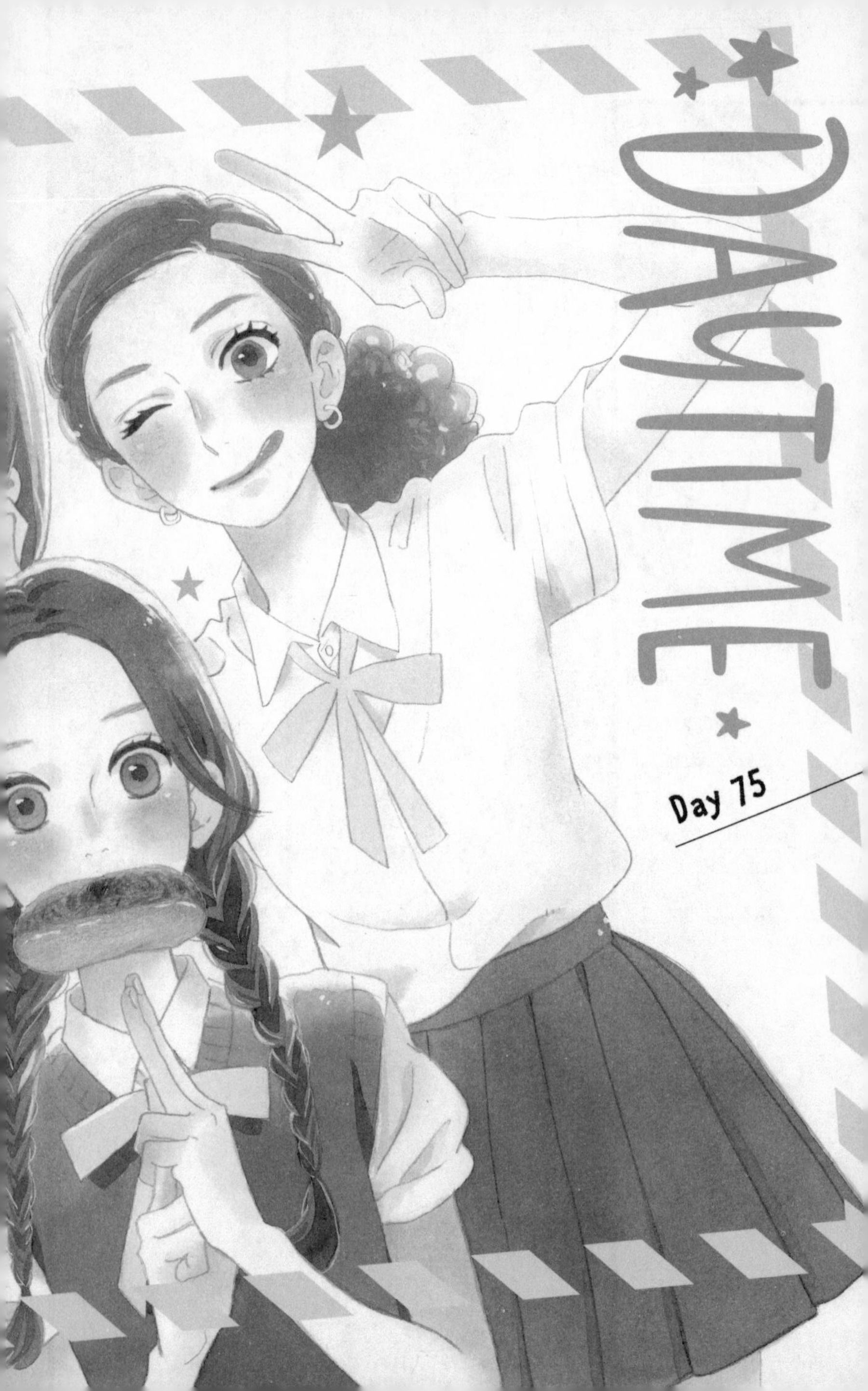
DAYTIME
Day 75

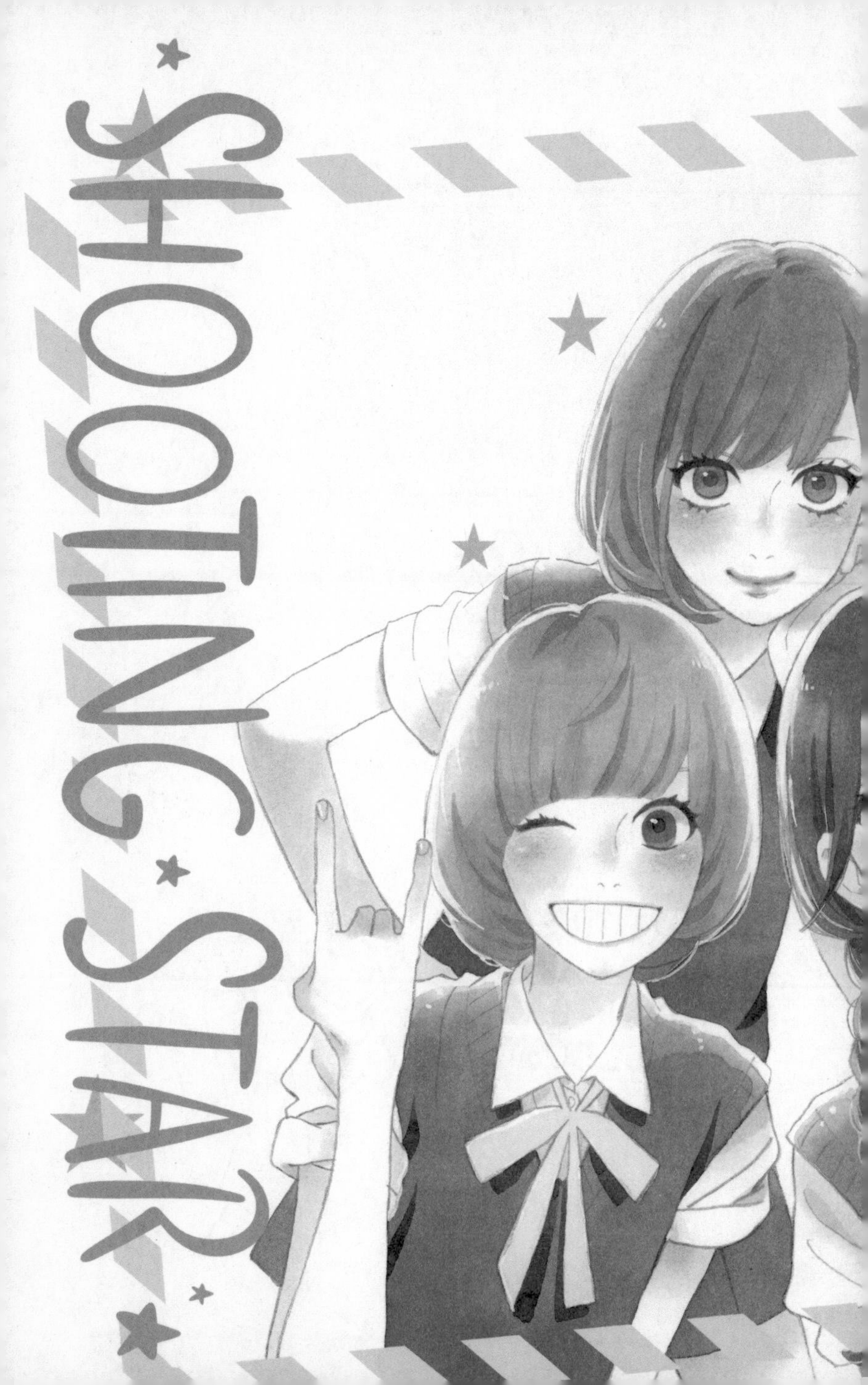
SHOOTING STAR

SHE TRIES TO AVOID CARRYING A BOOK BAG AT ALL COSTS.

Here goes...

STUFFING HER CELL PHONE AND WALLET INTO HER POCKETS.

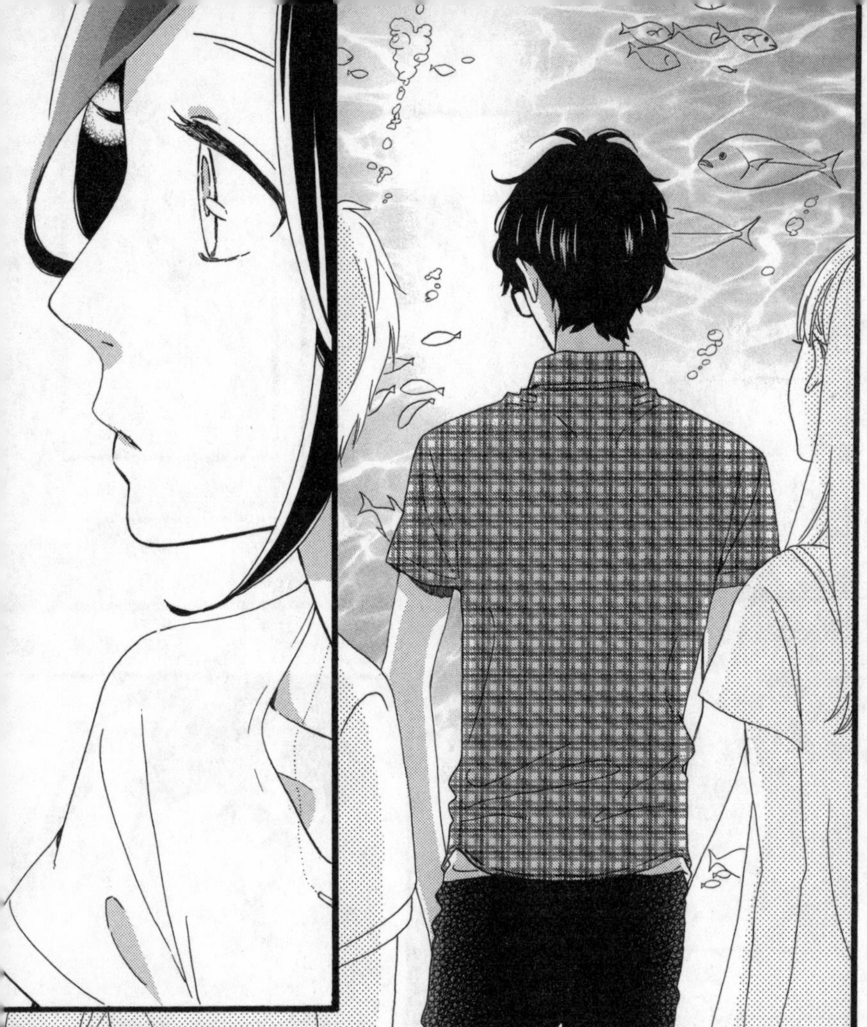

DAYTIME SHOOTING STAR

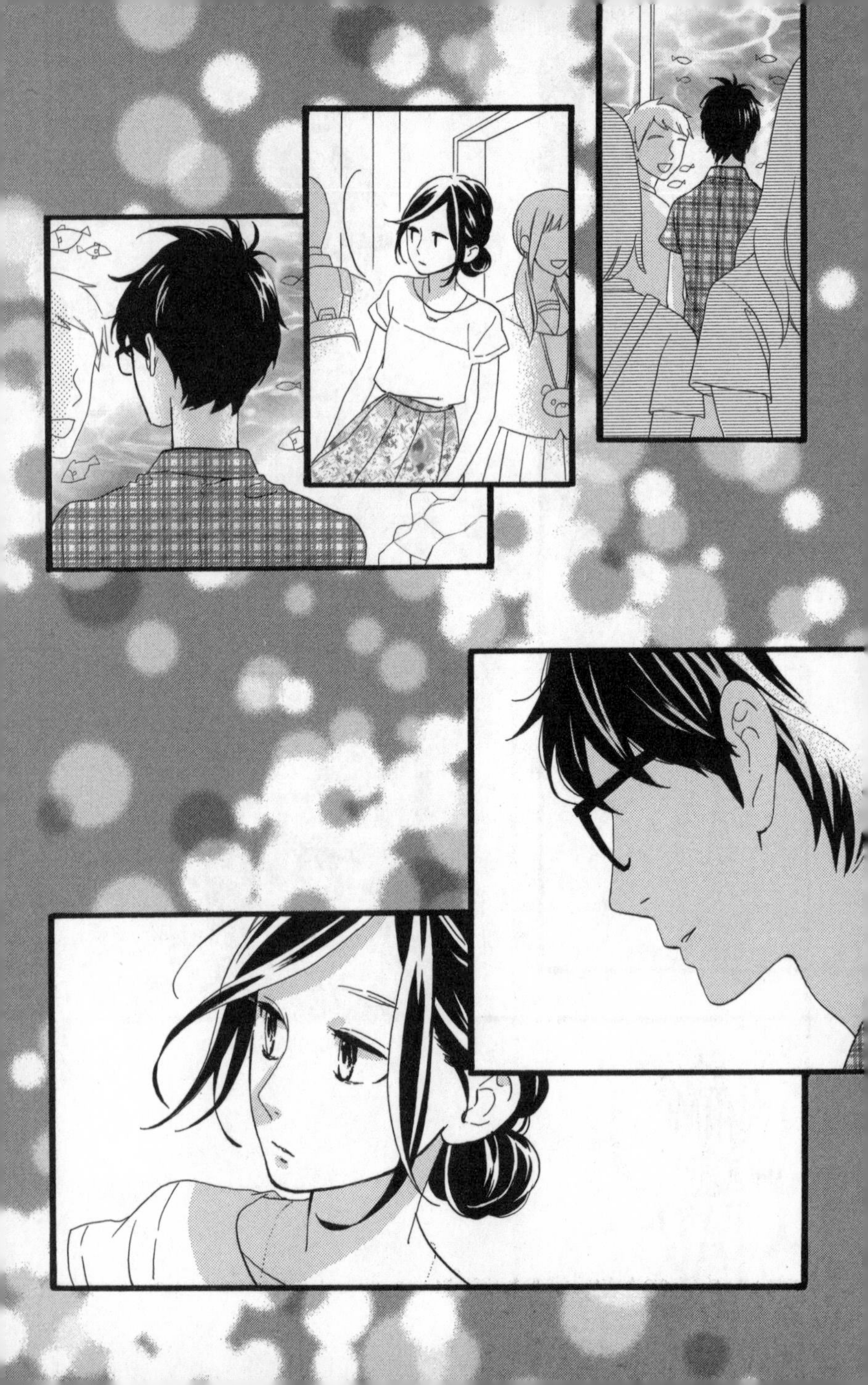

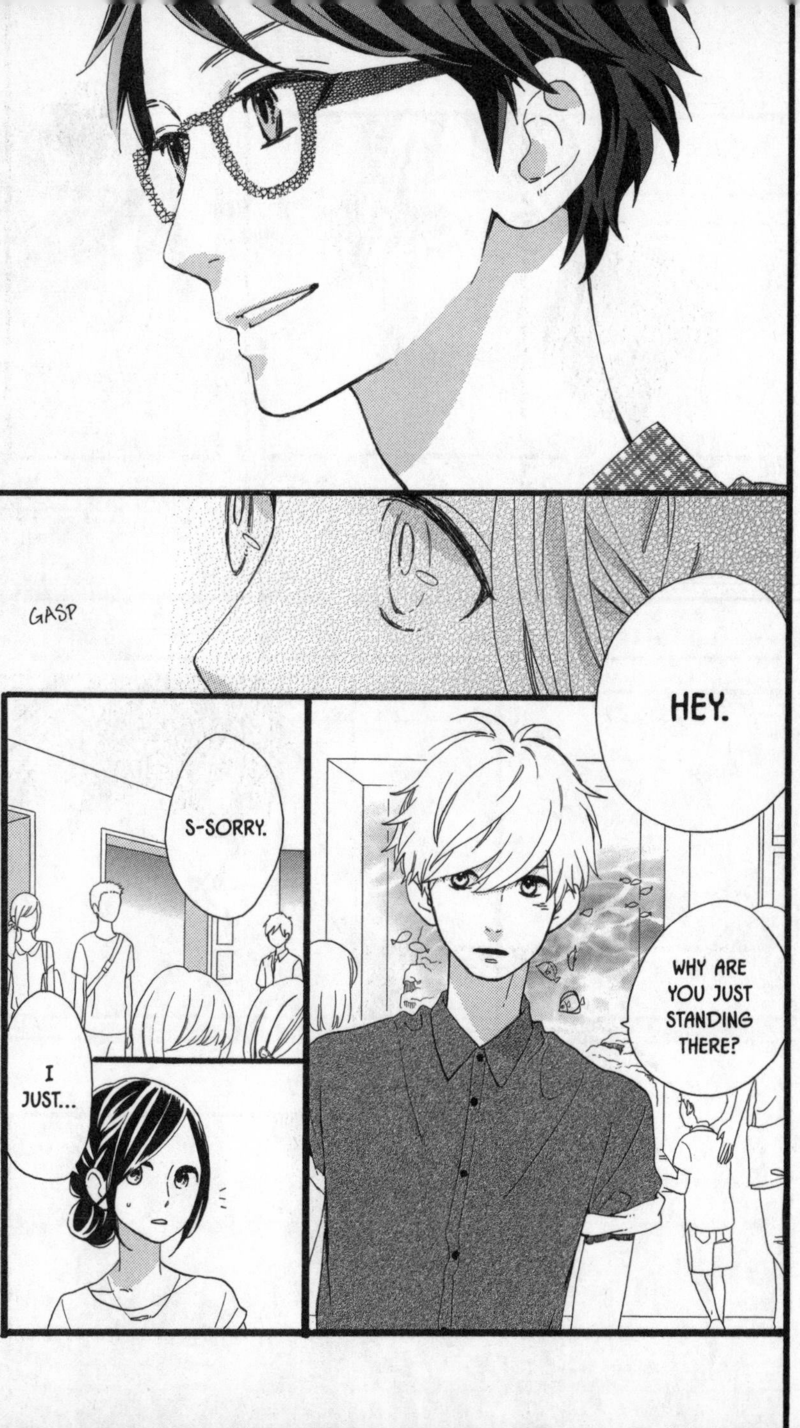
HEY.
GASP
WHY ARE YOU JUST STANDING THERE?
S-SORRY.
I JUST...

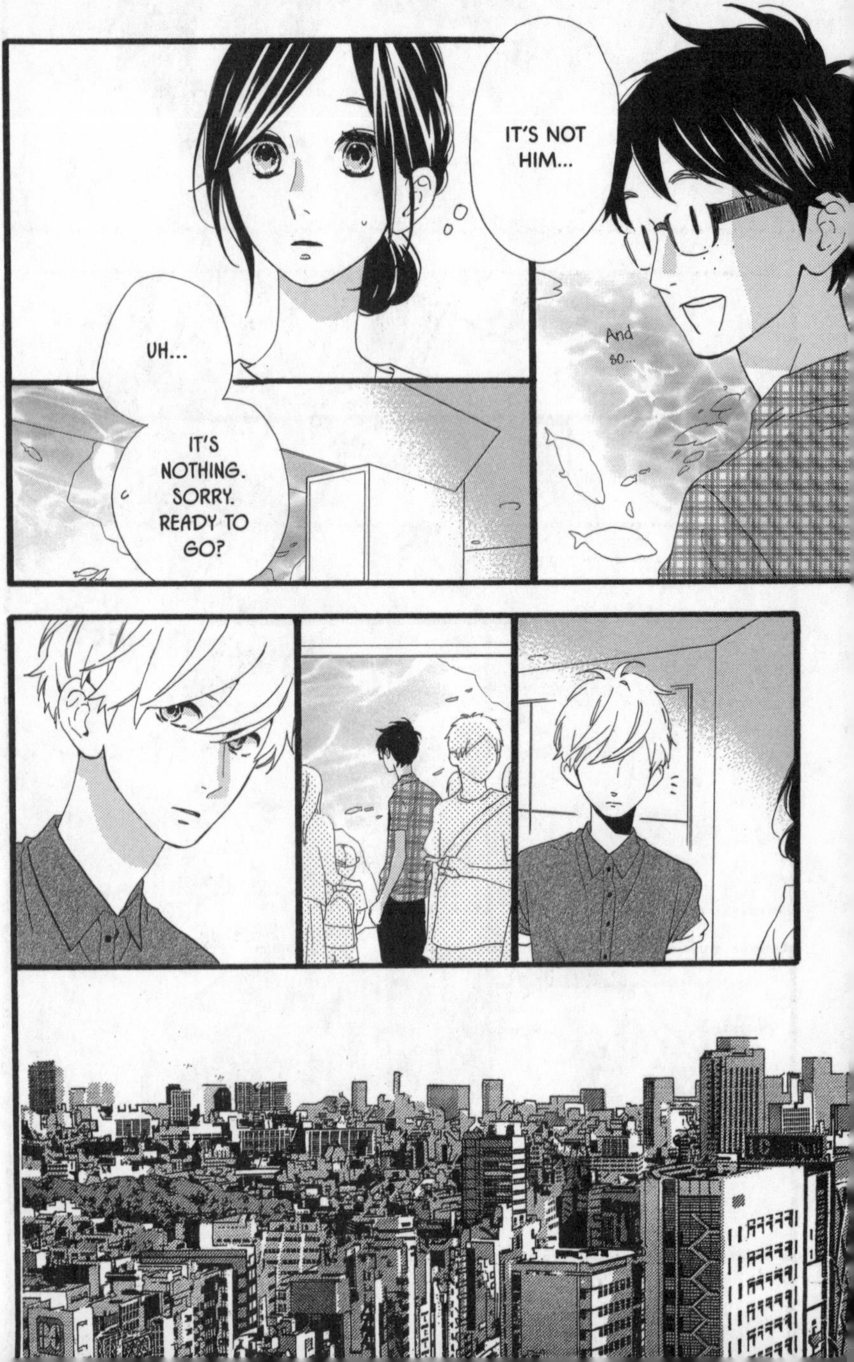
IT'S NOT HIM...
And so...
UH...
IT'S NOTHING. SORRY. READY TO GO?

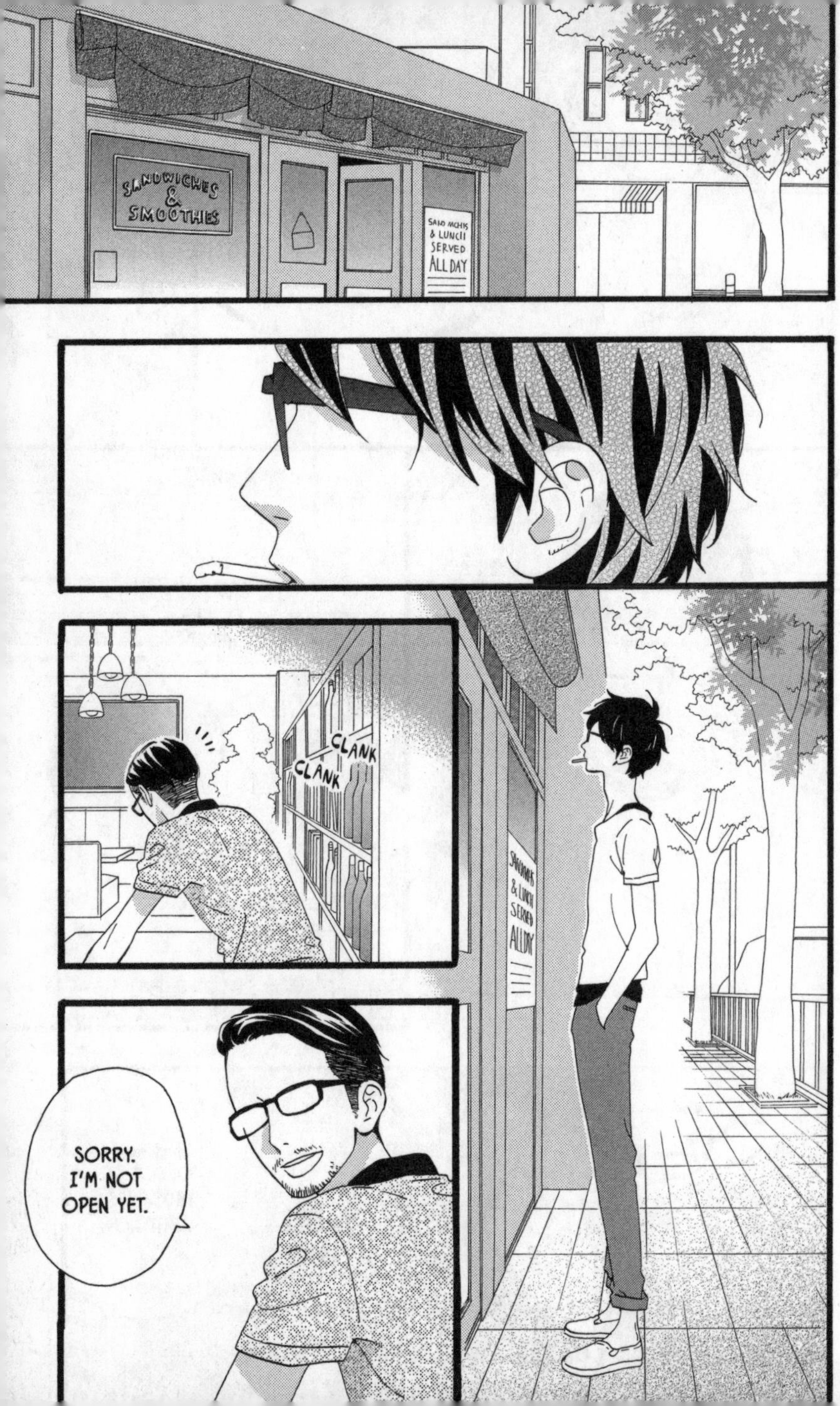
SANDWICHES & SMOOTHIES
SANDWICHES & LUNCH SERVED ALL DAY
CLANK
CLANK
SORRY. I'M NOT OPEN YET.

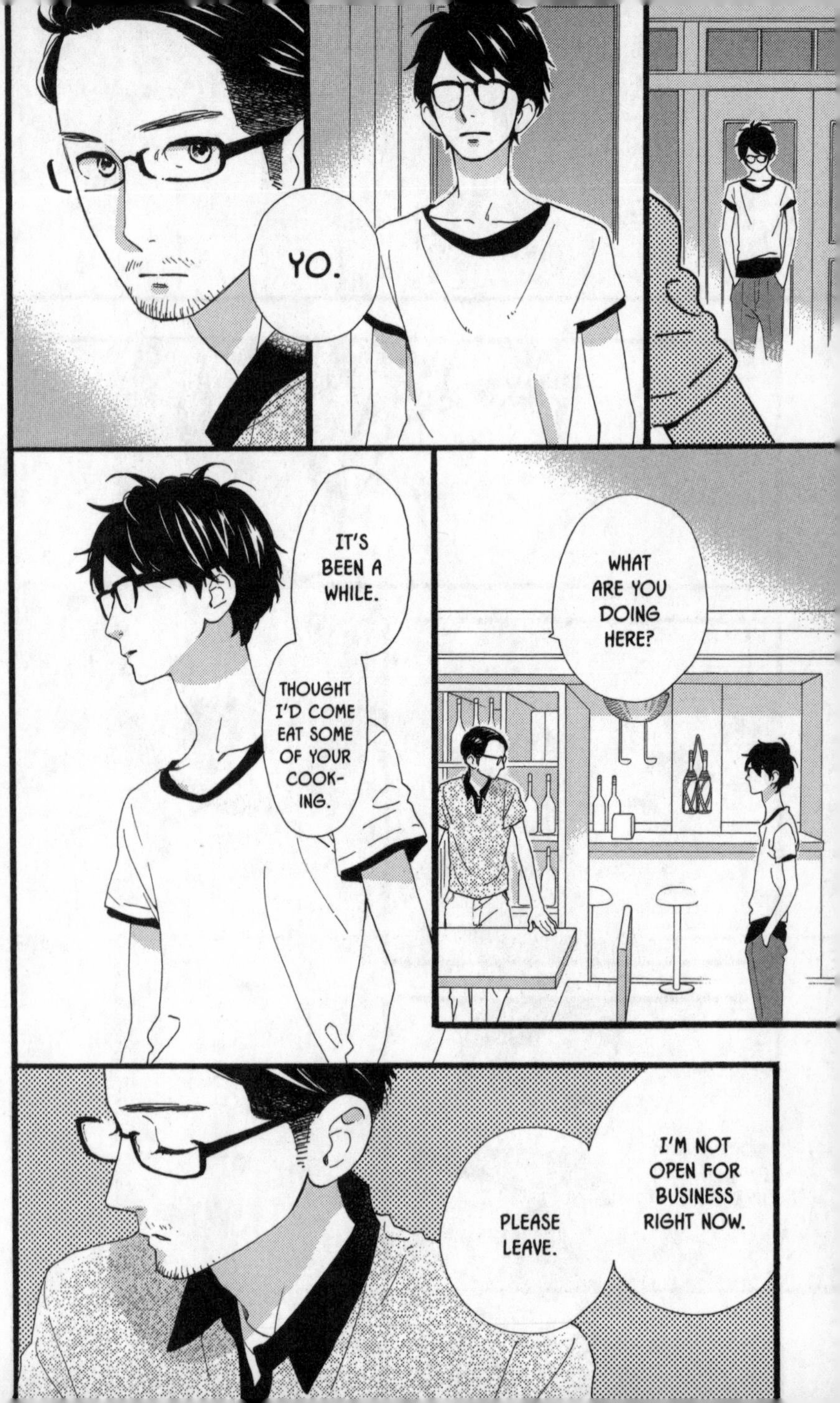
YO.
WHAT ARE YOU DOING HERE?
IT'S BEEN A WHILE.
THOUGHT I'D COME EAT SOME OF YOUR COOK-ING.
I'M NOT OPEN FOR BUSINESS RIGHT NOW.
PLEASE LEAVE.

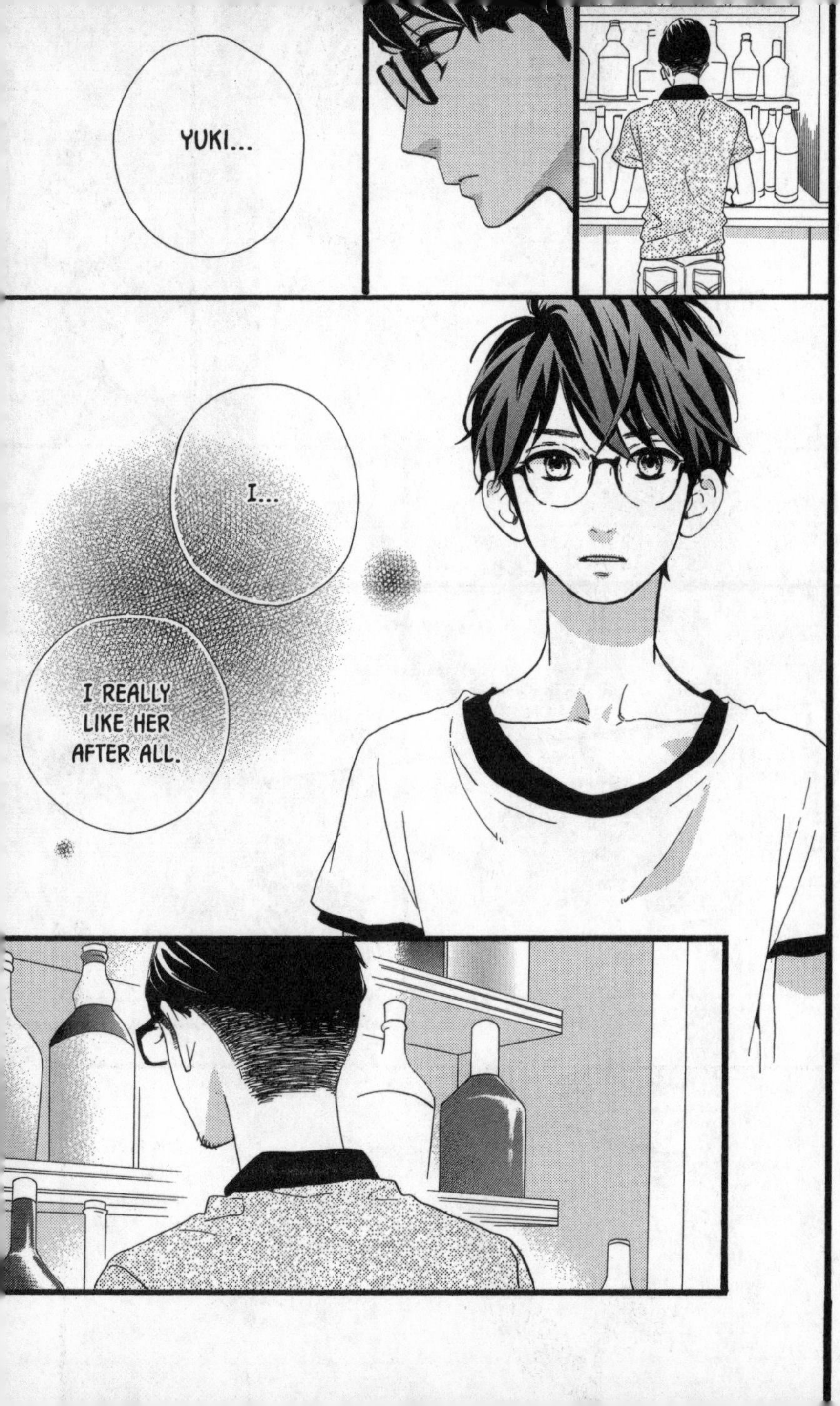
YUKI...
I...
I REALLY LIKE HER AFTER ALL.

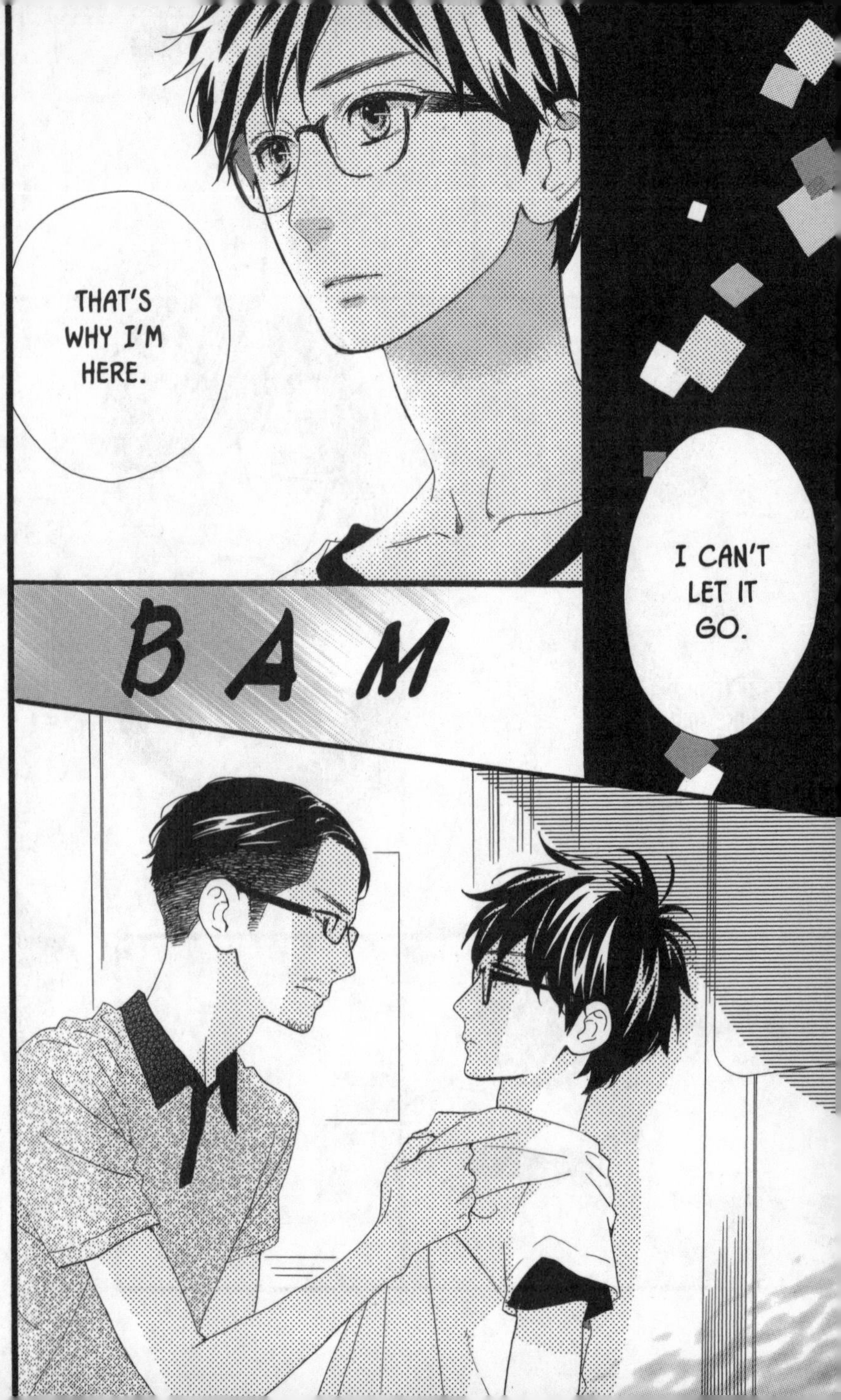
I CAN'T LET IT GO.
THAT'S WHY I'M HERE.
BAM

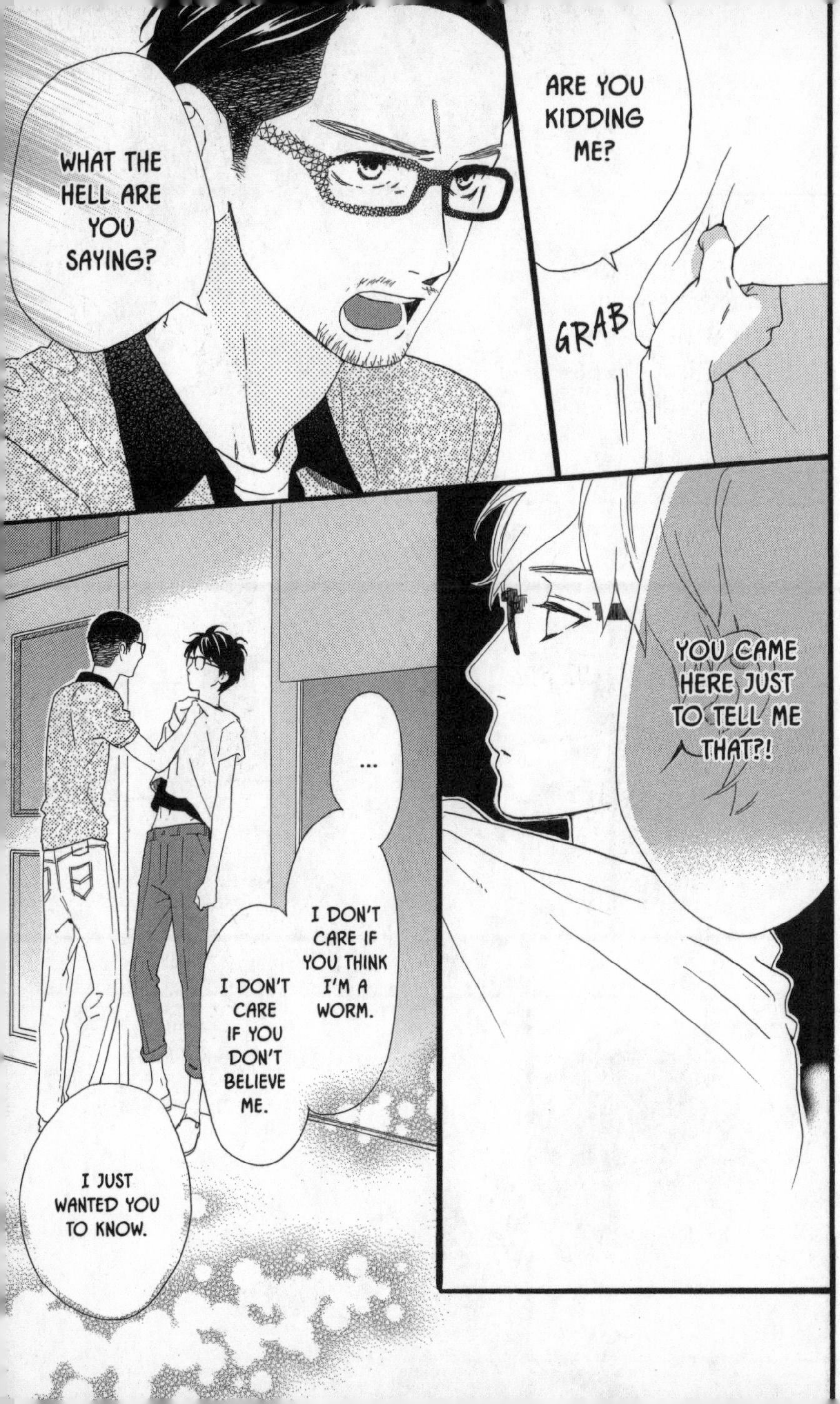
ARE YOU KIDDING ME?
GRAB
WHAT THE HELL ARE YOU SAYING?
YOU CAME HERE JUST TO TELL ME THAT?!
...
I DON'T CARE IF YOU THINK I'M A WORM.
I DON'T CARE IF YOU DON'T BELIEVE ME.
I JUST WANTED YOU TO KNOW.

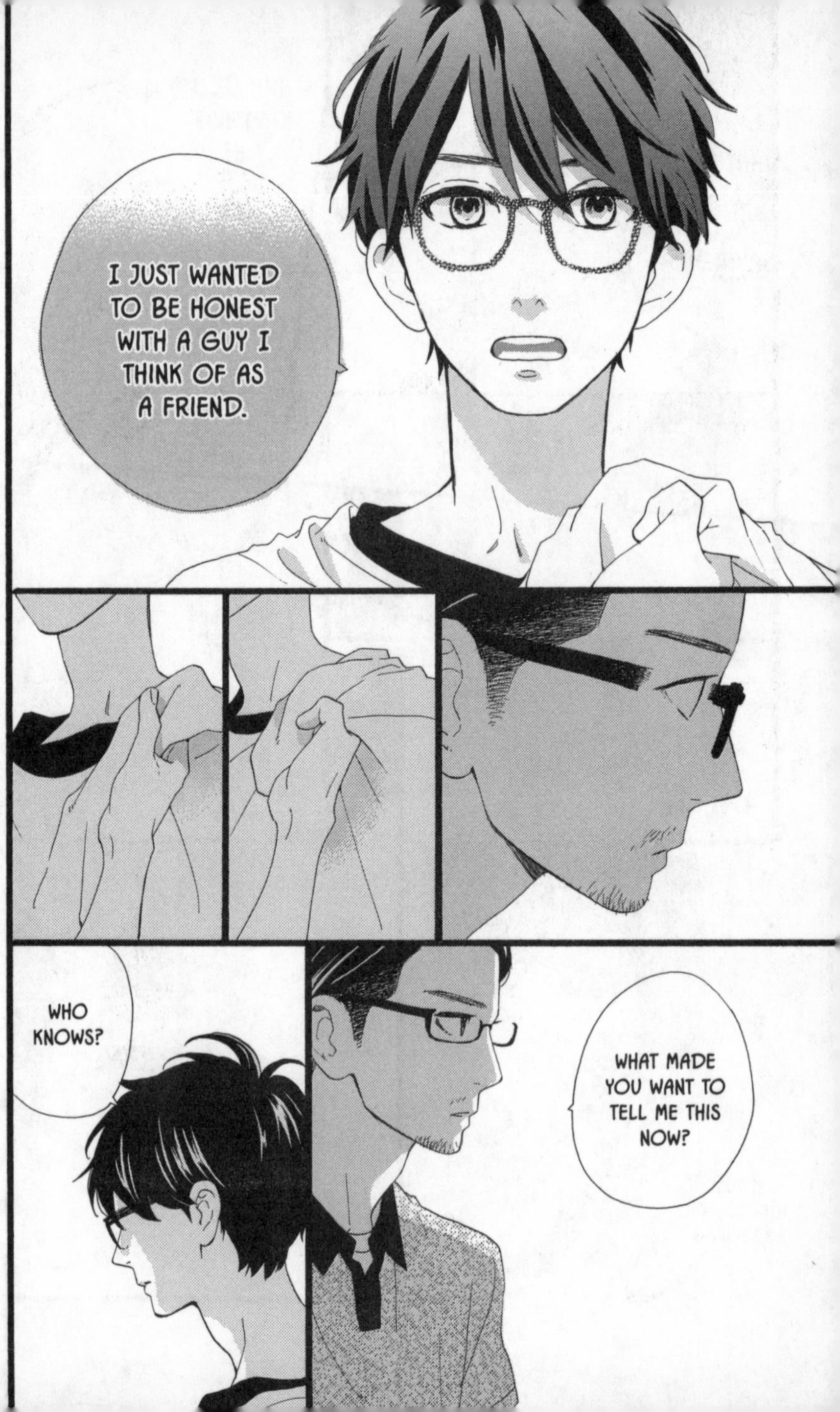
I JUST WANTED TO BE HONEST WITH A GUY I THINK OF AS A FRIEND.
WHAT MADE YOU WANT TO TELL ME THIS NOW?
WHO KNOWS?

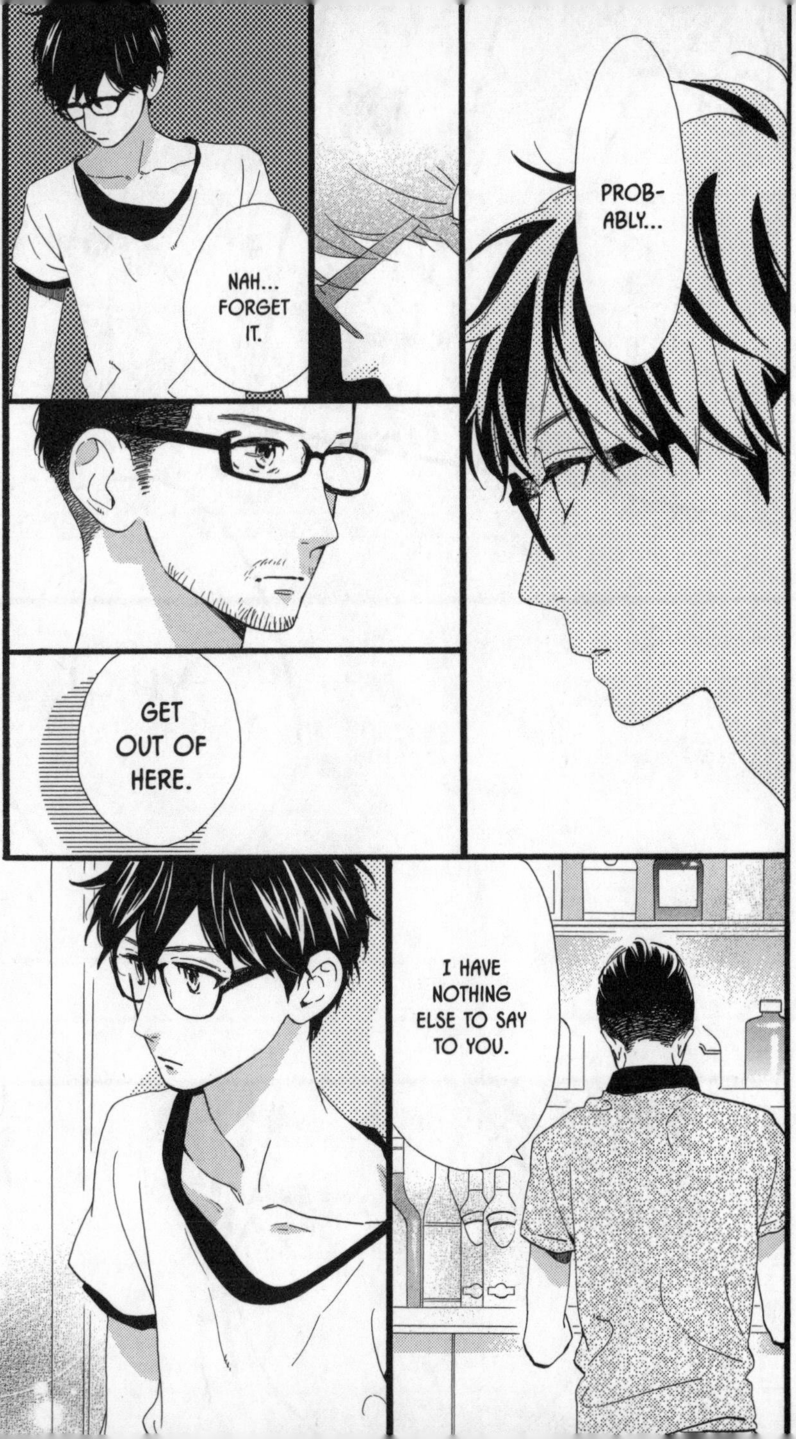
PROB-
ABLY...
NAH... FORGET IT.
GET OUT OF HERE.
I HAVE NOTHING ELSE TO SAY TO YOU.

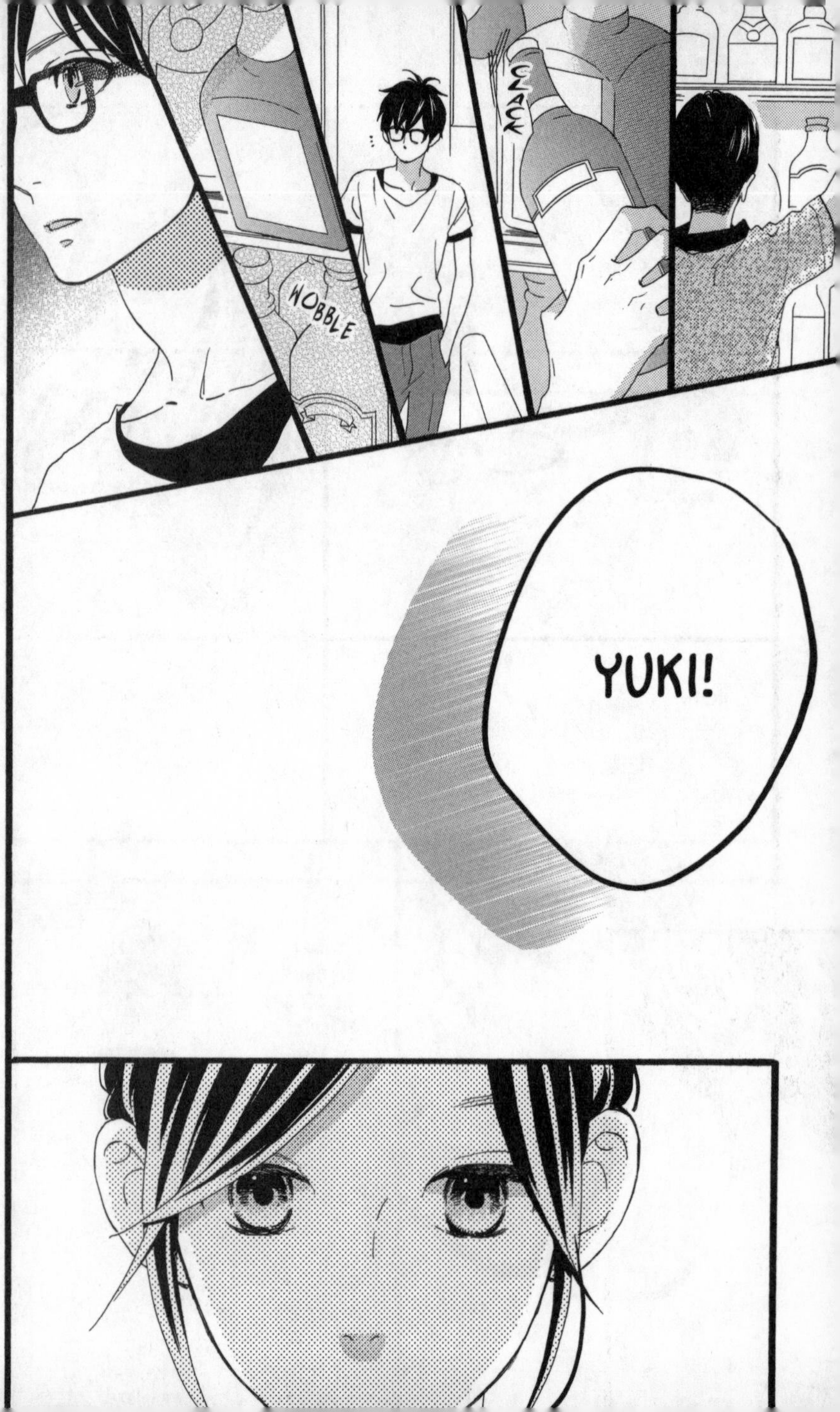
CLACK
WOBBLE
YUKI!

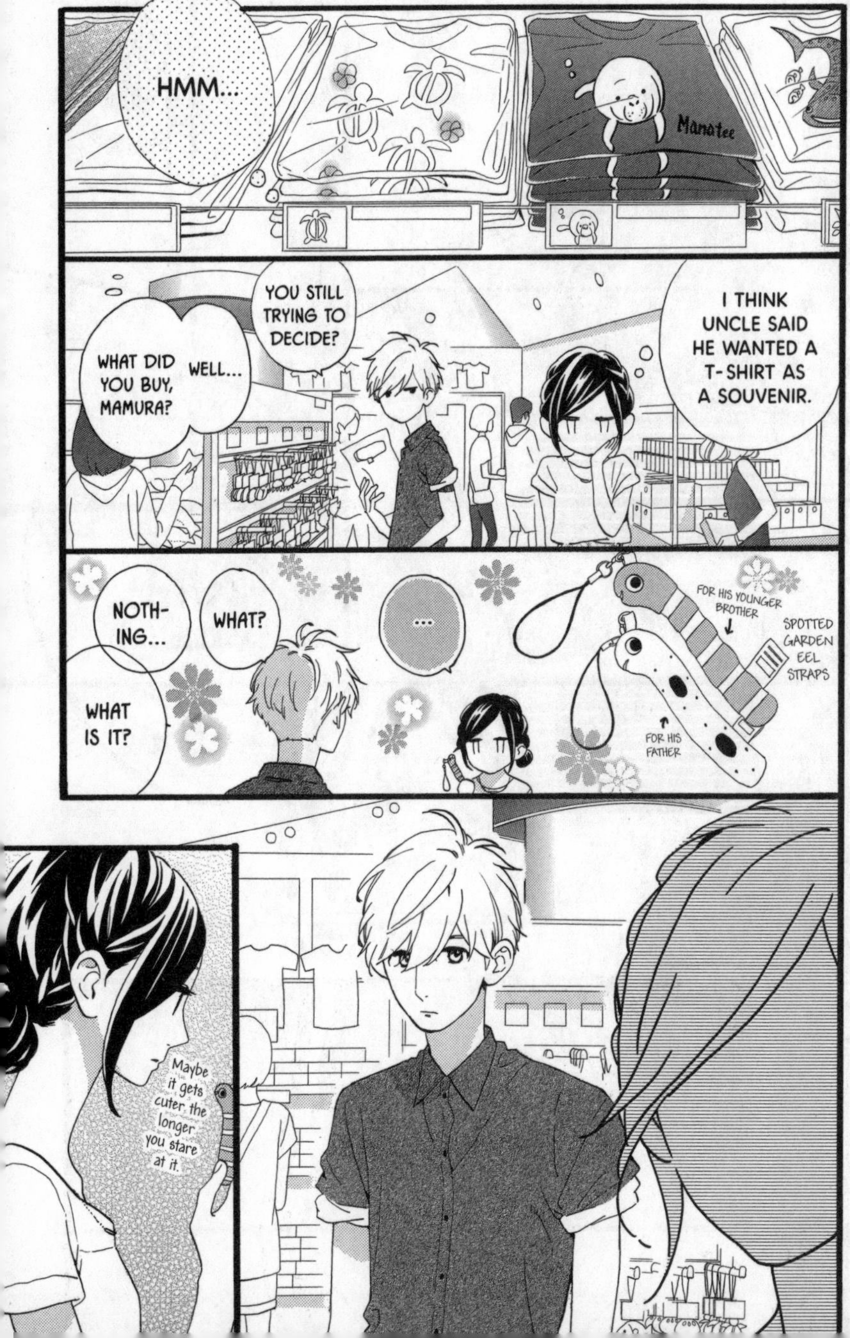
HMM...
Manatee
I THINK UNCLE SAID HE WANTED A T-SHIRT AS A SOUVENIR.
YOU STILL TRYING TO DECIDE?
WELL...
WHAT DID YOU BUY, MAMURA?
SPOTTED GARDEN EEL STRAPS
FOR HIS YOUNGER BROTHER
FOR HIS FATHER
...
WHAT?
NOTH-ING...
WHAT IS IT?
Maybe it gets cuter the longer you stare at it.

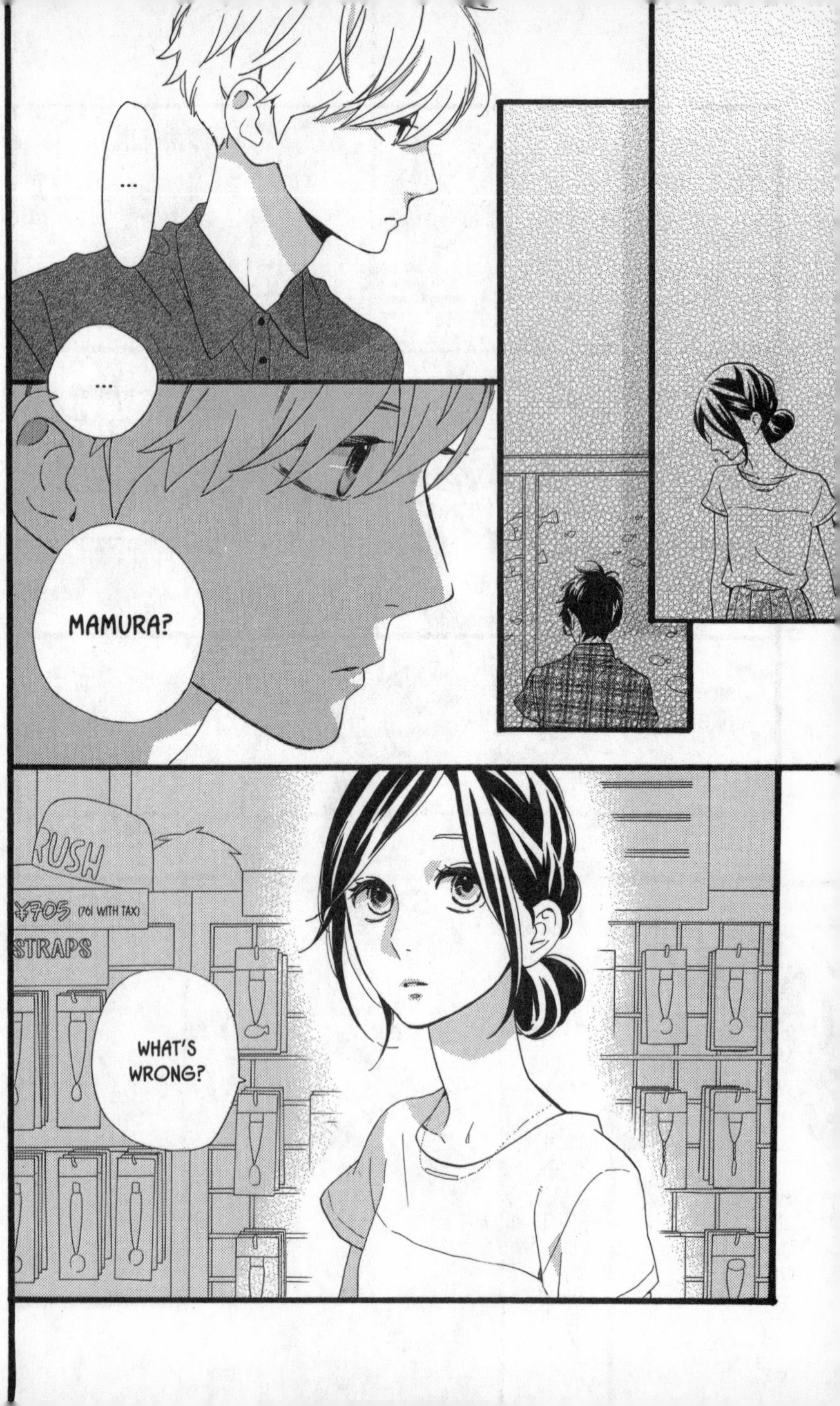
...
...
MAMURA?
RUSH
¥705 (761 WITH TAX)
STRAPS
WHAT'S WRONG?

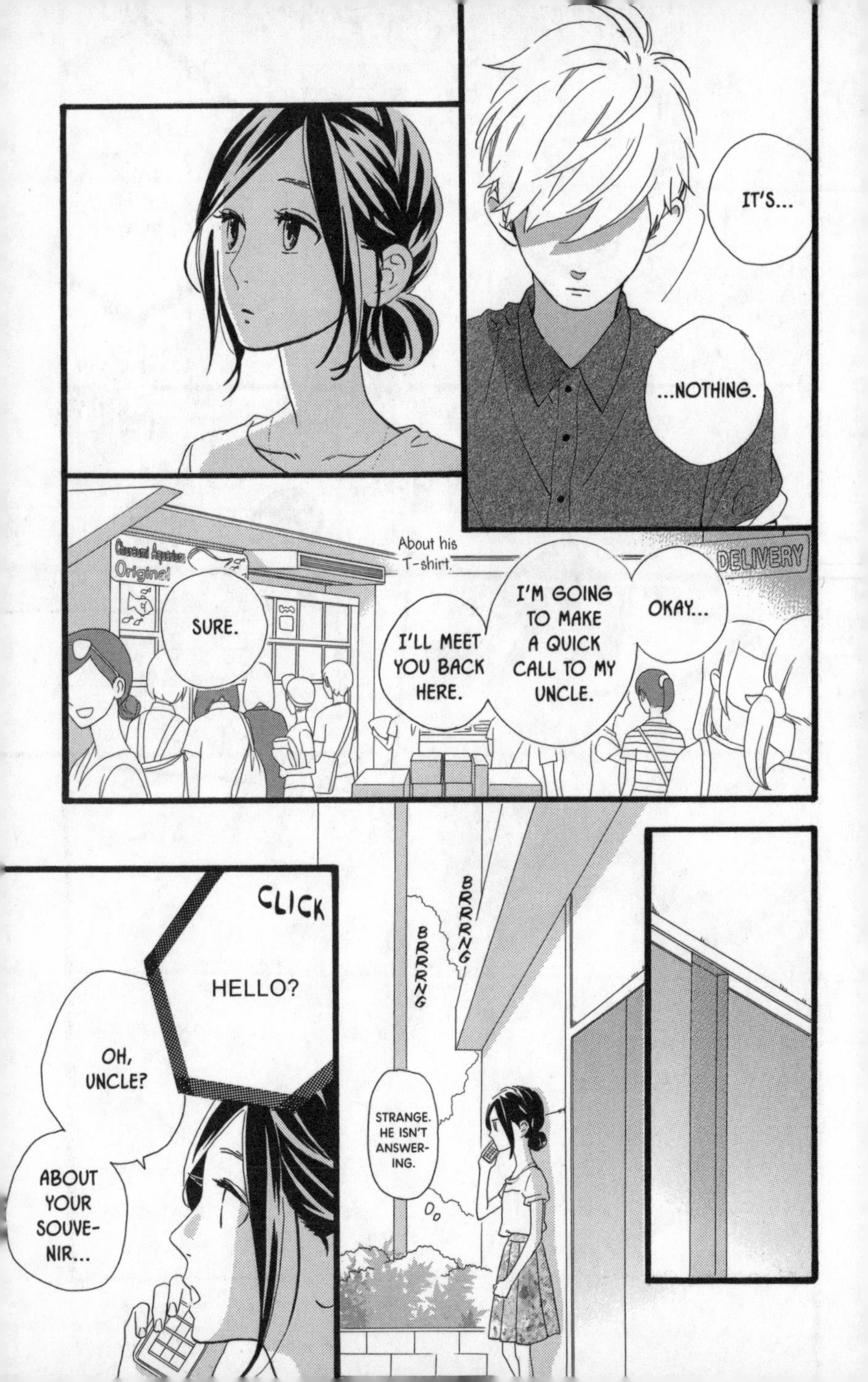
IT'S...
...NOTHING.
DELIVERY
OKAY...
About his T-shirt.
I'M GOING TO MAKE A QUICK CALL TO MY UNCLE.
I'LL MEET YOU BACK HERE.
SURE.
BRRRNG
BRRRNG
STRANGE. HE ISN'T ANSWER-ING.
CLICK
HELLO?
OH, UNCLE?
ABOUT YOUR SOUVE-NIR...

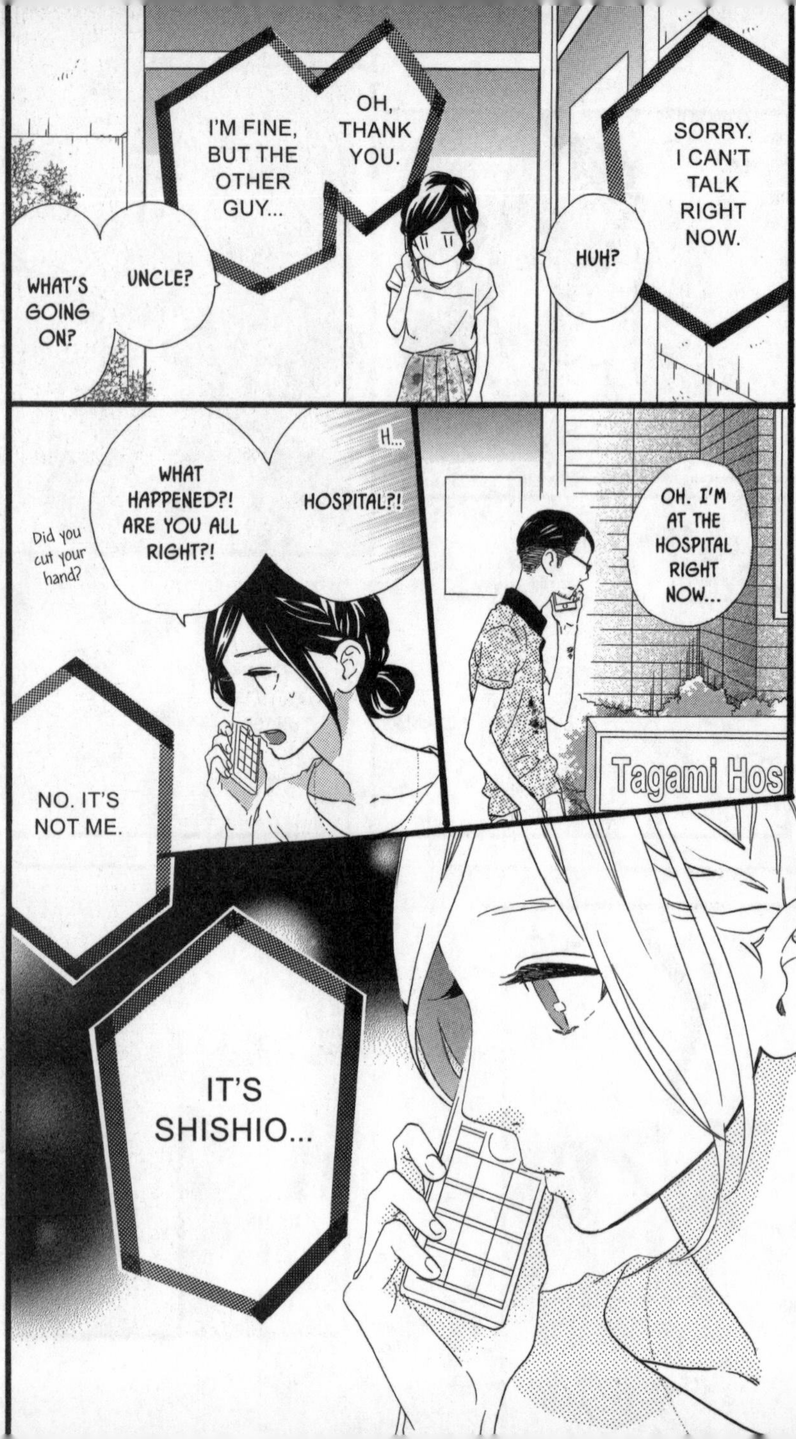
SORRY. I CAN'T TALK RIGHT NOW.
HUH?
OH, THANK YOU.
I'M FINE, BUT THE OTHER GUY...
UNCLE?
WHAT'S GOING ON?
OH. I'M AT THE HOSPITAL RIGHT NOW...
Tagami Hos
H...
HOSPITAL?!
WHAT HAPPENED?! ARE YOU ALL RIGHT?!
Did you cut your hand?
NO. IT'S NOT ME.
IT'S SHISHIO...

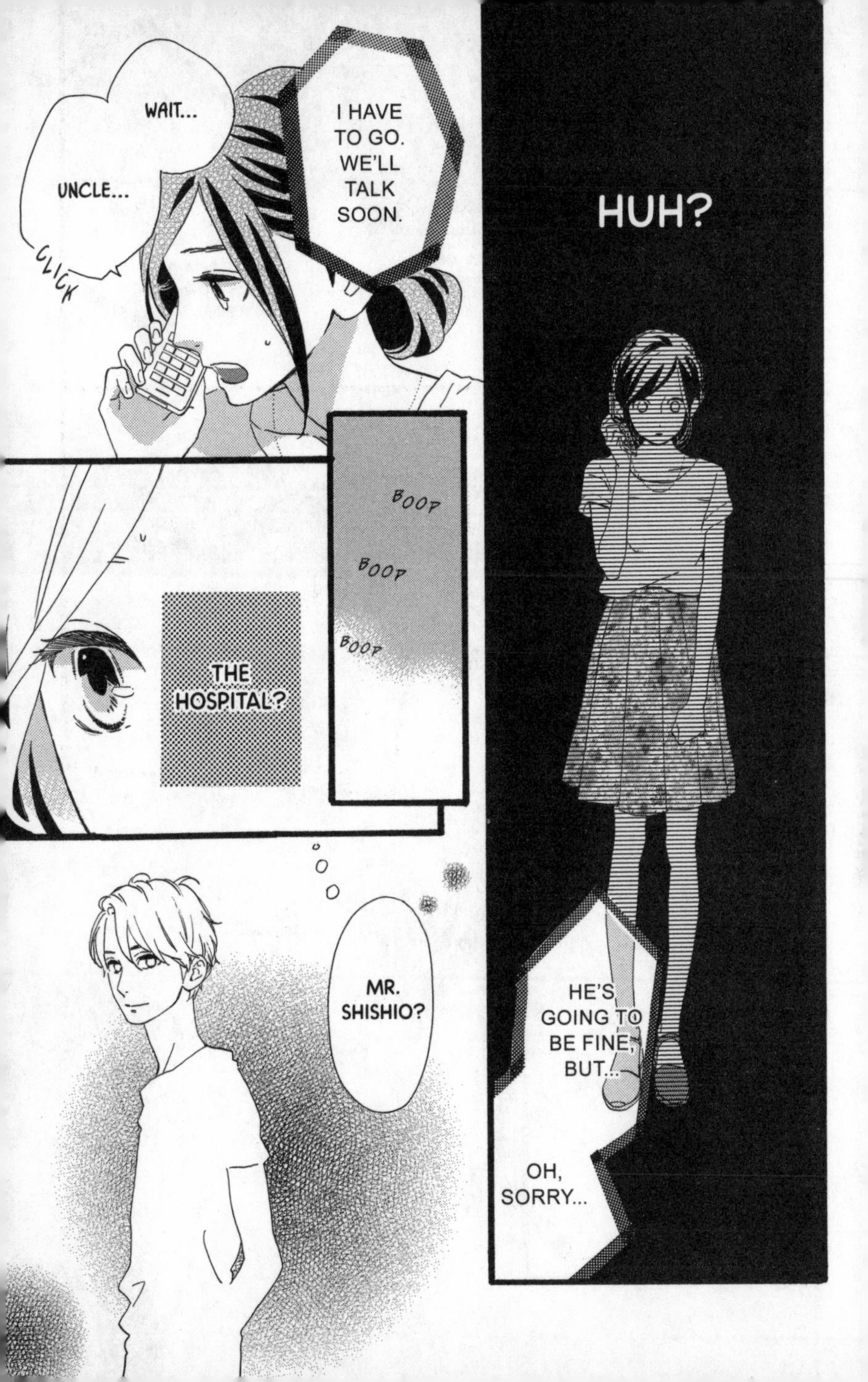
HUH?
HE'S GOING TO BE FINE, BUT...
OH, SORRY...
I HAVE TO GO. WE'LL TALK SOON.
WAIT...
UNCLE...
CLICK
BOOP
BOOP
BOOP
THE HOSPITAL?
MR. SHISHIO?

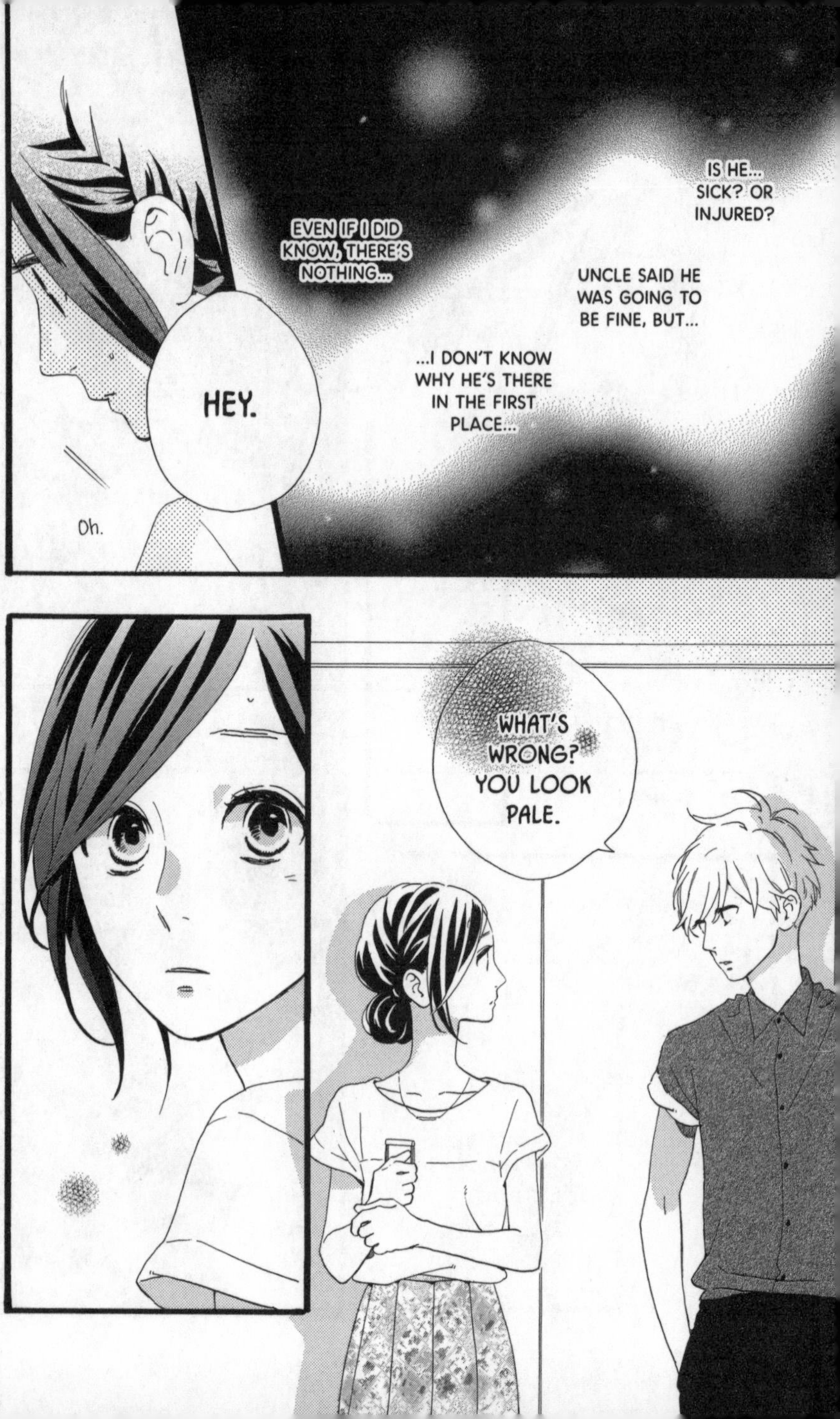
IS HE... SICK? OR INJURED?
UNCLE SAID HE WAS GOING TO BE FINE, BUT...
...I DON'T KNOW WHY HE'S THERE IN THE FIRST PLACE...
EVEN IF I DID KNOW, THERE'S NOTHING...
HEY.
Oh.
WHAT'S WRONG? YOU LOOK PALE.

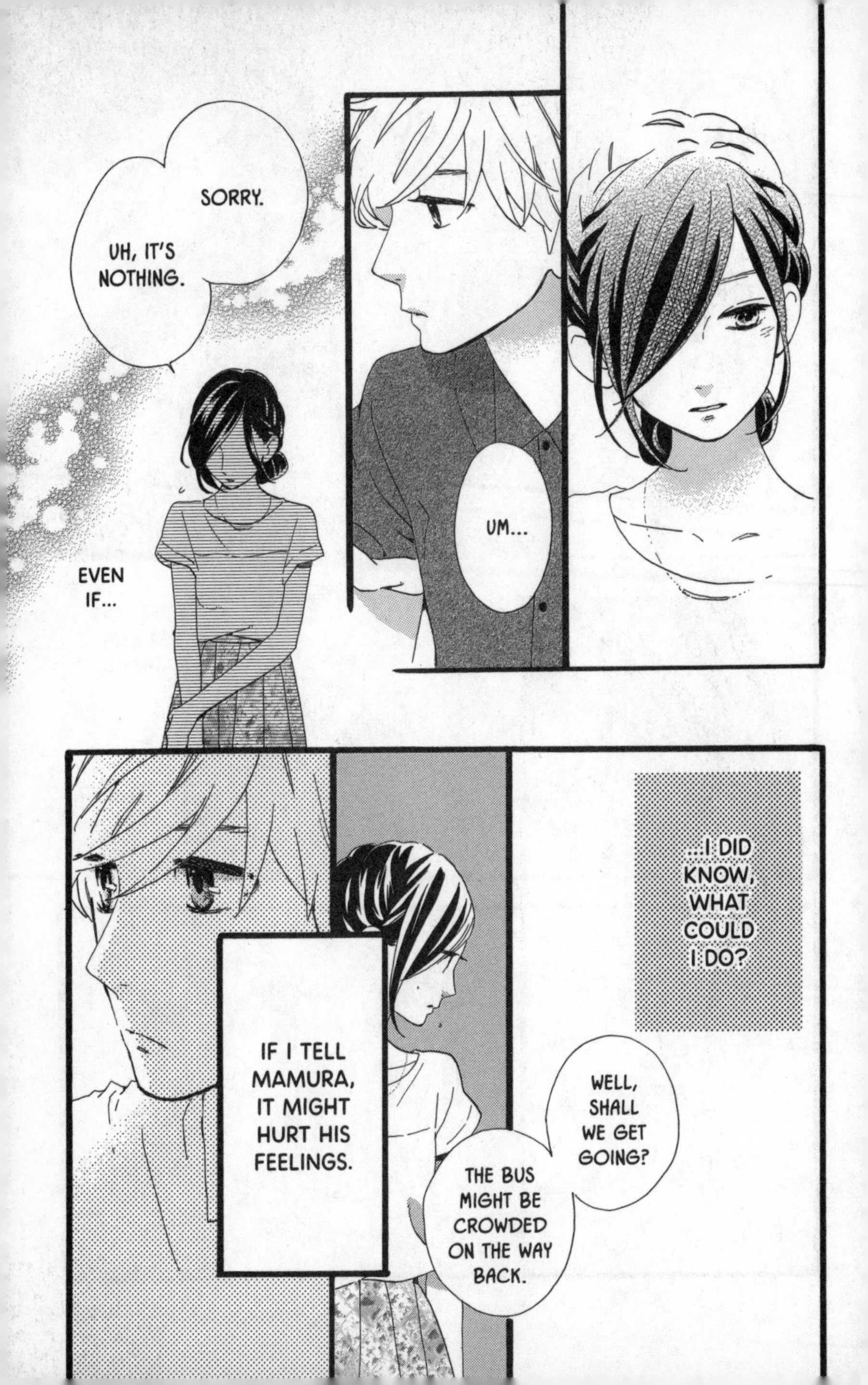
UM...
SORRY. UH, IT'S NOTHING.
EVEN IF...
...I DID KNOW, WHAT COULD I DO?
WELL, SHALL WE GET GOING?
THE BUS MIGHT BE CROWDED ON THE WAY BACK.
IF I TELL MAMURA, IT MIGHT HURT HIS FEELINGS.

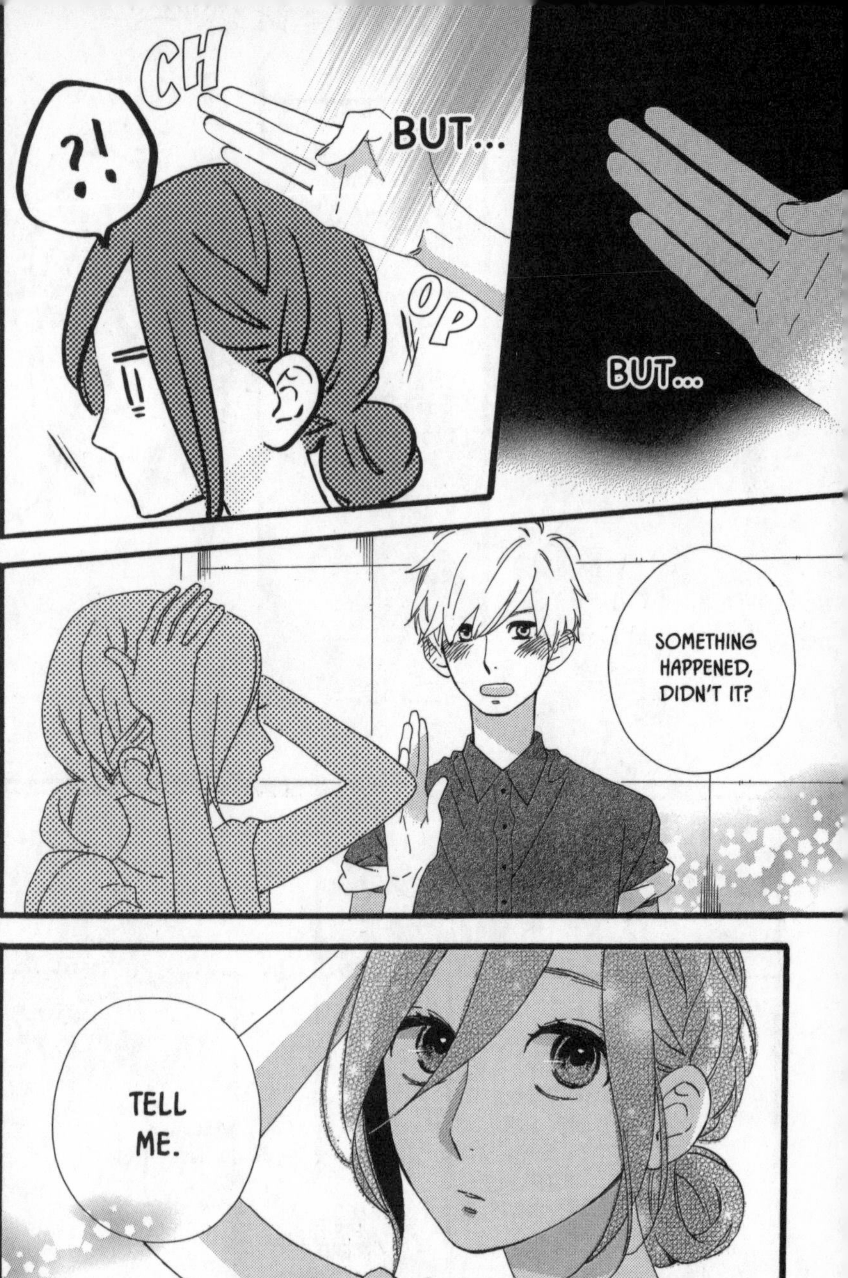
BUT...
BUT...
CH
?!
OP
SOMETHING HAPPENED, DIDN'T IT?
TELL ME.

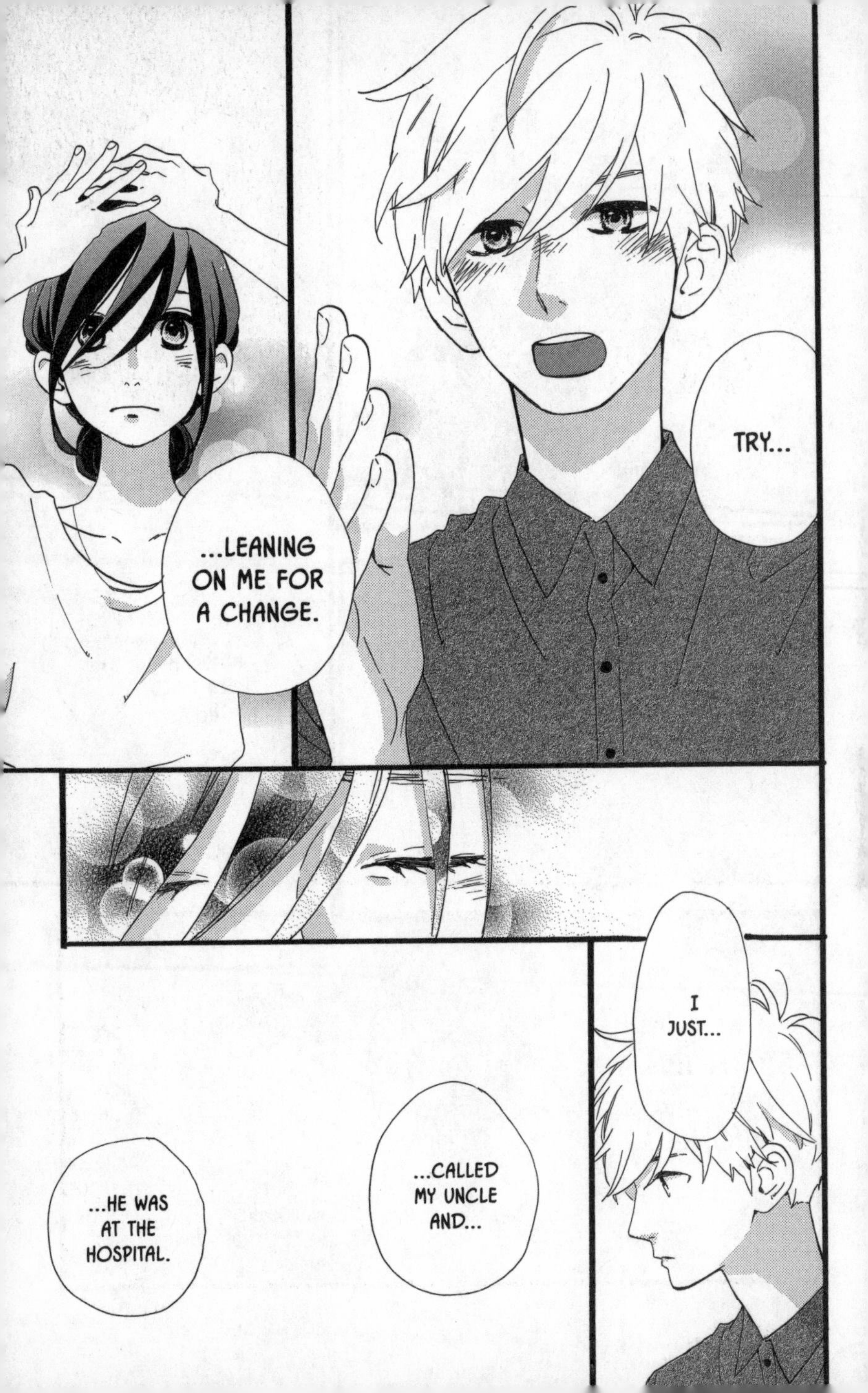
TRY...
...LEANING ON ME FOR A CHANGE.
I JUST...
...CALLED MY UNCLE AND...
...HE WAS AT THE HOSPITAL.

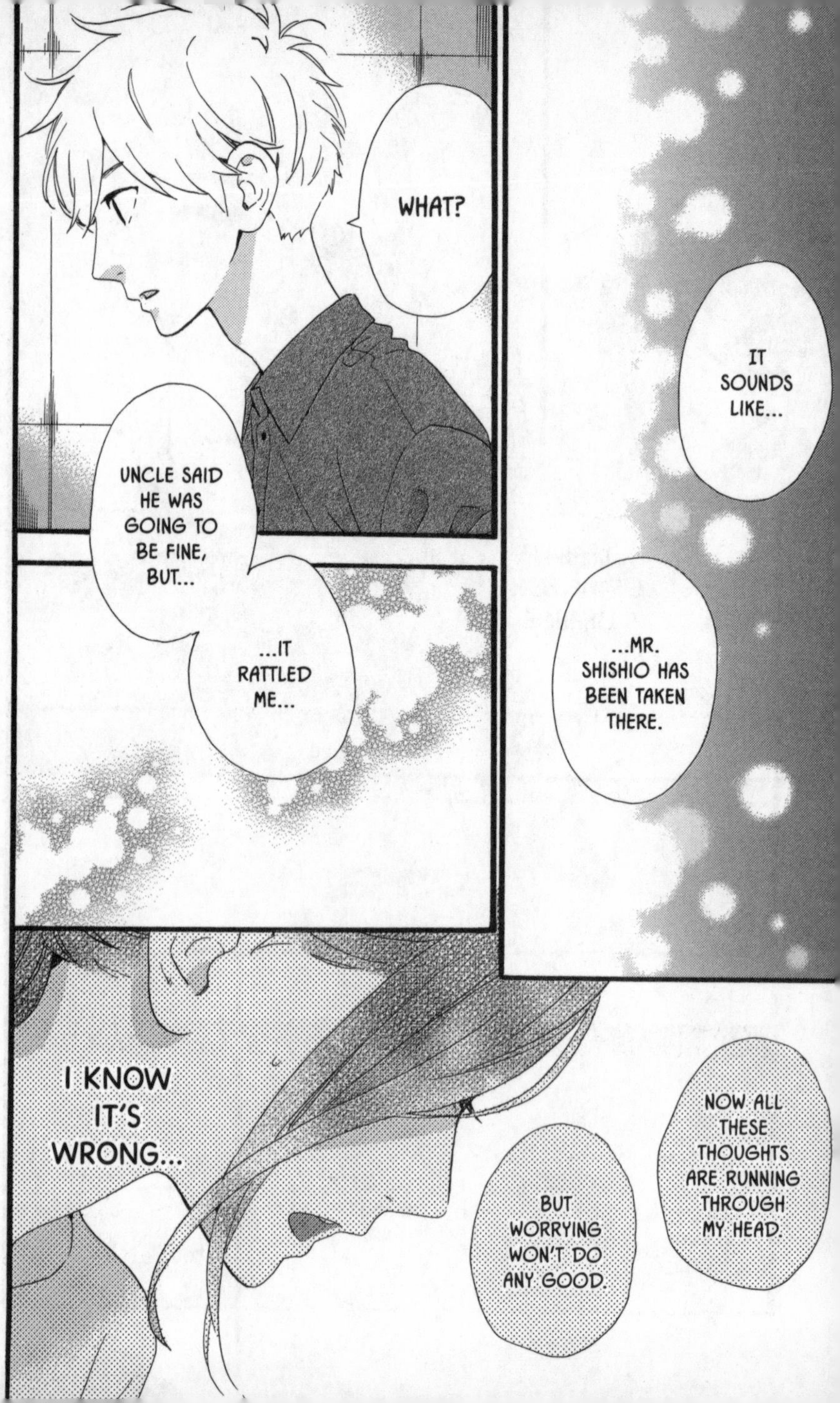
IT SOUNDS LIKE...
...MR. SHISHIO HAS BEEN TAKEN THERE.
WHAT?
UNCLE SAID HE WAS GOING TO BE FINE, BUT...
...IT RATTLED ME...
NOW ALL THESE THOUGHTS ARE RUNNING THROUGH MY HEAD.
BUT WORRYING WON'T DO ANY GOOD.
I KNOW IT'S WRONG...

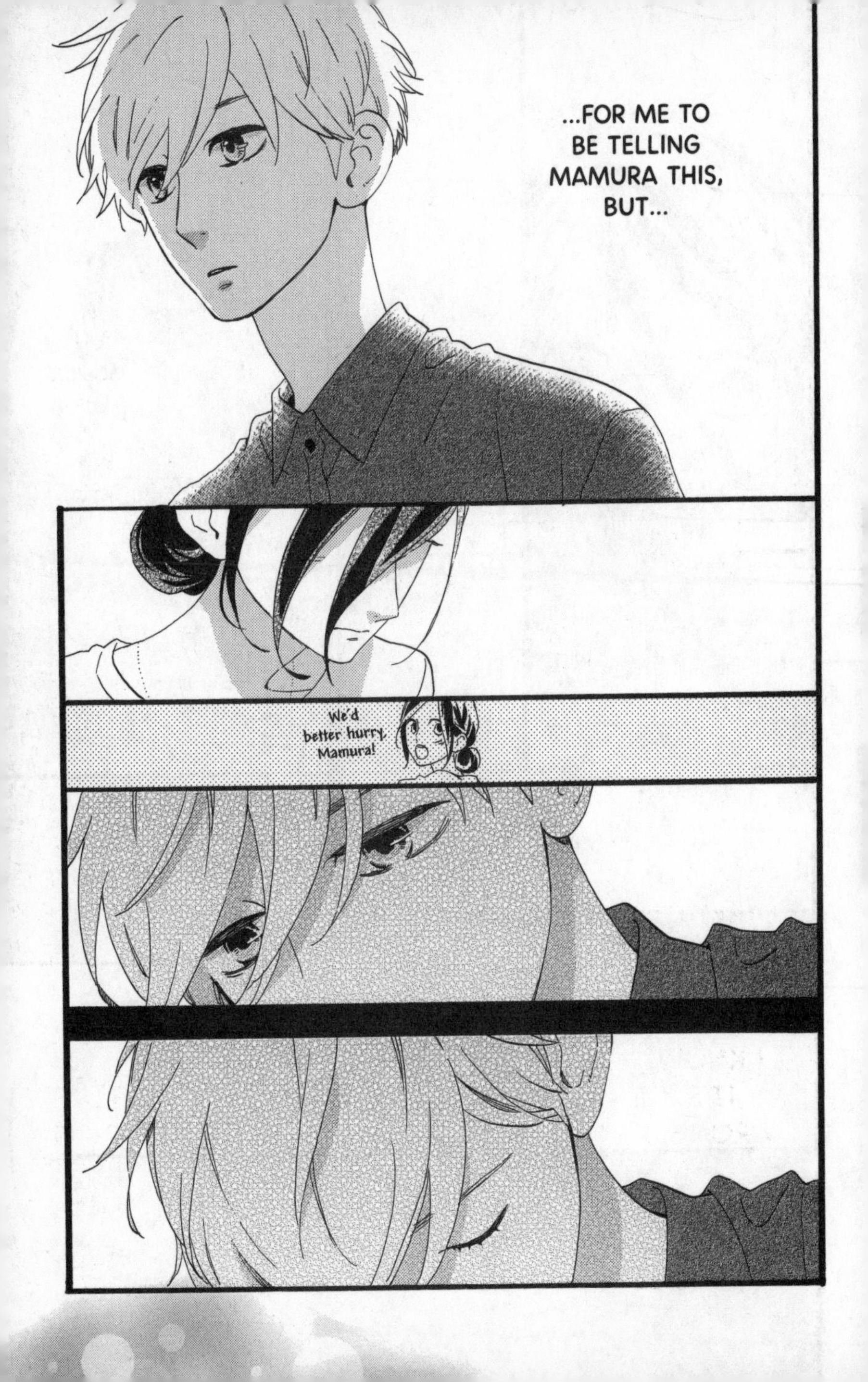
...FOR ME TO BE TELLING MAMURA THIS, BUT...
We'd better hurry, Mamura!

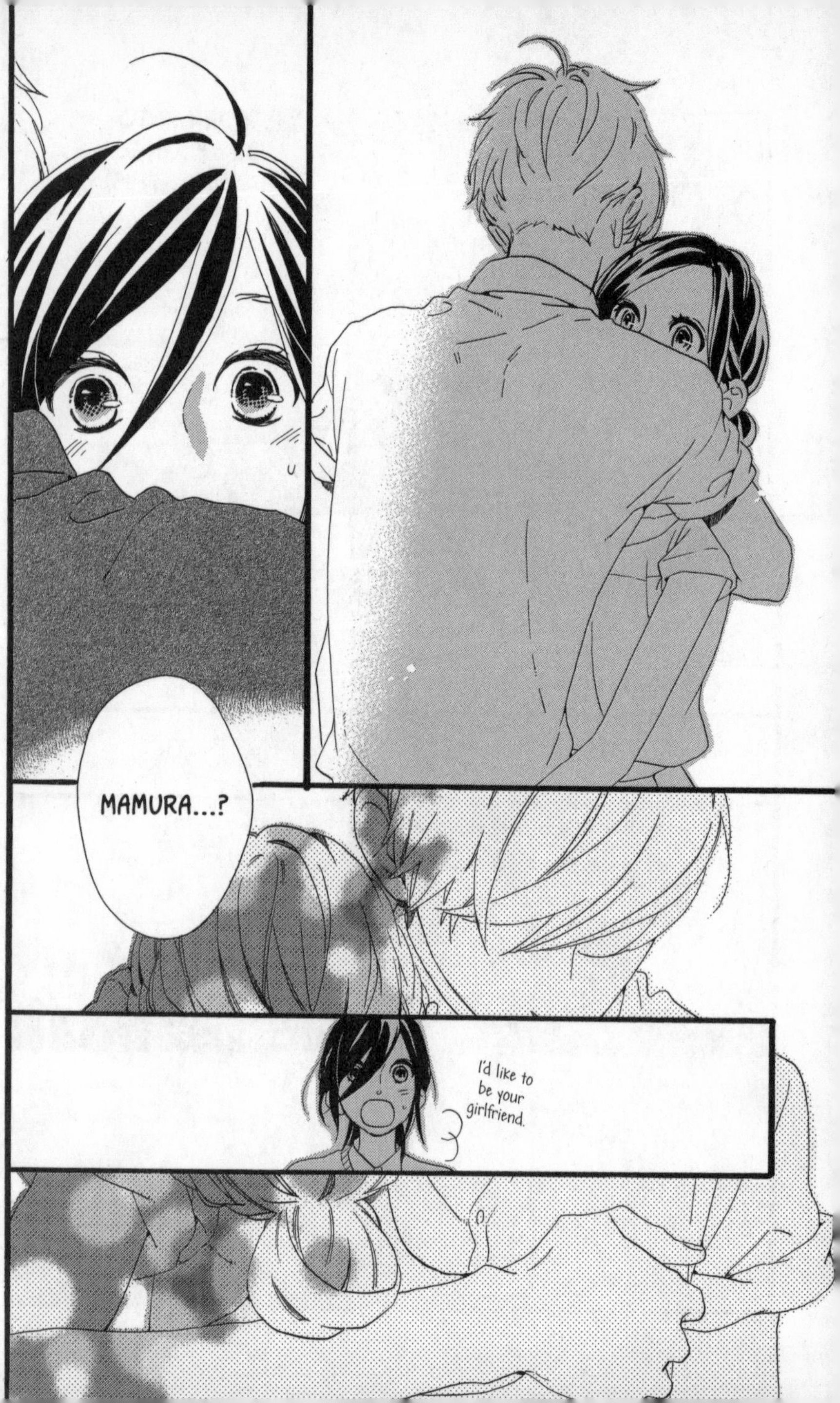
MAMURA...?
I'd like to be your girlfriend.

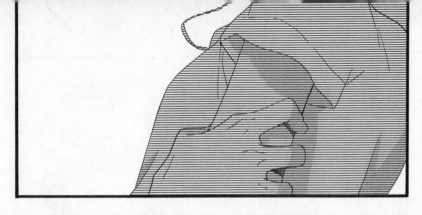

GO.

☆Special Thanks☆

Editor Kirimi
Previous Editor Katan

Sanae Kameyama, Sachie Noborio,
Nils Machimura

The Editorial Staff Designer Kawatani The Printer Staff

My family, friends, and all of my readers!

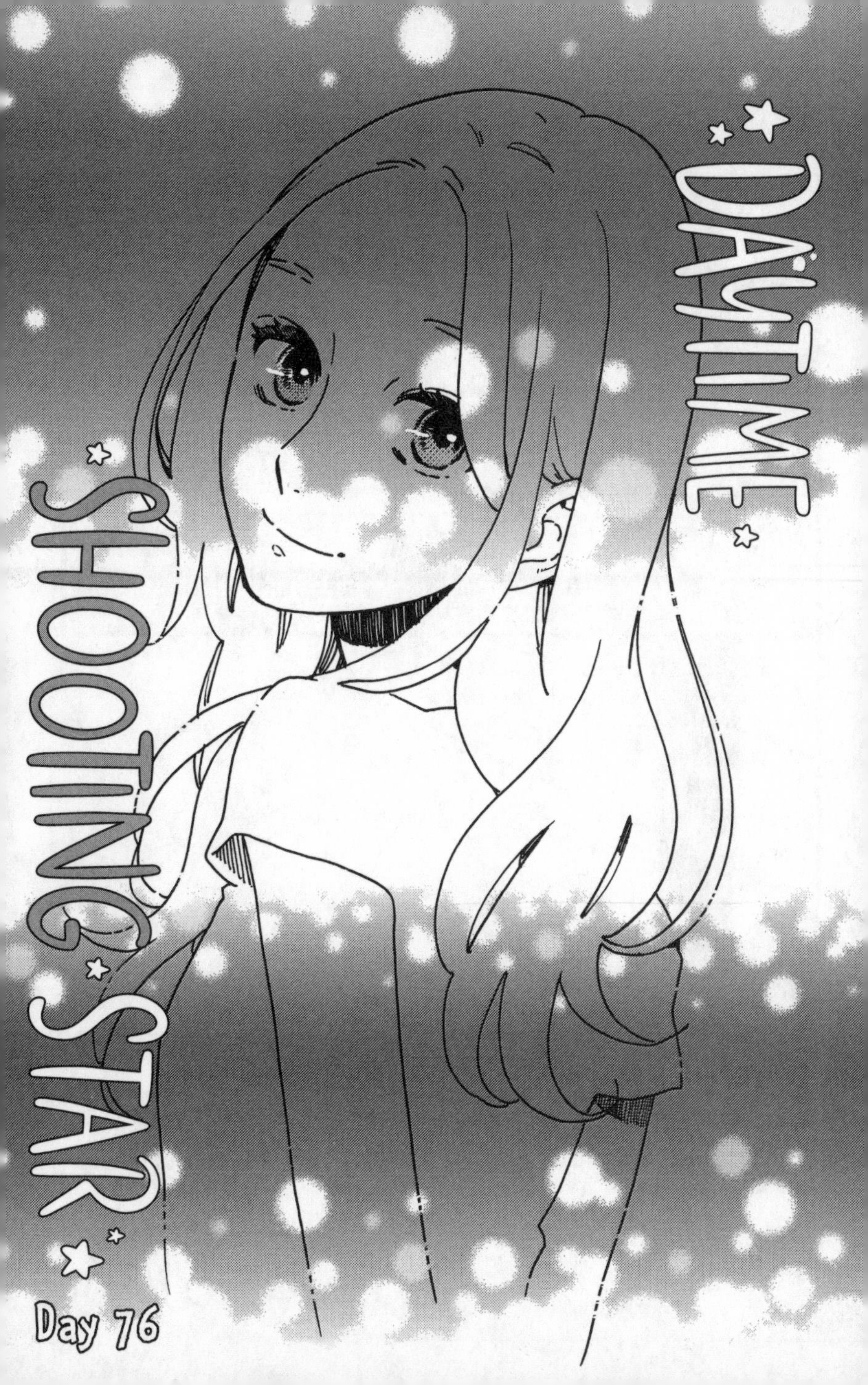
DAYTIME
SHOOTING STAR
Day 76

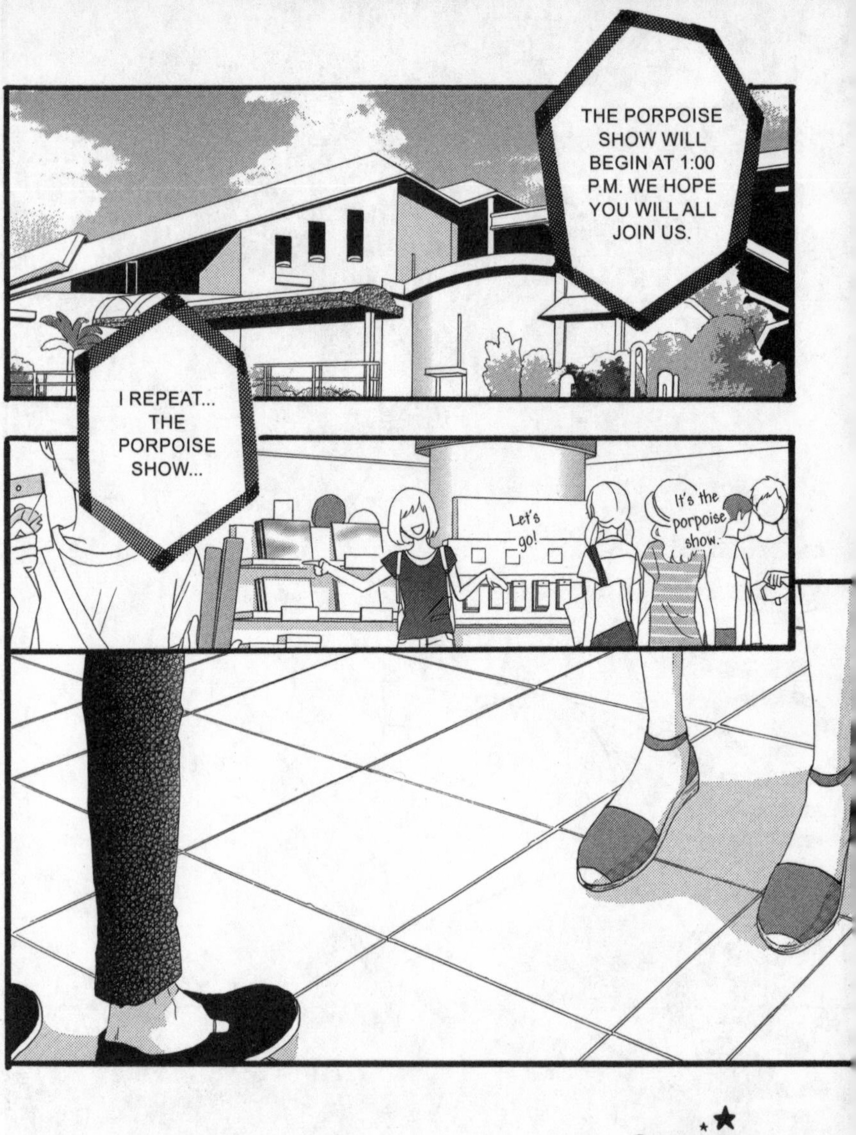
THE PORPOISE SHOW WILL BEGIN AT 1:00 P.M. WE HOPE YOU WILL ALL JOIN US.
I REPEAT... THE PORPOISE SHOW...
It's the porpoise show.
Let's go!

DAYTIME SHOOTING STAR

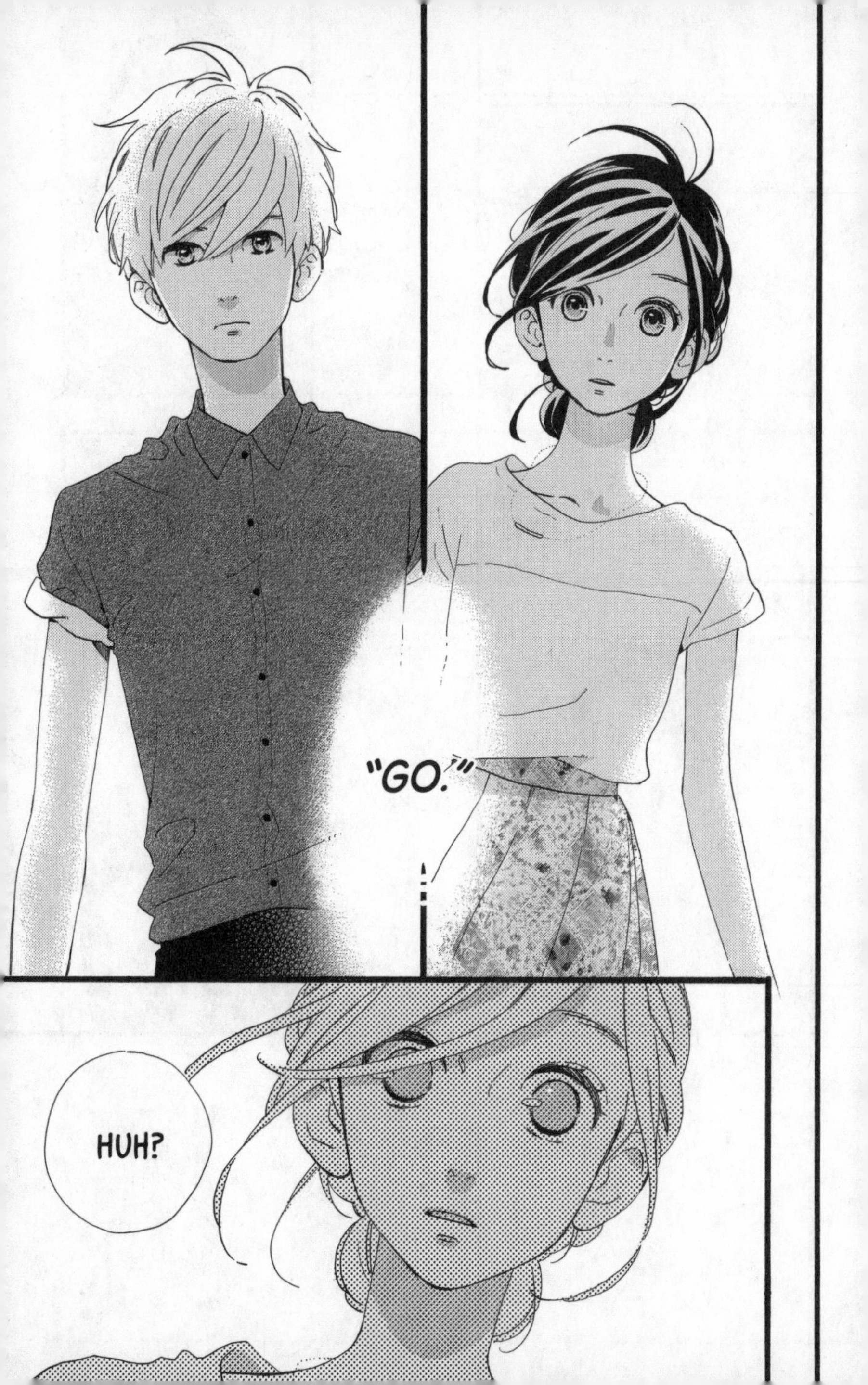
"GO."
HUH?

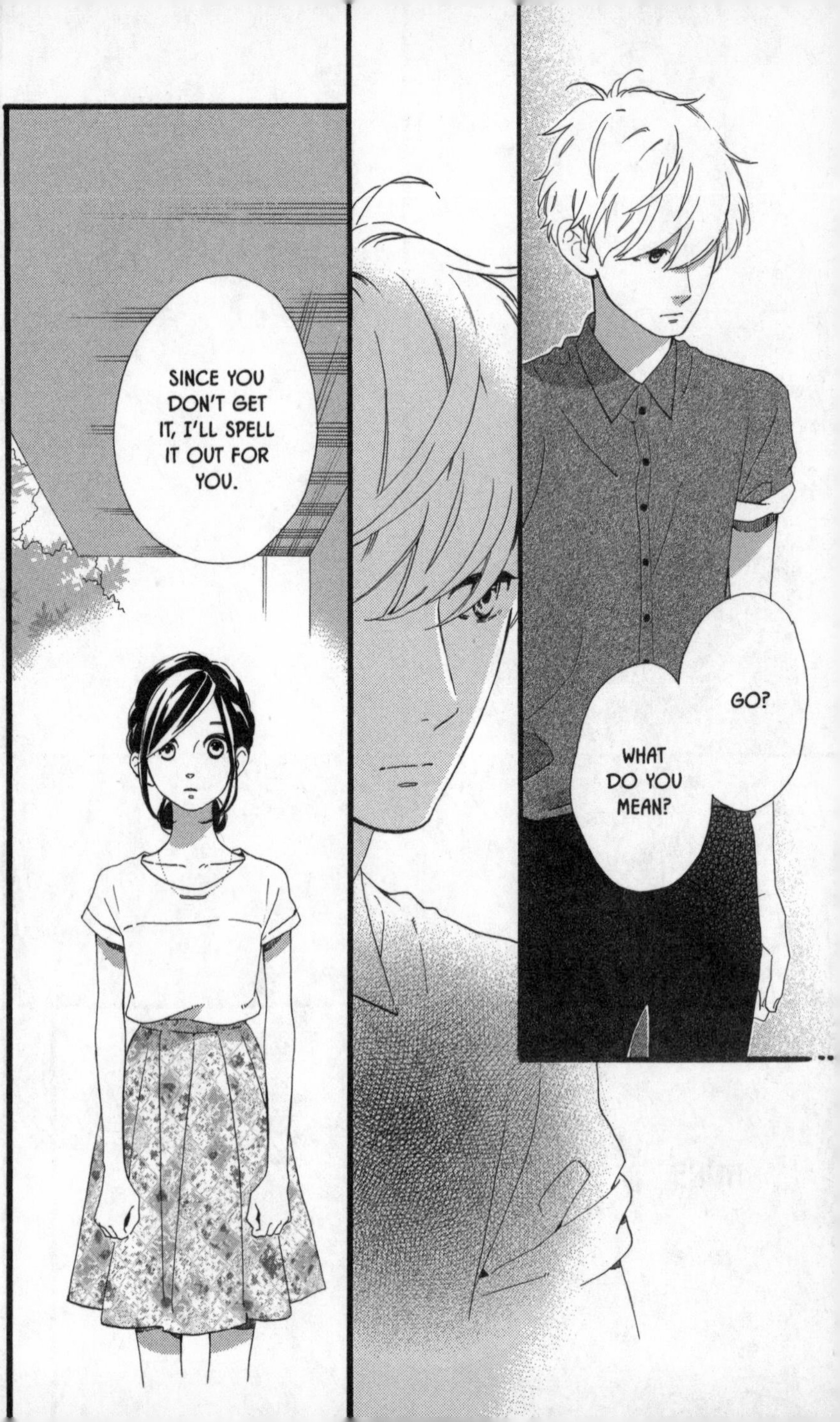
GO?
WHAT DO YOU MEAN?
SINCE YOU DON'T GET IT, I'LL SPELL IT OUT FOR YOU.

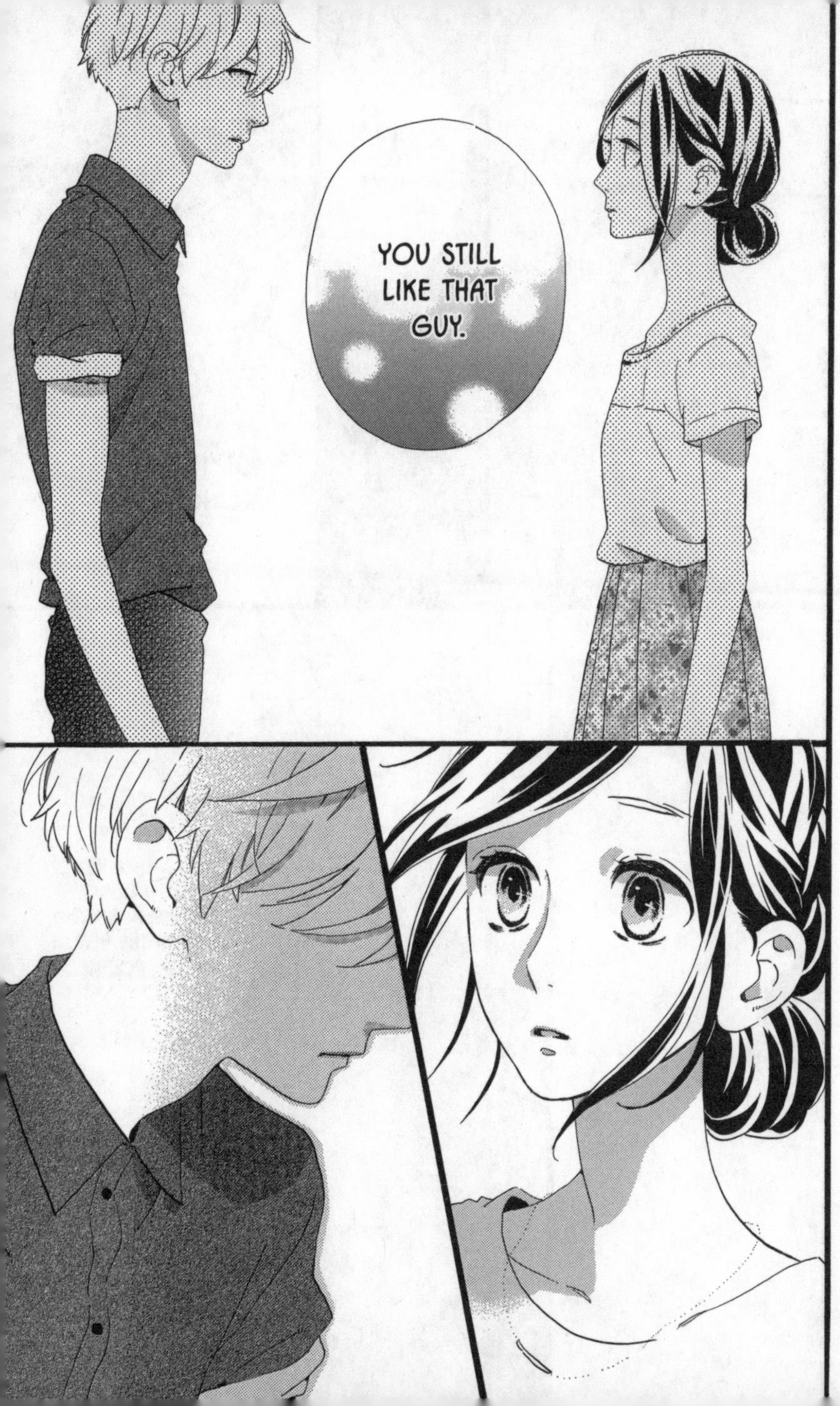
YOU STILL LIKE THAT GUY.

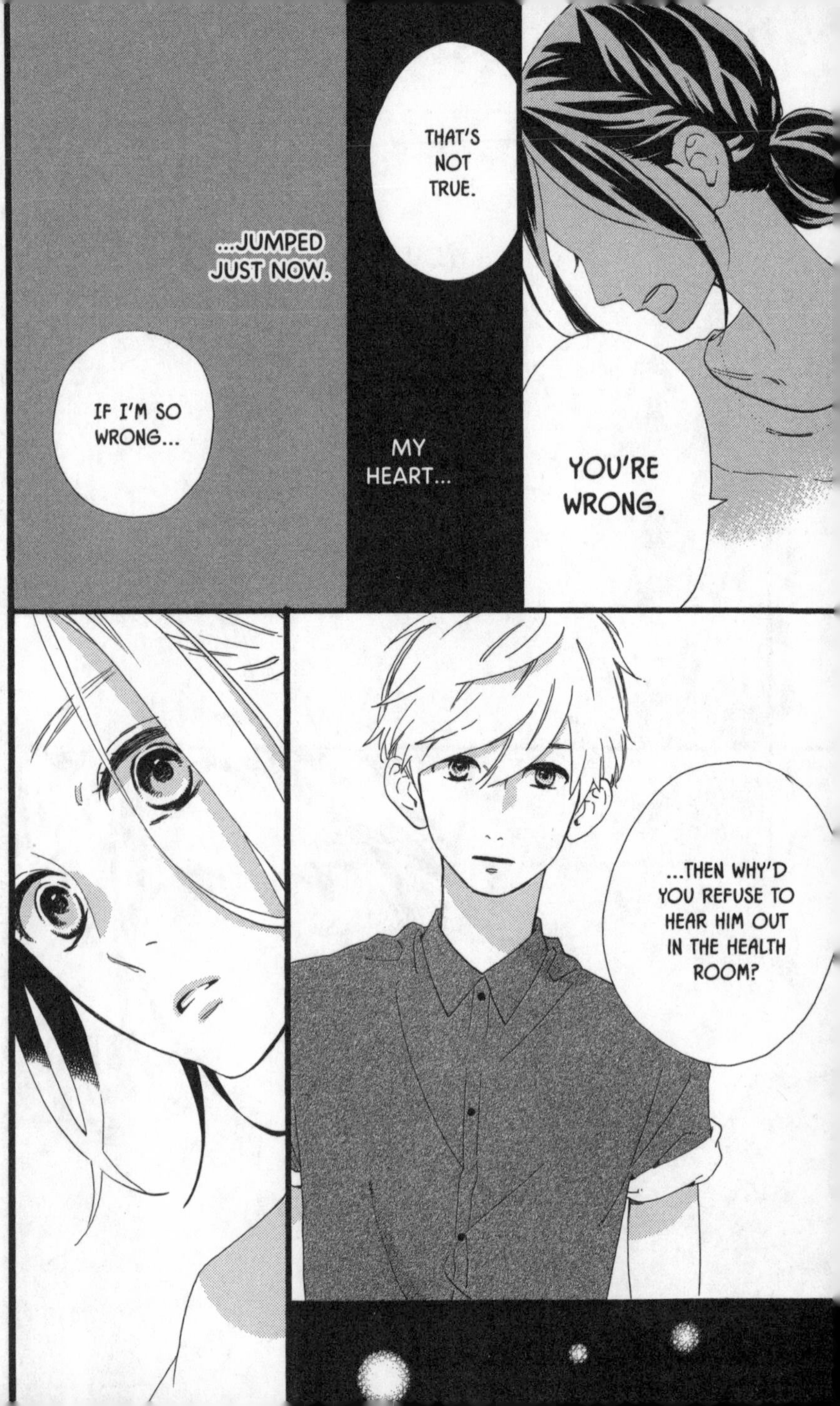
YOU'RE WRONG.
THAT'S NOT TRUE.
MY HEART...
...JUMPED JUST NOW.
IF I'M SO WRONG...
...THEN WHY'D YOU REFUSE TO HEAR HIM OUT IN THE HEALTH ROOM?

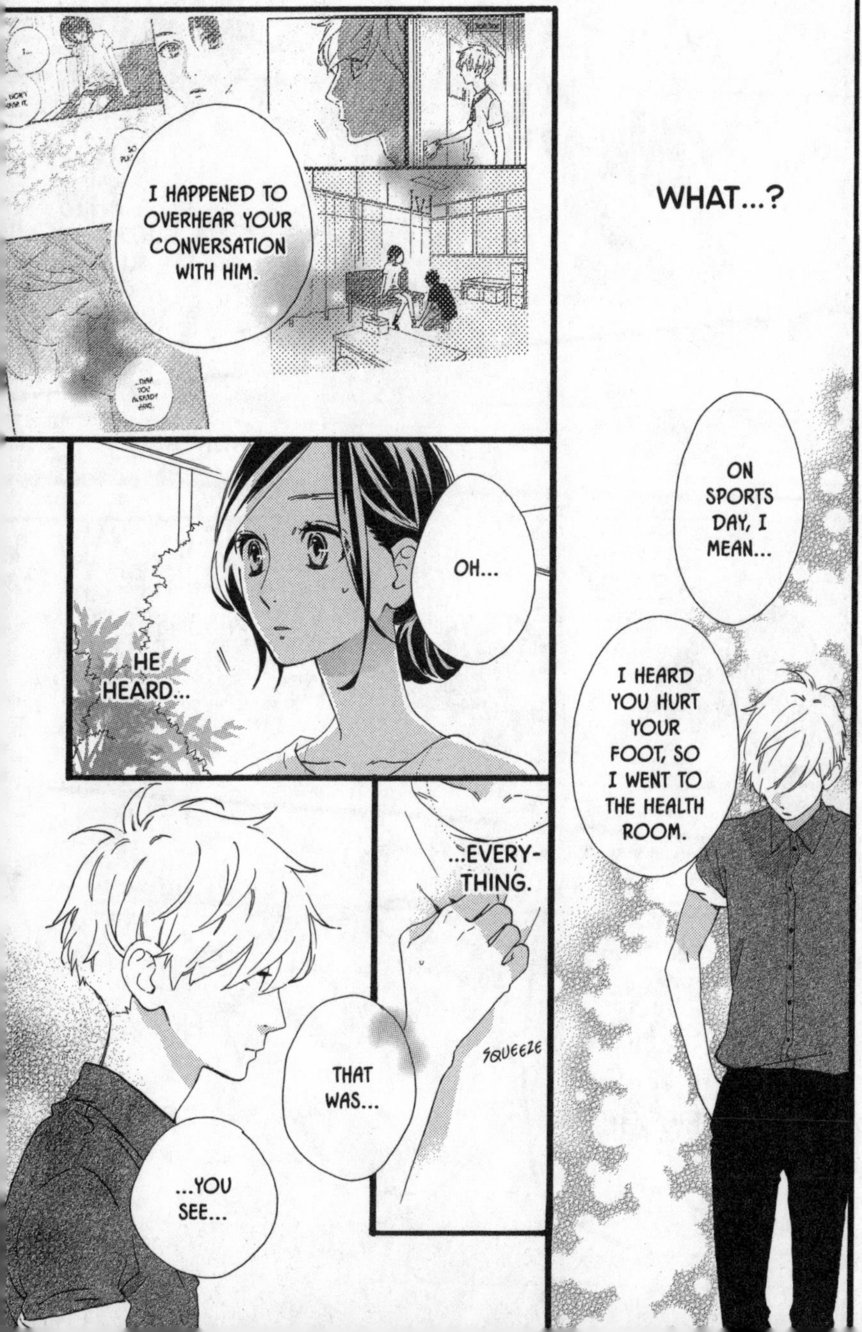
WHAT...?
ON SPORTS DAY, I MEAN...
I HEARD YOU HURT YOUR FOOT, SO I WENT TO THE HEALTH ROOM.
I HAPPENED TO OVERHEAR YOUR CONVERSATION WITH HIM.
OH...
HE HEARD...
...EVERY-THING.
SQUEEZE
THAT WAS...
...YOU SEE...

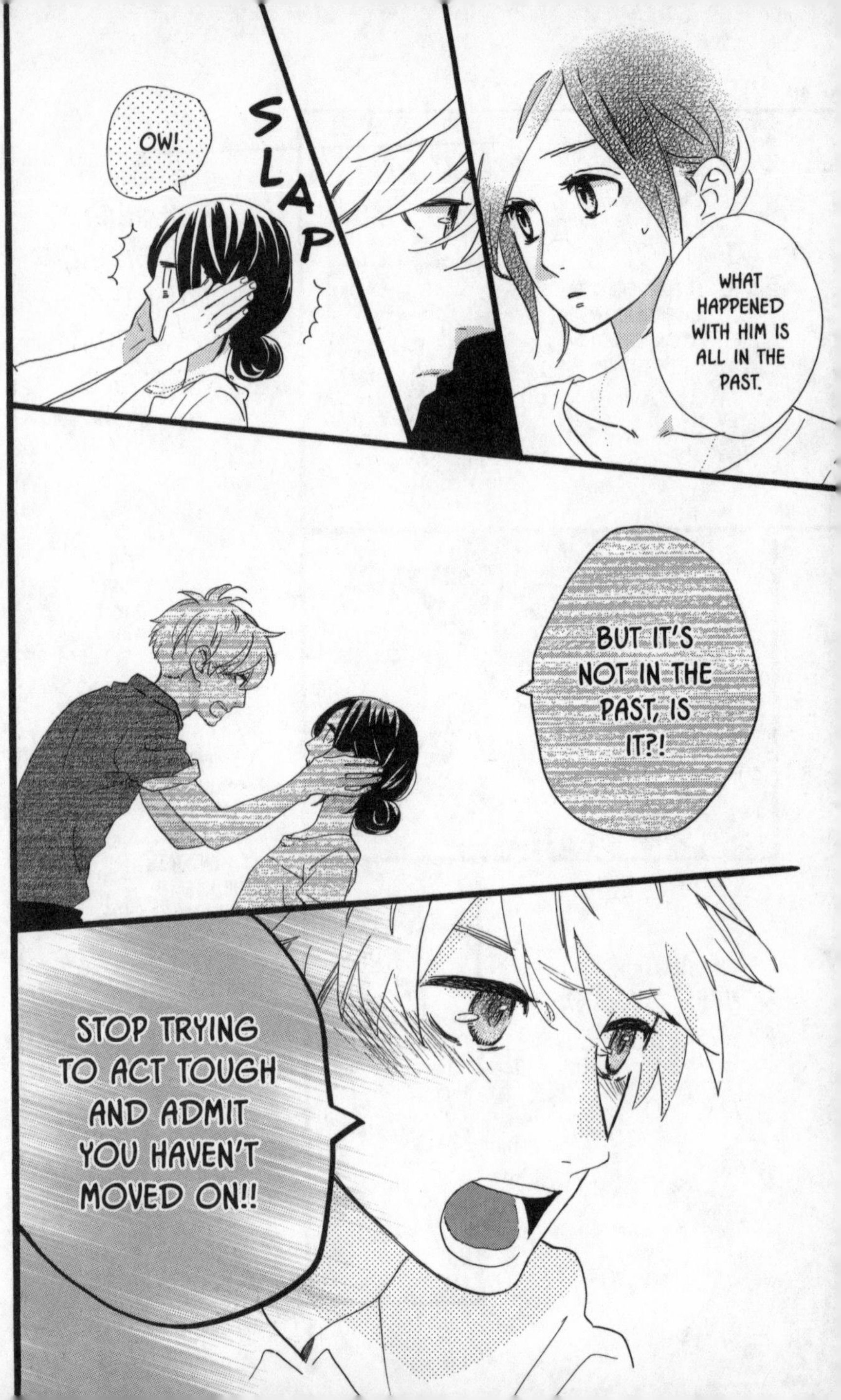
WHAT HAPPENED WITH HIM IS ALL IN THE PAST.
SLAP
OW!
BUT IT'S NOT IN THE PAST, IS IT?!
STOP TRYING TO ACT TOUGH AND ADMIT YOU HAVEN'T MOVED ON!!

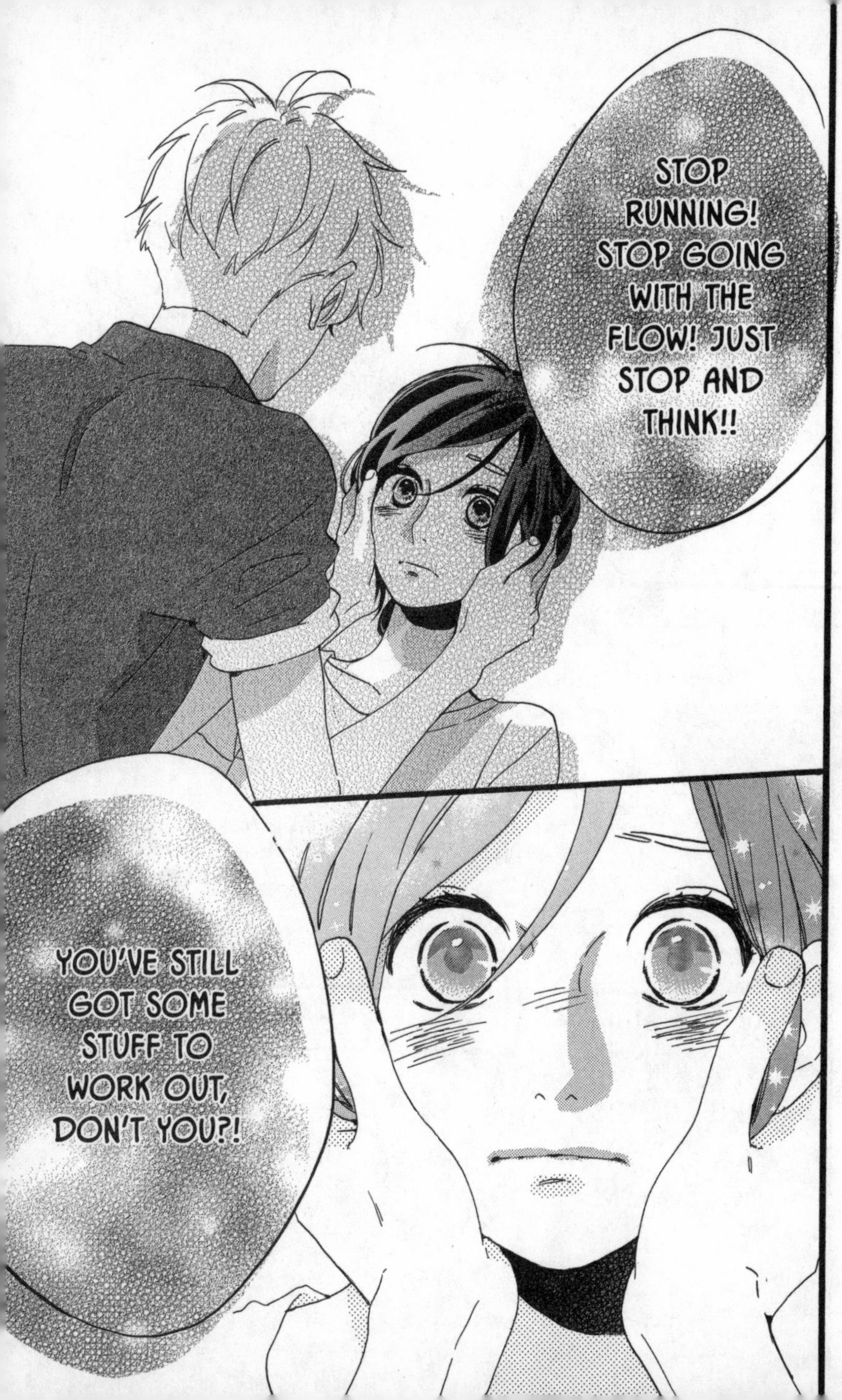
STOP RUNNING! STOP GOING WITH THE FLOW! JUST STOP AND THINK!!
YOU'VE STILL GOT SOME STUFF TO WORK OUT, DON'T YOU?!

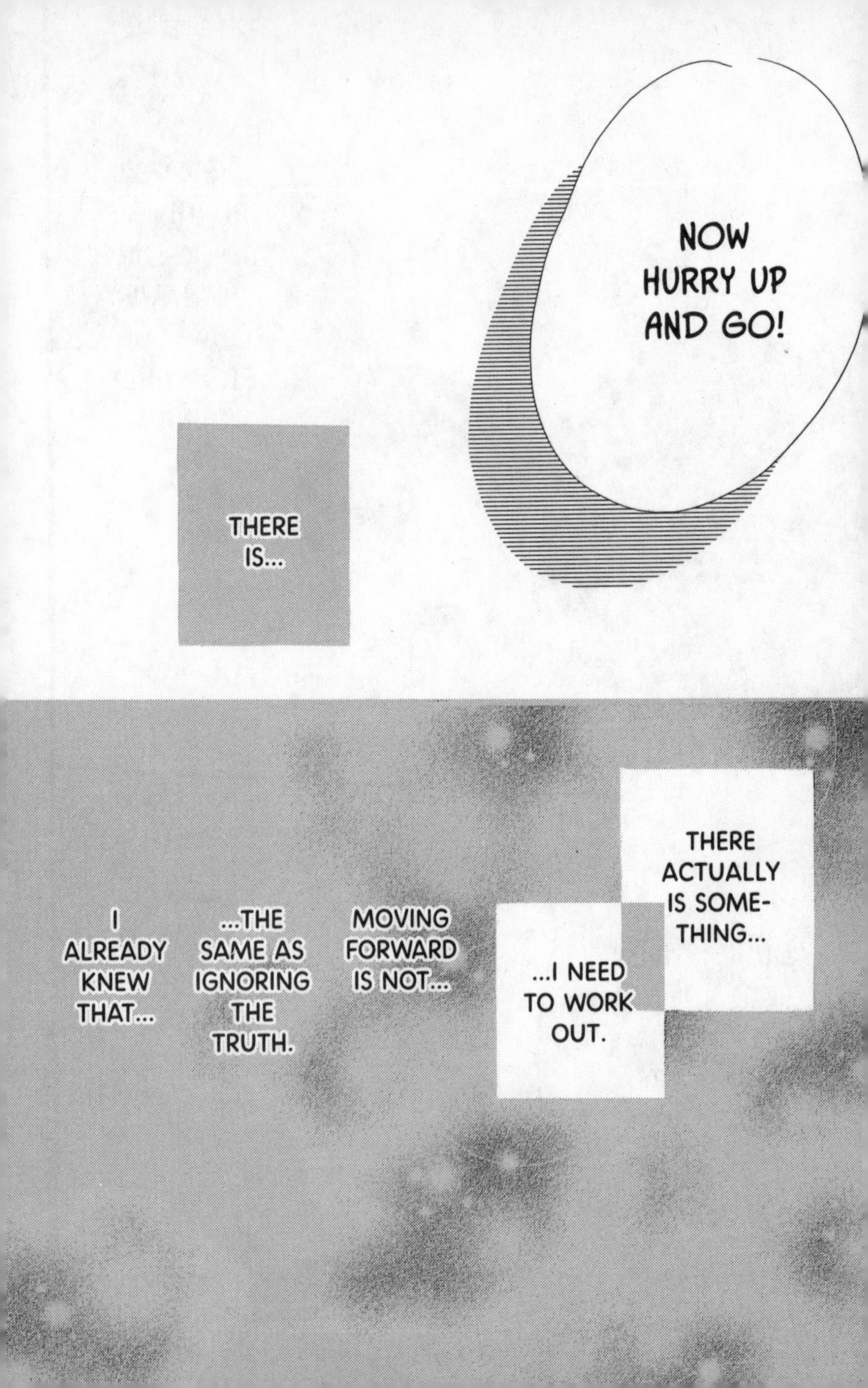
NOW HURRY UP AND GO!
THERE IS...
THERE ACTUALLY IS SOME-THING...
...I NEED TO WORK OUT.
MOVING FORWARD IS NOT...
...THE SAME AS IGNORING THE TRUTH.
I ALREADY KNEW THAT...

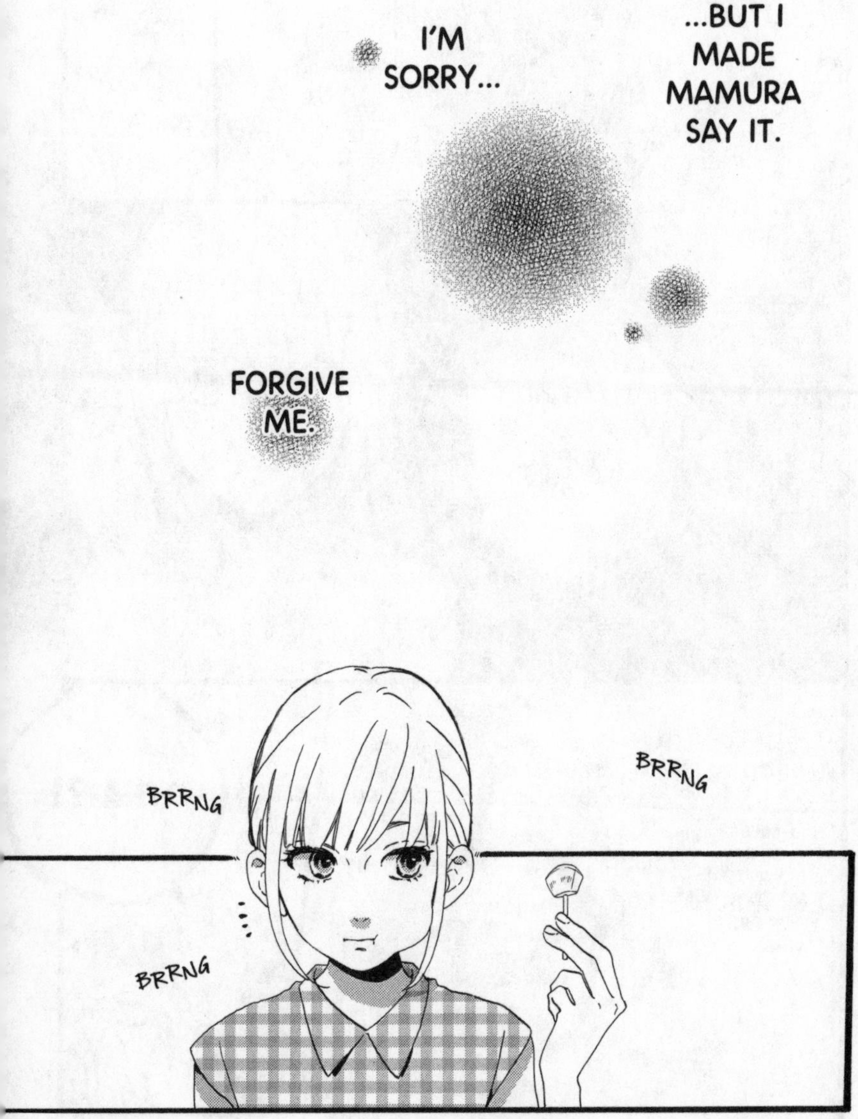
...BUT I MADE MAMURA SAY IT.
I'M SORRY...
FORGIVE ME.
BRRNG
BRRNG
BRRNG
...

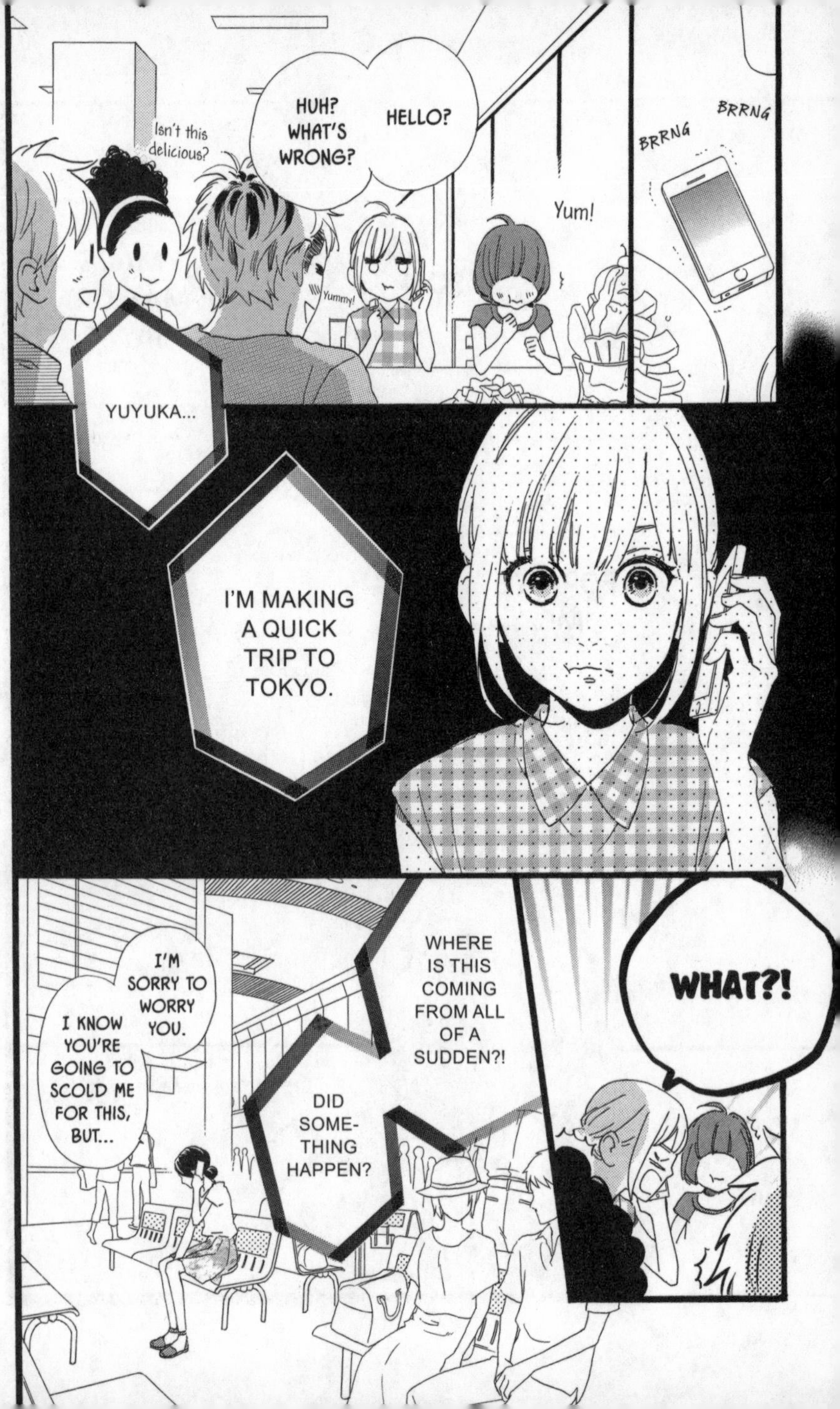
BRRNG
BRRNG
HELLO?
HUH? WHAT'S WRONG?
Yum!
Yummy!
Isn't this delicious?
YUYUKA...
I'M MAKING A QUICK TRIP TO TOKYO.
WHAT?!
WHERE IS THIS COMING FROM ALL OF A SUDDEN?!
DID SOME-THING HAPPEN?
I'M SORRY TO WORRY YOU.
I KNOW YOU'RE GOING TO SCOLD ME FOR THIS, BUT...

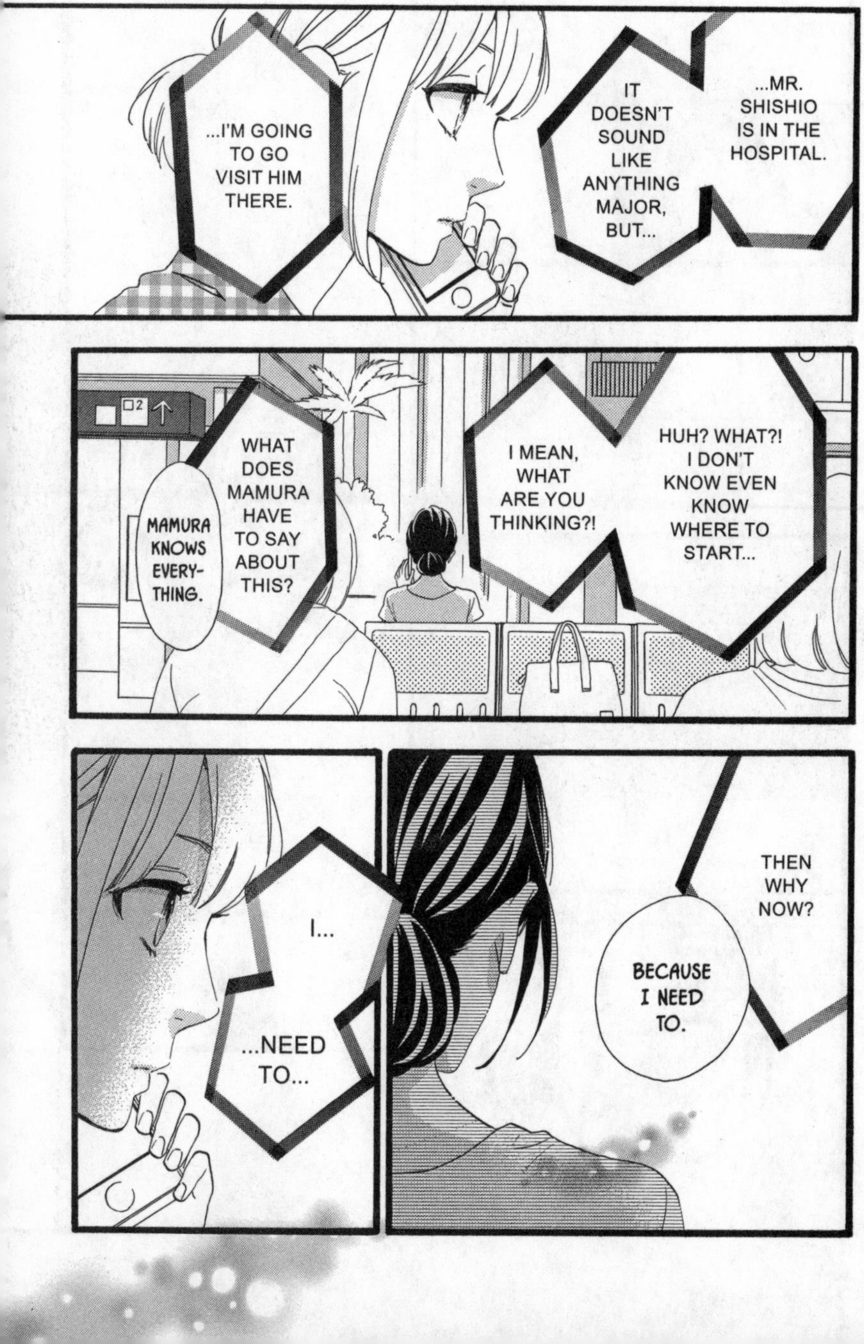
...MR. SHISHIO IS IN THE HOSPITAL.
IT DOESN'T SOUND LIKE ANYTHING MAJOR, BUT...
...I'M GOING TO GO VISIT HIM THERE.
HUH? WHAT?! I DON'T KNOW EVEN KNOW WHERE TO START...
I MEAN, WHAT ARE YOU THINKING?!
WHAT DOES MAMURA HAVE TO SAY ABOUT THIS?
MAMURA KNOWS EVERYTHING.
THEN WHY NOW?
BECAUSE I NEED TO.
I...
...NEED TO...

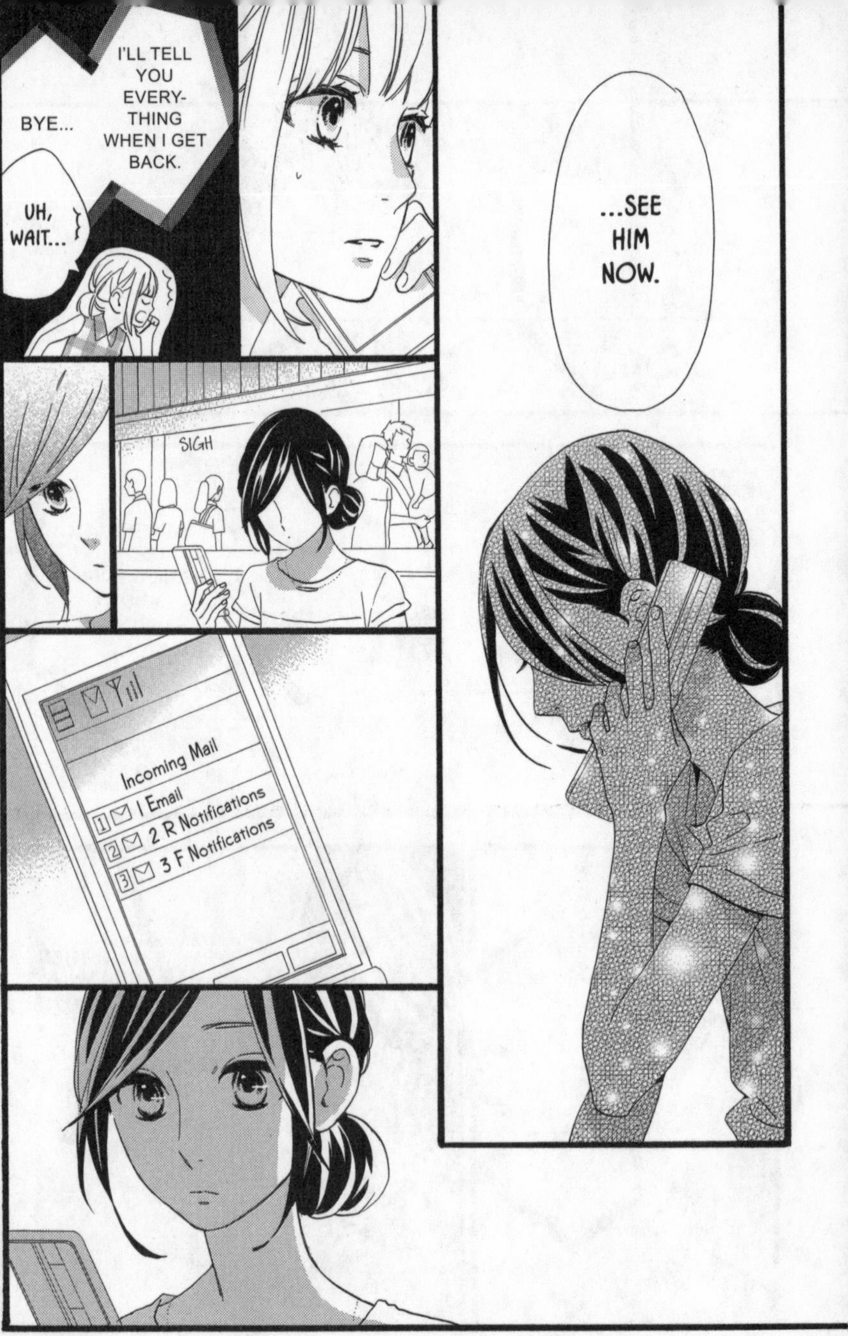
...SEE HIM NOW.
I'LL TELL YOU EVERY-THING WHEN I GET BACK.
BYE...
UH, WAIT...
SIGH
Incoming Mail
1 1 Email
2 2 R Notifications
3 3 F Notifications

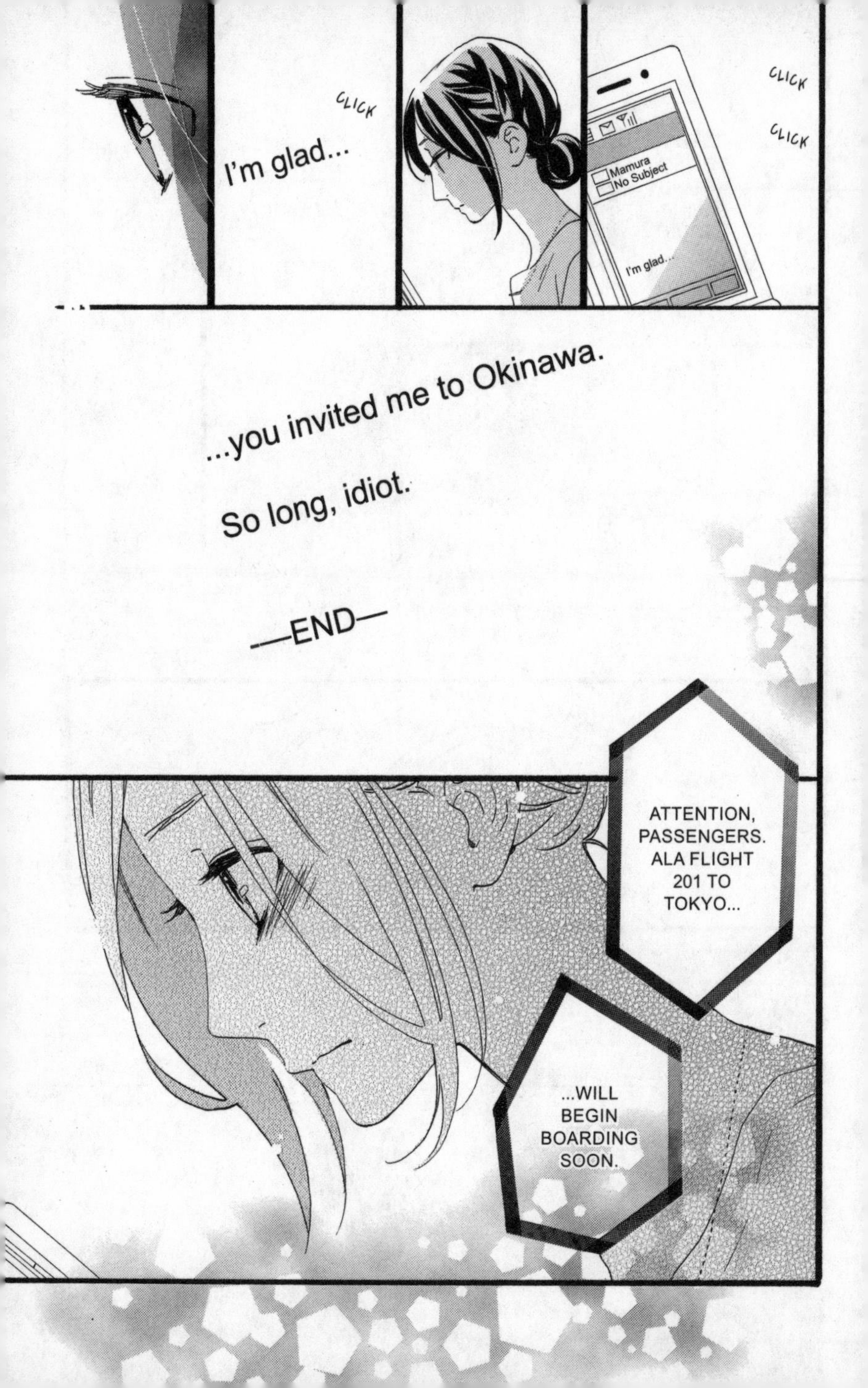
CLICK
CLICK
Mamura
No Subject
I'm glad...
CLICK
I'm glad...
...you invited me to Okinawa.
So long, idiot.
—END—
ATTENTION, PASSENGERS. ALA FLIGHT 201 TO TOKYO...
...WILL BEGIN BOARDING SOON.

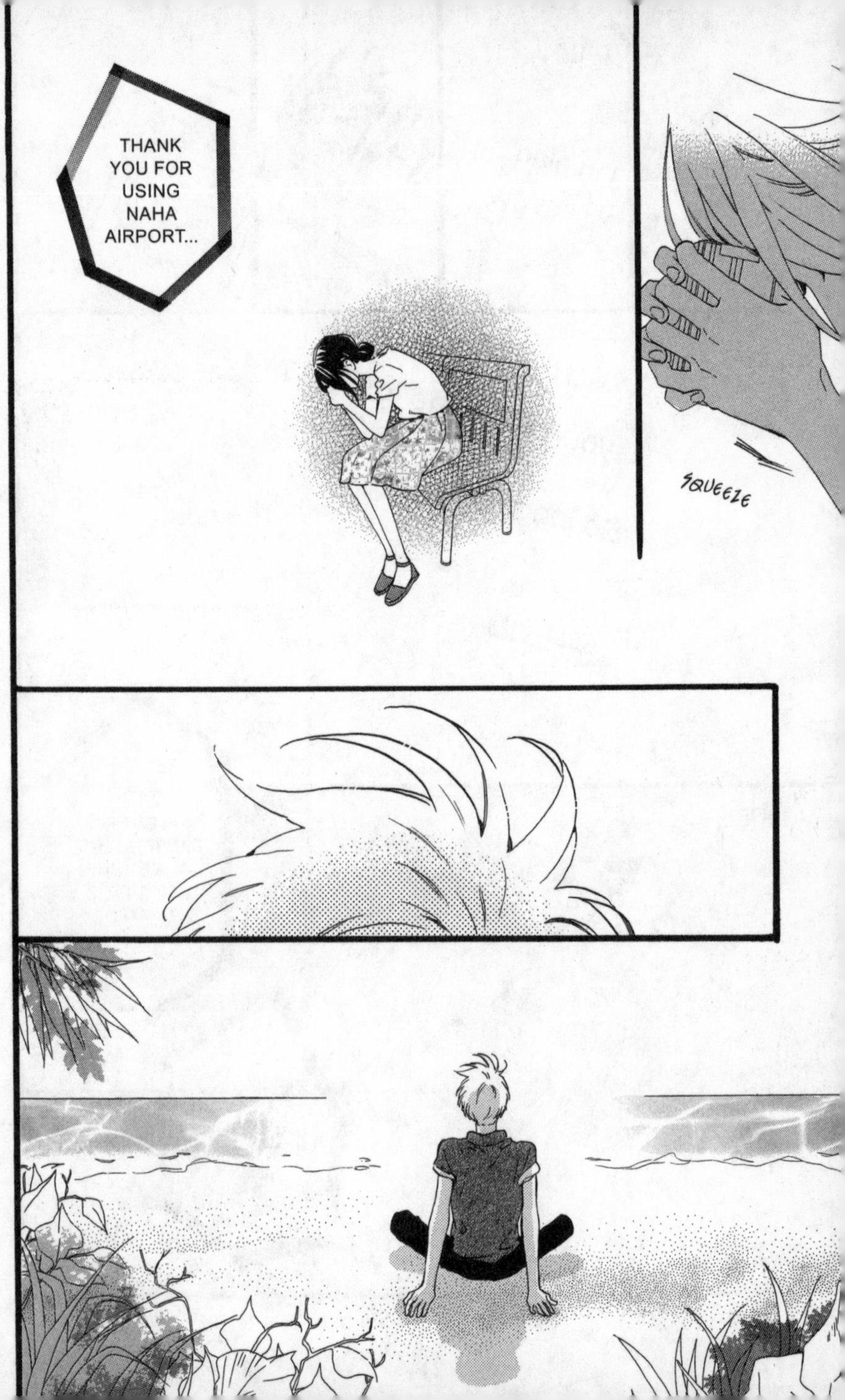
SQUEEZE
THANK YOU FOR USING NAHA AIRPORT...

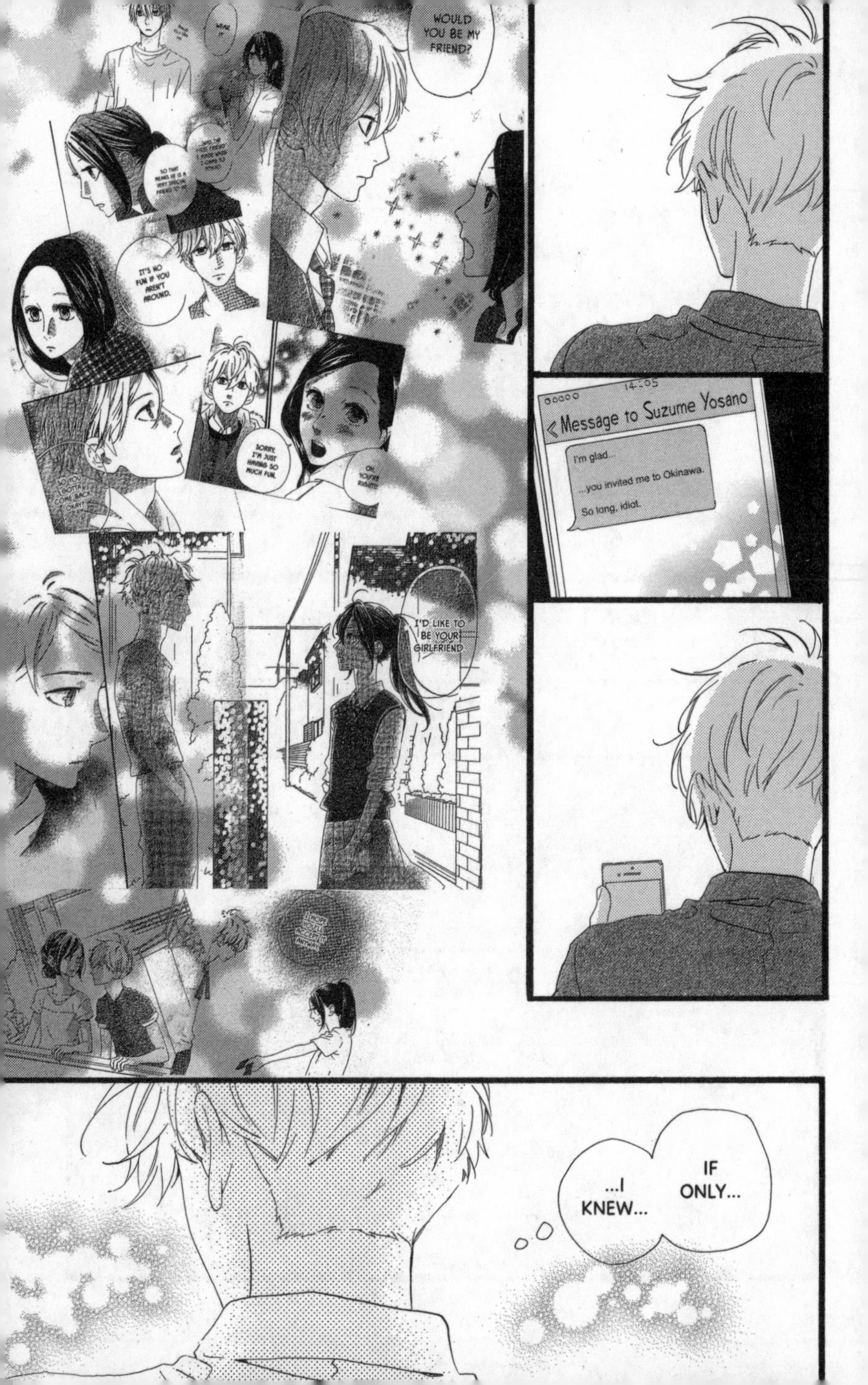

14:05
Message to Suzume Yosano
I'm glad...
...you invited me to Okinawa.
So long, idiot.
WOULD YOU BE MY FRIEND?
SO THAT MEANS HE IS A VERY SPECIAL FRIEND TO HIM.
IT'S NO FUN IF YOU AREN'T AROUND.
OH, YOU'RE RIGHT!
SORRY. I'M JUST HAVING SO MUCH FUN.
SO YOU GOTTA COME BACK, OKAY?
I'D LIKE TO BE YOUR GIRLFRIEND.
I HOPE YOU'LL ACCEPT IT ANYWAY.
IF ONLY...
...I KNEW...

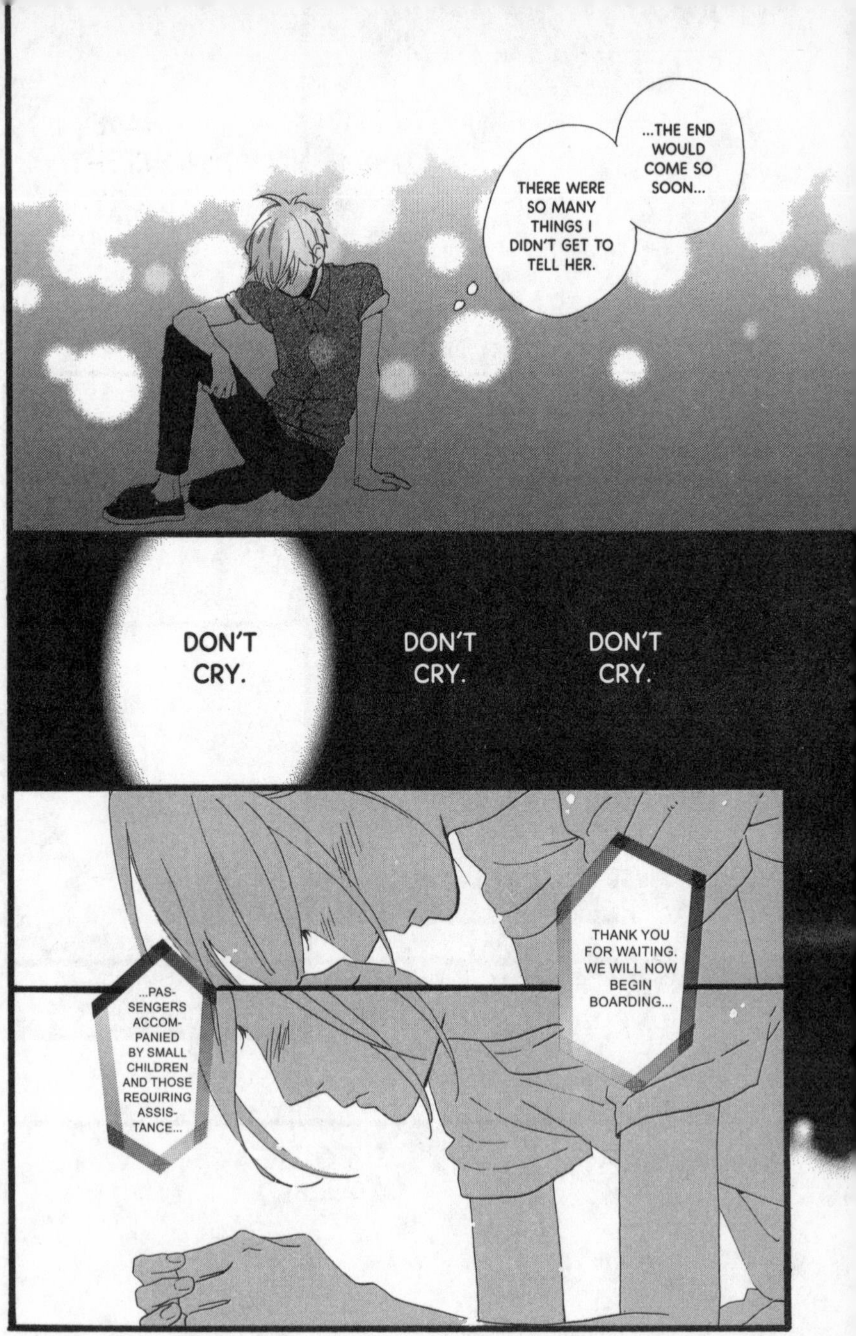

...THE END WOULD COME SO SOON...
THERE WERE SO MANY THINGS I DIDN'T GET TO TELL HER.
DON'T CRY.
DON'T CRY.
DON'T CRY.
THANK YOU FOR WAITING. WE WILL NOW BEGIN BOARDING...
...PAS-SENGERS ACCOM-PANIED BY SMALL CHILDREN AND THOSE REQUIRING ASSIS-TANCE...

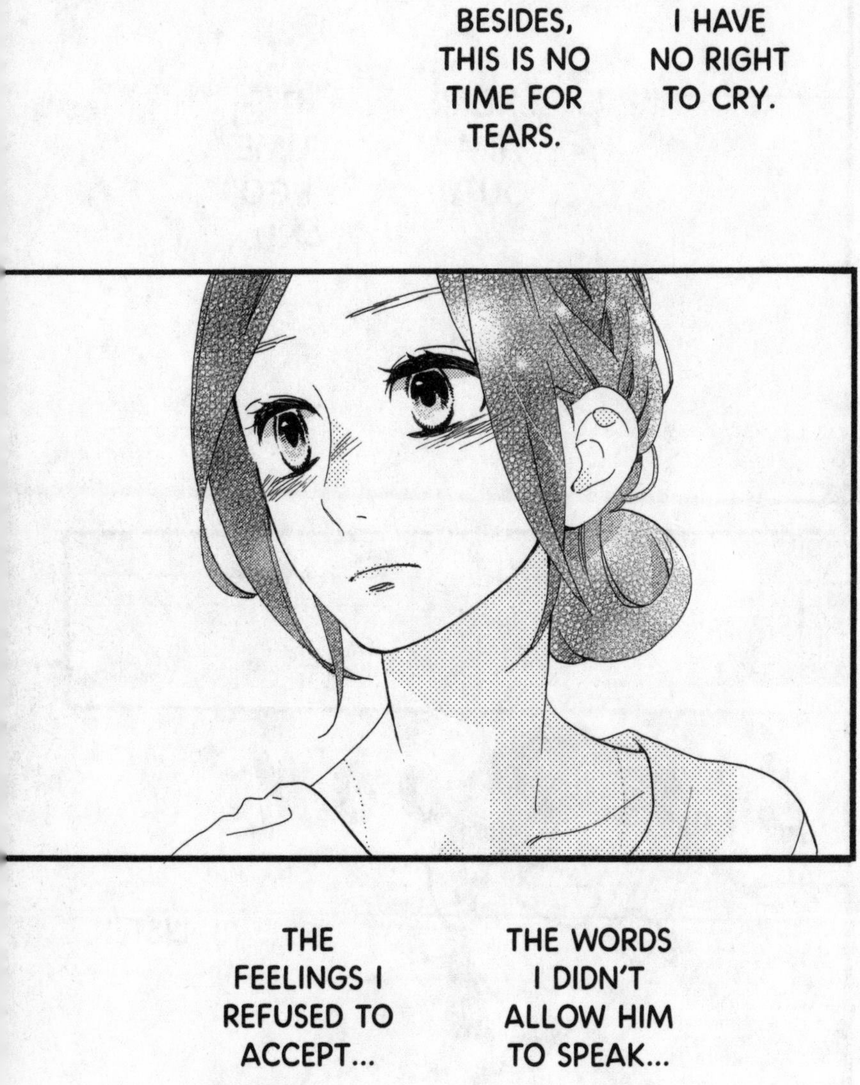
I HAVE NO RIGHT TO CRY.
BESIDES, THIS IS NO TIME FOR TEARS.
THE WORDS I DIDN'T ALLOW HIM TO SPEAK...
THE FEELINGS I REFUSED TO ACCEPT...

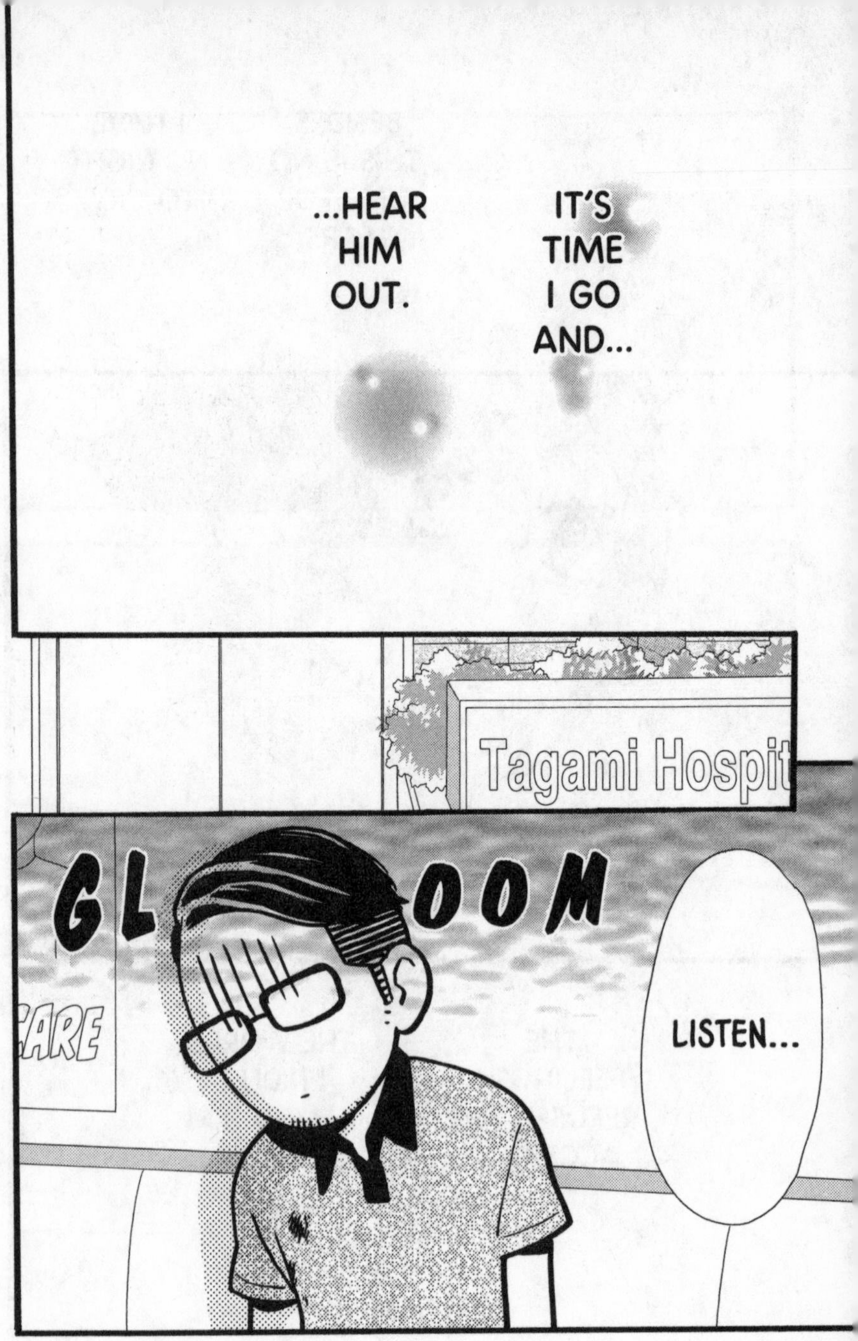
IT'S TIME I GO AND...
...HEAR HIM OUT.
Tagami Hospit
LISTEN...
GLOOM

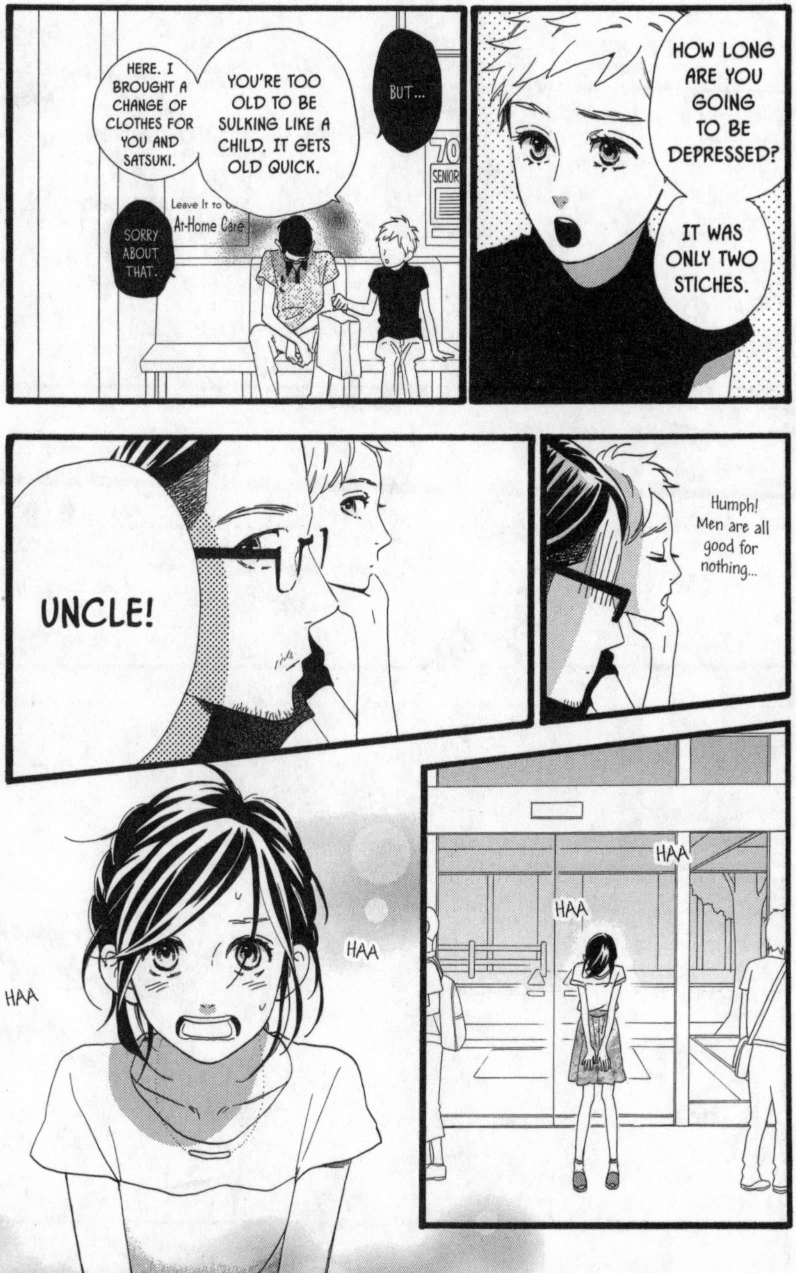
HOW LONG ARE YOU GOING TO BE DEPRESSED?
IT WAS ONLY TWO STICHES.
BUT...
YOU'RE TOO OLD TO BE SULKING LIKE A CHILD. IT GETS OLD QUICK.
HERE. I BROUGHT A CHANGE OF CLOTHES FOR YOU AND SATSUKI.
70
SENIOR
Leave It to
At-Home Care
SORRY ABOUT THAT.
Humph! Men are all good for nothing...
UNCLE!
HAA
HAA
HAA
HAA

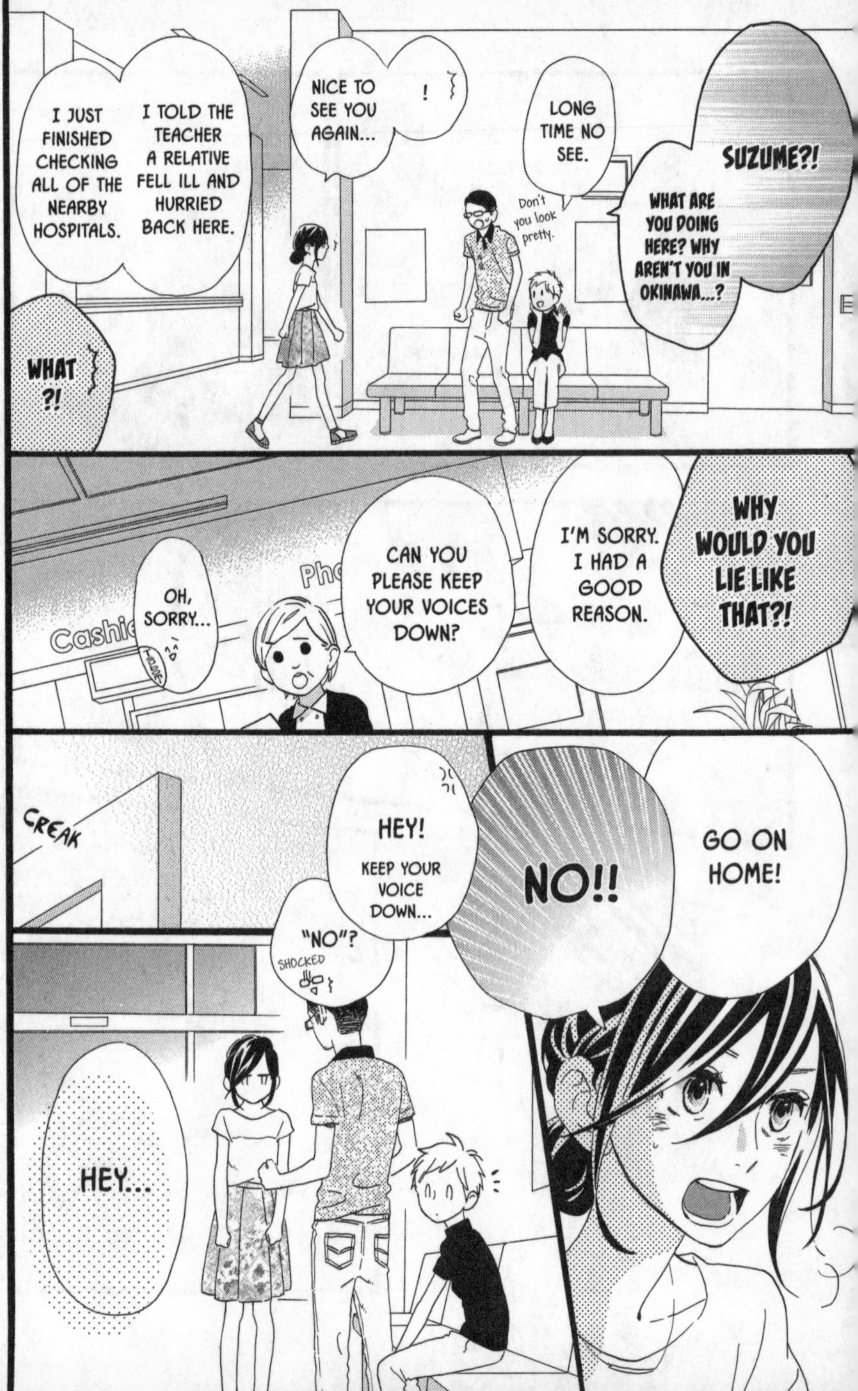

SUZUME?!
WHAT ARE YOU DOING HERE? WHY AREN'T YOU IN OKINAWA...?
LONG TIME NO SEE.
Don't you look pretty.
!
NICE TO SEE YOU AGAIN...
I TOLD THE TEACHER A RELATIVE FELL ILL AND HURRIED BACK HERE.
I JUST FINISHED CHECKING ALL OF THE NEARBY HOSPITALS.
WHAT?!
WHY WOULD YOU LIE LIKE THAT?!
I'M SORRY. I HAD A GOOD REASON.
CAN YOU PLEASE KEEP YOUR VOICES DOWN?
OH, SORRY...
GO ON HOME!
NO!!
HEY!
KEEP YOUR VOICE DOWN...
CREAK
"NO"?
SHOCKED
HEY...

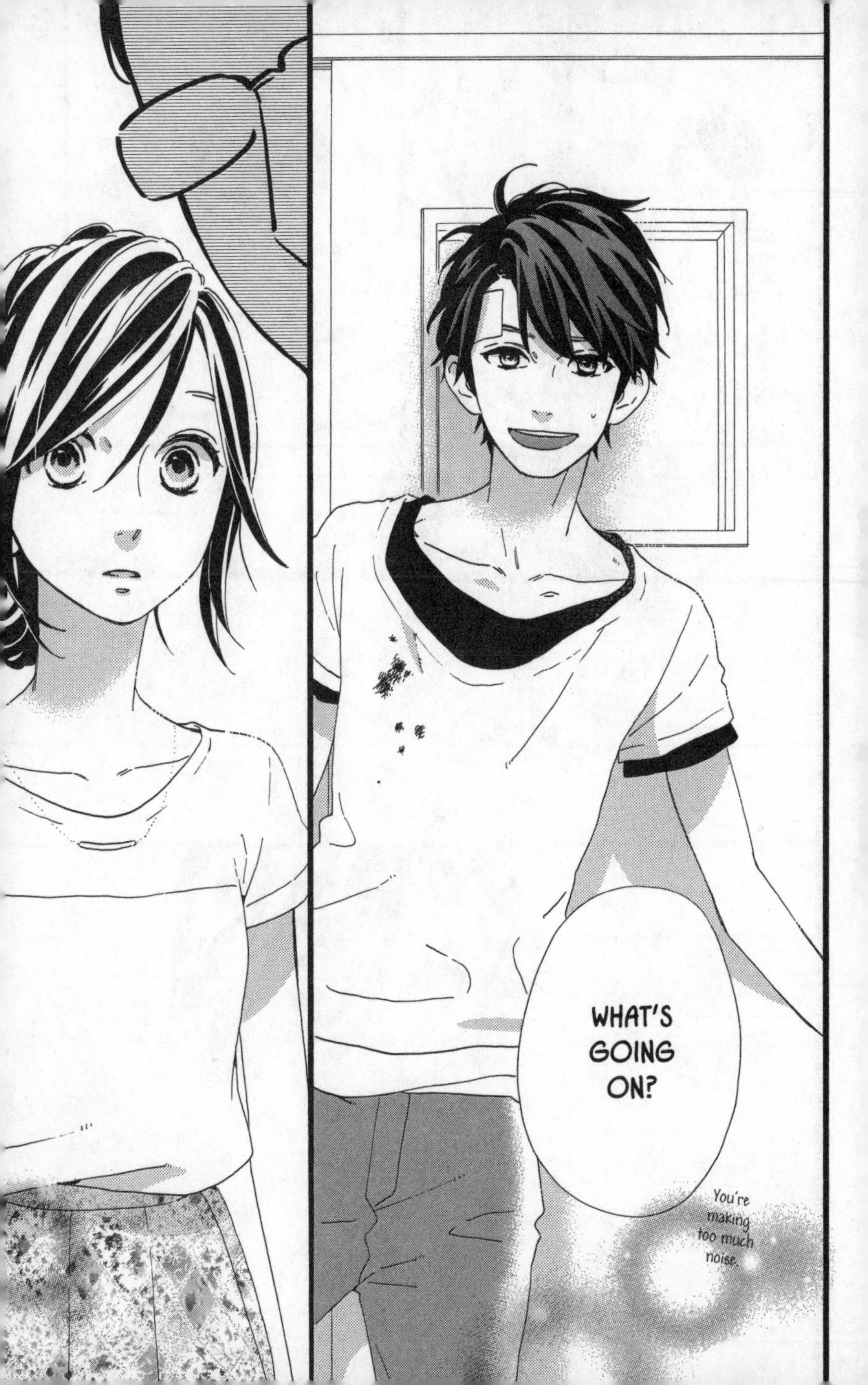
WHAT'S GOING ON?
You're making too much noise.

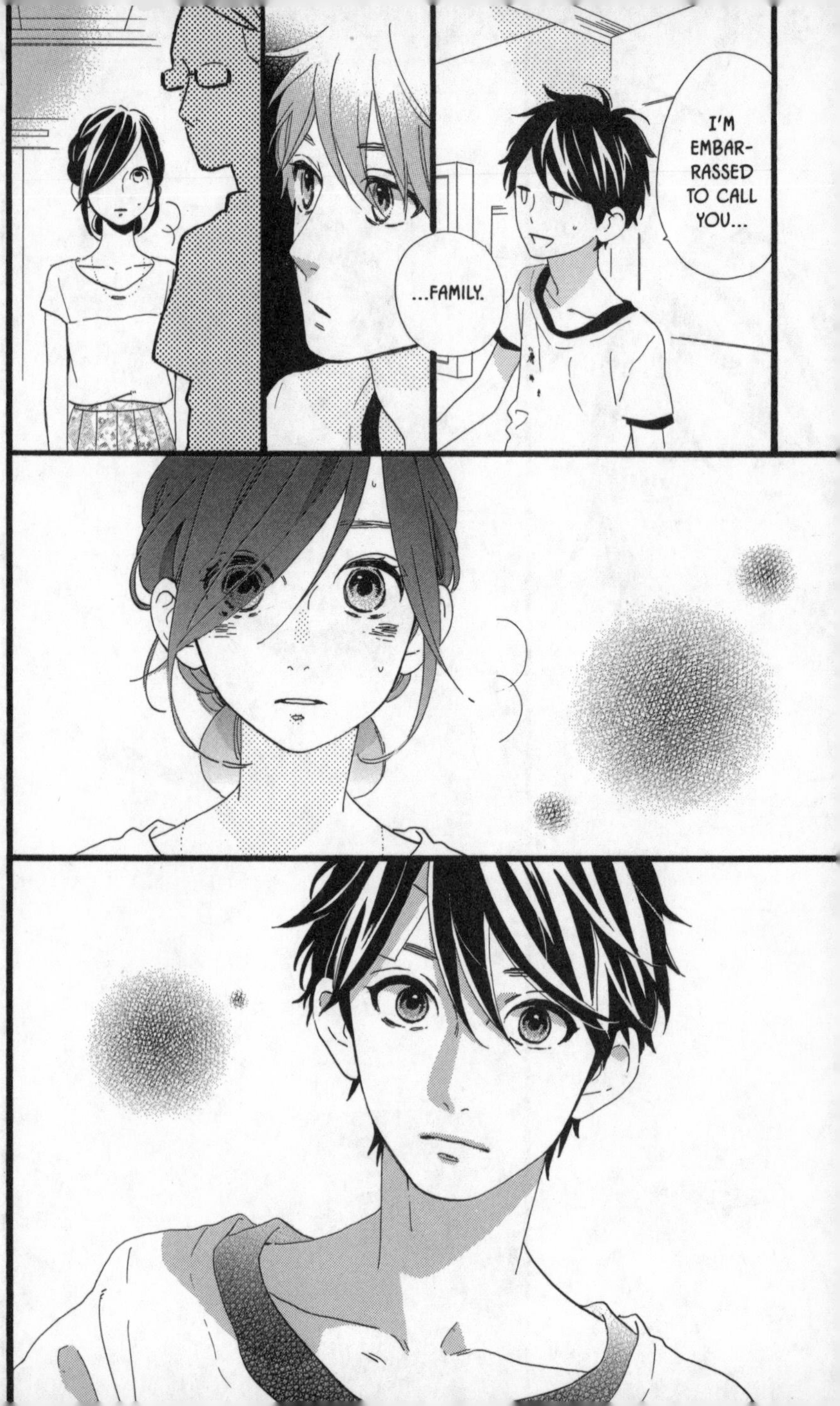
I'M EMBAR-RASSED TO CALL YOU...
...FAMILY.

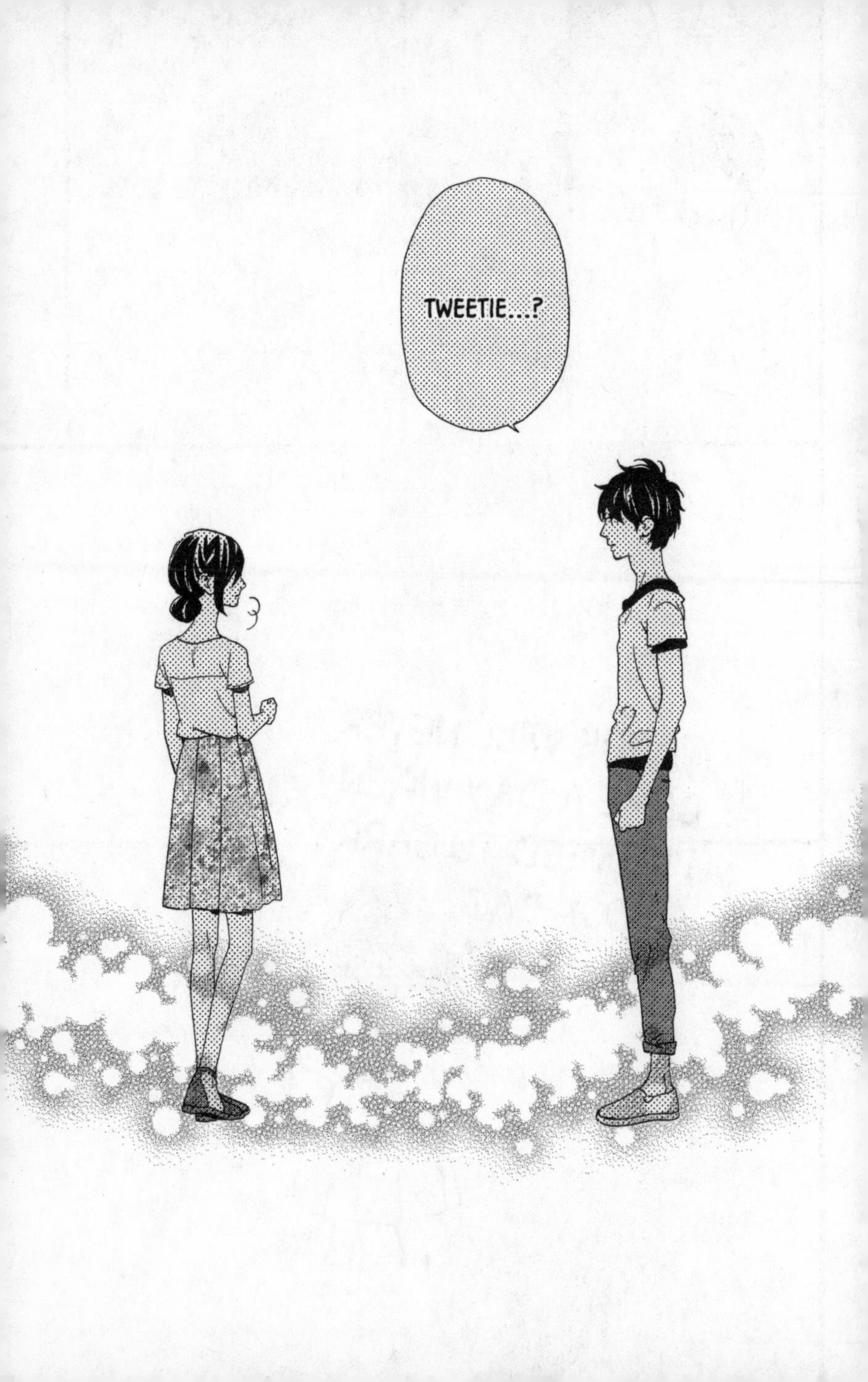
TWEETIE...?

THERE WILL NEVER COME A DAY WHEN I'LL NEED TO CARRY A BOOK BAG.

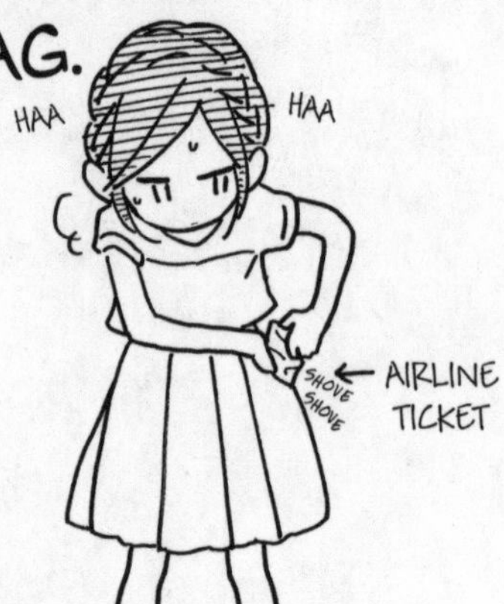
HAA
HAA
SHOVE SHOVE
AIRLINE TICKET

Day 77

DAYTIME
SHOOTING
STAR

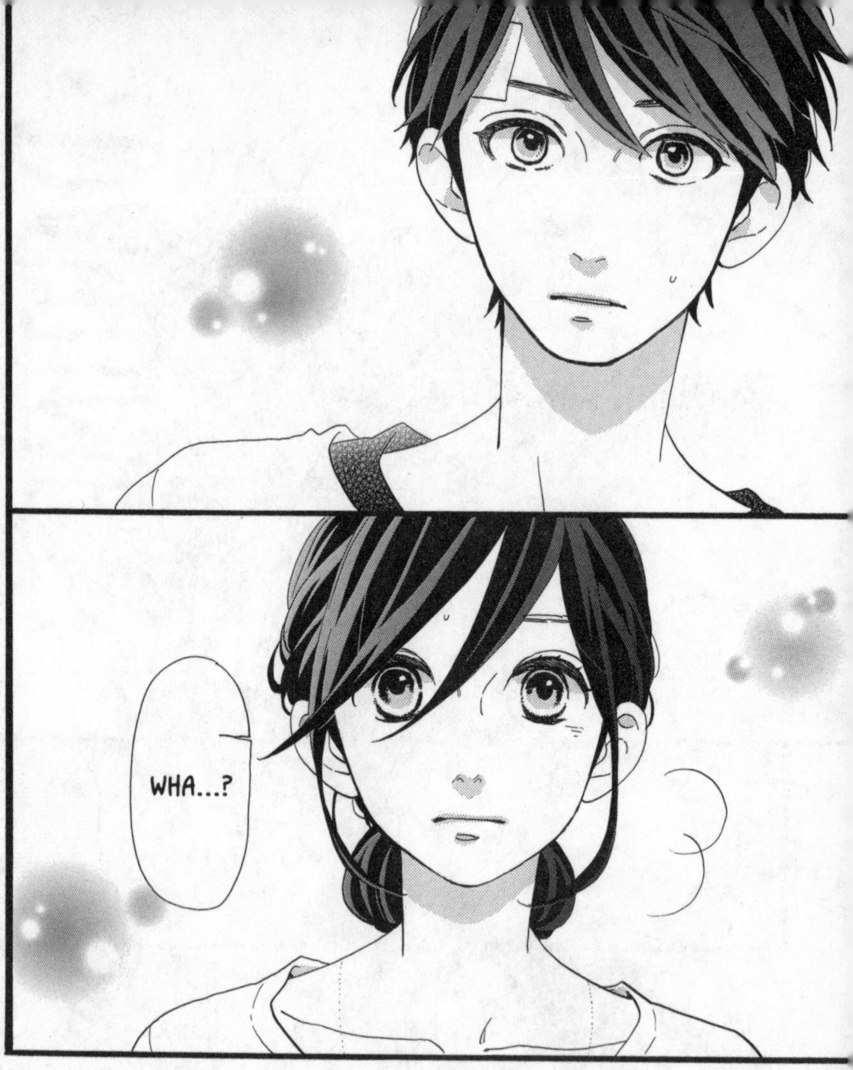
WHA...?

DAYTIME SHOOTING STAR

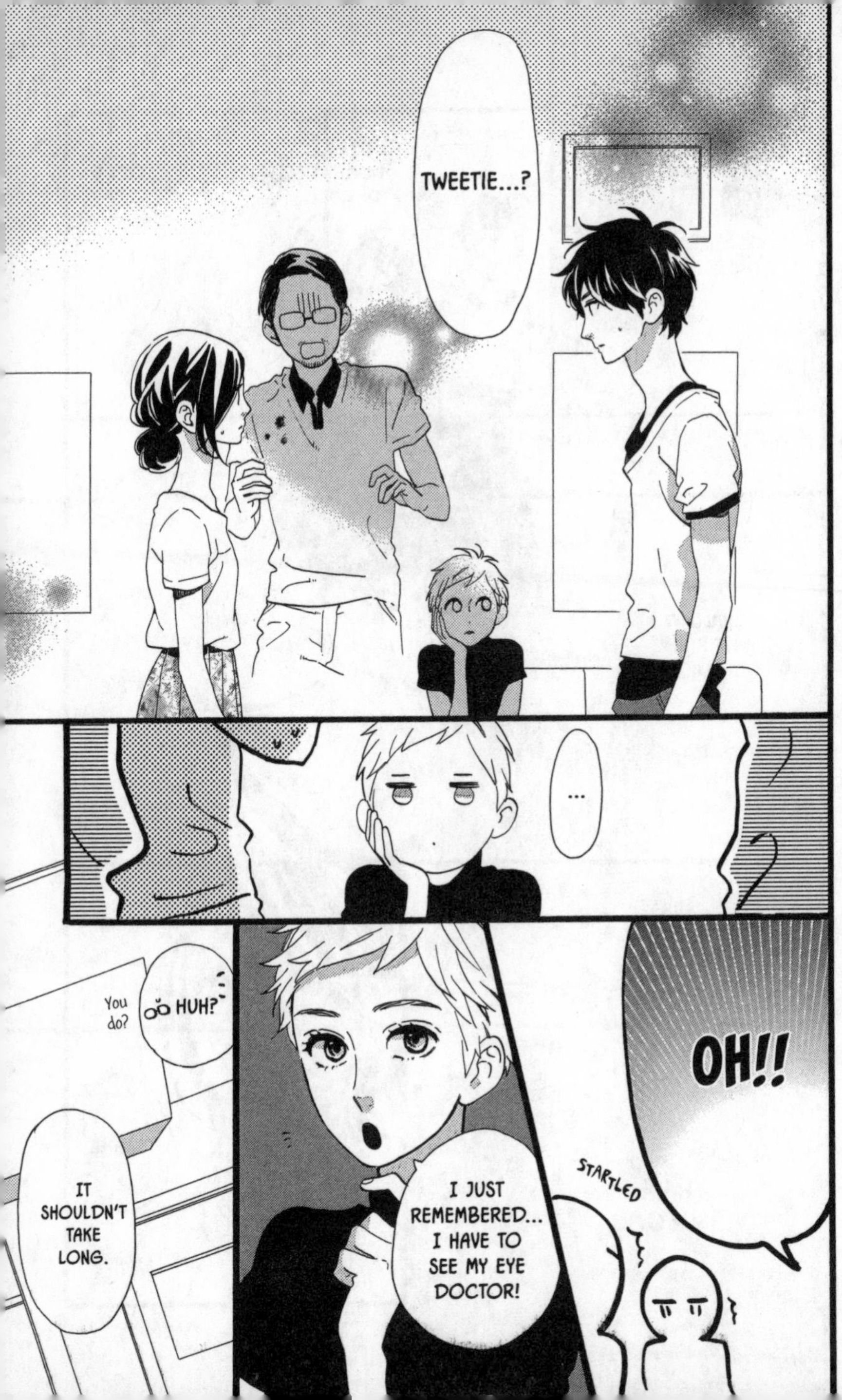
TWEETIE...?
...
OH!!
STARTLED
I JUST REMEMBERED... I HAVE TO SEE MY EYE DOCTOR!
HUH?
You do?
IT SHOULDN'T TAKE LONG.

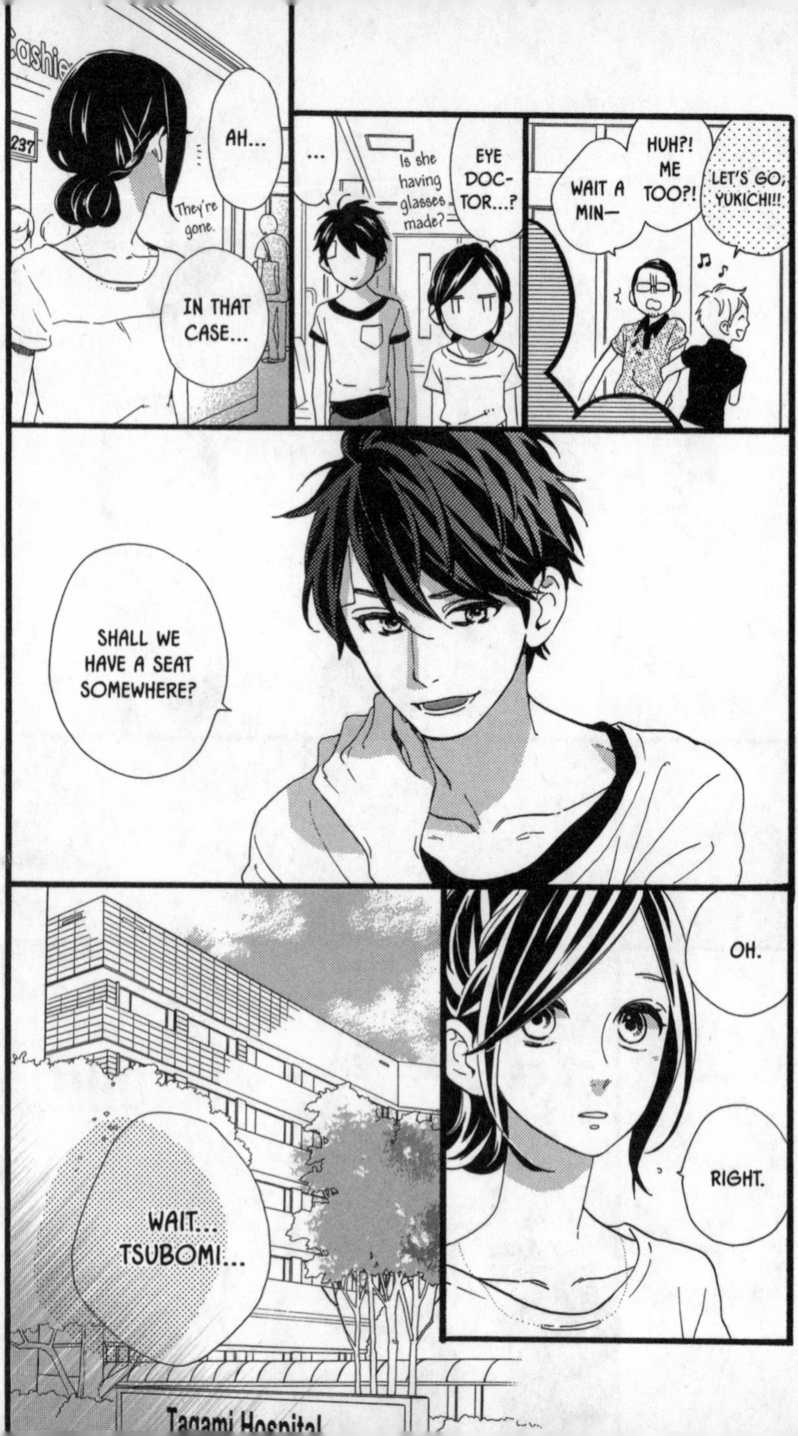
LET'S GO, YUKICHI!!!
HUH?! ME TOO?!
WAIT A MIN—
EYE DOCTOR...?
Is she having glasses made?
...
AH...
They're gone.
IN THAT CASE...
SHALL WE HAVE A SEAT SOMEWHERE?
OH.
RIGHT.
WAIT... TSUBOMI...
Tagami Hospital

OH, I'M SORRY.

PAT

It's dangerous.

I GOT IT, TSUBOMI. YOU CAN LET GO.

TUG TUG

I WAS READY...

...TO GIVE THOSE TWO SOME SPACE TO TALK THINGS OUT.

...

Humph!

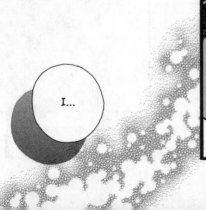

I...

THAT'S RIGHT.

Pretty much...

OH, IS THAT SO?

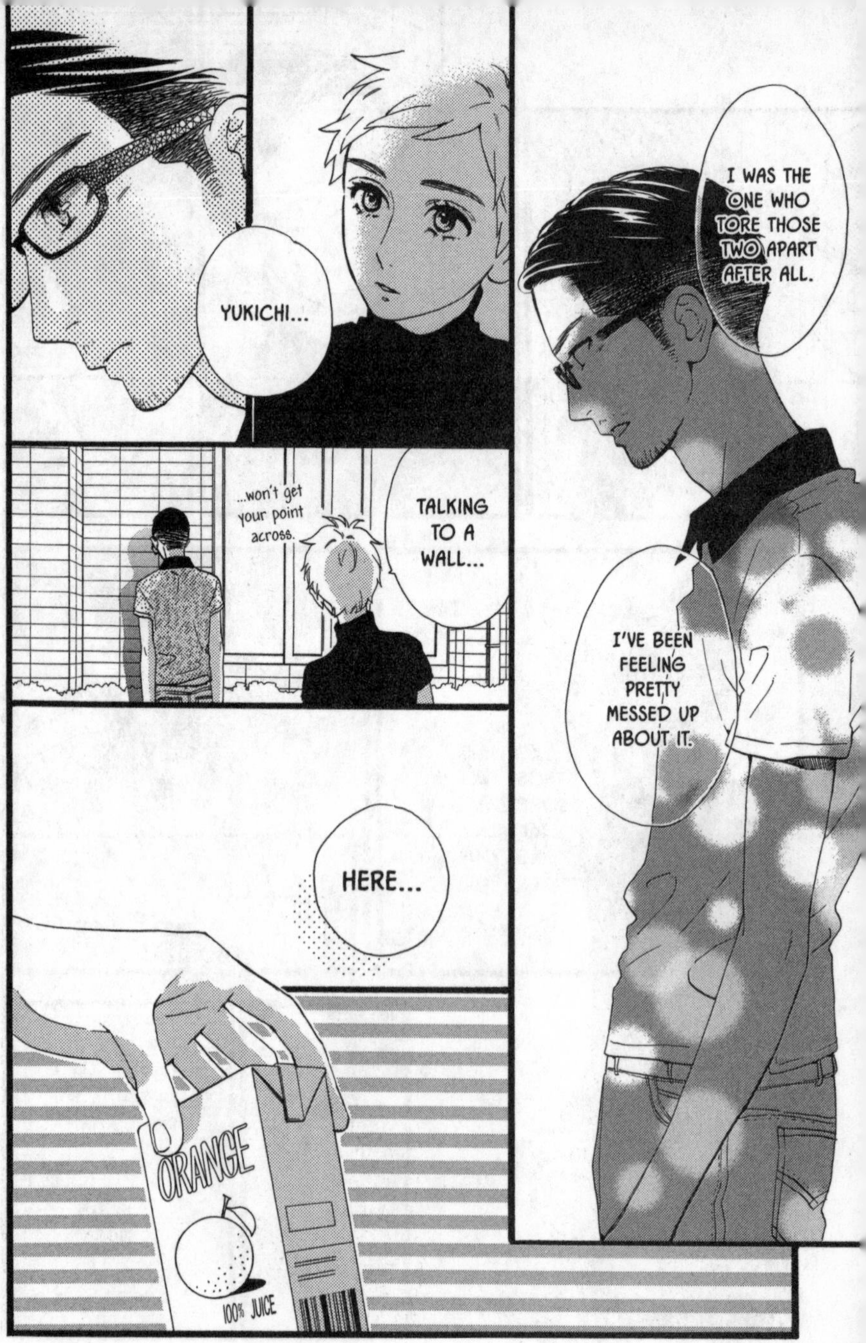
I WAS THE ONE WHO TORE THOSE TWO APART AFTER ALL.
I'VE BEEN FEELING PRETTY MESSED UP ABOUT IT.
YUKICHI...
TALKING TO A WALL...
...won't get your point across.
HERE...
ORANGE
100% JUICE

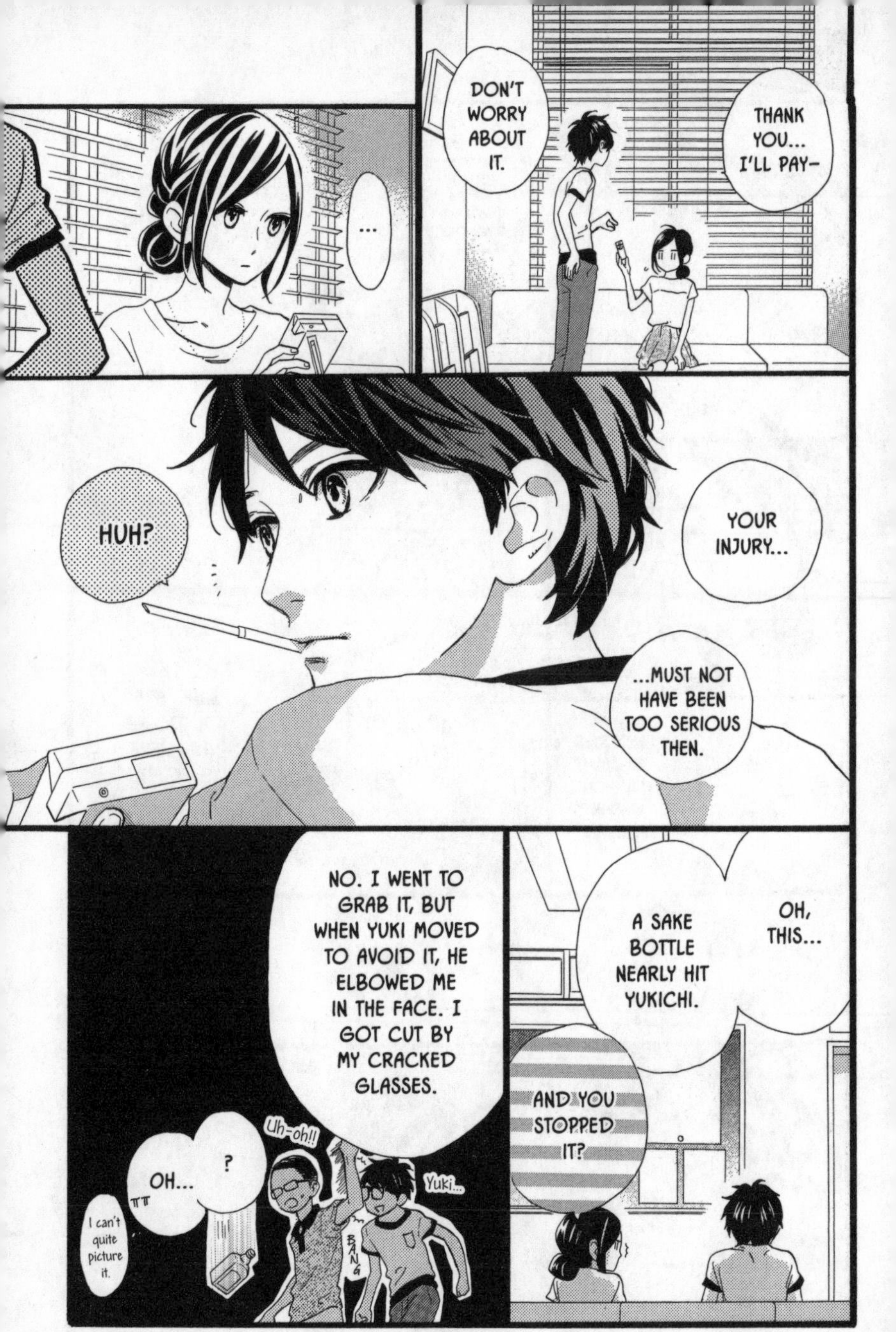
THANK YOU... I'LL PAY–
DON'T WORRY ABOUT IT.
...
YOUR INJURY...
...MUST NOT HAVE BEEN TOO SERIOUS THEN.
HUH?
OH, THIS...
A SAKE BOTTLE NEARLY HIT YUKICHI.
AND YOU STOPPED IT?
NO. I WENT TO GRAB IT, BUT WHEN YUKI MOVED TO AVOID IT, HE ELBOWED ME IN THE FACE. I GOT CUT BY MY CRACKED GLASSES.
Uh-oh!!
Yuki...
BANG
?
OH...
I can't quite picture it.

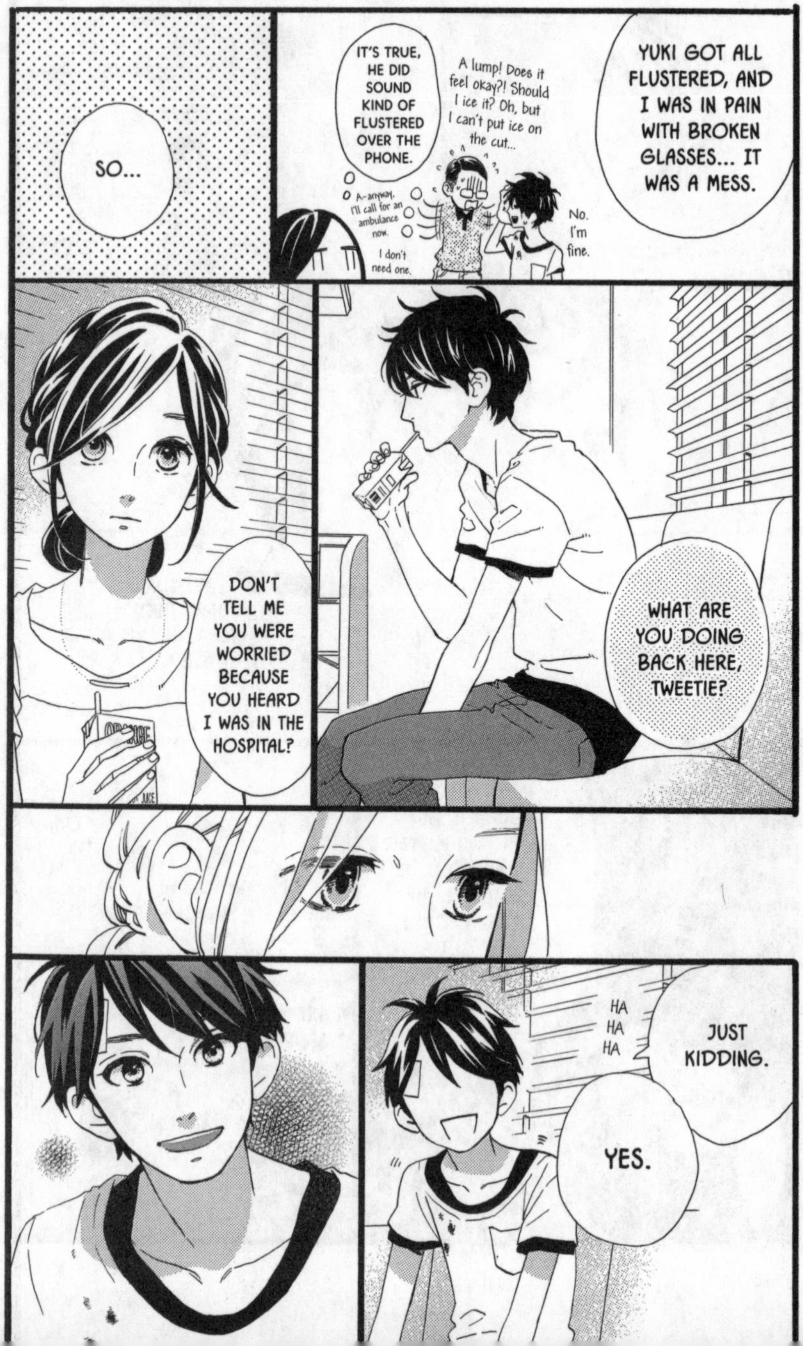
YUKI GOT ALL FLUSTERED, AND I WAS IN PAIN WITH BROKEN GLASSES... IT WAS A MESS.
A lump! Does it feel okay?! Should I ice it? Oh, but I can't put ice on the cut...
No. I'm fine.
IT'S TRUE, HE DID SOUND KIND OF FLUSTERED OVER THE PHONE.
A-anyway, I'll call for an ambulance now.
I don't need one.
SO...
WHAT ARE YOU DOING BACK HERE, TWEETIE?
DON'T TELL ME YOU WERE WORRIED BECAUSE YOU HEARD I WAS IN THE HOSPITAL?
JUST KIDDING.
HA HA HA
YES.

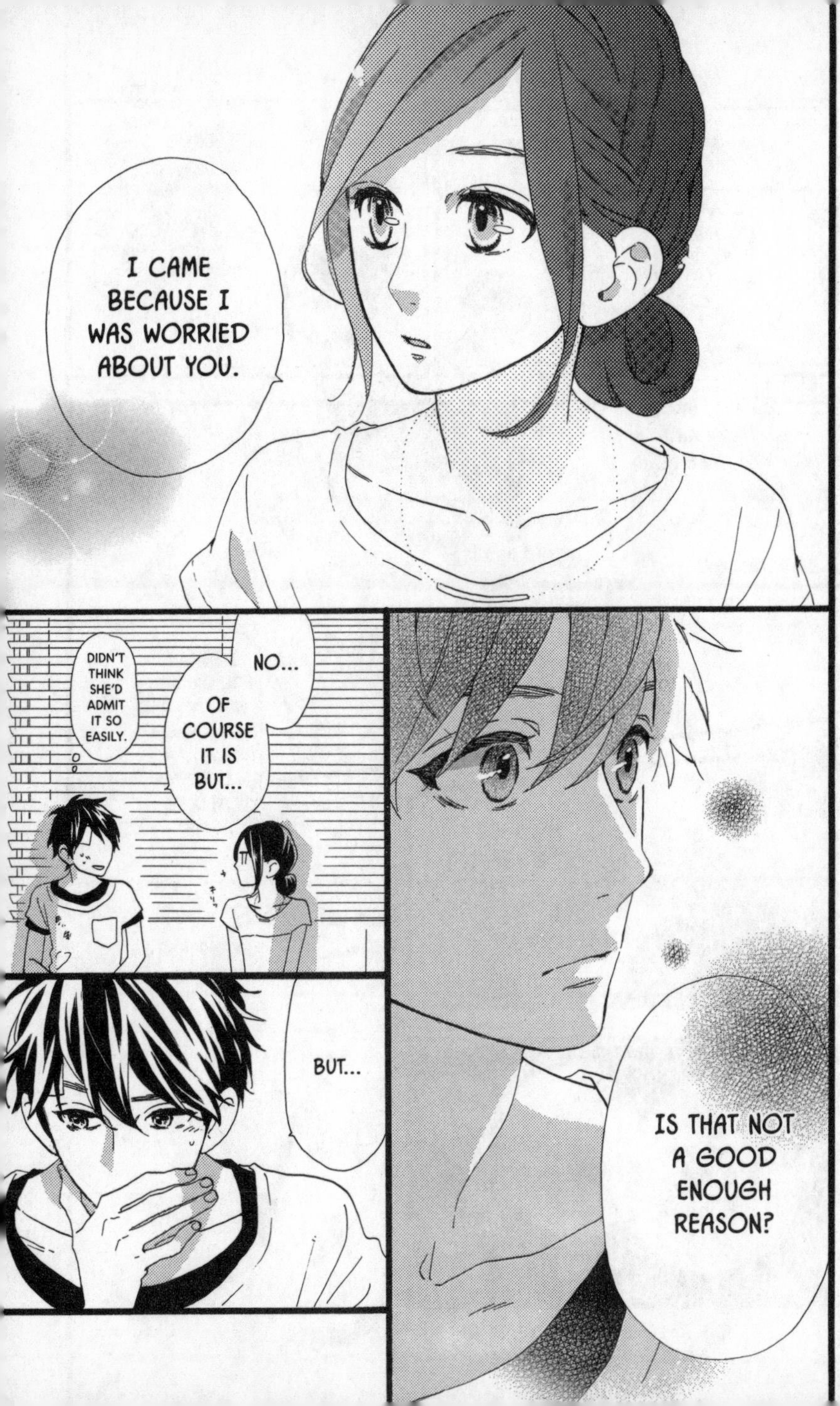
I CAME BECAUSE I WAS WORRIED ABOUT YOU.
IS THAT NOT A GOOD ENOUGH REASON?
NO... OF COURSE IT IS BUT...
DIDN'T THINK SHE'D ADMIT IT SO EASILY.
BUT...

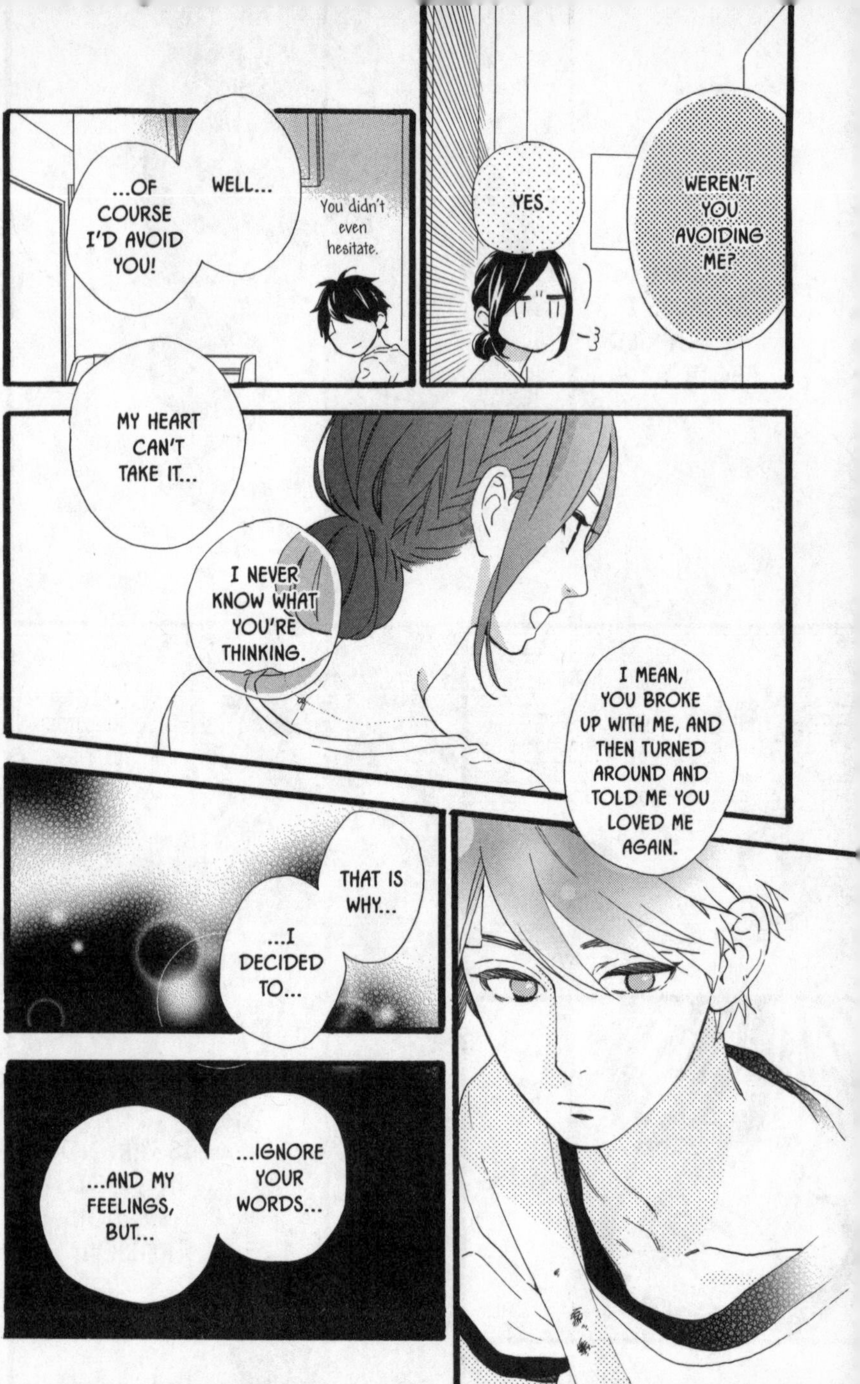
WEREN'T YOU AVOIDING ME?
YES.
WELL...
...OF COURSE I'D AVOID YOU!
You didn't even hesitate.
MY HEART CAN'T TAKE IT...
I NEVER KNOW WHAT YOU'RE THINKING.
I MEAN, YOU BROKE UP WITH ME, AND THEN TURNED AROUND AND TOLD ME YOU LOVED ME AGAIN.
THAT IS WHY...
...I DECIDED TO...
...IGNORE YOUR WORDS...
...AND MY FEELINGS, BUT...

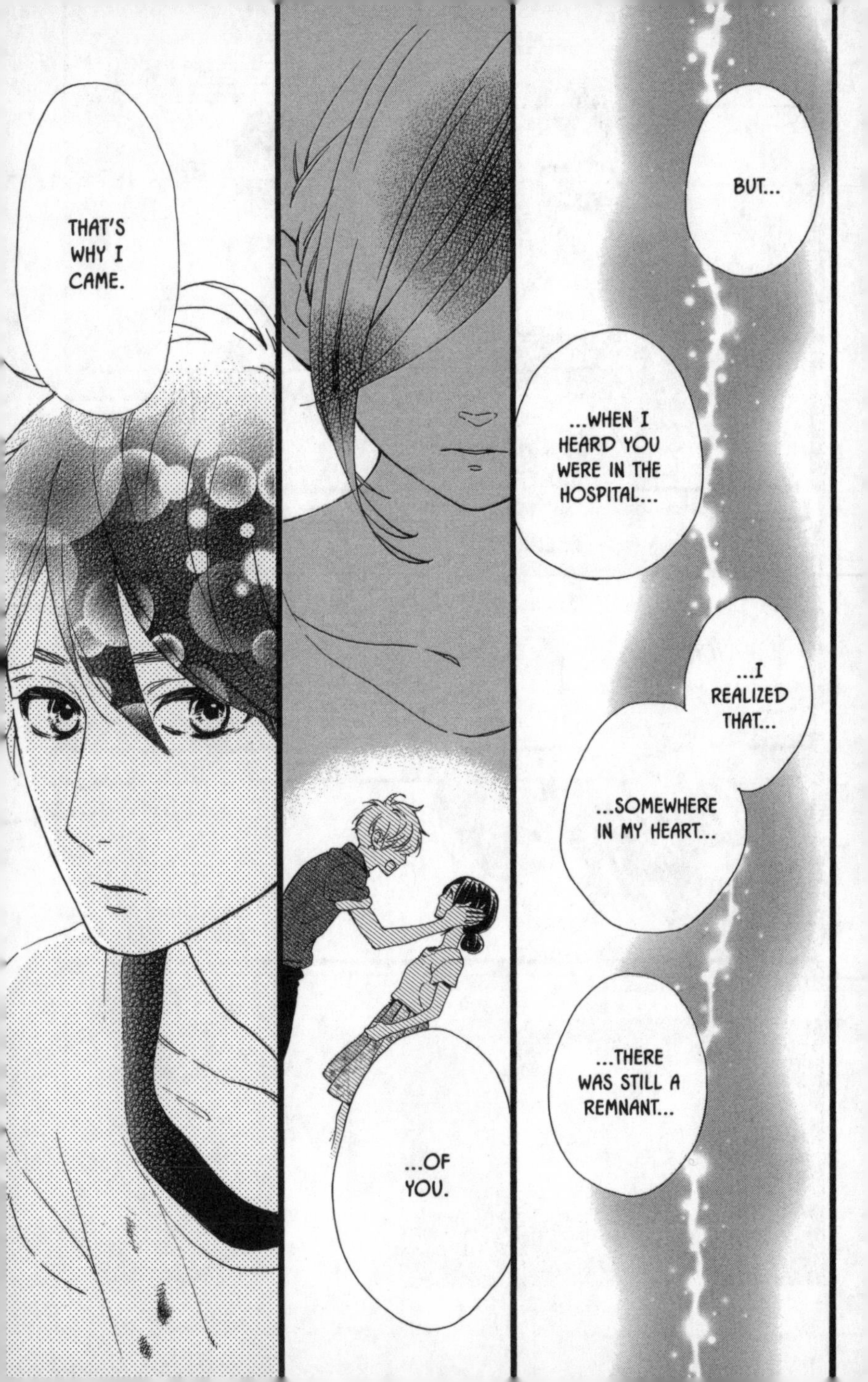
BUT...
...WHEN I HEARD YOU WERE IN THE HOSPITAL...
...I REALIZED THAT...
...SOMEWHERE IN MY HEART...
...THERE WAS STILL A REMNANT...
...OF YOU.
THAT'S WHY I CAME.

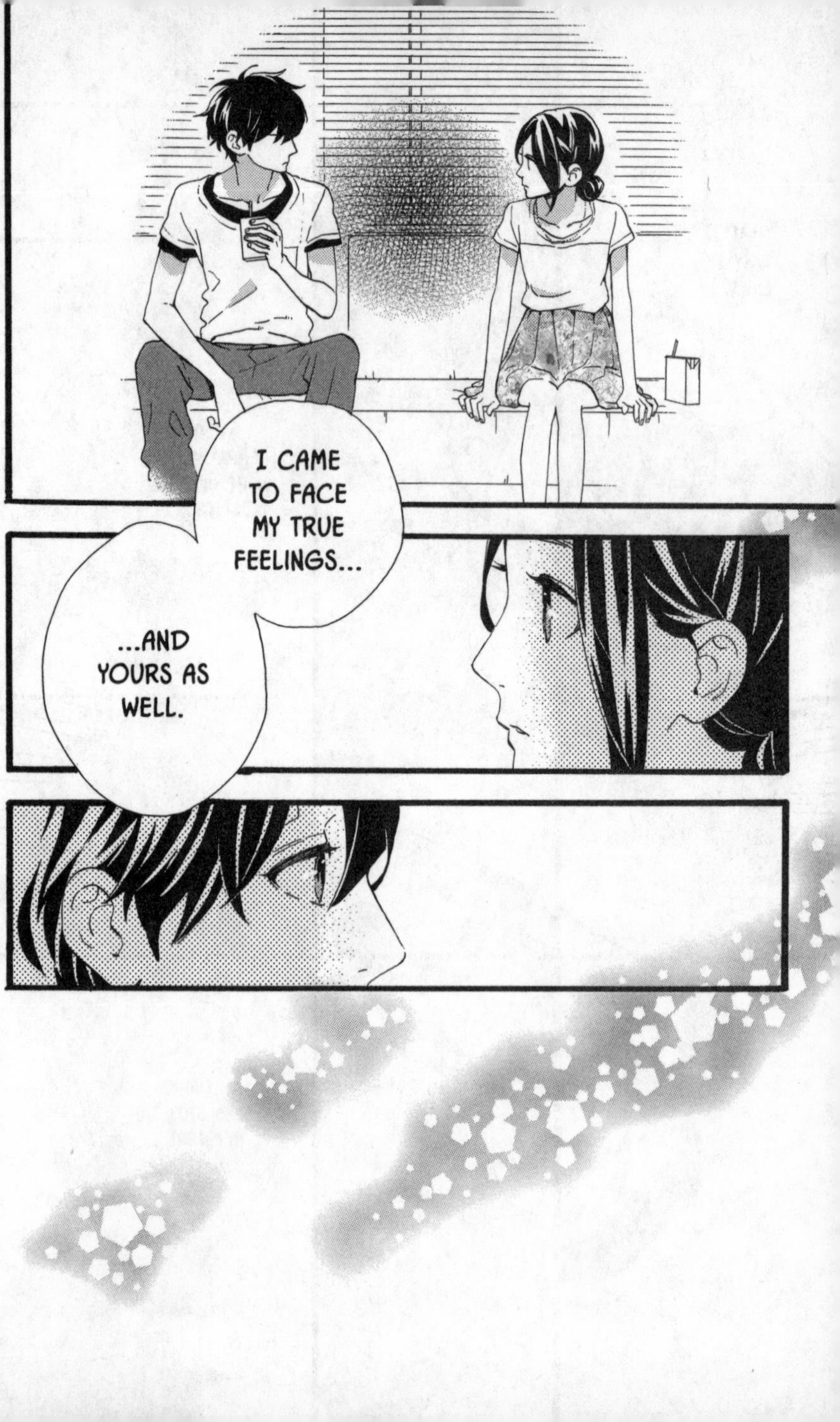
I CAME TO FACE MY TRUE FEELINGS...
...AND YOURS AS WELL.

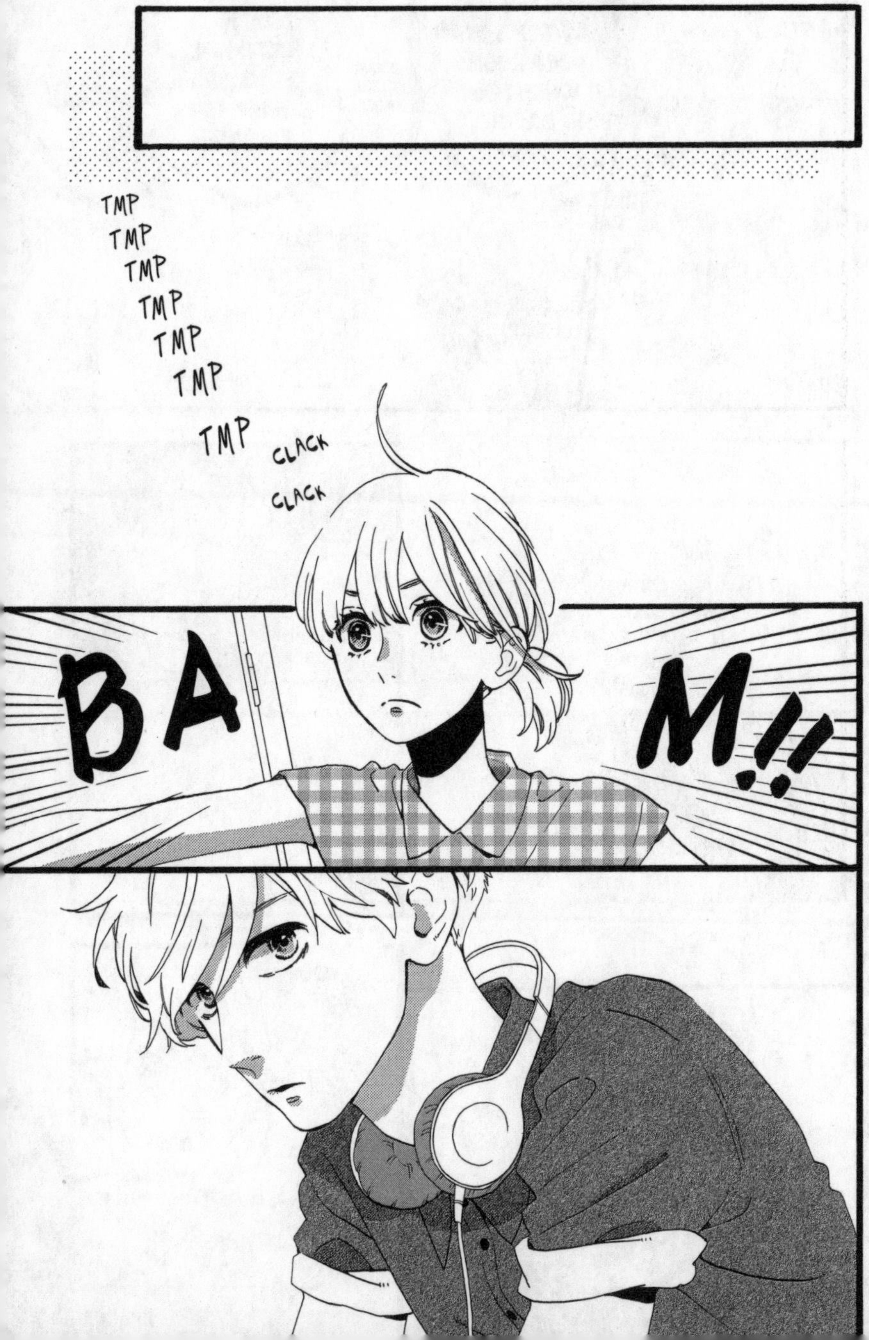
TMP
TMP
TMP
TMP
TMP
TMP
TMP
CLACK
CLACK
BAM!!

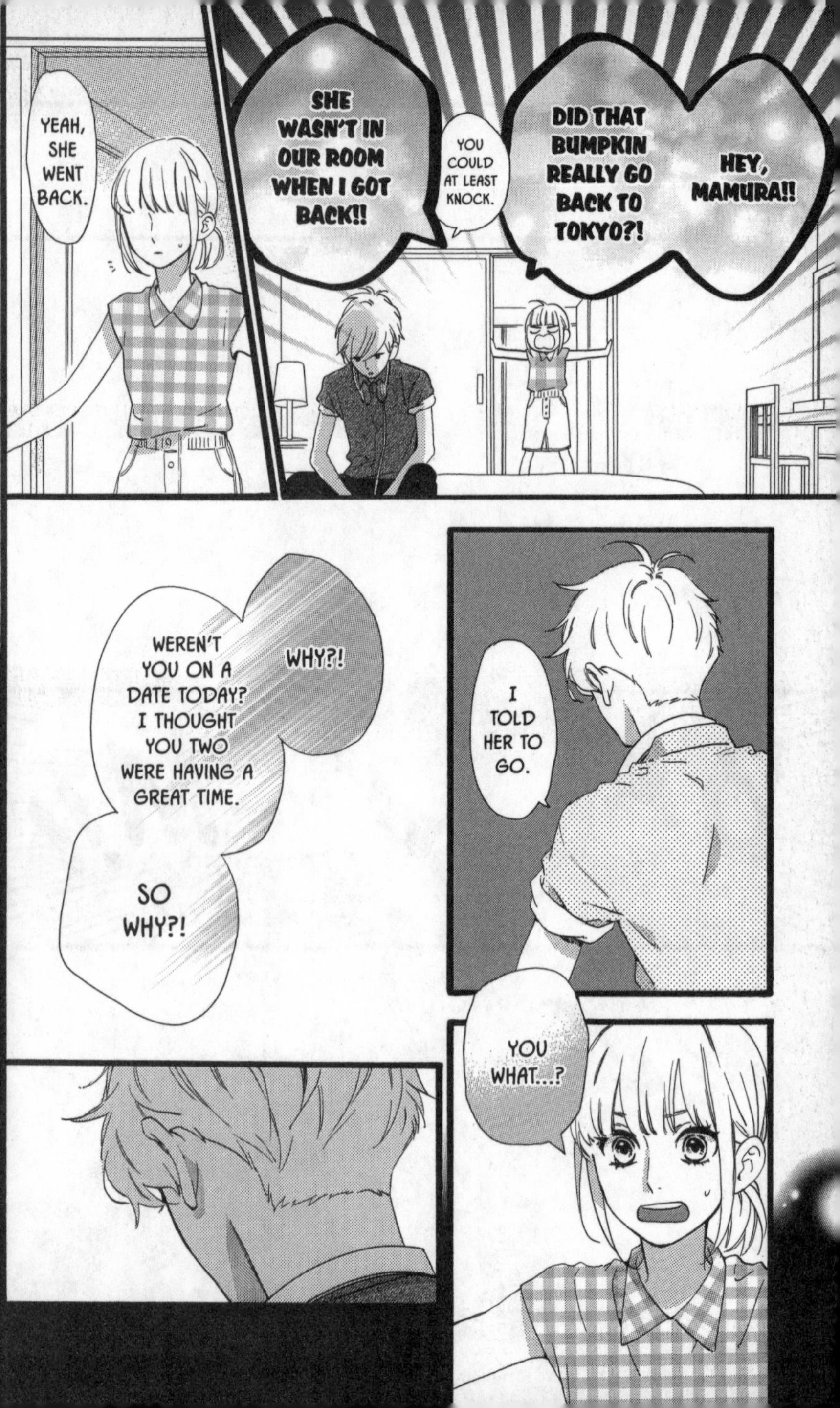
HEY, MAMURA!!
DID THAT BUMPKIN REALLY GO BACK TO TOKYO?!
YOU COULD AT LEAST KNOCK.
SHE WASN'T IN OUR ROOM WHEN I GOT BACK!!
YEAH, SHE WENT BACK.
I TOLD HER TO GO.
YOU WHAT...?
WHY?!
WEREN'T YOU ON A DATE TODAY? I THOUGHT YOU TWO WERE HAVING A GREAT TIME.
SO WHY?!

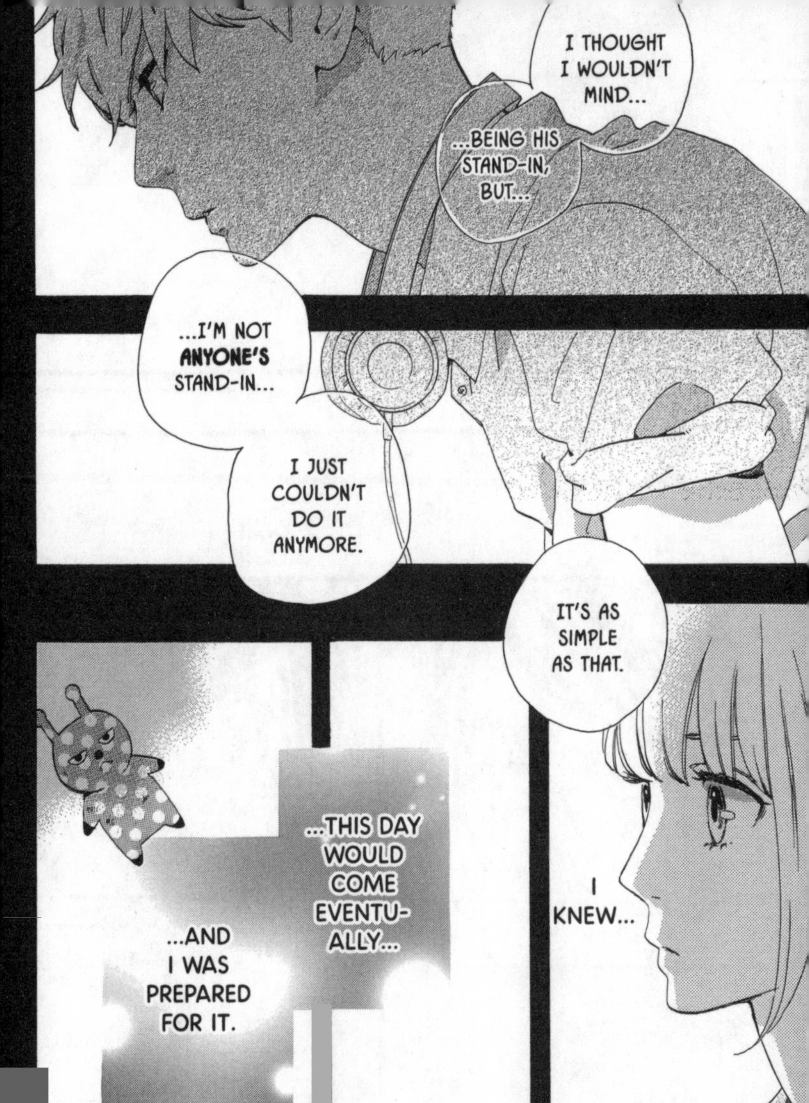
I THOUGHT I WOULDN'T MIND...
...BEING HIS STAND-IN, BUT...
...I'M NOT **ANYONE'S** STAND-IN...
I JUST COULDN'T DO IT ANYMORE.
IT'S AS SIMPLE AS THAT.
I KNEW...
...THIS DAY WOULD COME EVENTU-ALLY...
...AND I WAS PREPARED FOR IT.

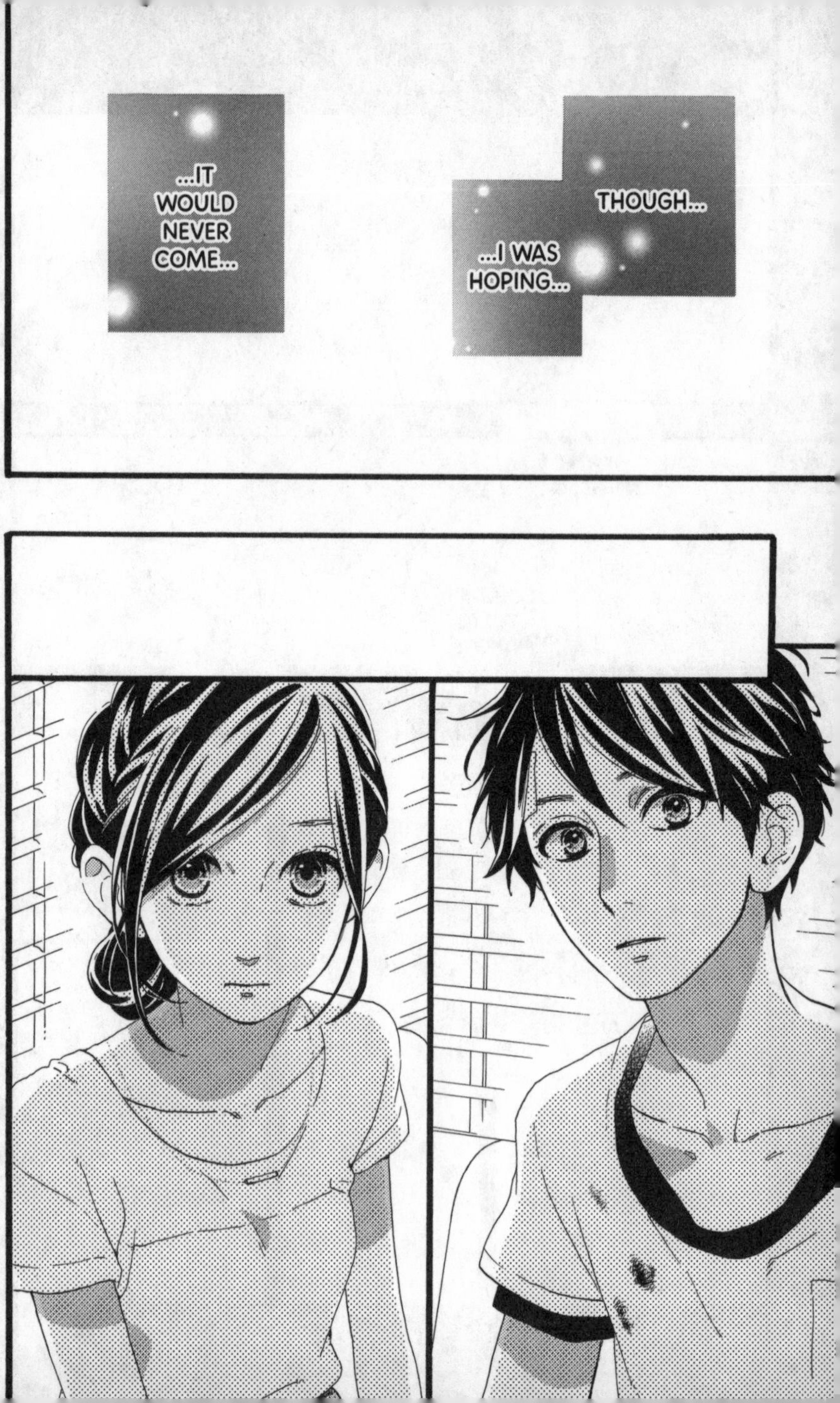
THOUGH...
...I WAS HOPING...
...IT WOULD NEVER COME...

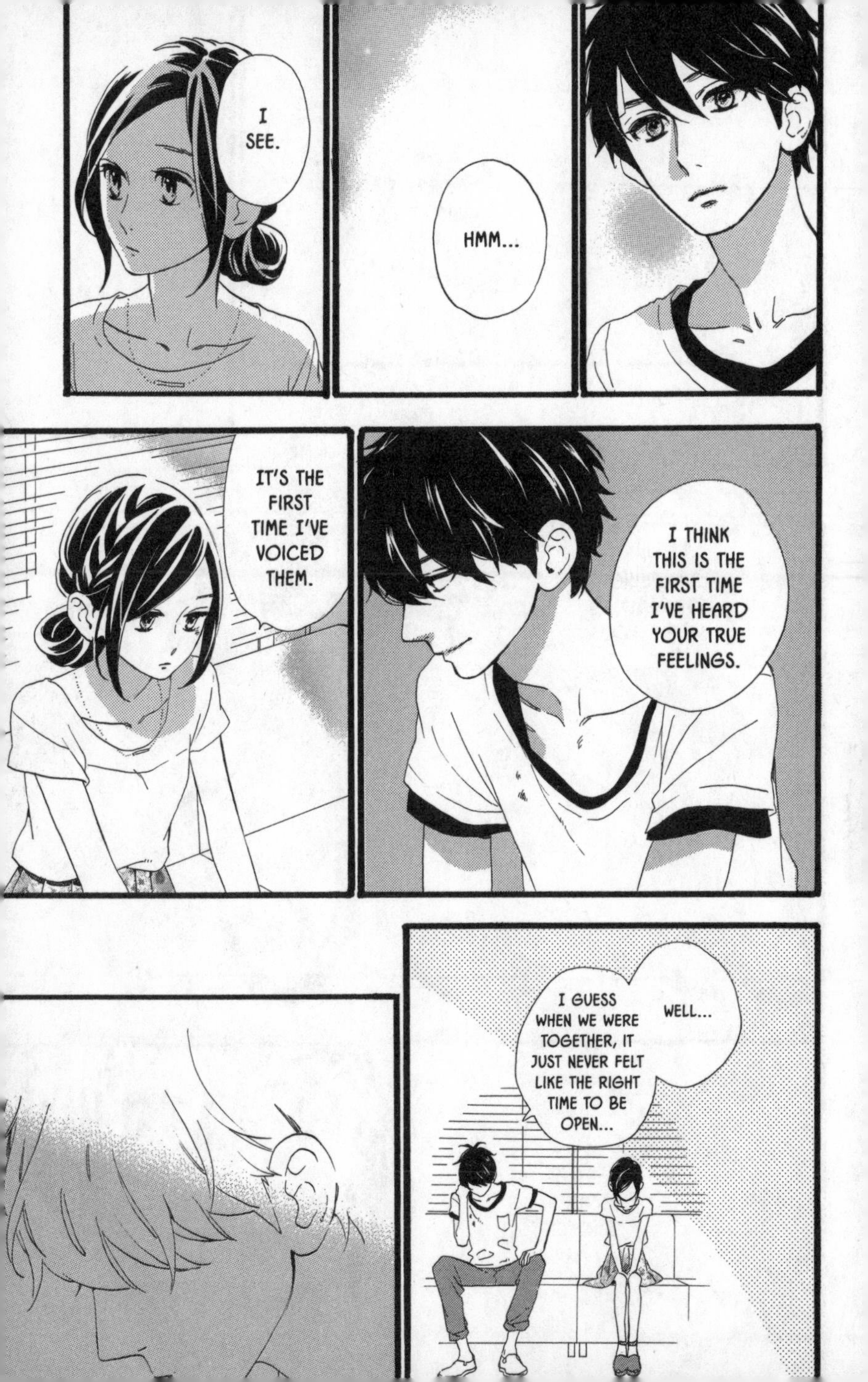
HMM...
I SEE.
I THINK THIS IS THE FIRST TIME I'VE HEARD YOUR TRUE FEELINGS.
IT'S THE FIRST TIME I'VE VOICED THEM.
WELL...
I GUESS WHEN WE WERE TOGETHER, IT JUST NEVER FELT LIKE THE RIGHT TIME TO BE OPEN...

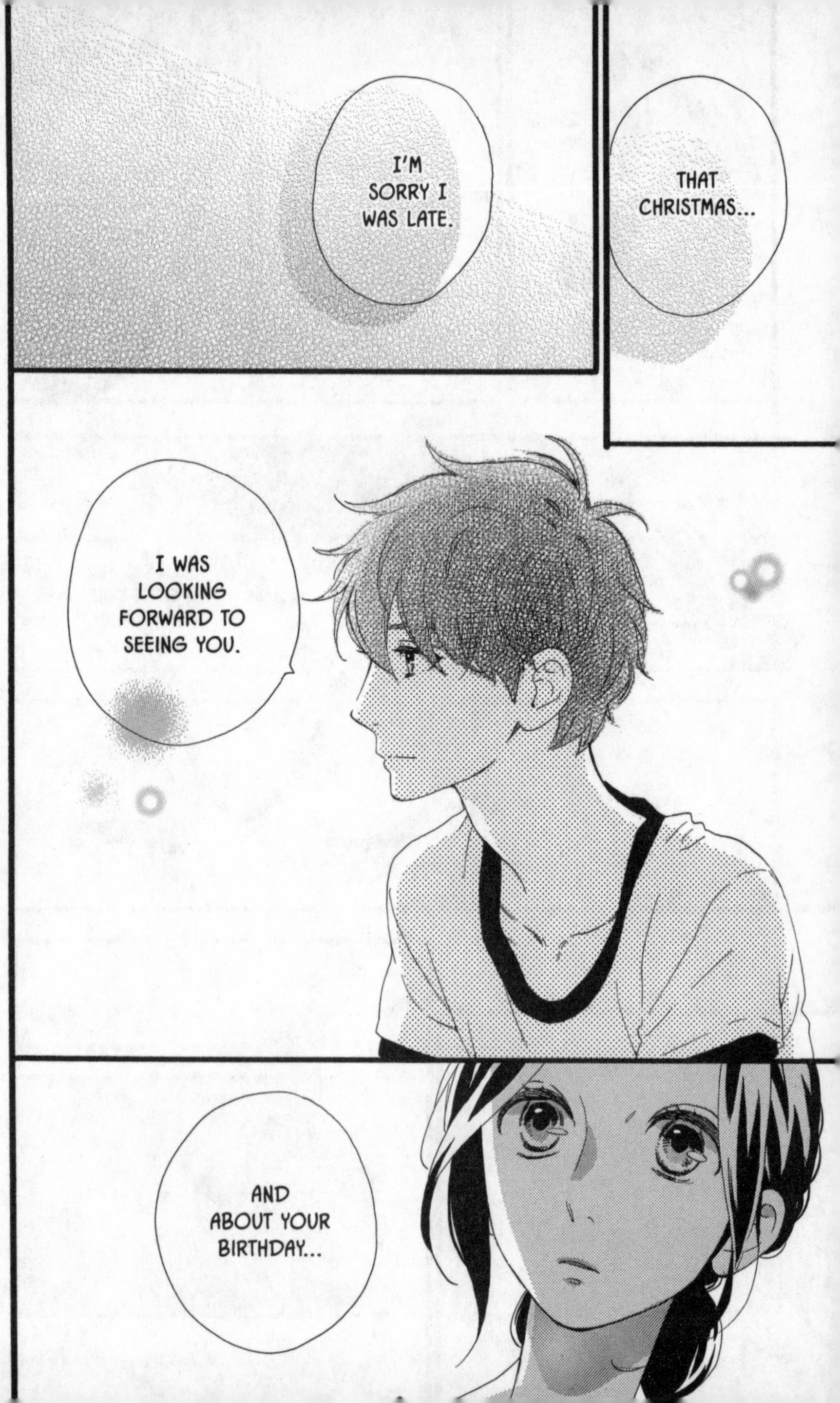
THAT CHRISTMAS...
I'M SORRY I WAS LATE.
I WAS LOOKING FORWARD TO SEEING YOU.
AND ABOUT YOUR BIRTHDAY...

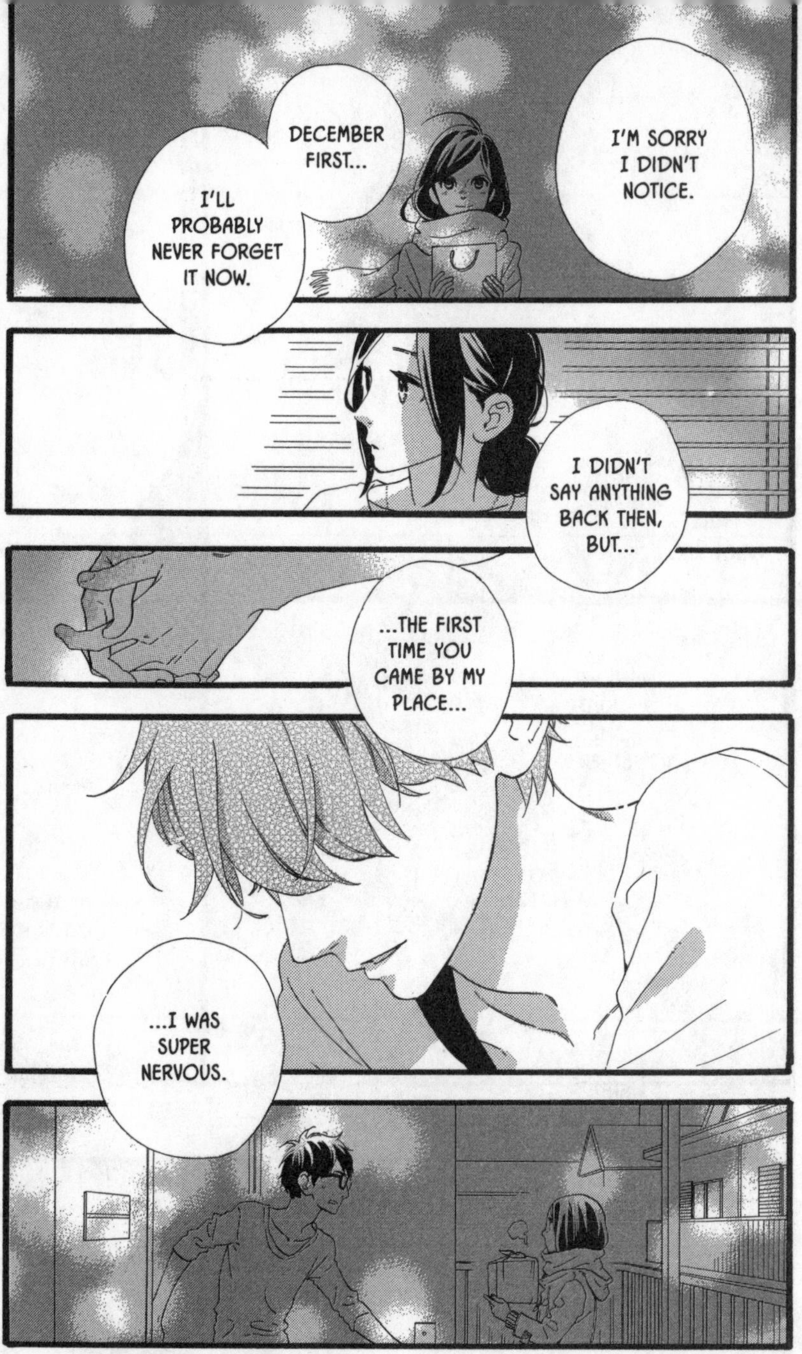
I'M SORRY I DIDN'T NOTICE.
DECEMBER FIRST...
I'LL PROBABLY NEVER FORGET IT NOW.
I DIDN'T SAY ANYTHING BACK THEN, BUT...
...THE FIRST TIME YOU CAME BY MY PLACE...
...I WAS SUPER NERVOUS.

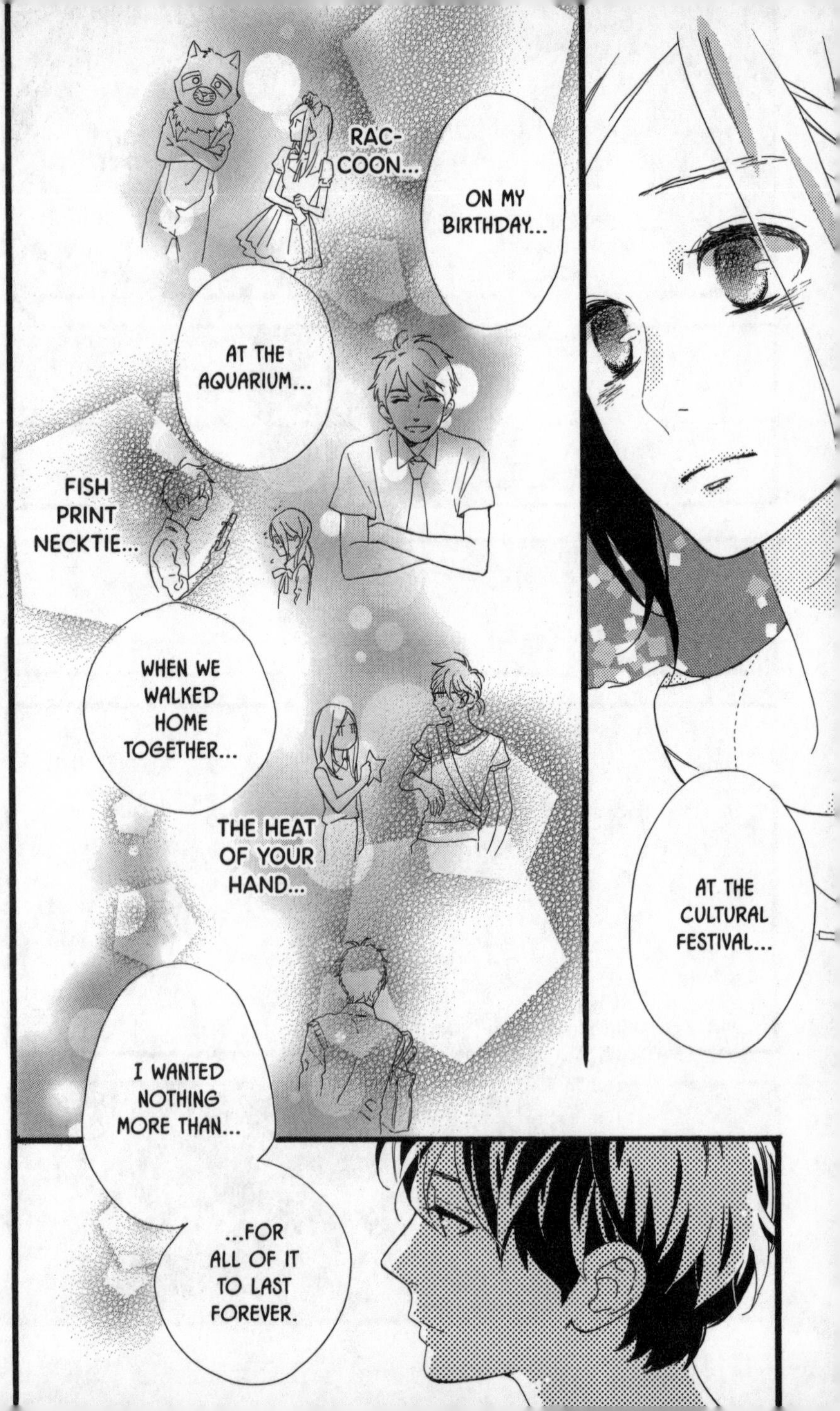
AT THE CULTURAL FESTIVAL...
ON MY BIRTHDAY...
RAC-COON...
AT THE AQUARIUM...
FISH PRINT NECKTIE...
WHEN WE WALKED HOME TOGETHER...
THE HEAT OF YOUR HAND...
I WANTED NOTHING MORE THAN...
...FOR ALL OF IT TO LAST FOREVER.

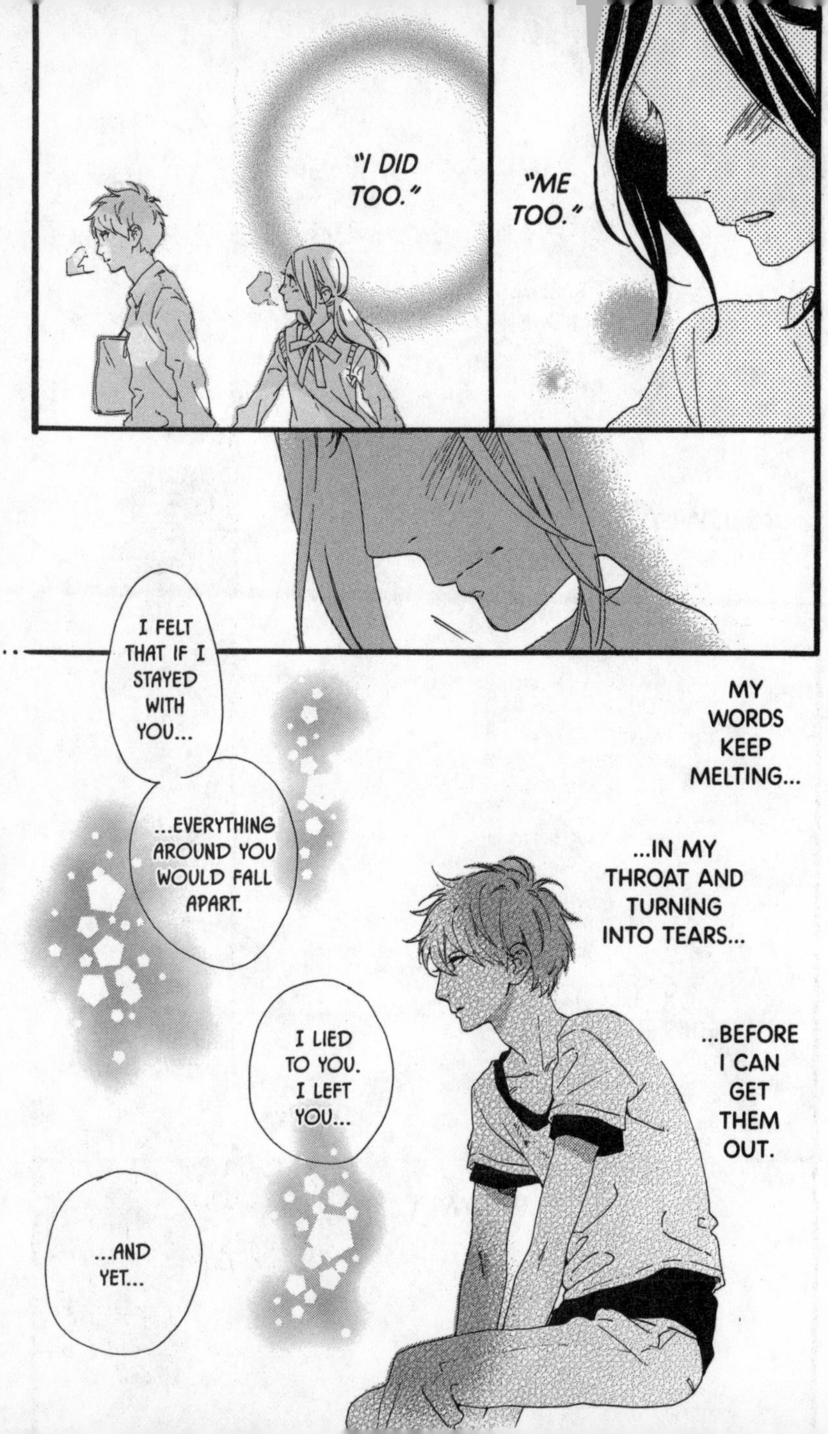
"ME TOO."
"I DID TOO."
MY WORDS KEEP MELTING...
...IN MY THROAT AND TURNING INTO TEARS...
...BEFORE I CAN GET THEM OUT.
I FELT THAT IF I STAYED WITH YOU...
...EVERYTHING AROUND YOU WOULD FALL APART.
I LIED TO YOU. I LEFT YOU...
...AND YET...

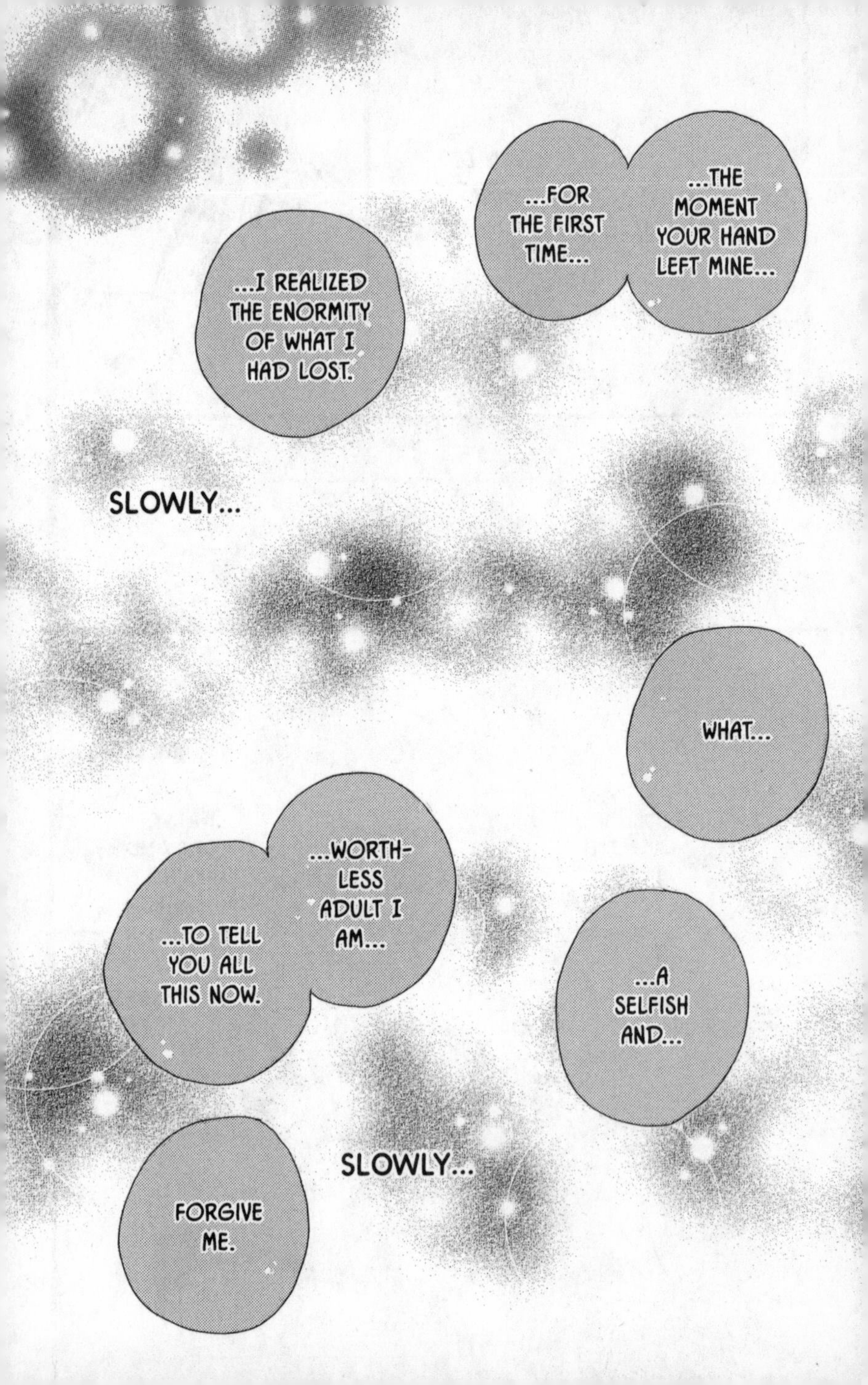
...THE MOMENT YOUR HAND LEFT MINE...
...FOR THE FIRST TIME...
...I REALIZED THE ENORMITY OF WHAT I HAD LOST.
SLOWLY...
WHAT...
...A SELFISH AND...
...WORTH-LESS ADULT I AM...
...TO TELL YOU ALL THIS NOW.
SLOWLY...
FORGIVE ME.

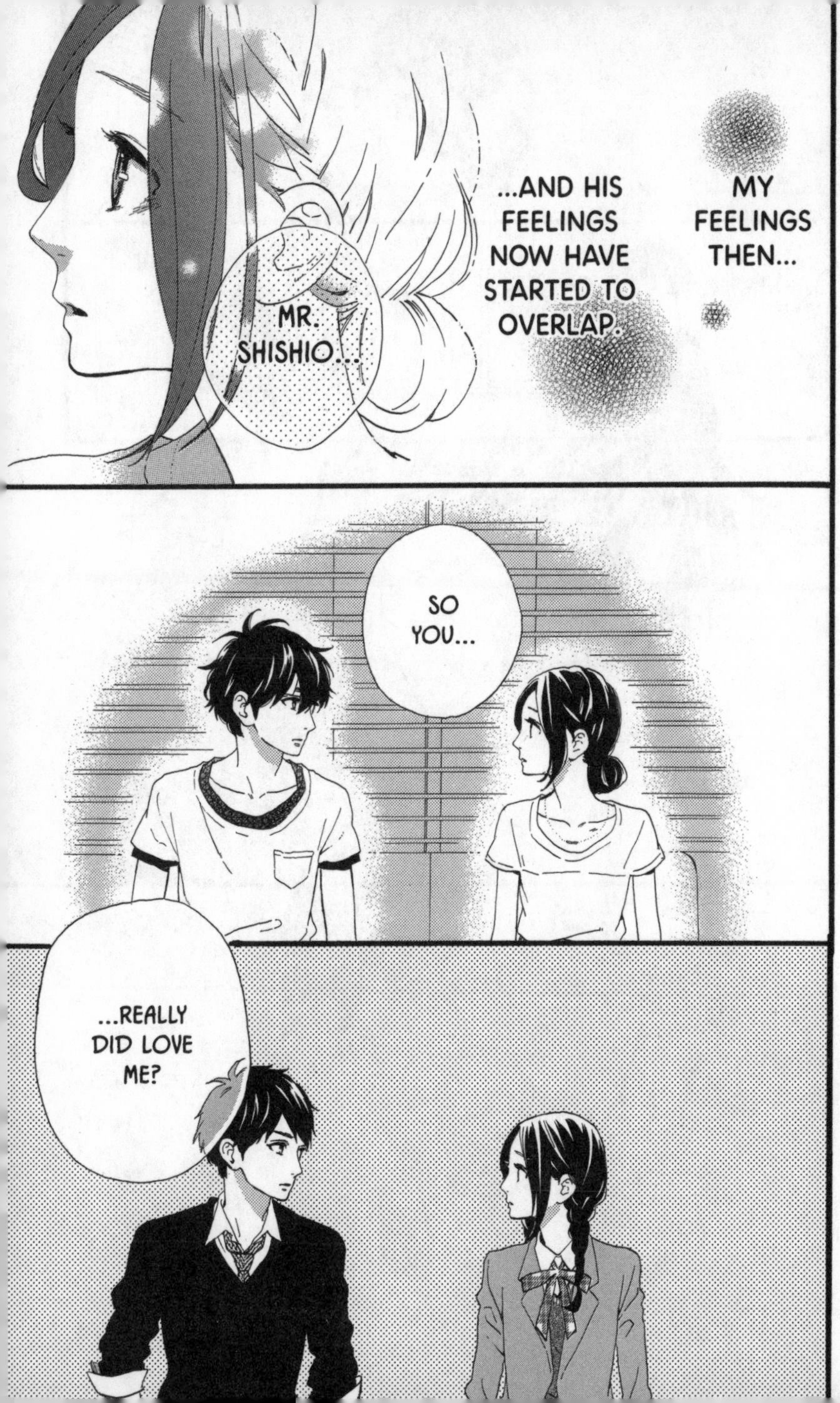
MY FEELINGS THEN...
...AND HIS FEELINGS NOW HAVE STARTED TO OVERLAP.
MR. SHISHIO...
SO YOU...
...REALLY DID LOVE ME?

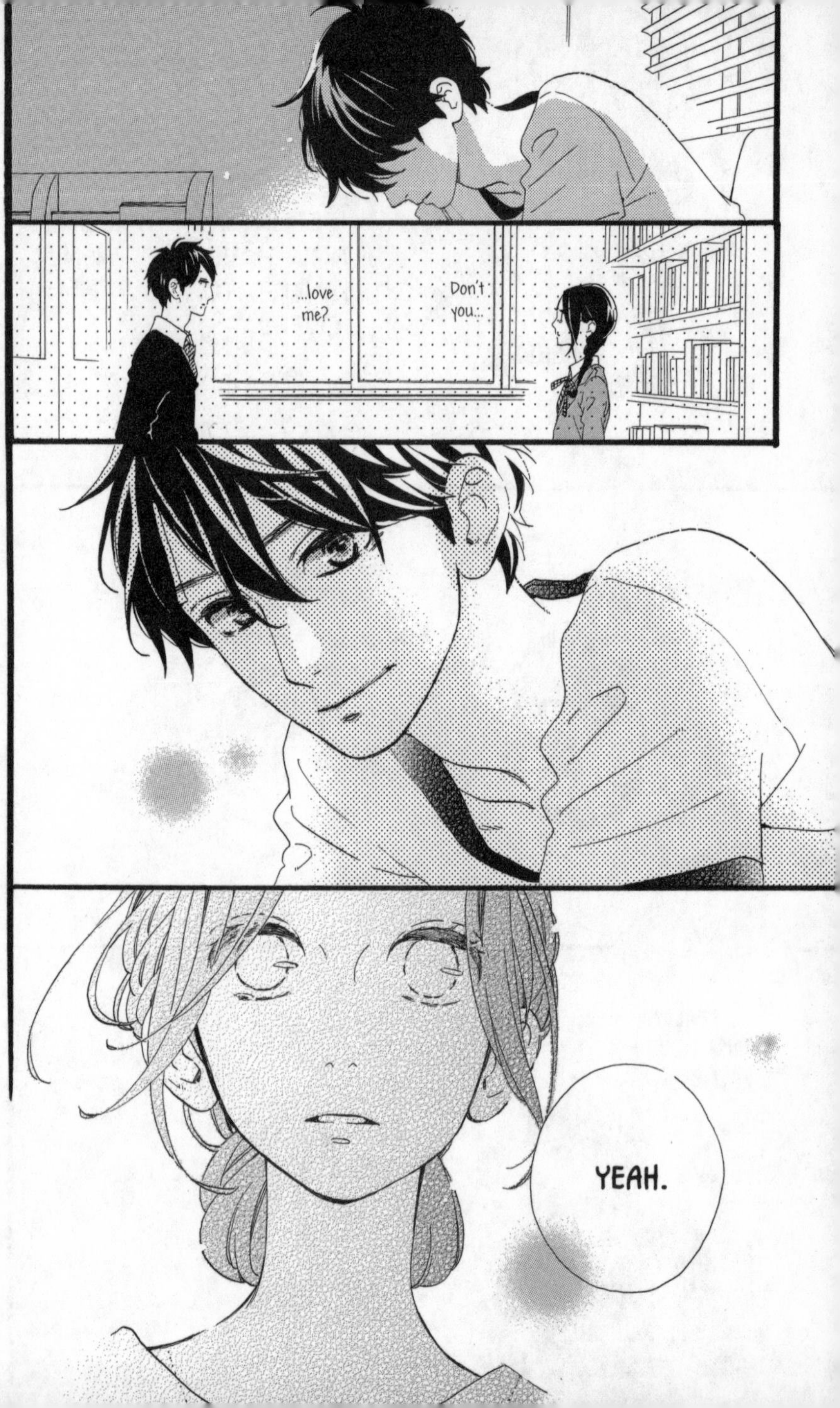
Don't you...
...love me?
YEAH.

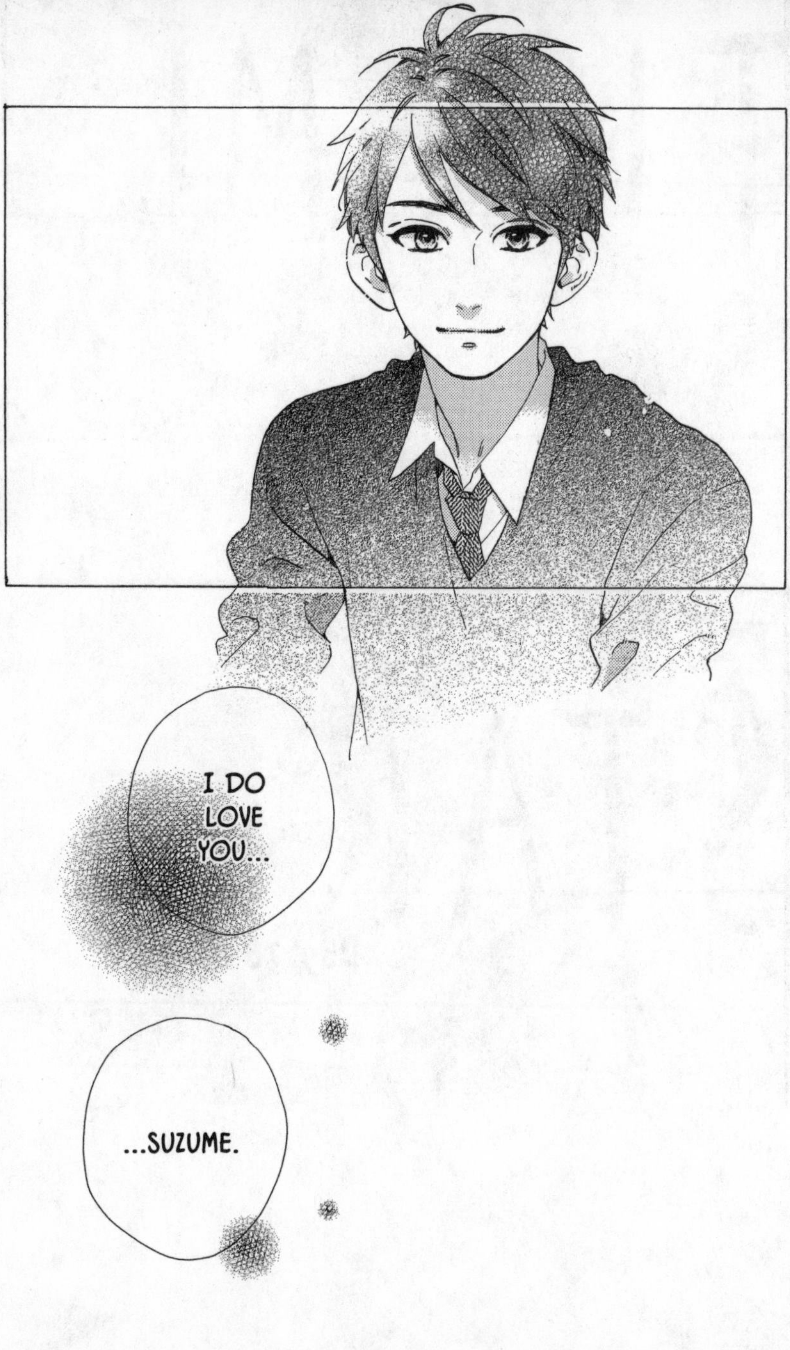
I DO LOVE YOU...
...SUZUME.

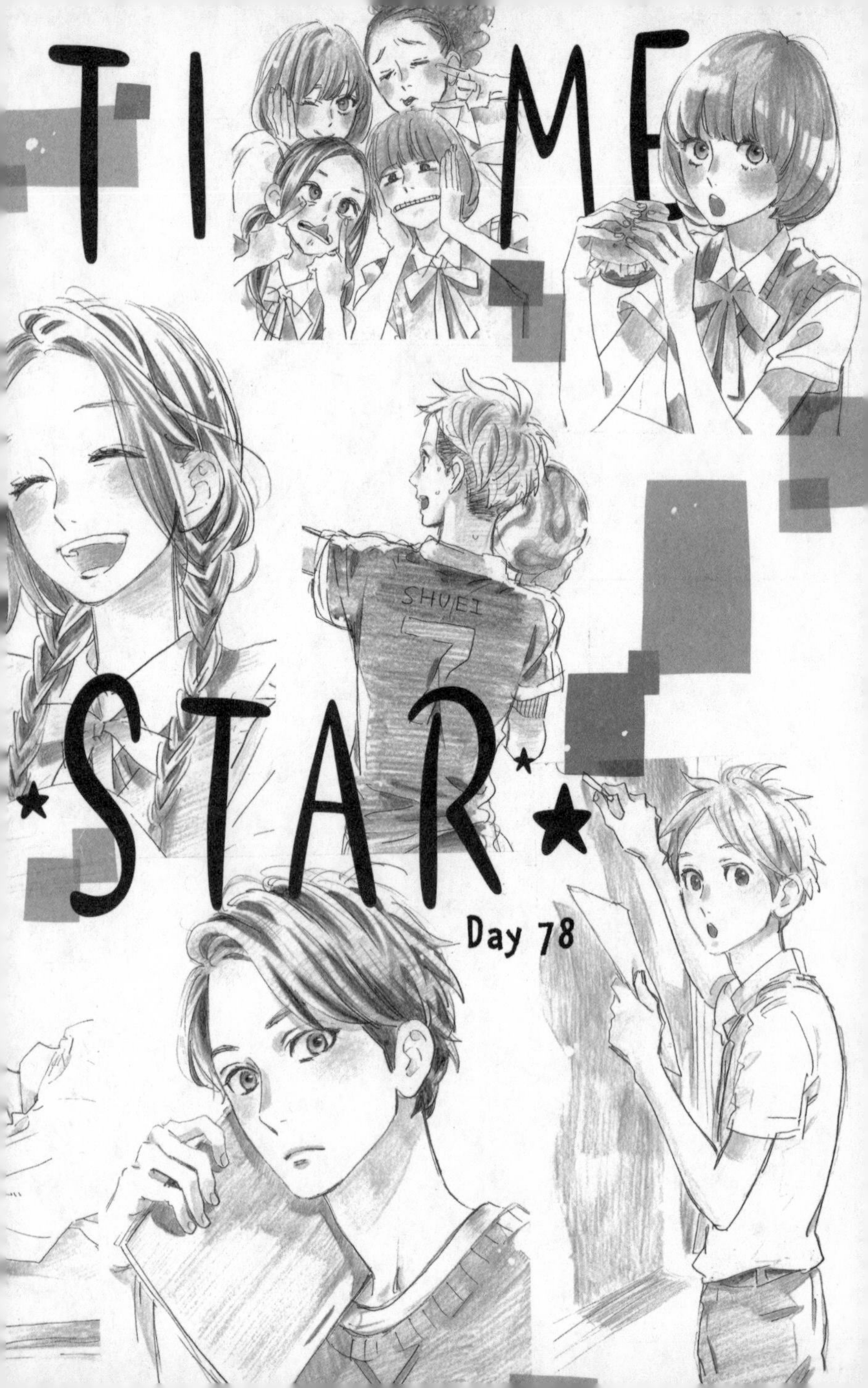
TIME STAR
Day 78
SHUEI
7

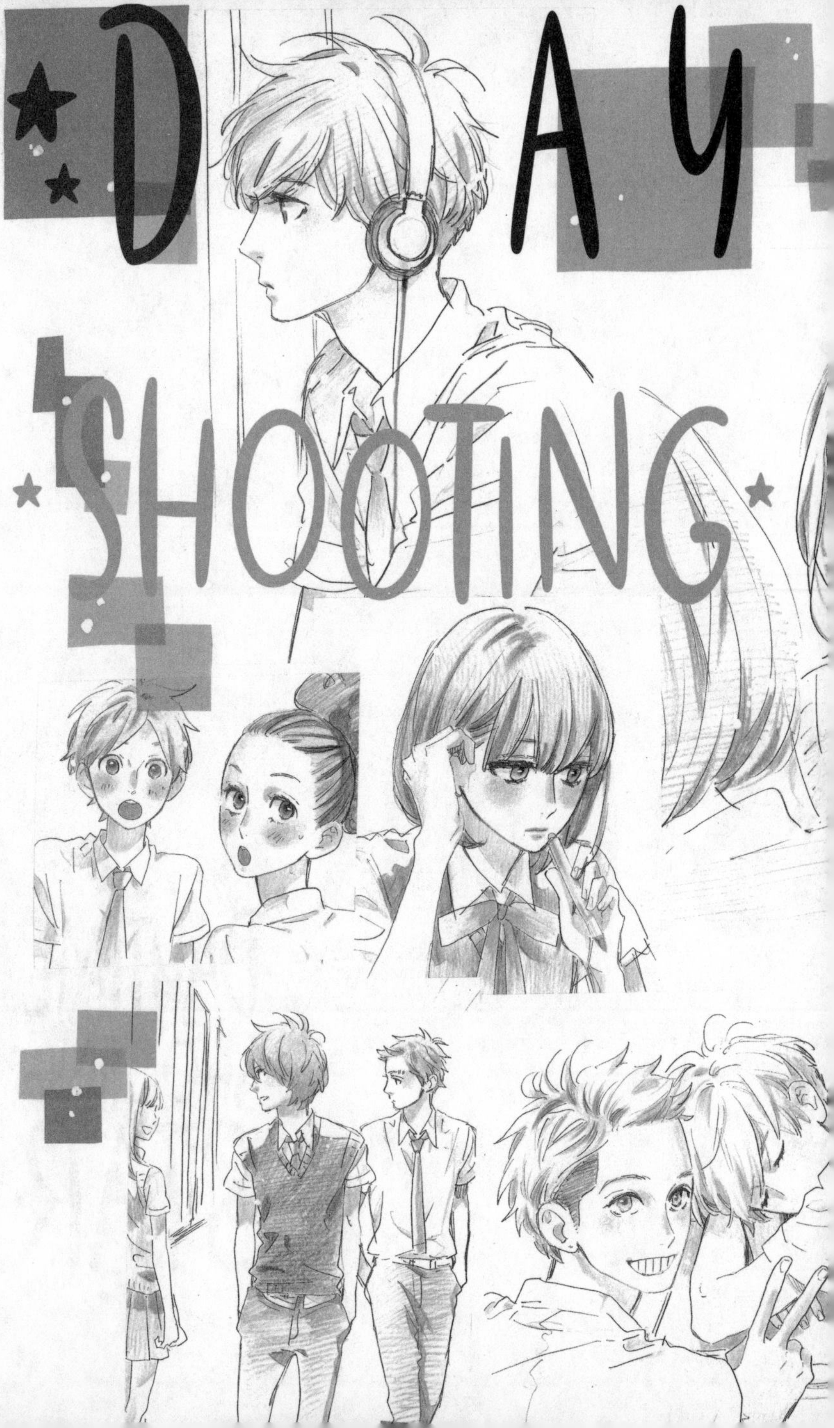
DAY
SHOOTING

DAYTIME SHOOTING STAR

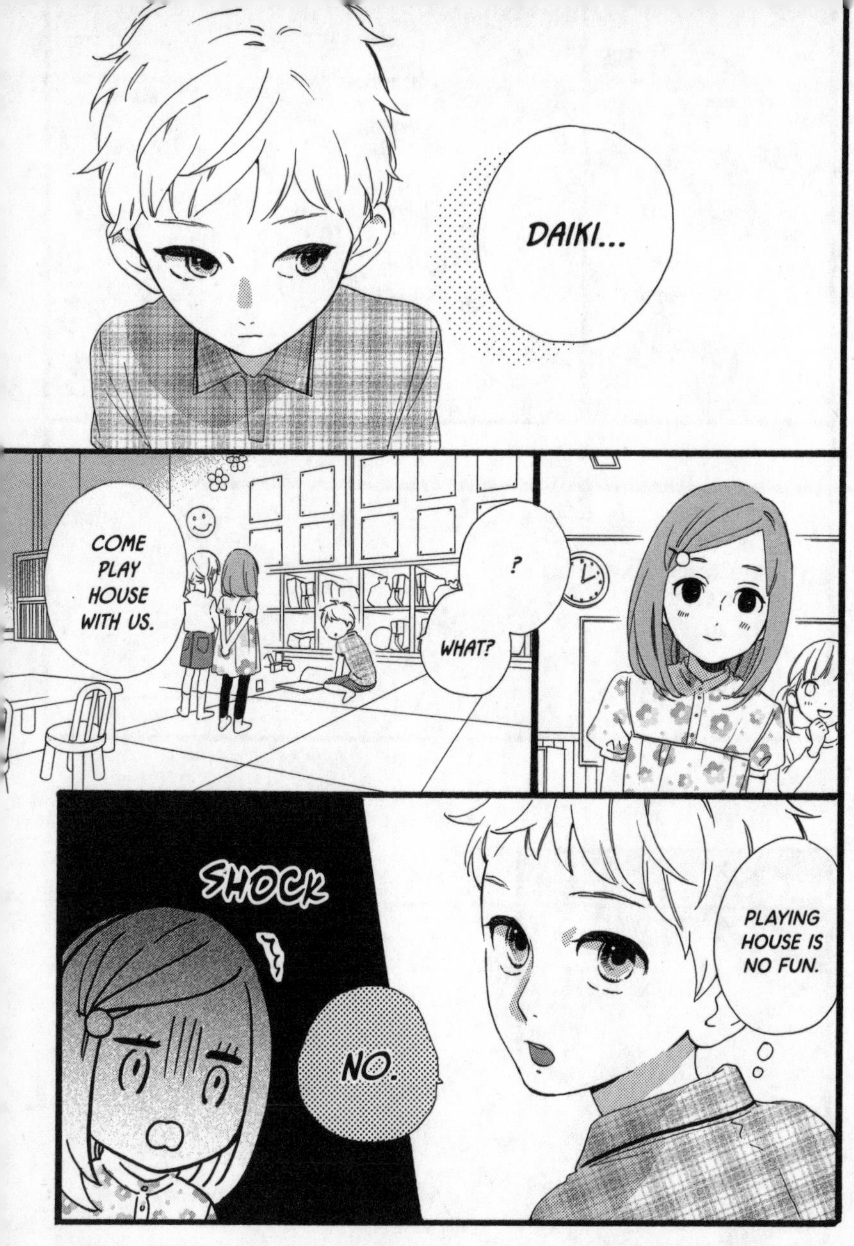
DAIKI...
?
WHAT?
COME PLAY HOUSE WITH US.
PLAYING HOUSE IS NO FUN.
SHOCK
NO.

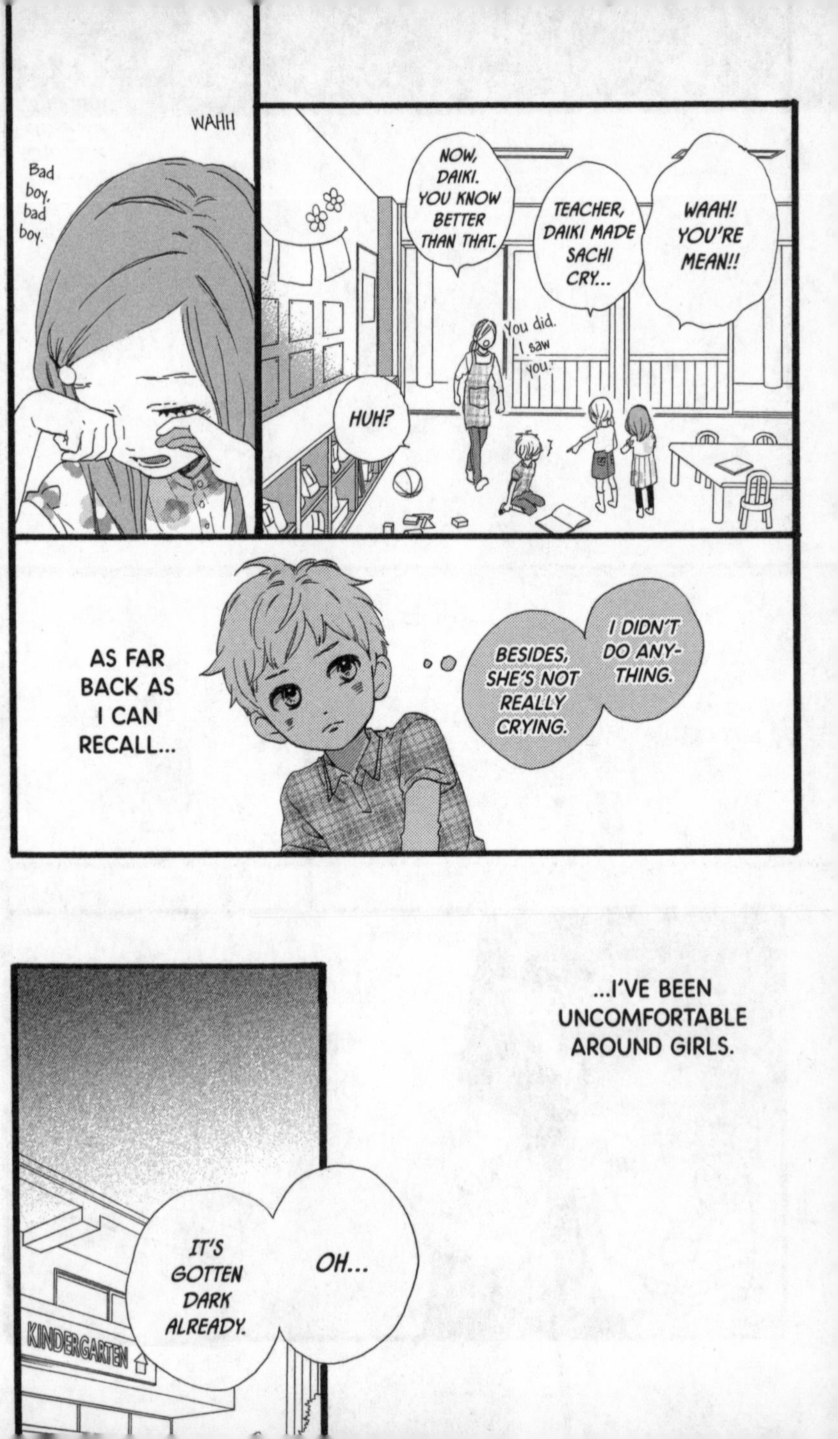
WAAH! YOU'RE MEAN!!
TEACHER, DAIKI MADE SACHI CRY...
NOW, DAIKI. YOU KNOW BETTER THAN THAT.
You did. I saw you.
HUH?
WAHH
Bad boy, bad boy.
I DIDN'T DO ANY-THING.
BESIDES, SHE'S NOT REALLY CRYING.
AS FAR BACK AS I CAN RECALL...
...I'VE BEEN UNCOMFORTABLE AROUND GIRLS.
OH...
IT'S GOTTEN DARK ALREADY.
KINDERGARTEN

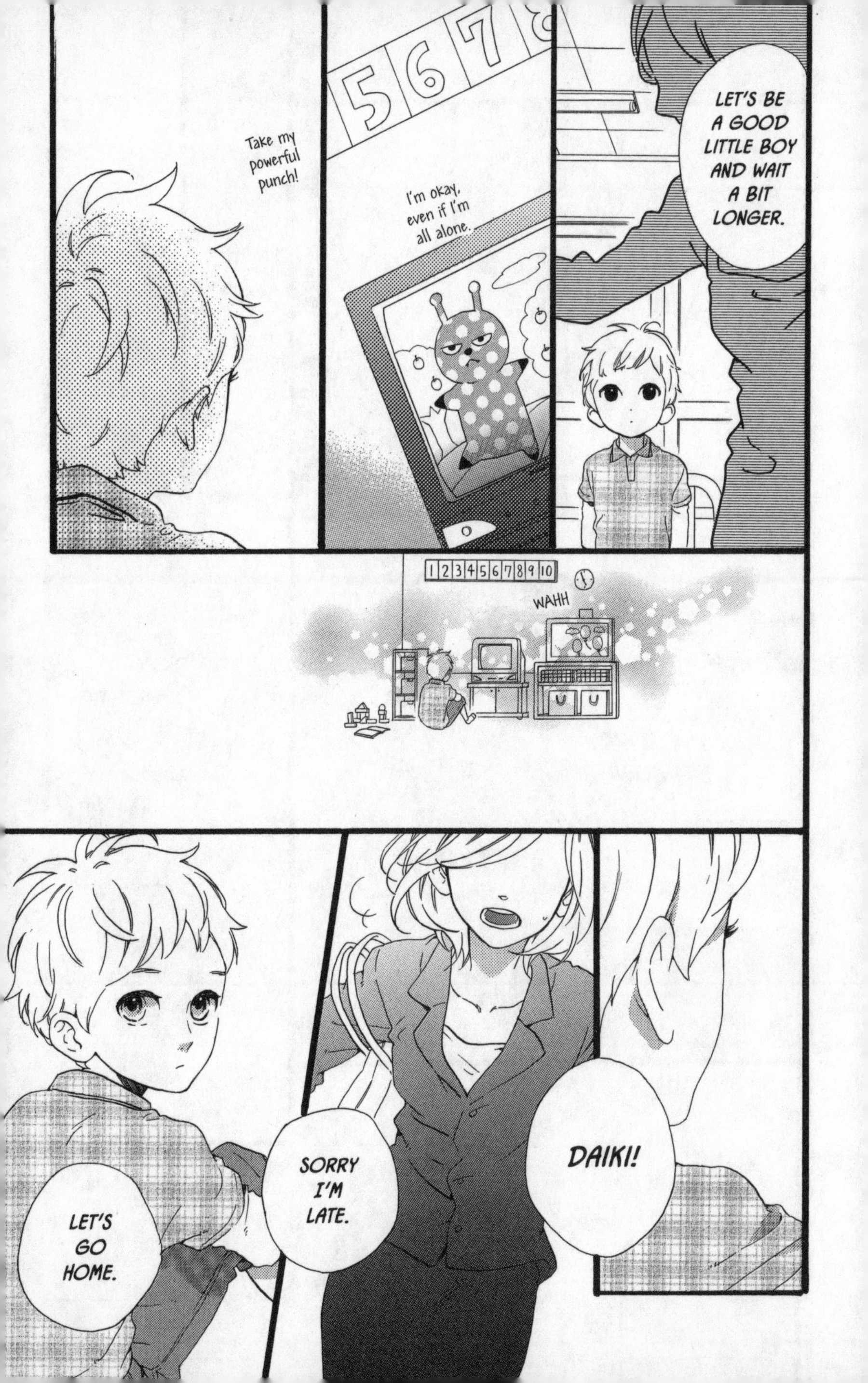
LET'S BE A GOOD LITTLE BOY AND WAIT A BIT LONGER.
I'm okay, even if I'm all alone.
Take my powerful punch!
WAHH
DAIKI!
SORRY I'M LATE.
LET'S GO HOME.

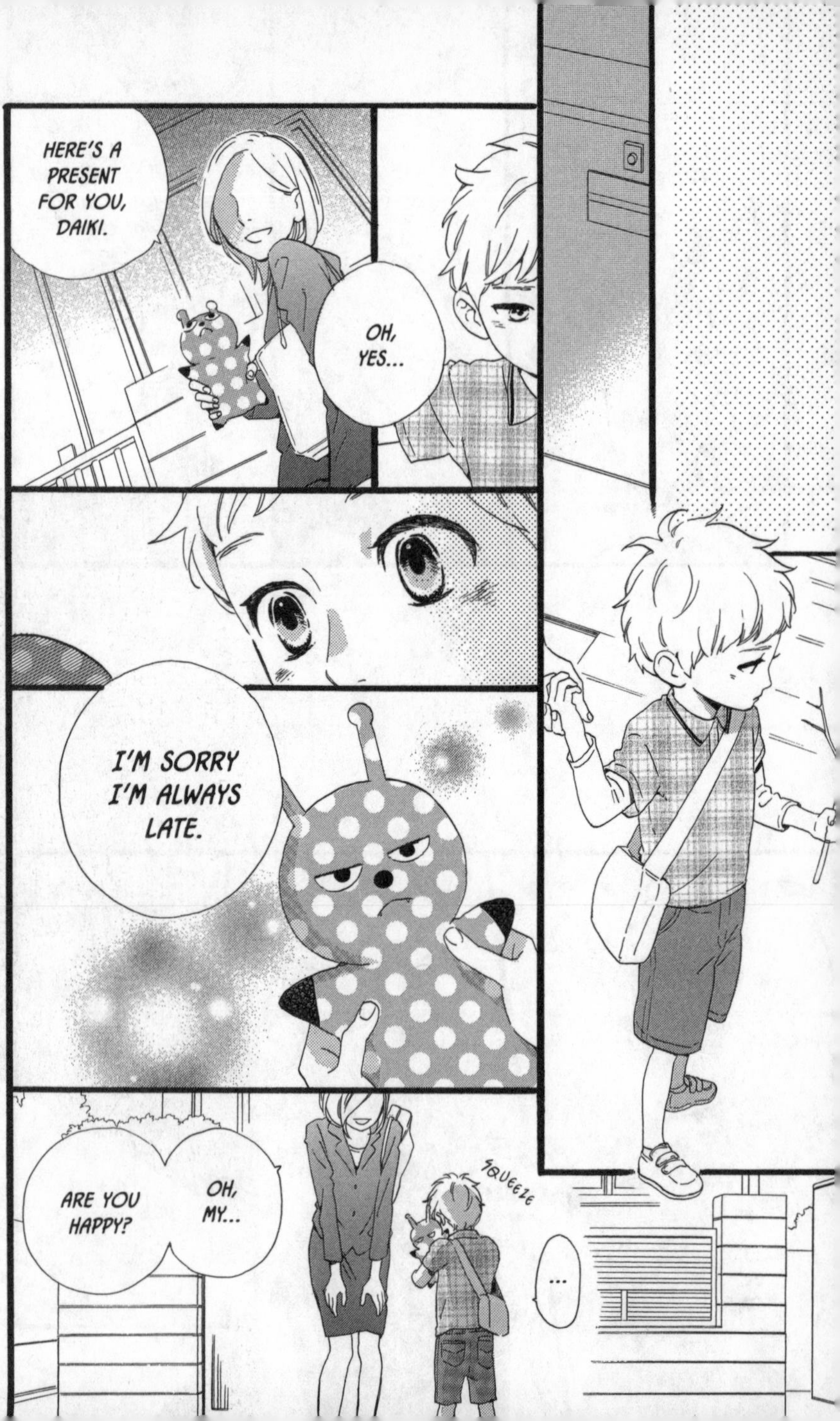
OH, YES...
HERE'S A PRESENT FOR YOU, DAIKI.
I'M SORRY I'M ALWAYS LATE.
SQUEEZE
...
OH, MY...
ARE YOU HAPPY?

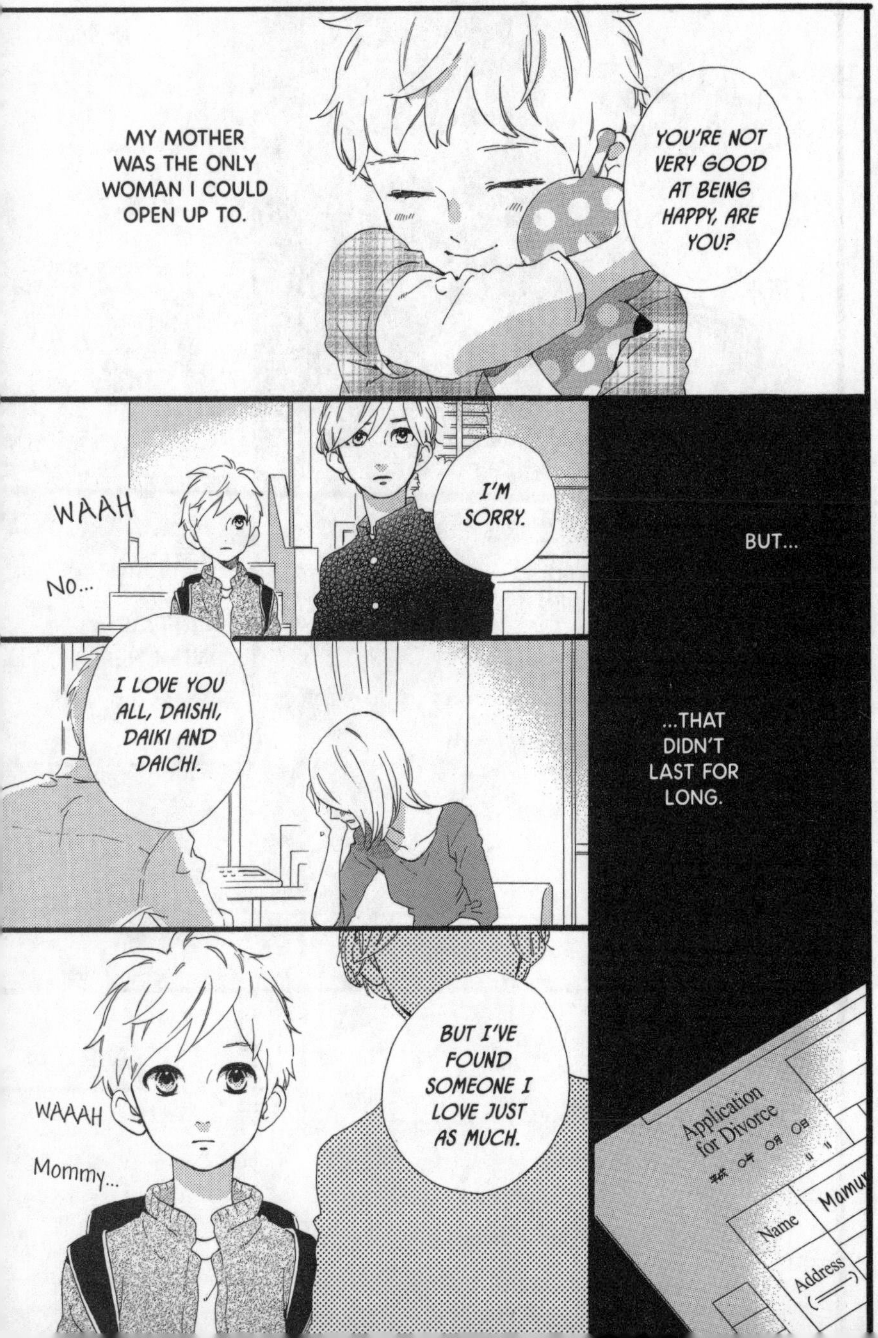
YOU'RE NOT VERY GOOD AT BEING HAPPY, ARE YOU?
MY MOTHER WAS THE ONLY WOMAN I COULD OPEN UP TO.
BUT...
...THAT DIDN'T LAST FOR LONG.
Application for Divorce
Name
Address
I'M SORRY.
WAAH
No...
I LOVE YOU ALL, DAISHI, DAIKI AND DAICHI.
BUT I'VE FOUND SOMEONE I LOVE JUST AS MUCH.
WAAAH
Mommy...

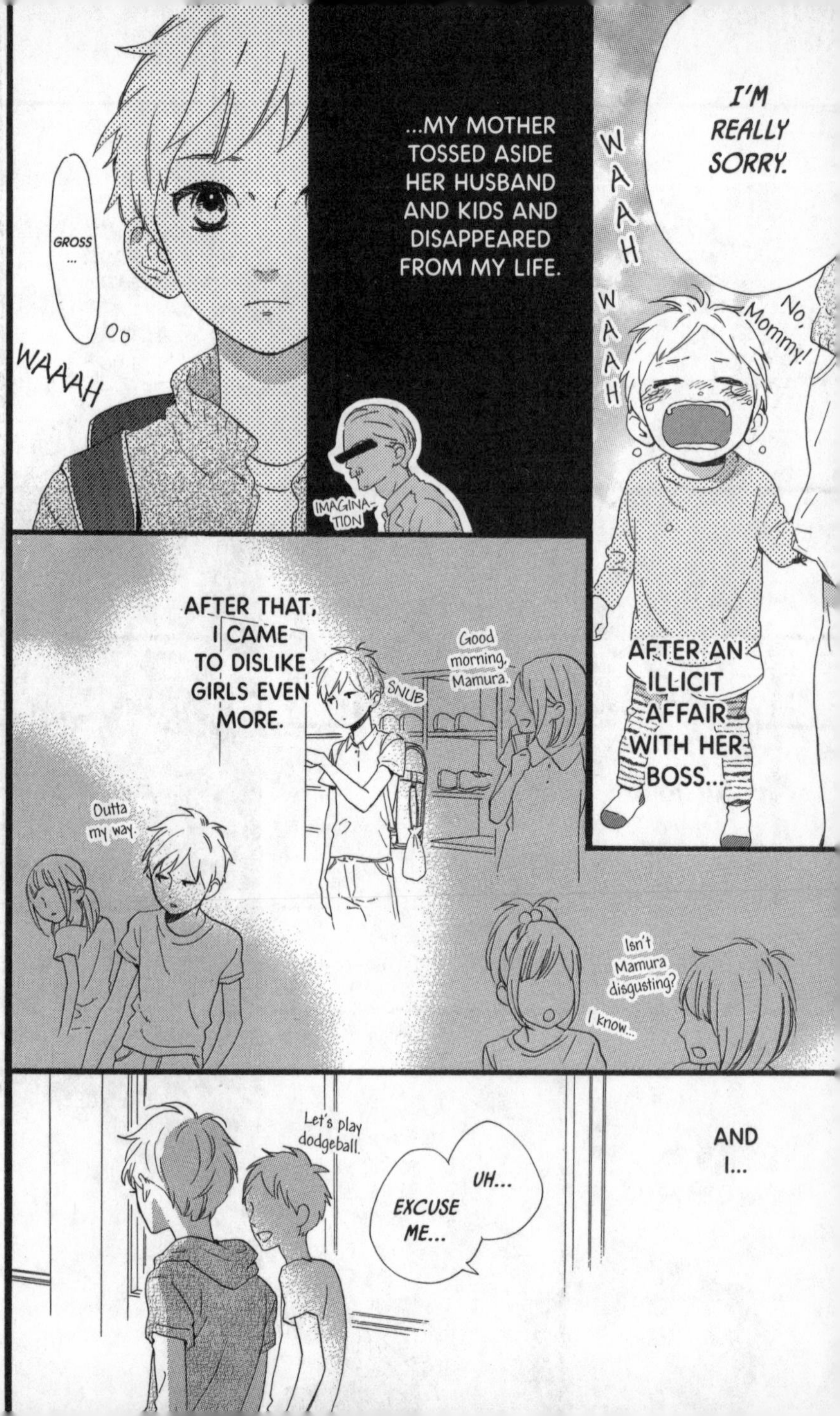
I'M REALLY SORRY.
WAAH
WAAH
No, Mommy!
AFTER AN ILLICIT AFFAIR WITH HER BOSS...
...MY MOTHER TOSSED ASIDE HER HUSBAND AND KIDS AND DISAPPEARED FROM MY LIFE.
IMAGINATION
GROSS...
WAAAH
Good morning, Mamura.
AFTER THAT, I CAME TO DISLIKE GIRLS EVEN MORE.
SNUB
Isn't Mamura disgusting?
I know...
Outta my way.
AND I...
UH... EXCUSE ME...
Let's play dodgeball.

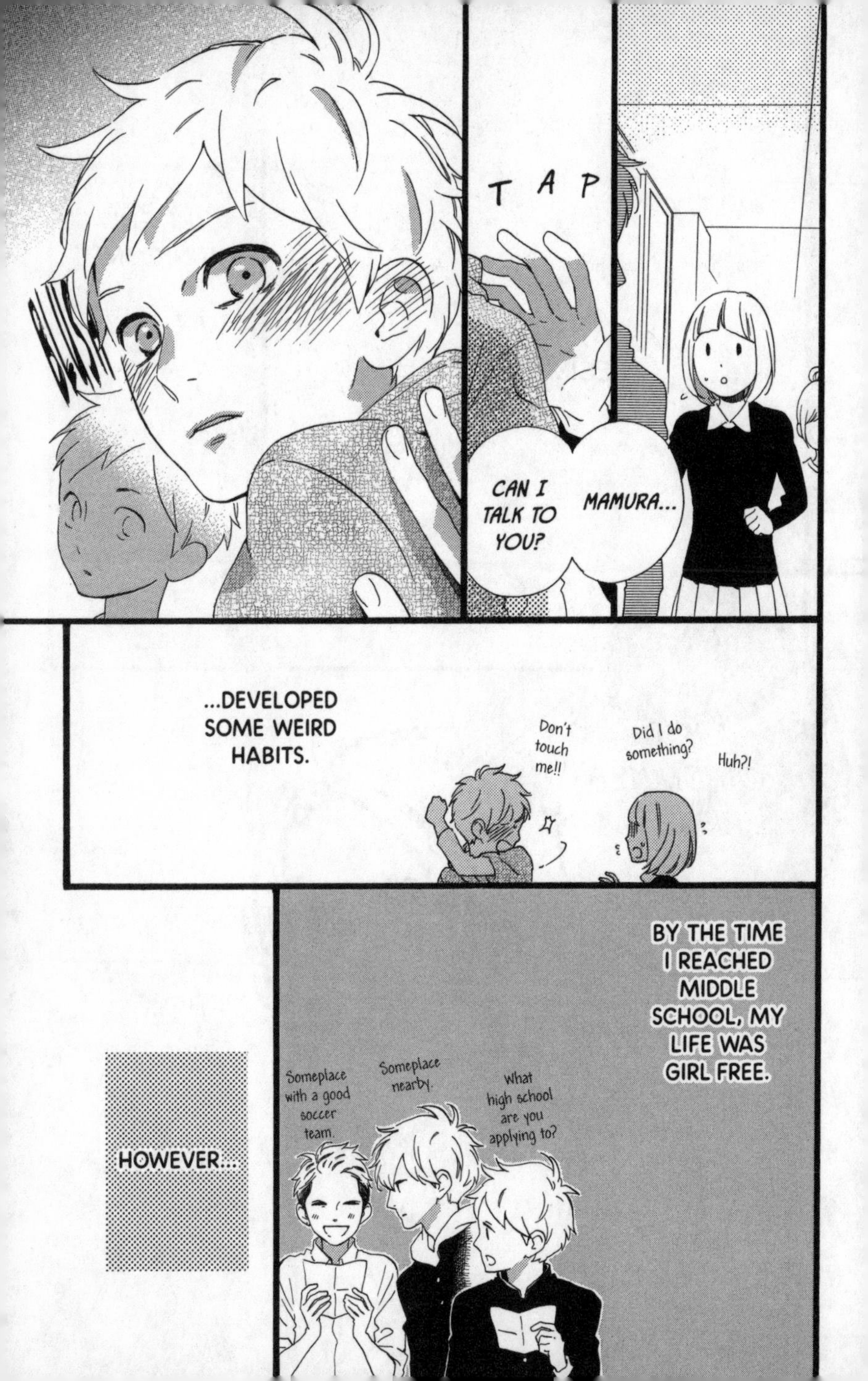
T A P
MAMURA...
CAN I TALK TO YOU?
Huh?!
Did I do something?
Don't touch me!!
...DEVELOPED SOME WEIRD HABITS.
BY THE TIME I REACHED MIDDLE SCHOOL, MY LIFE WAS GIRL FREE.
What high school are you applying to?
Someplace nearby.
Someplace with a good soccer team.
HOWEVER...

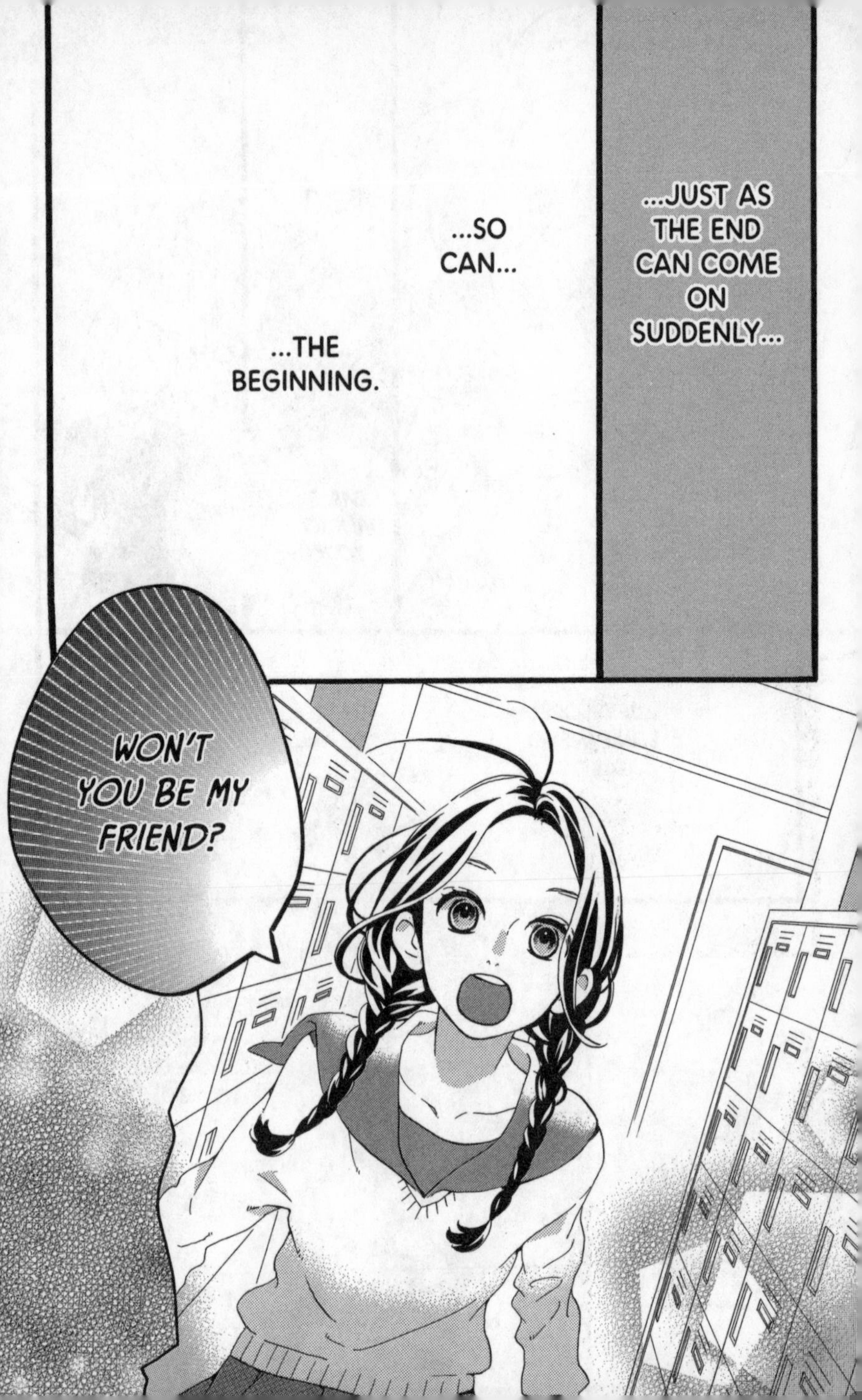
...JUST AS THE END CAN COME ON SUDDENLY...
...SO CAN...
...THE BEGINNING.
WON'T YOU BE MY FRIEND?

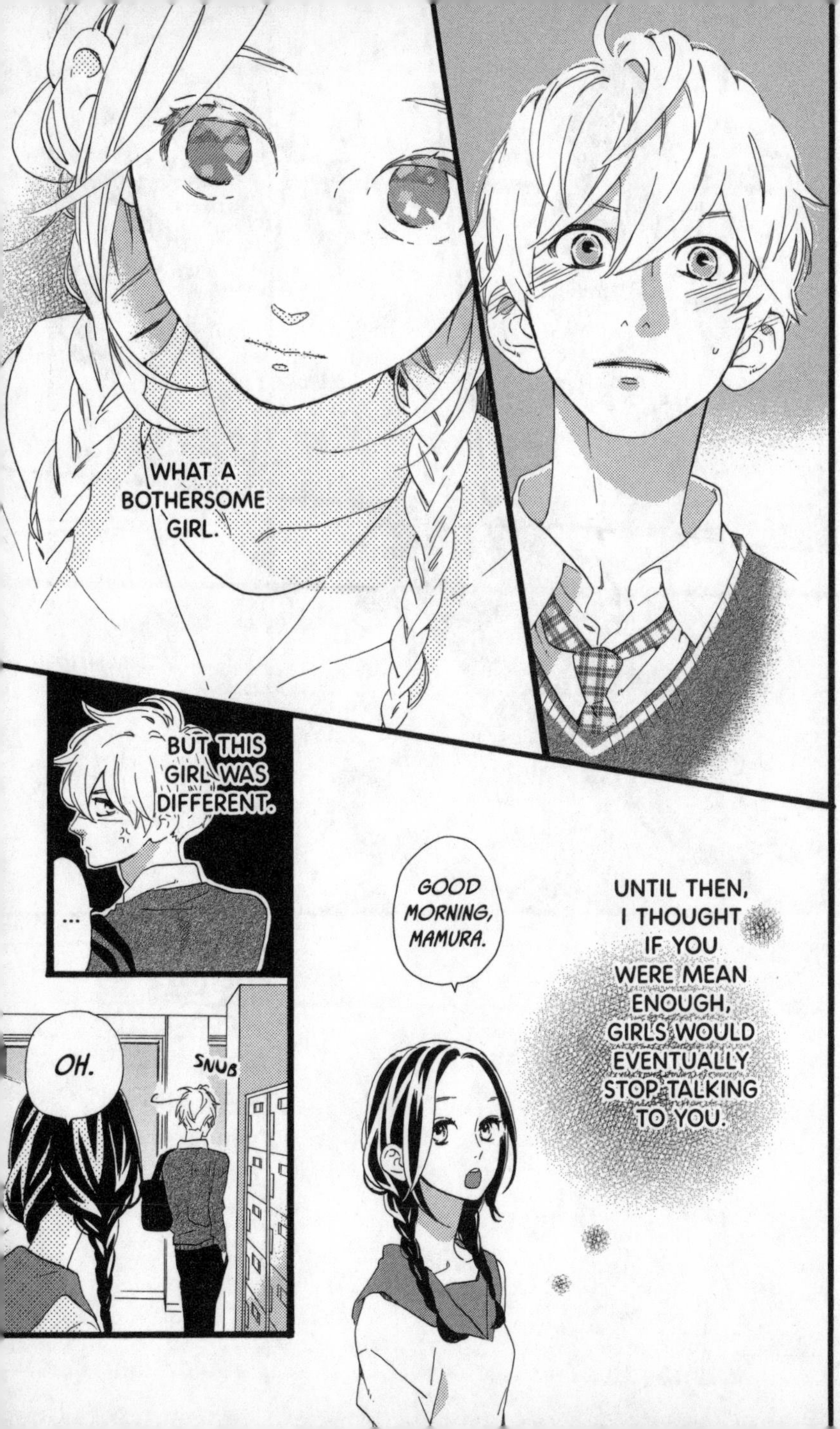
WHAT A BOTHERSOME GIRL.
UNTIL THEN, I THOUGHT IF YOU WERE MEAN ENOUGH, GIRLS WOULD EVENTUALLY STOP TALKING TO YOU.
GOOD MORNING, MAMURA.
BUT THIS GIRL WAS DIFFERENT.
...
SNUB
OH.

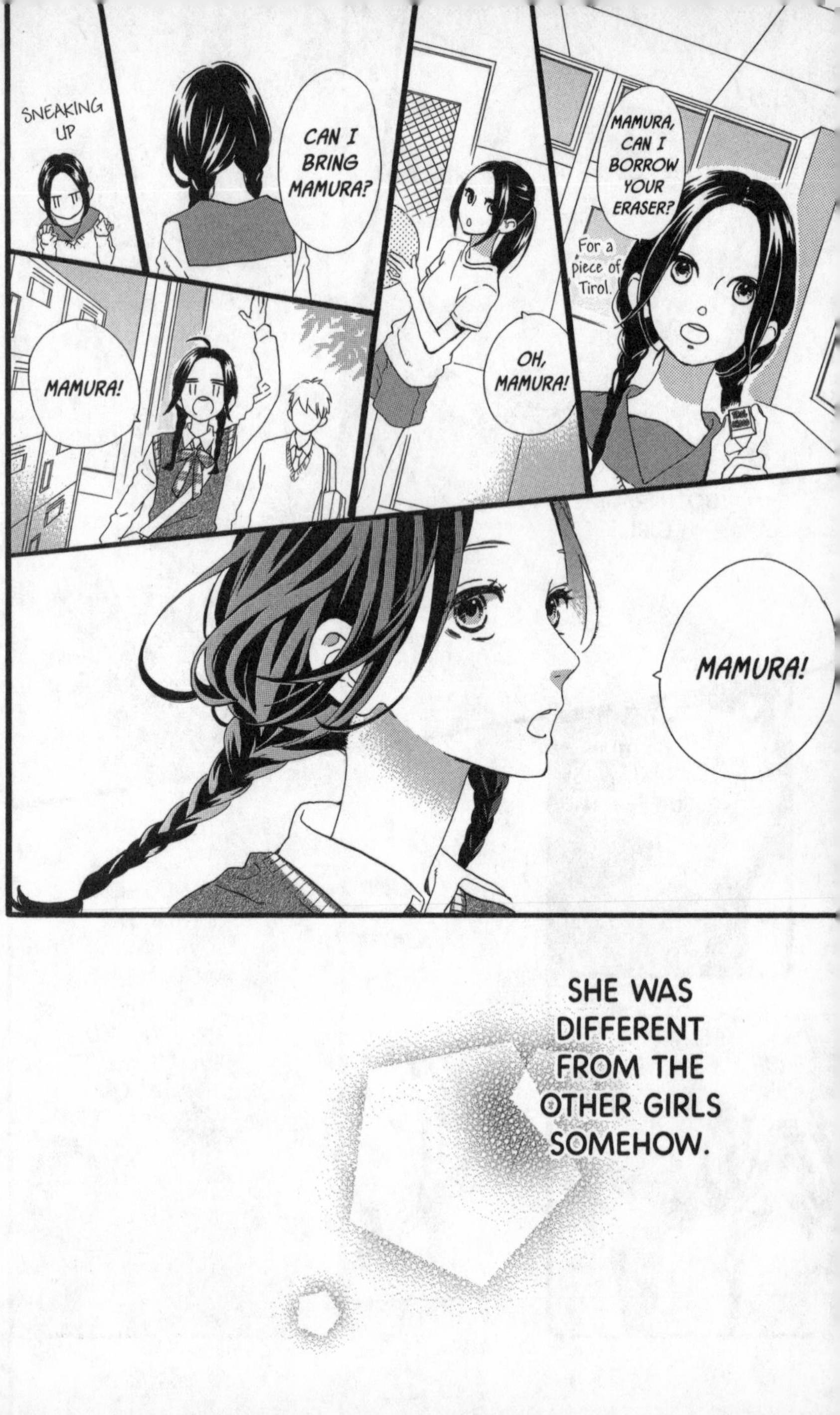
MAMURA, CAN I BORROW YOUR ERASER?
For a piece of Tirol.
OH, MAMURA!
CAN I BRING MAMURA?
SNEAKING UP
MAMURA!
MAMURA!
SHE WAS DIFFERENT FROM THE OTHER GIRLS SOMEHOW.

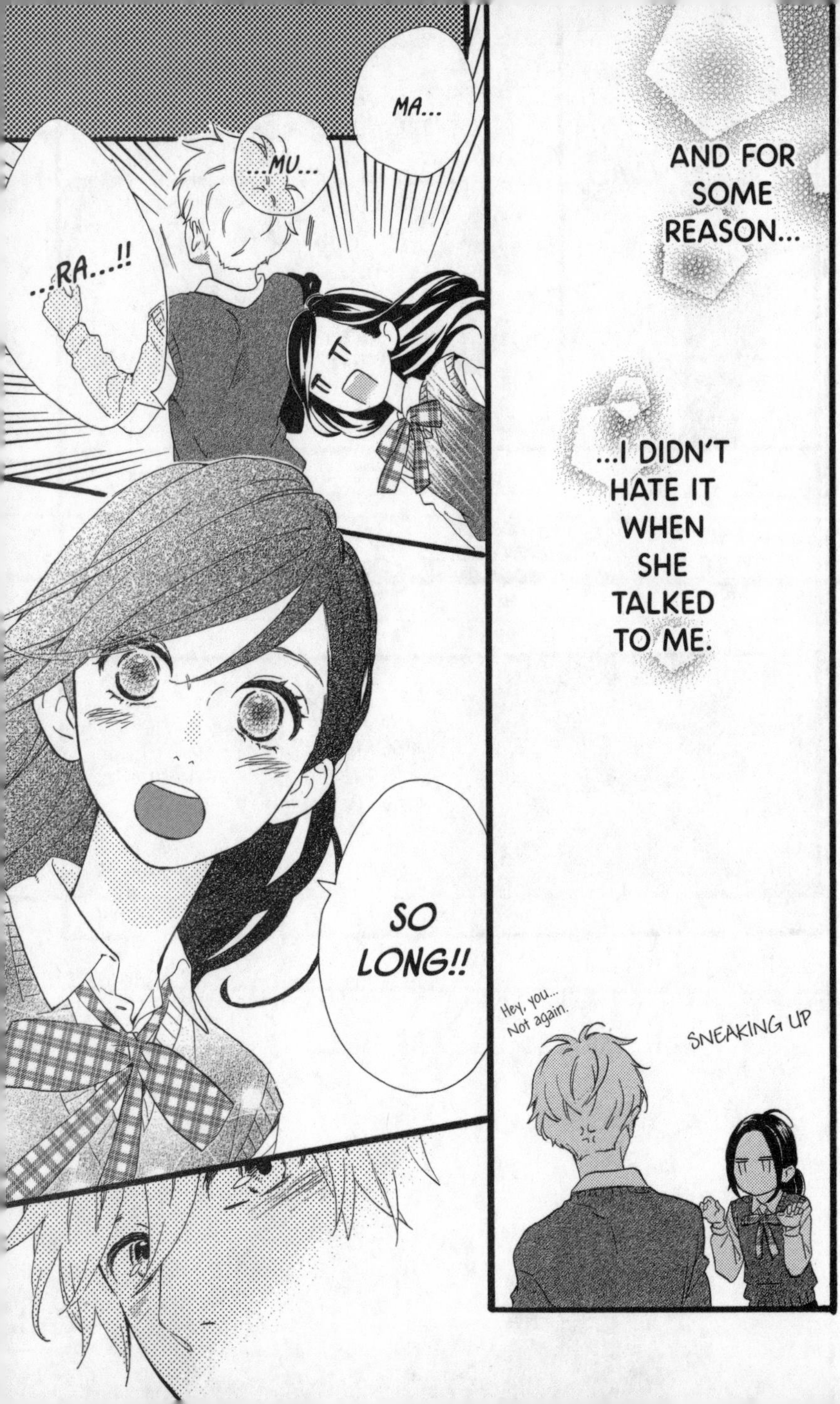
AND FOR SOME REASON...
...I DIDN'T HATE IT WHEN SHE TALKED TO ME.
SNEAKING UP
Hey, you... Not again.
MA...
...MU...
...RA...!!
SO LONG!!

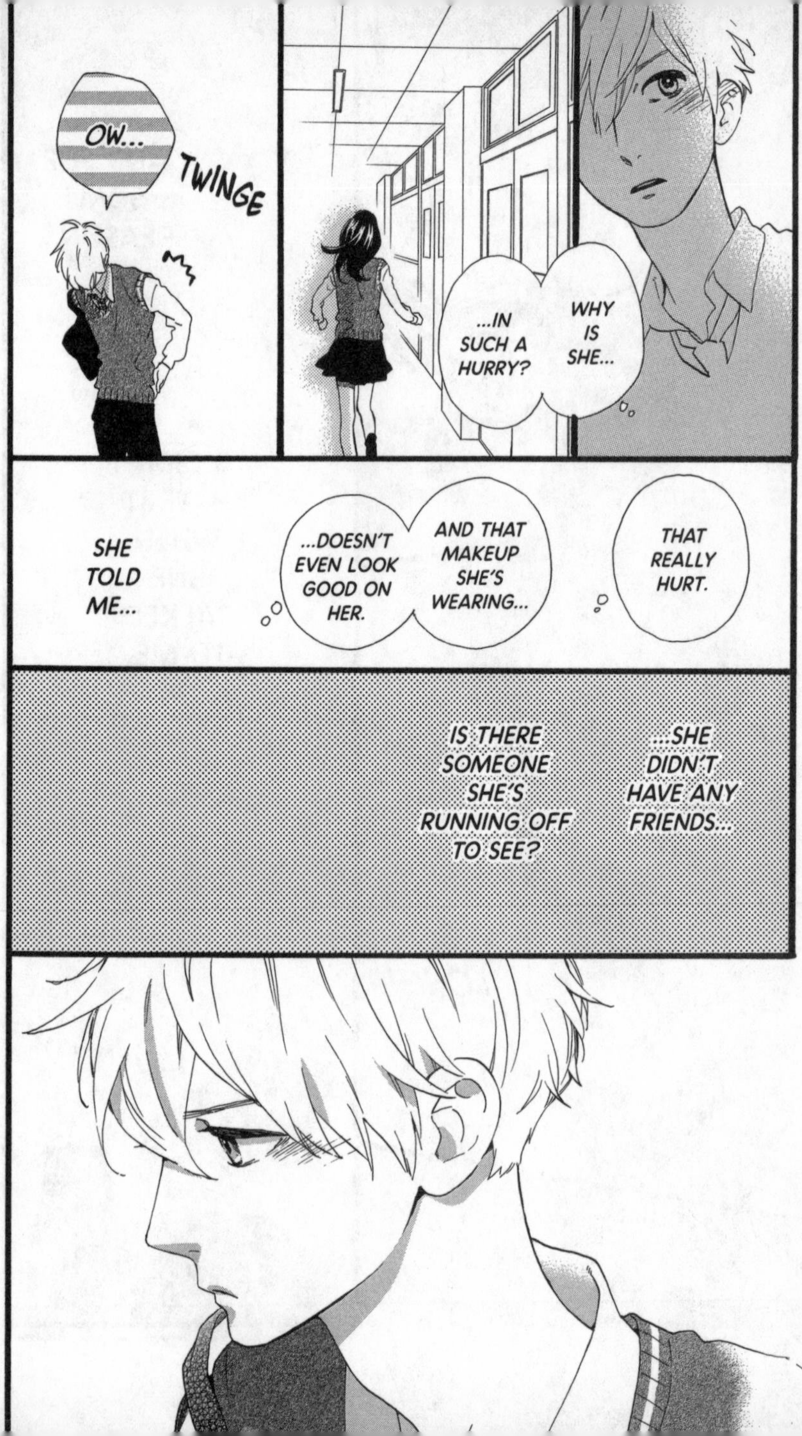
WHY IS SHE...
...IN SUCH A HURRY?
OW...
TWINGE
THAT REALLY HURT.
AND THAT MAKEUP SHE'S WEARING...
...DOESN'T EVEN LOOK GOOD ON HER.
SHE TOLD ME...
...SHE DIDN'T HAVE ANY FRIENDS...
IS THERE SOMEONE SHE'S RUNNING OFF TO SEE?

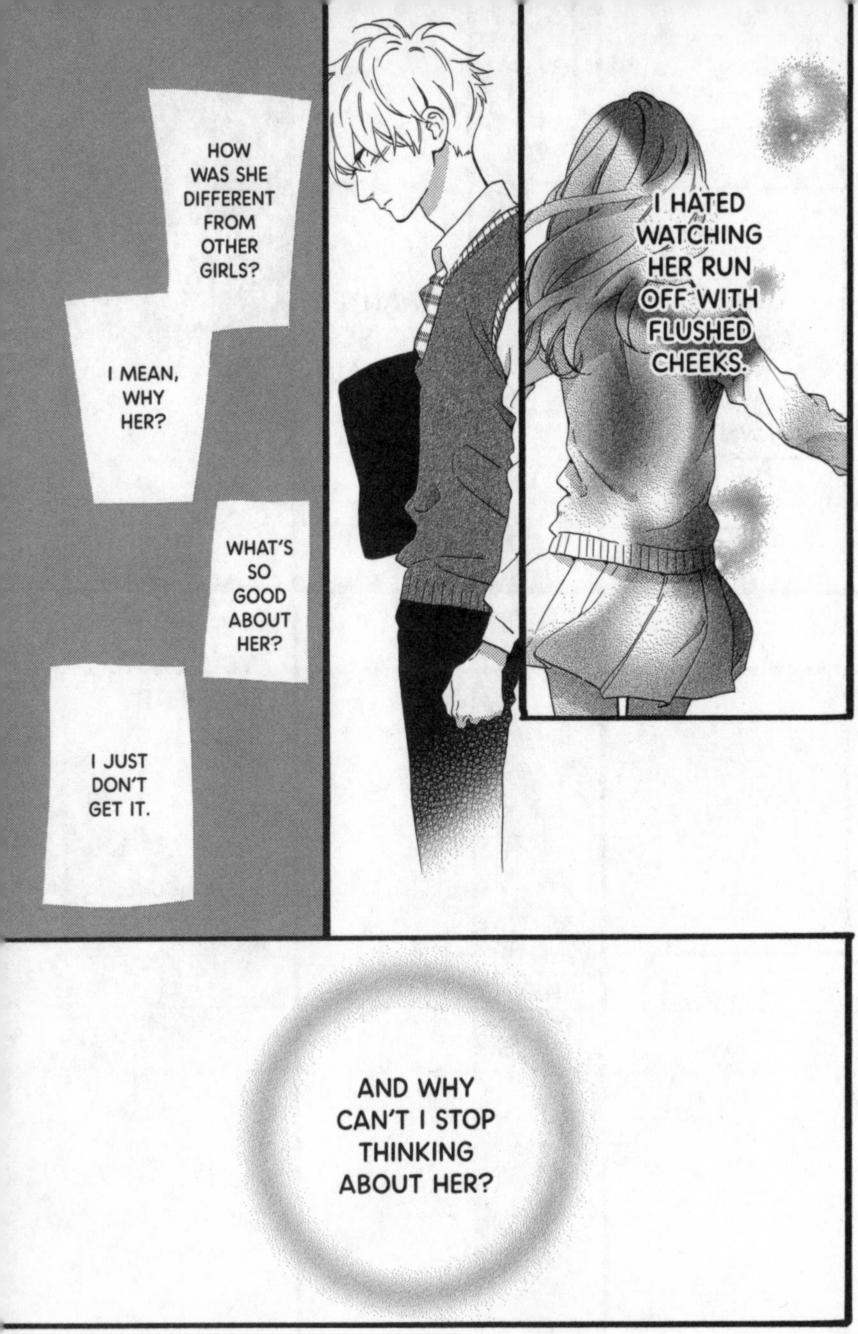
I HATED WATCHING HER RUN OFF WITH FLUSHED CHEEKS.
HOW WAS SHE DIFFERENT FROM OTHER GIRLS?
I MEAN, WHY HER?
WHAT'S SO GOOD ABOUT HER?
I JUST DON'T GET IT.
AND WHY CAN'T I STOP THINKING ABOUT HER?

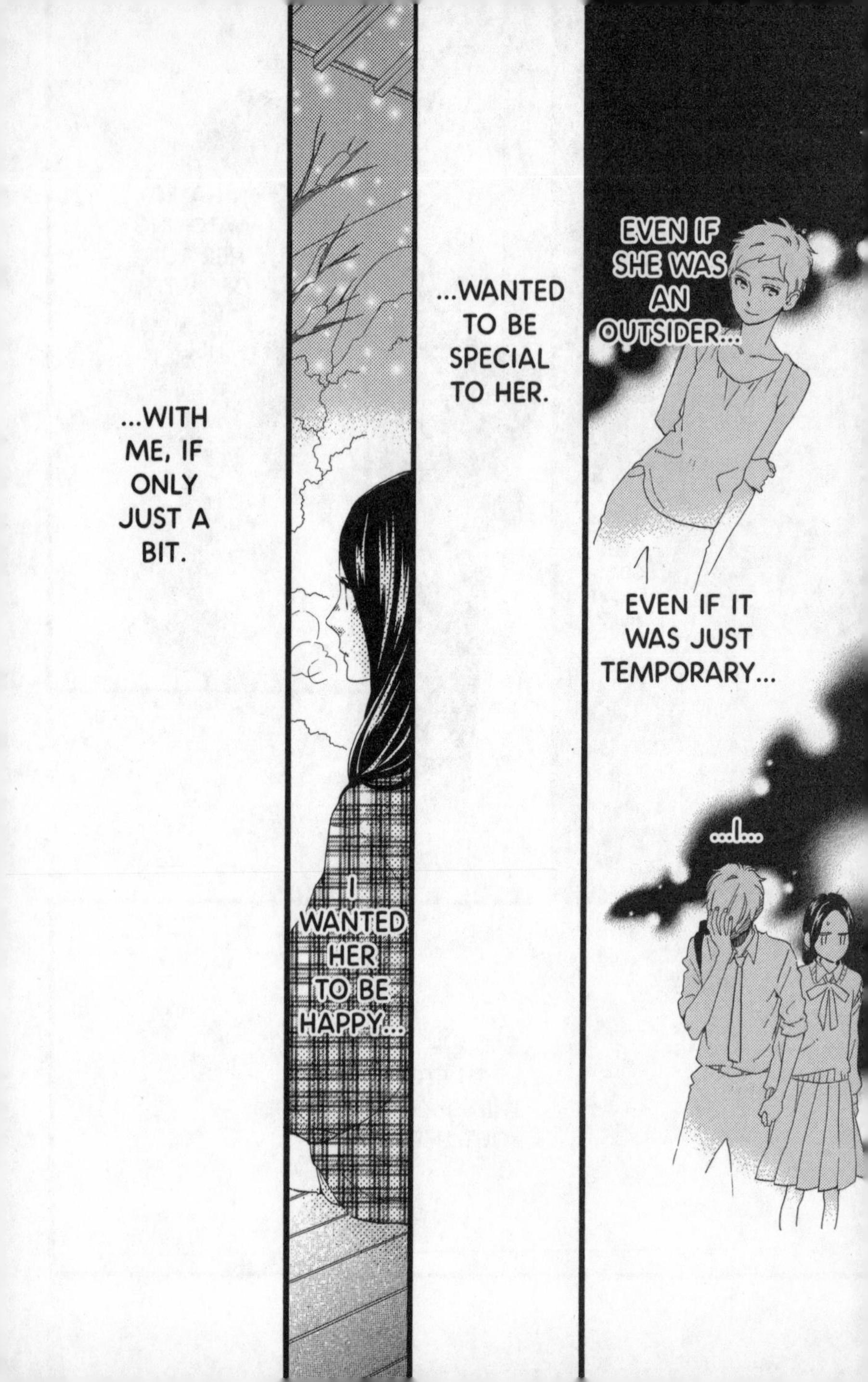
EVEN IF SHE WAS AN OUTSIDER...
EVEN IF IT WAS JUST TEMPORARY...
...I...
...WANTED TO BE SPECIAL TO HER.
I WANTED HER TO BE HAPPY...
...WITH ME, IF ONLY JUST A BIT.

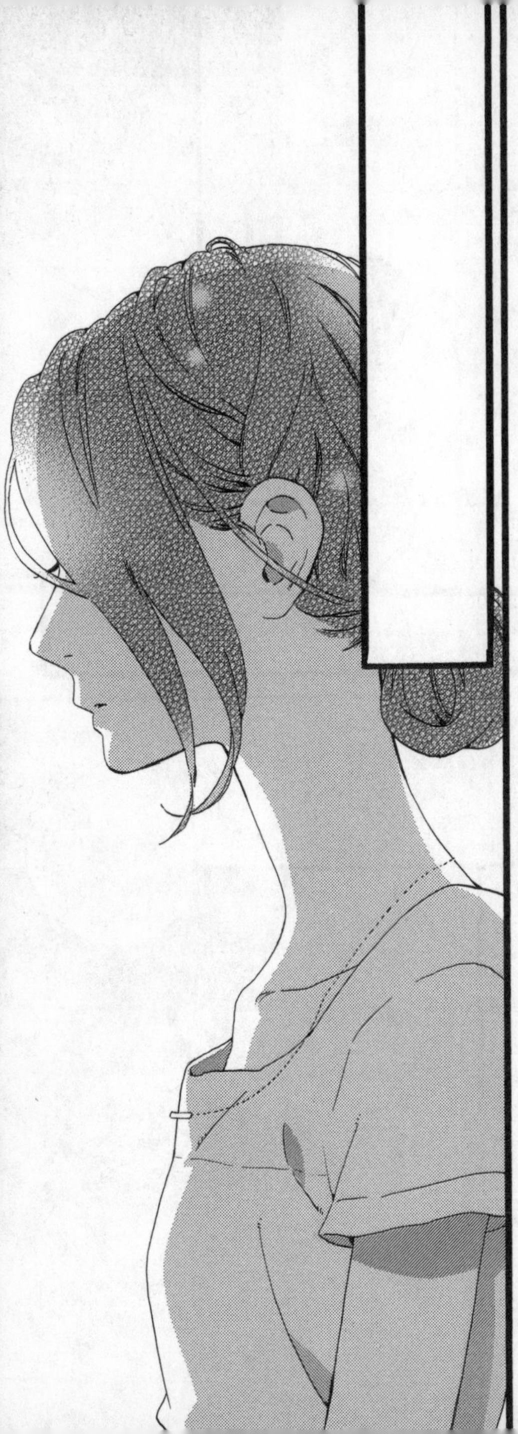

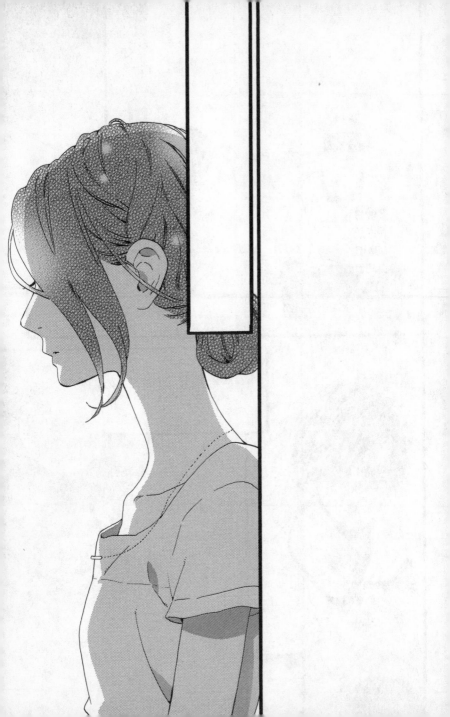

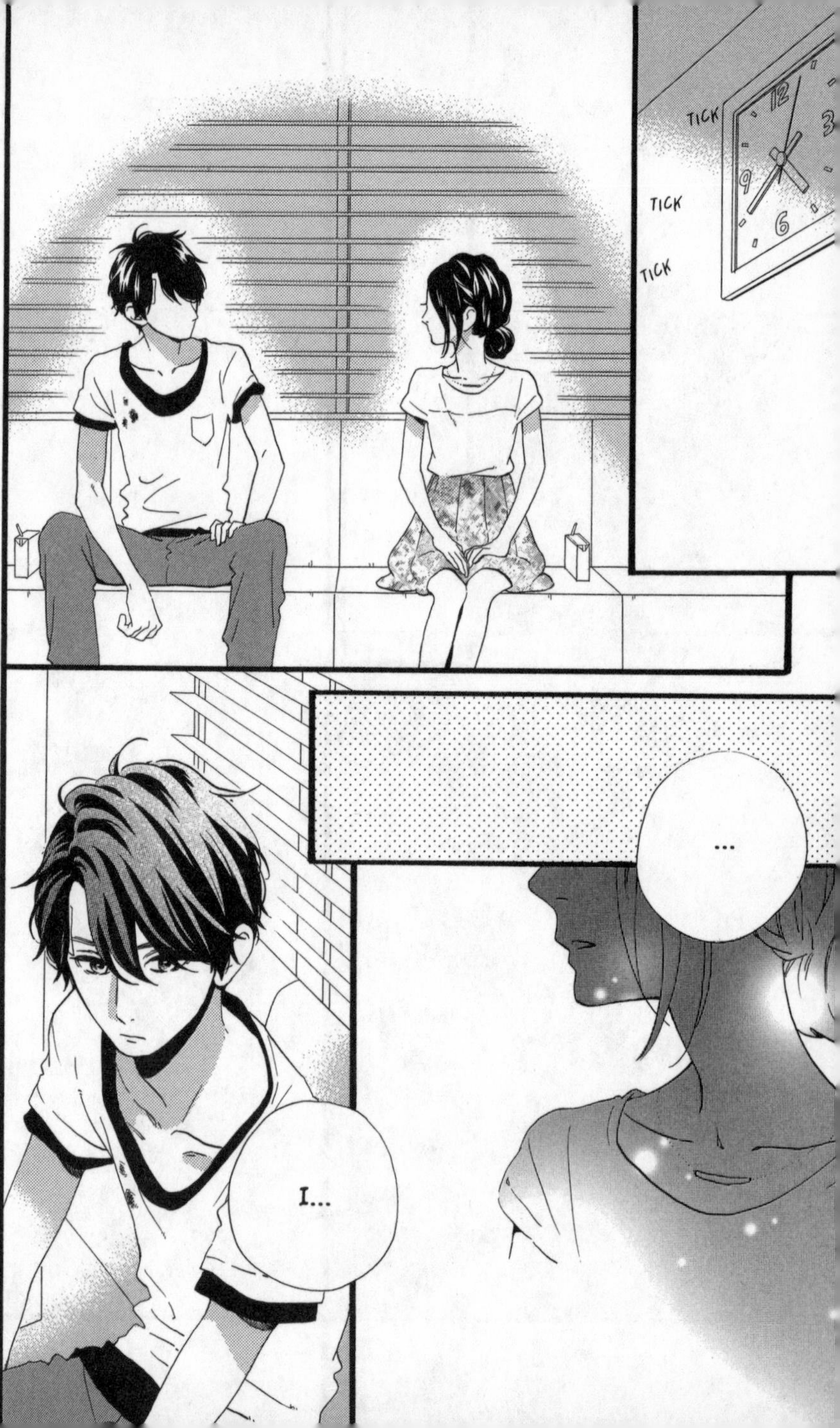
TICK
TICK
TICK
...
I...

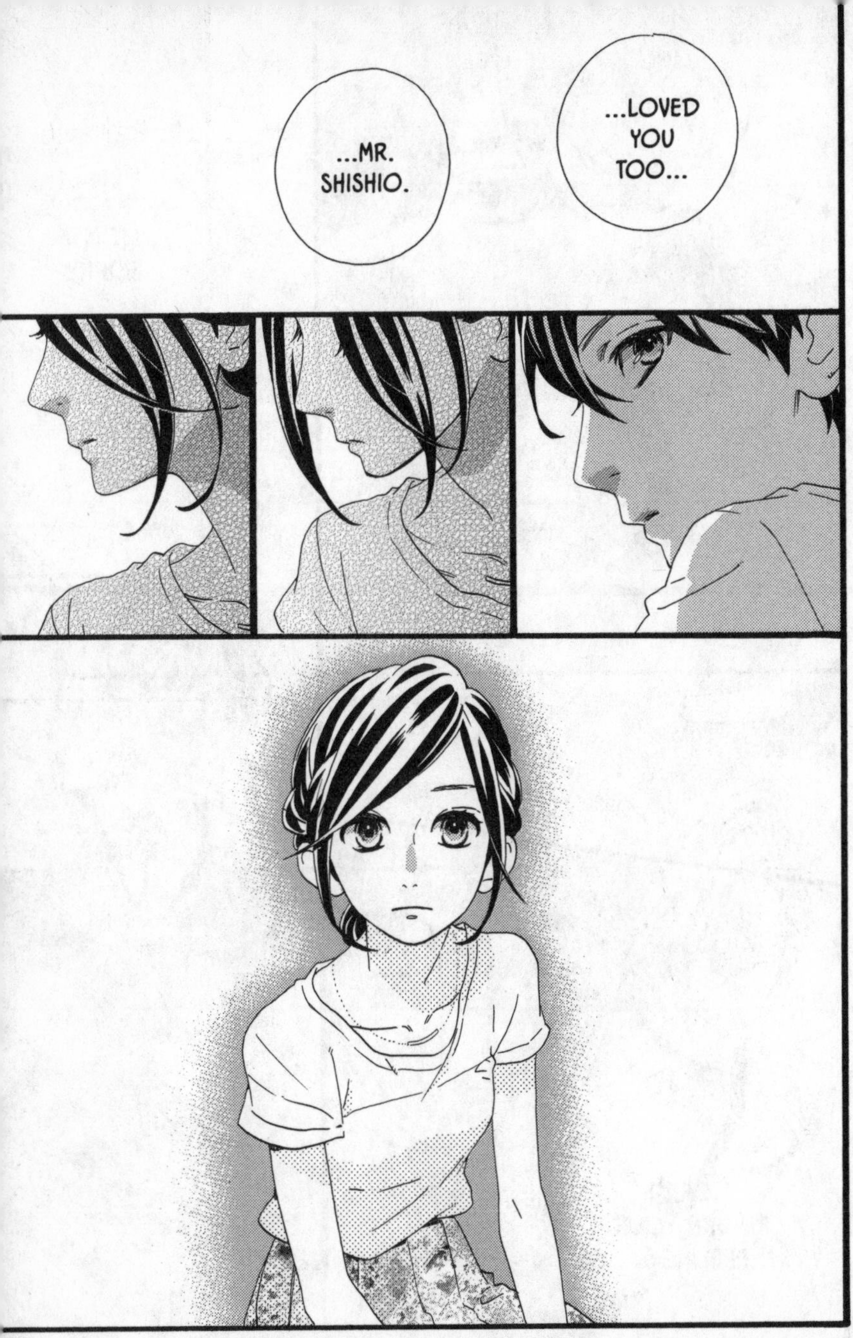
...LOVED YOU TOO...
...MR. SHISHIO.

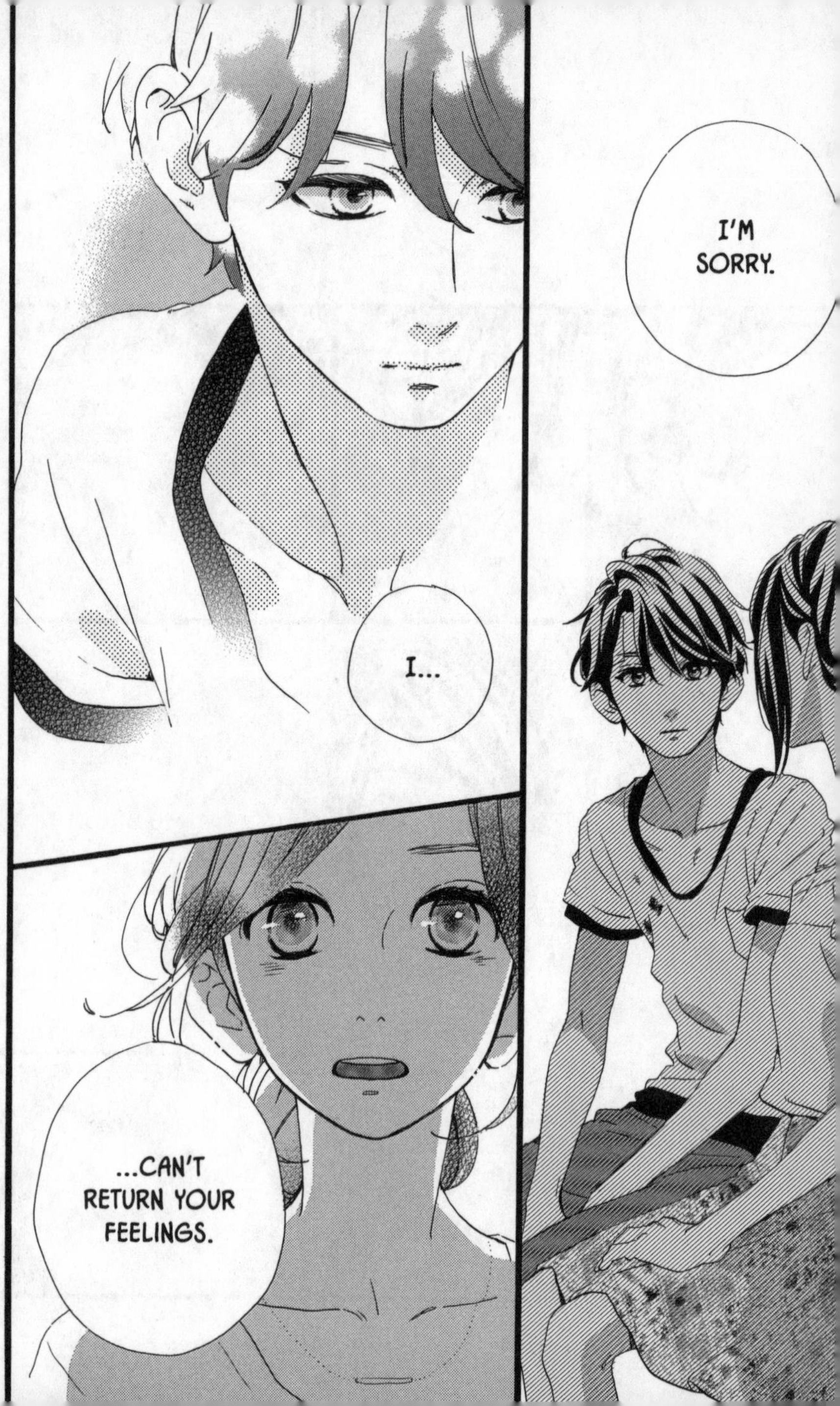
I'M SORRY.
I...
...CAN'T RETURN YOUR FEELINGS.

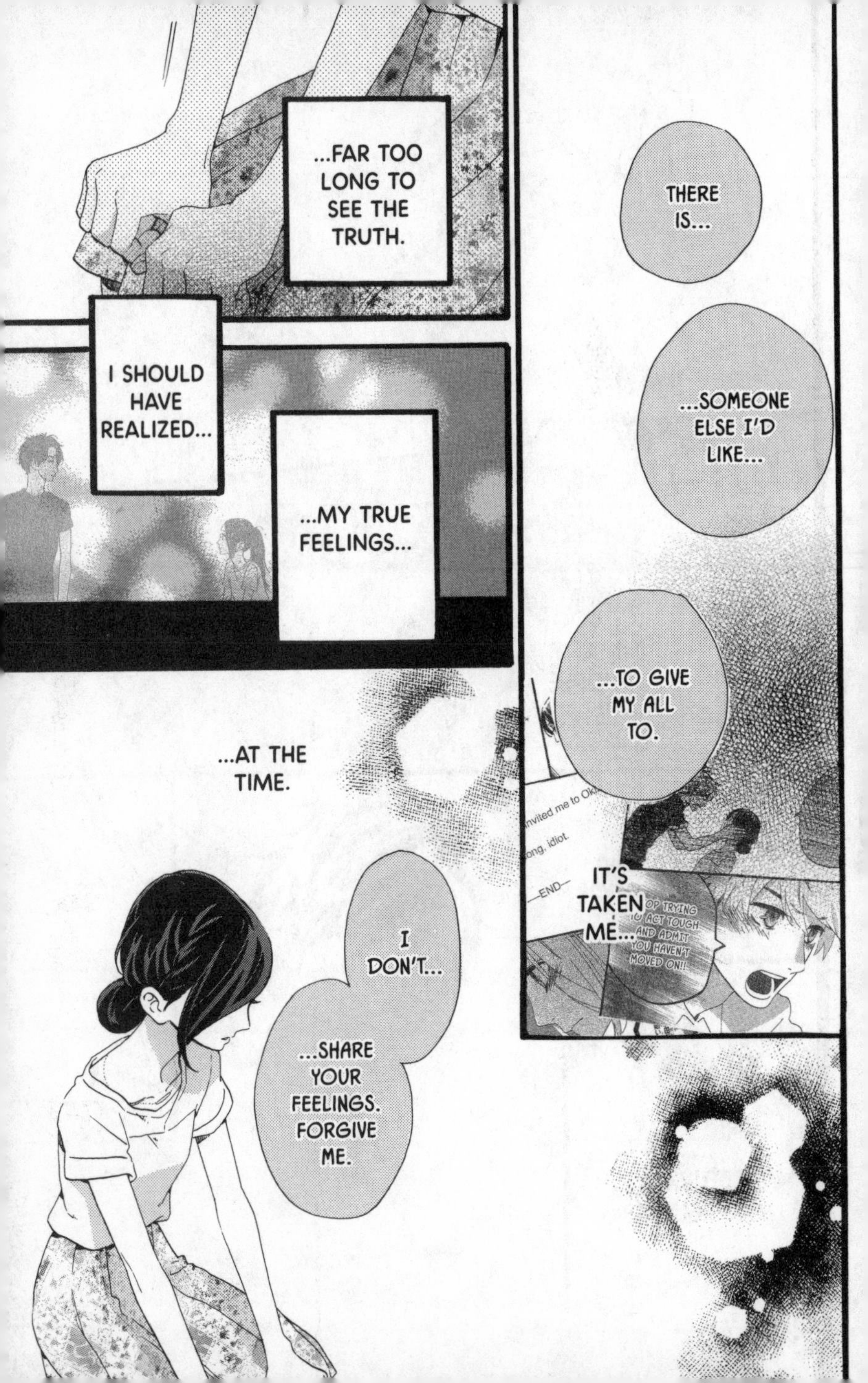
THERE IS...
...SOMEONE ELSE I'D LIKE...
...TO GIVE MY ALL TO.
invited me to Ok
ong, idiot.
—END—
IT'S TAKEN ME...
OP TRYING TO ACT TOUGH AND ADMIT YOU HAVEN'T MOVED ON!!
...FAR TOO LONG TO SEE THE TRUTH.
I SHOULD HAVE REALIZED...
...MY TRUE FEELINGS...
...AT THE TIME.
I DON'T...
...SHARE YOUR FEELINGS. FORGIVE ME.

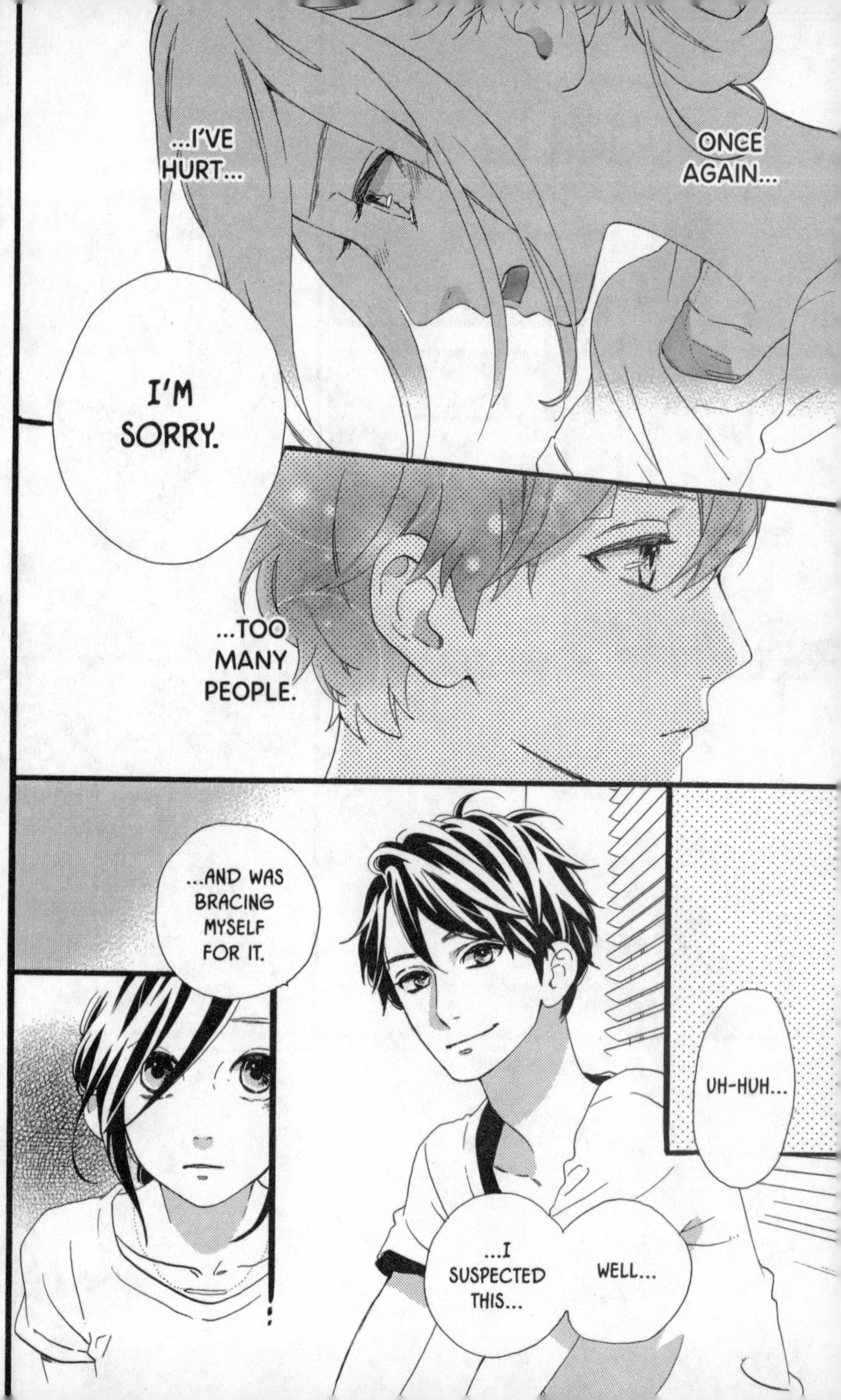
ONCE AGAIN...
...I'VE HURT...
I'M SORRY.
...TOO MANY PEOPLE.
UH-HUH...
WELL...
...I SUSPECTED THIS...
...AND WAS BRACING MYSELF FOR IT.

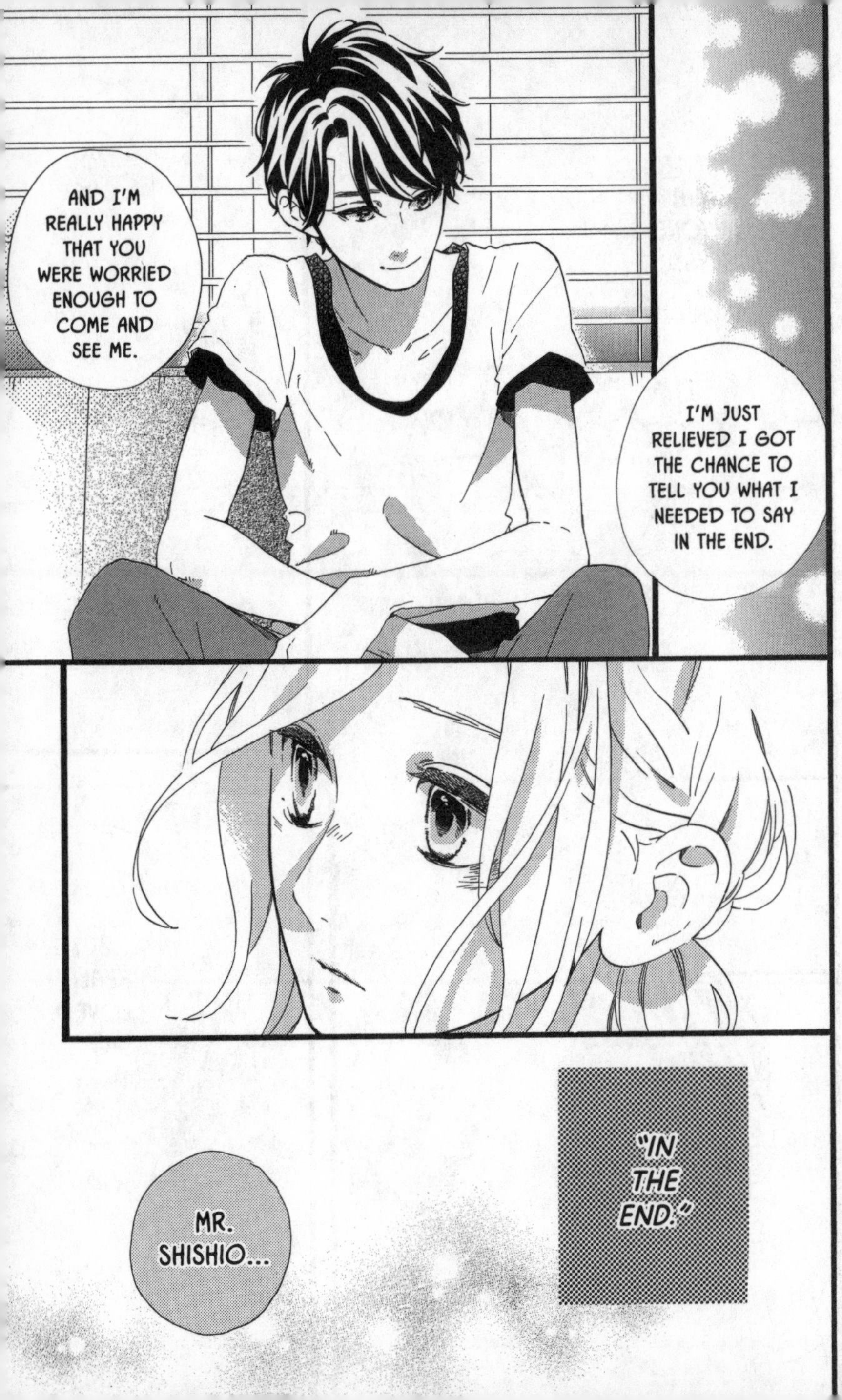
I'M JUST RELIEVED I GOT THE CHANCE TO TELL YOU WHAT I NEEDED TO SAY IN THE END.
AND I'M REALLY HAPPY THAT YOU WERE WORRIED ENOUGH TO COME AND SEE ME.
"IN THE END."
MR. SHISHIO...

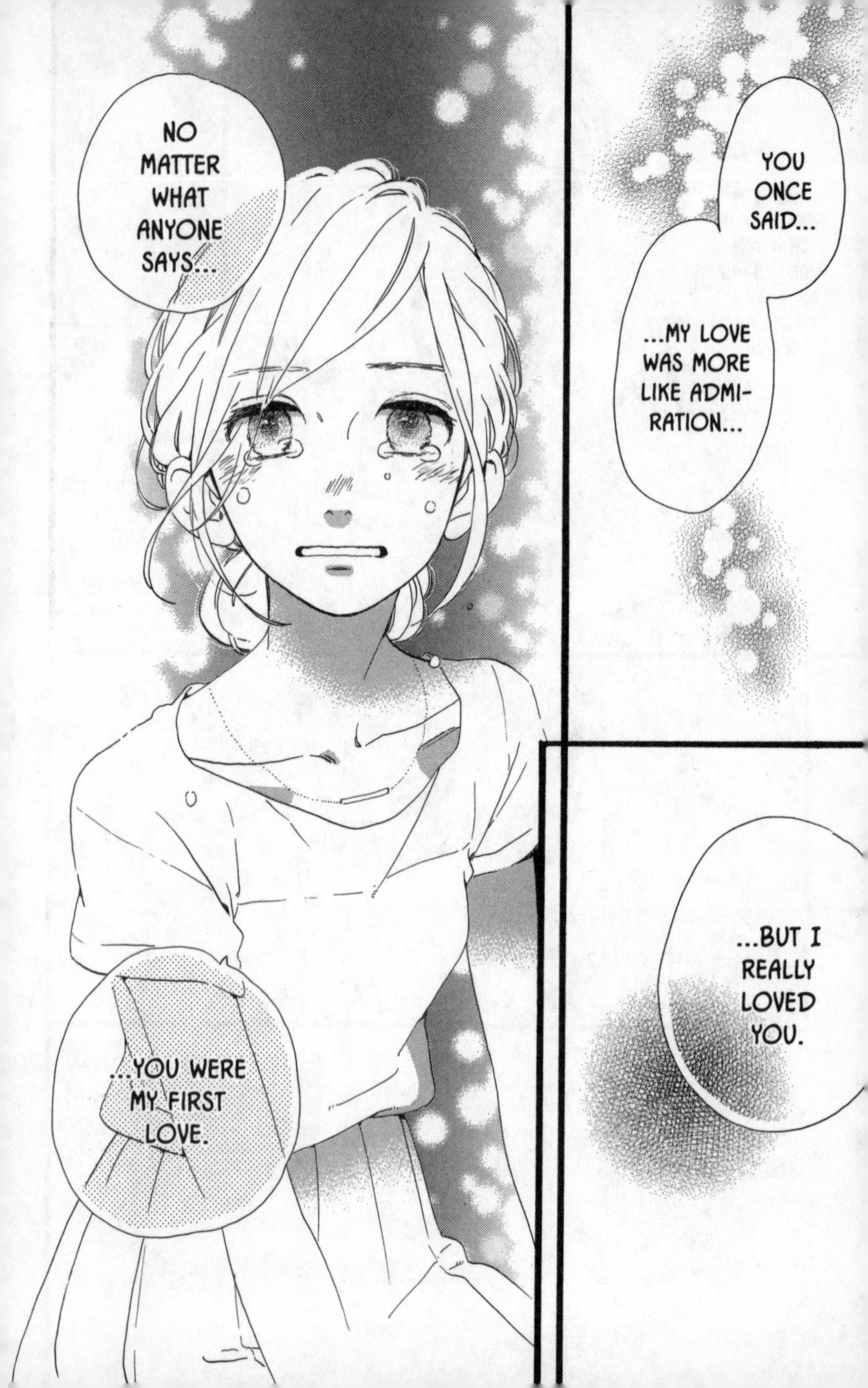
YOU ONCE SAID...
...MY LOVE WAS MORE LIKE ADMIRATION...
...BUT I REALLY LOVED YOU.
NO MATTER WHAT ANYONE SAYS...
...YOU WERE MY FIRST LOVE.

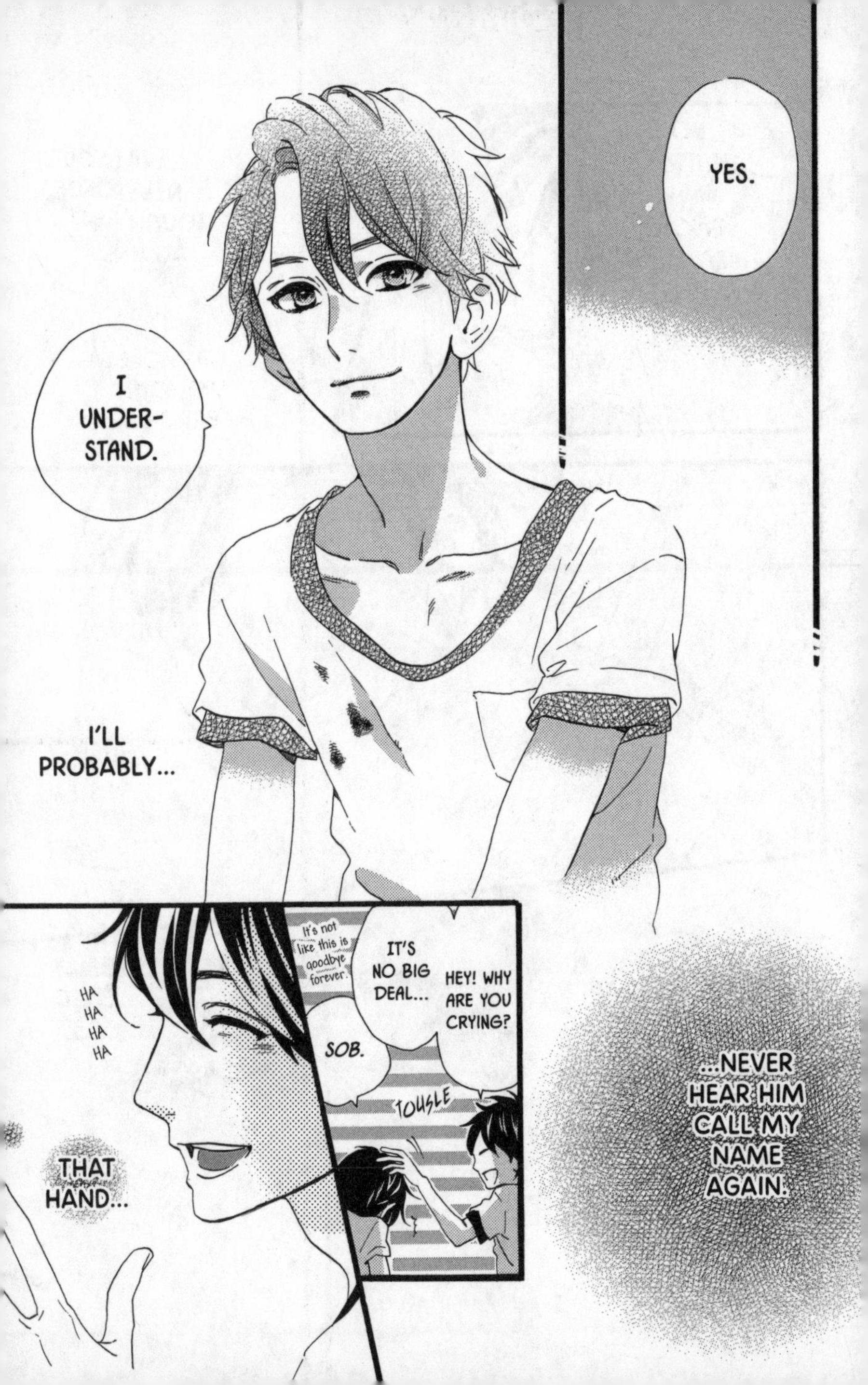
YES.
I UNDERSTAND.
I'LL PROBABLY...
...NEVER HEAR HIM CALL MY NAME AGAIN.
HEY! WHY ARE YOU CRYING?
IT'S NO BIG DEAL...
It's not like this is goodbye forever.
SOB.
TOUSLE
HA HA HA HA
THAT HAND...

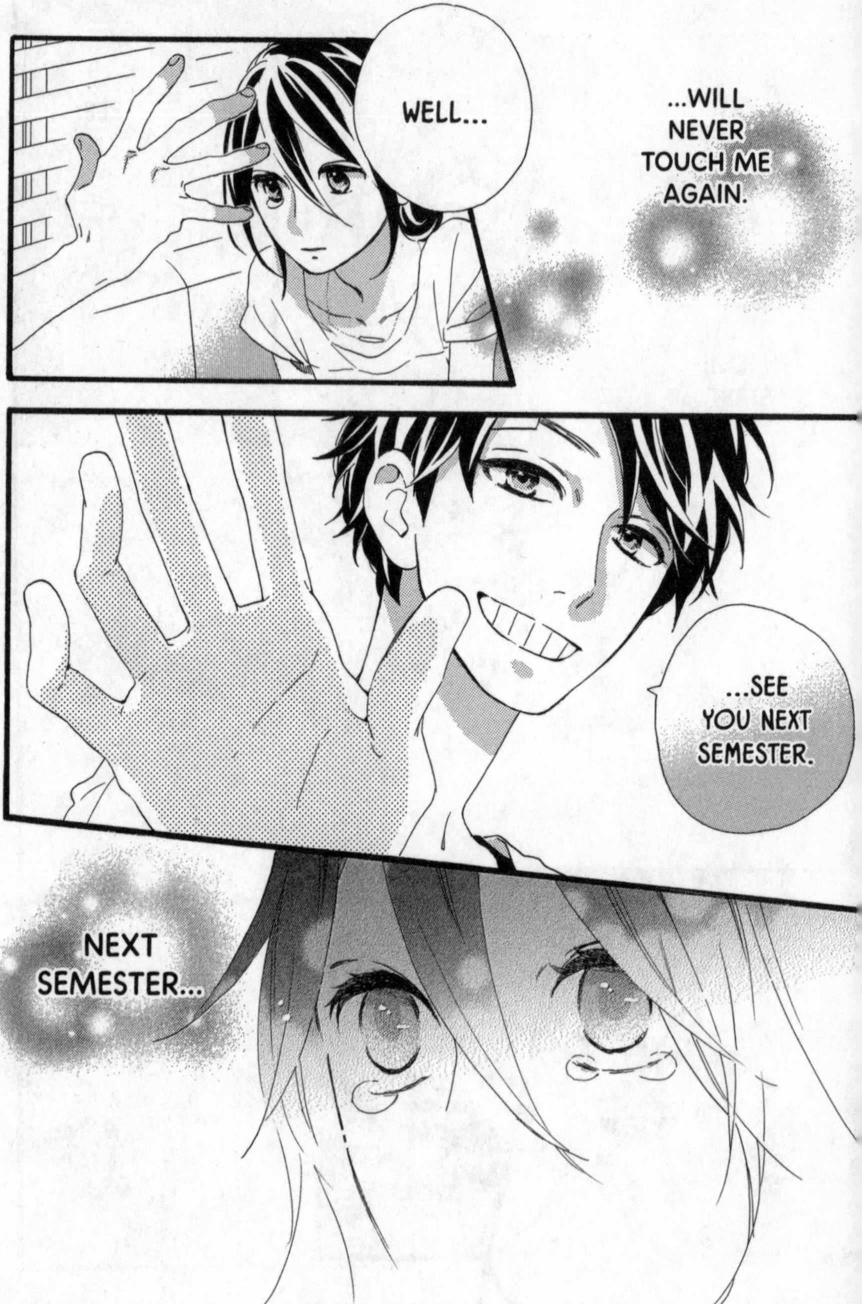
...WILL NEVER TOUCH ME AGAIN.
WELL...
...SEE YOU NEXT SEMESTER.
NEXT SEMESTER...

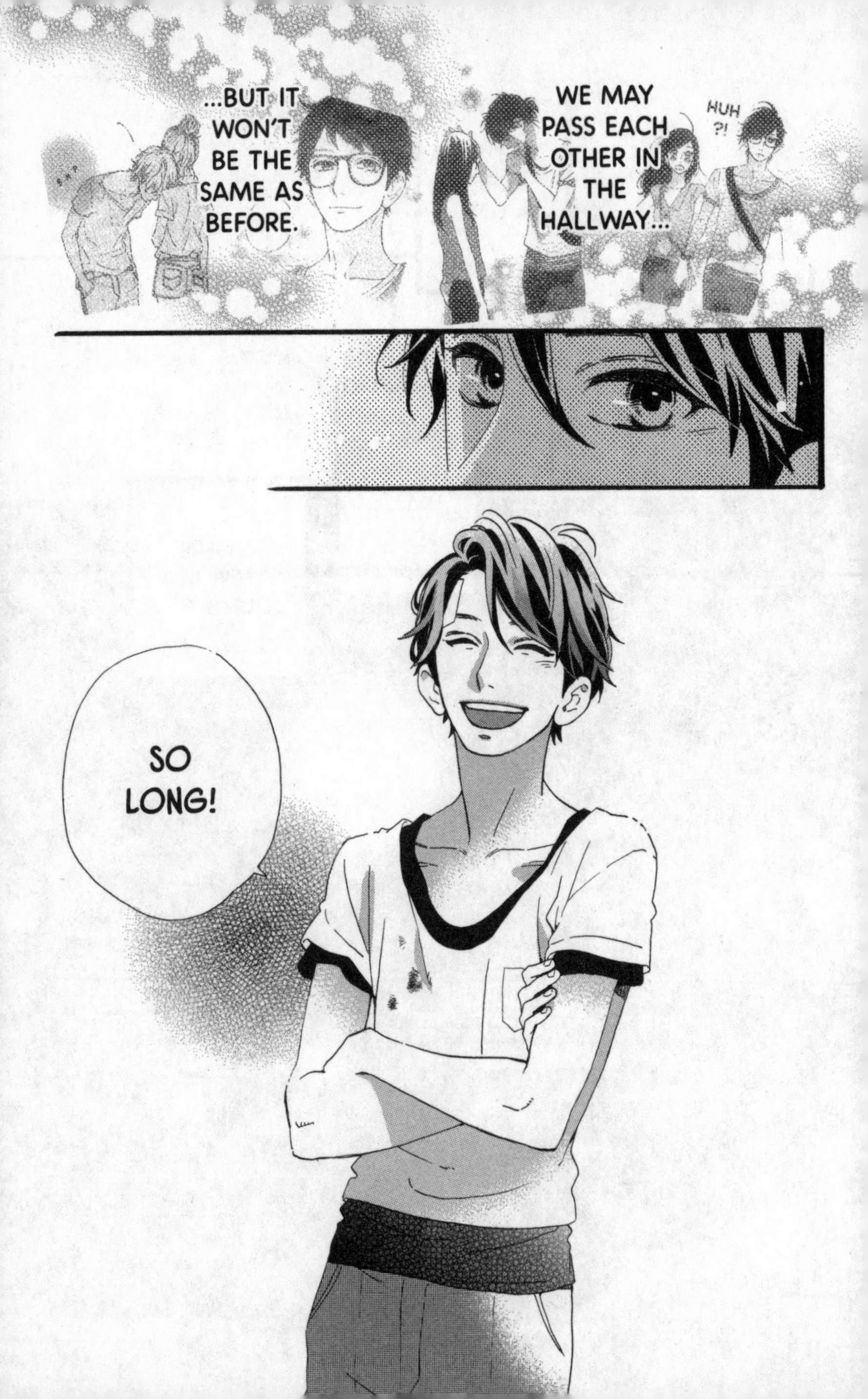
HUH ?!
WE MAY PASS EACH OTHER IN THE HALLWAY...
...BUT IT WON'T BE THE SAME AS BEFORE.
SO LONG!

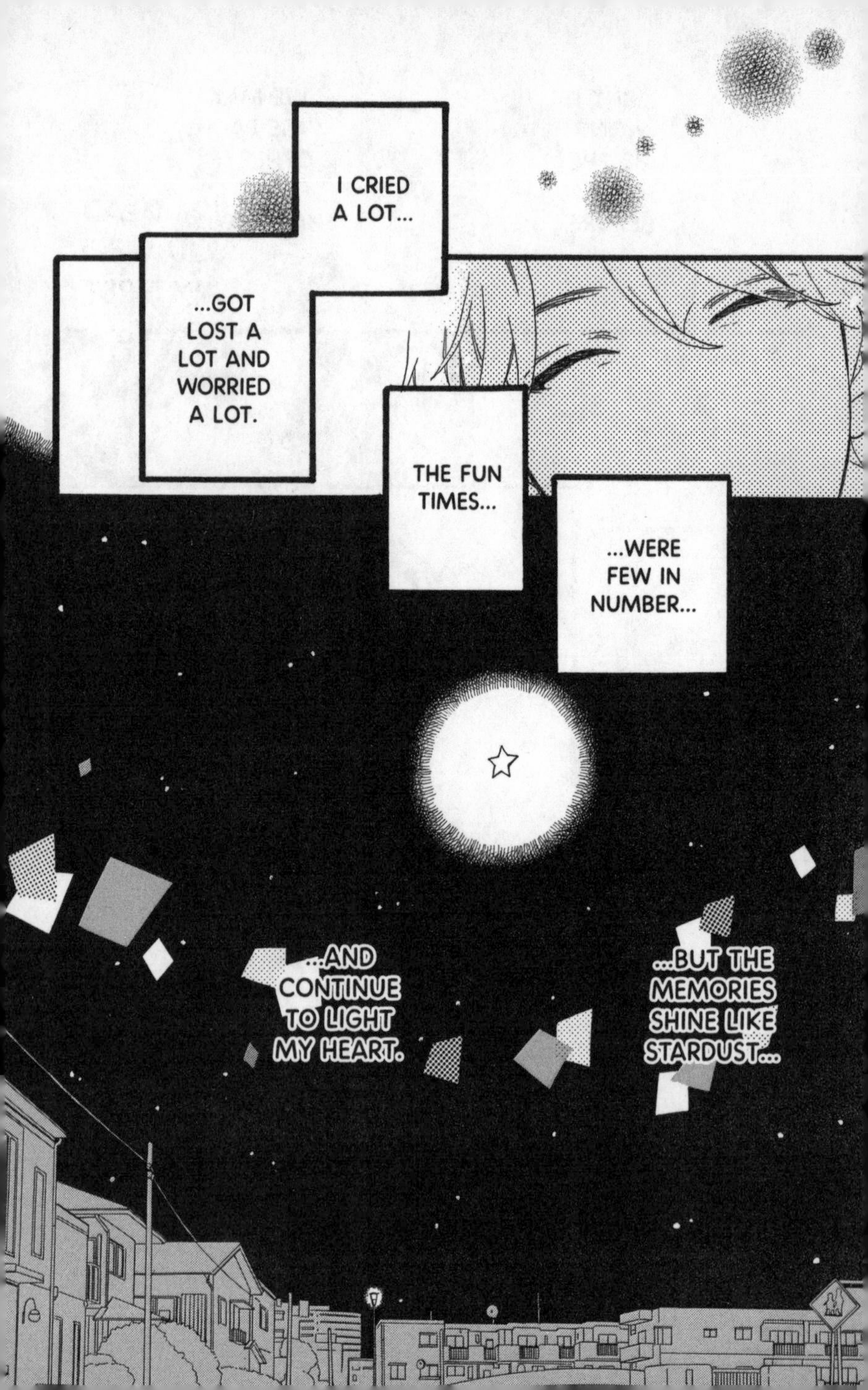
I CRIED A LOT...
...GOT LOST A LOT AND WORRIED A LOT.
THE FUN TIMES...
...WERE FEW IN NUMBER...
...BUT THE MEMORIES SHINE LIKE STARDUST...
...AND CONTINUE TO LIGHT MY HEART.

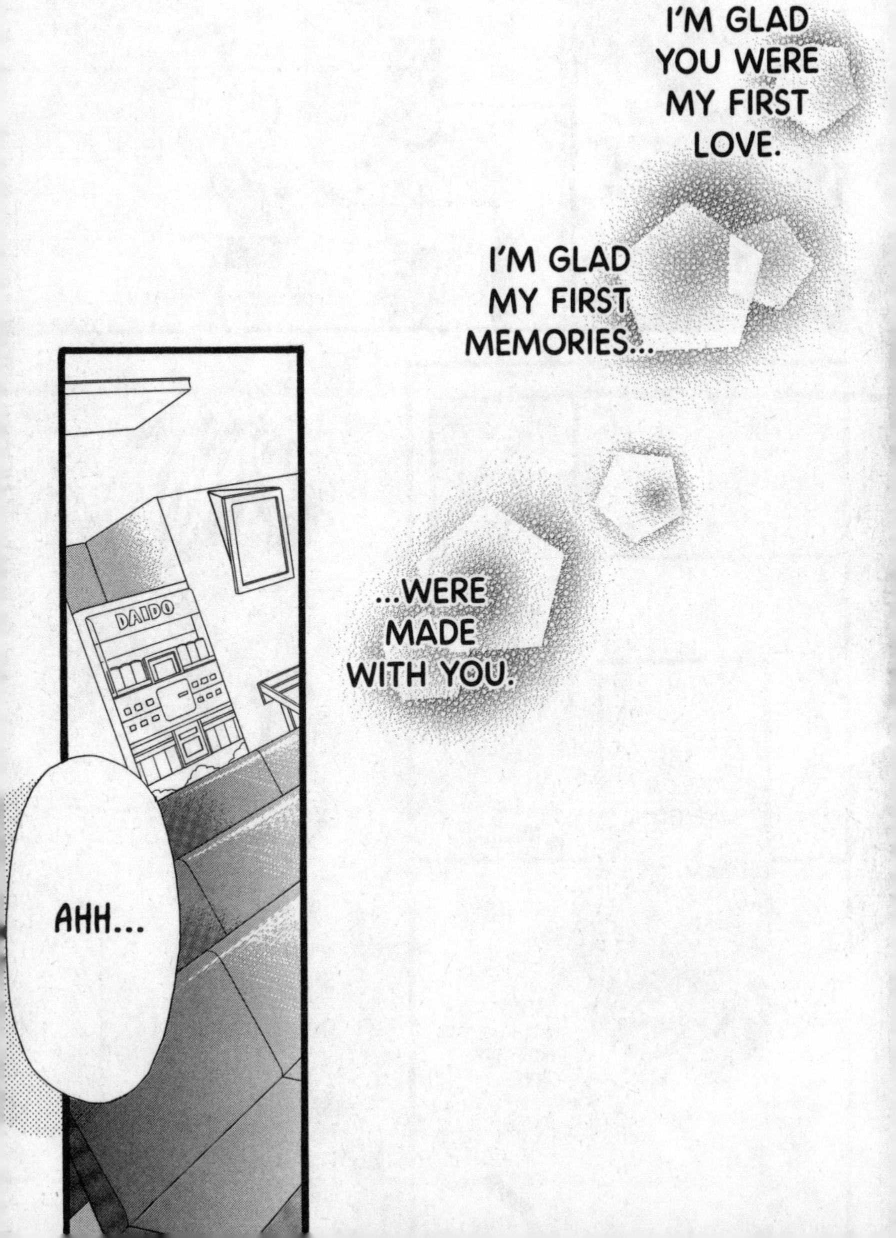
I'M GLAD YOU WERE MY FIRST LOVE.
I'M GLAD MY FIRST MEMORIES...
...WERE MADE WITH YOU.
DAIDO
AHH...

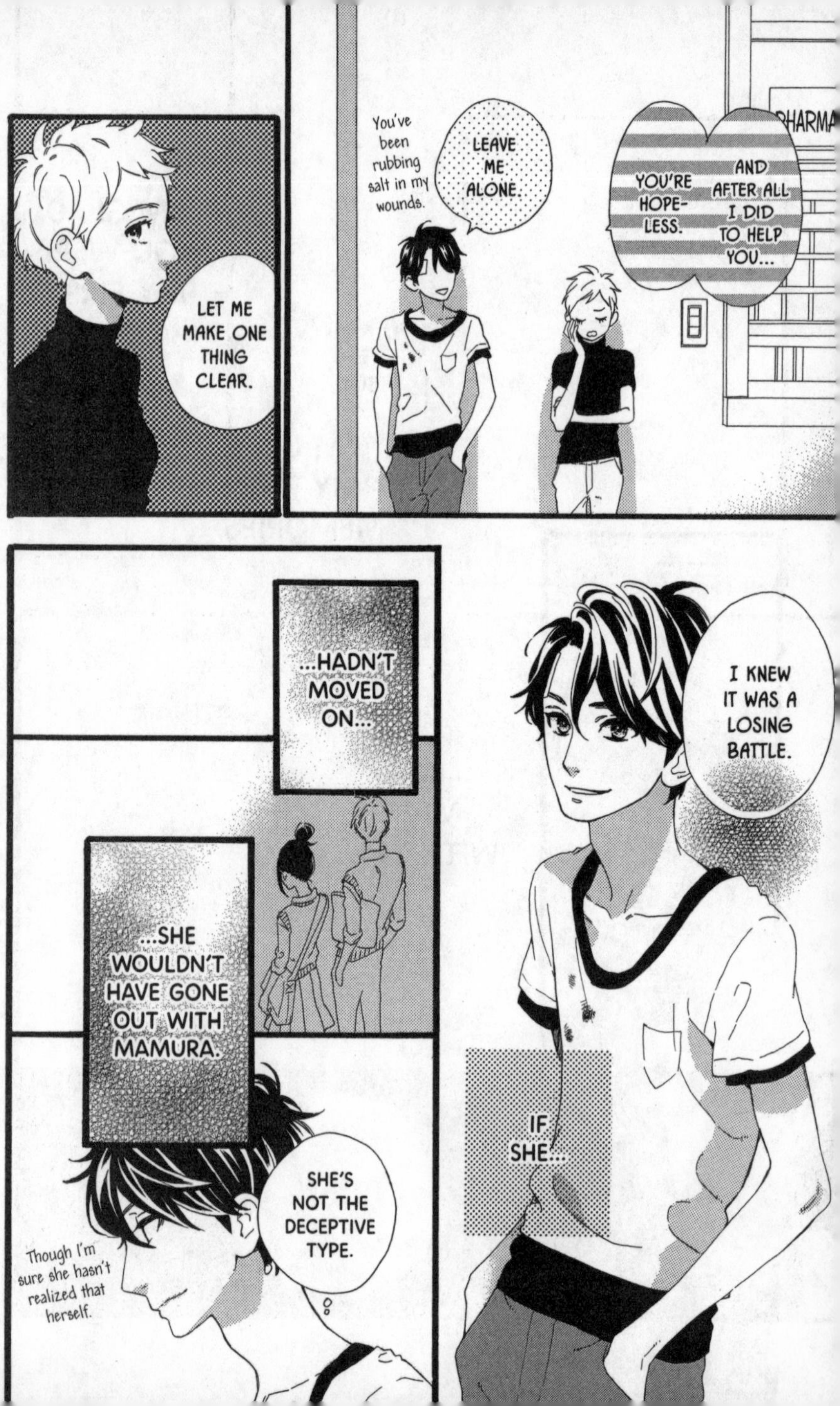
PHARMA
YOU'RE HOPE-LESS.
AND AFTER ALL I DID TO HELP YOU...
LEAVE ME ALONE.
You've been rubbing salt in my wounds.
LET ME MAKE ONE THING CLEAR.
I KNEW IT WAS A LOSING BATTLE.
IF SHE...
...HADN'T MOVED ON...
...SHE WOULDN'T HAVE GONE OUT WITH MAMURA.
SHE'S NOT THE DECEPTIVE TYPE.
Though I'm sure she hasn't realized that herself.

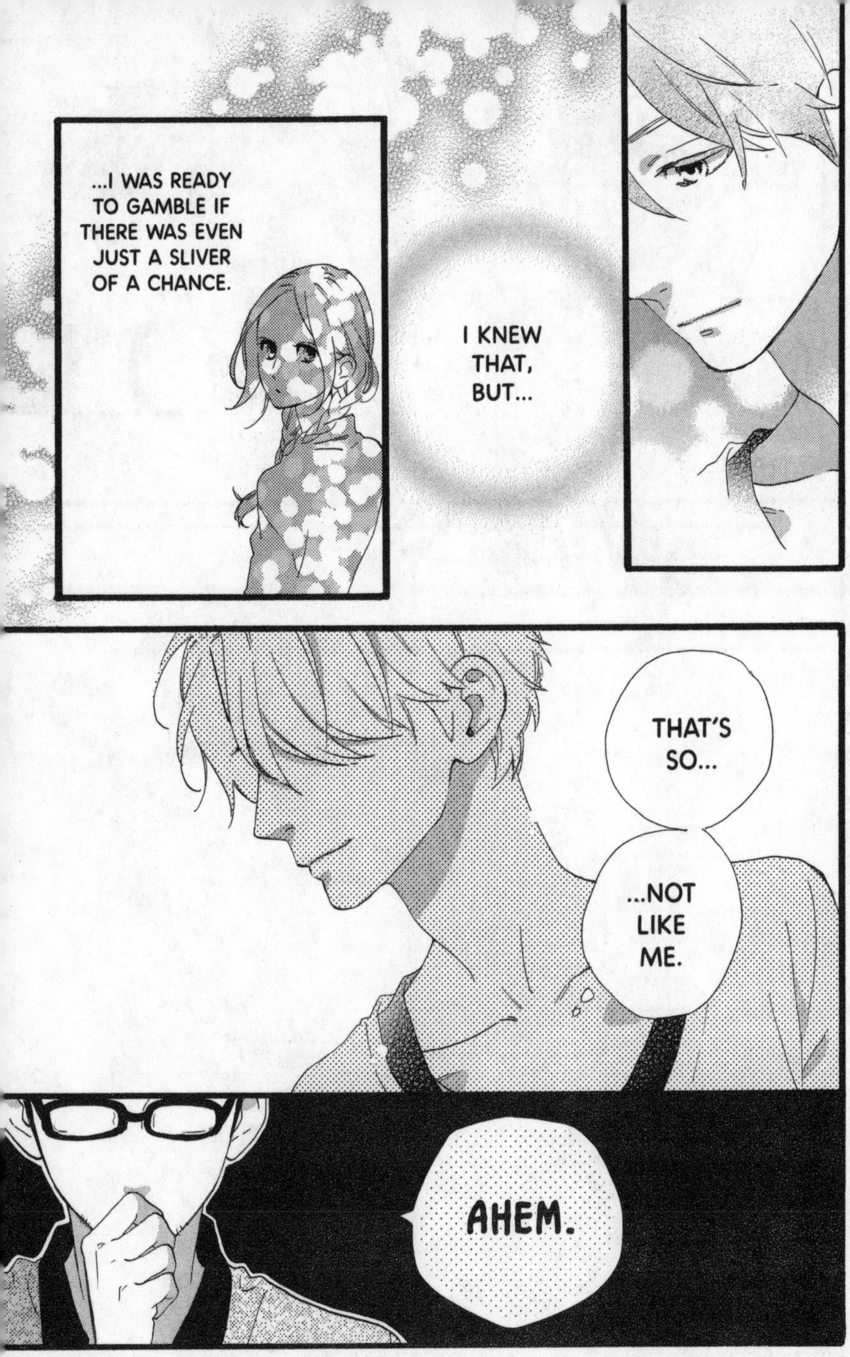
I KNEW THAT, BUT...
...I WAS READY TO GAMBLE IF THERE WAS EVEN JUST A SLIVER OF A CHANCE.
THAT'S SO...
...NOT LIKE ME.
AHEM.

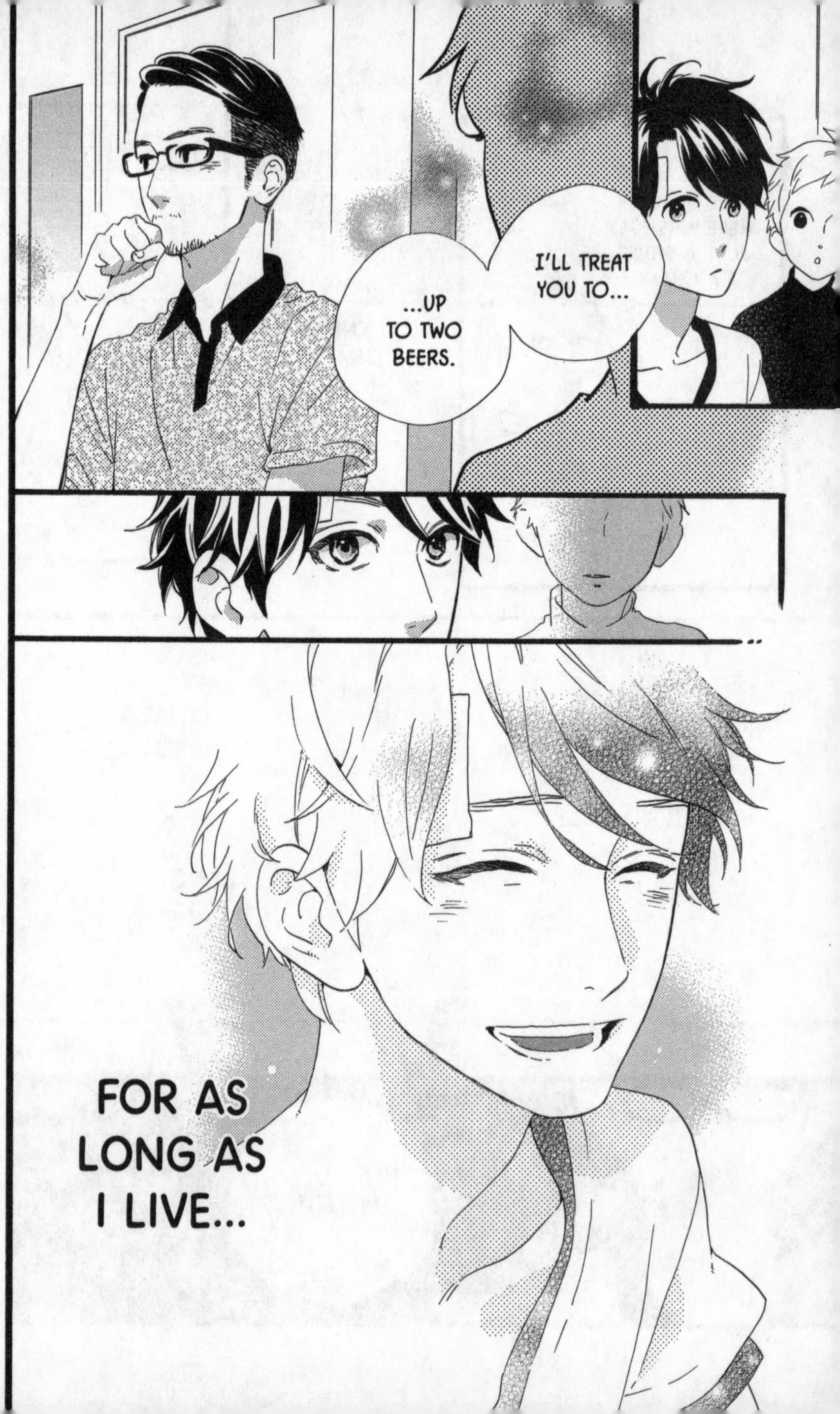
I'LL TREAT YOU TO...
...UP TO TWO BEERS.
FOR AS LONG AS I LIVE...

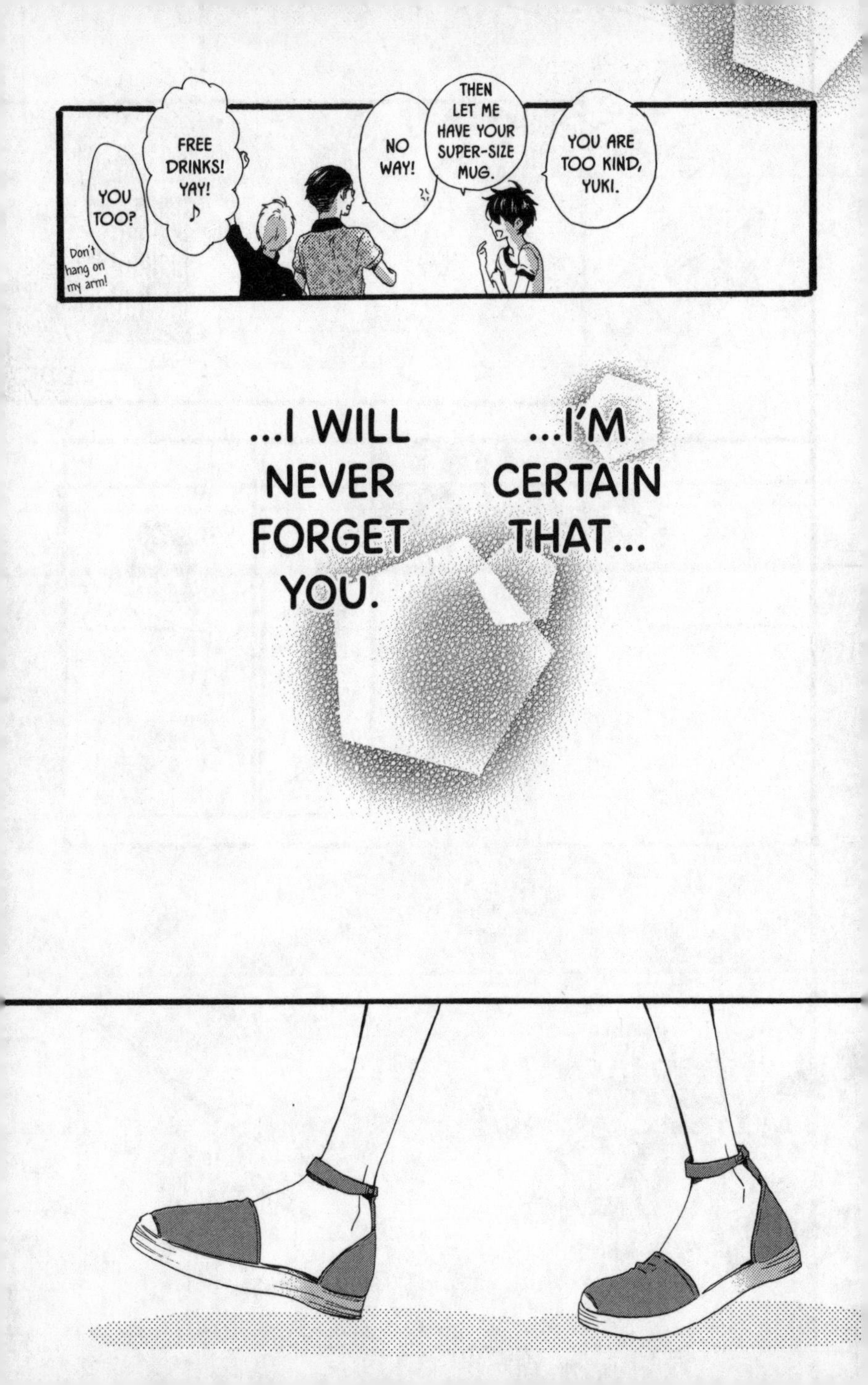
YOU ARE TOO KIND, YUKI.
THEN LET ME HAVE YOUR SUPER-SIZE MUG.
NO WAY!
FREE DRINKS! YAY! ♪
YOU TOO?
Don't hang on my arm!
...I'M CERTAIN THAT...
...I WILL NEVER FORGET YOU.

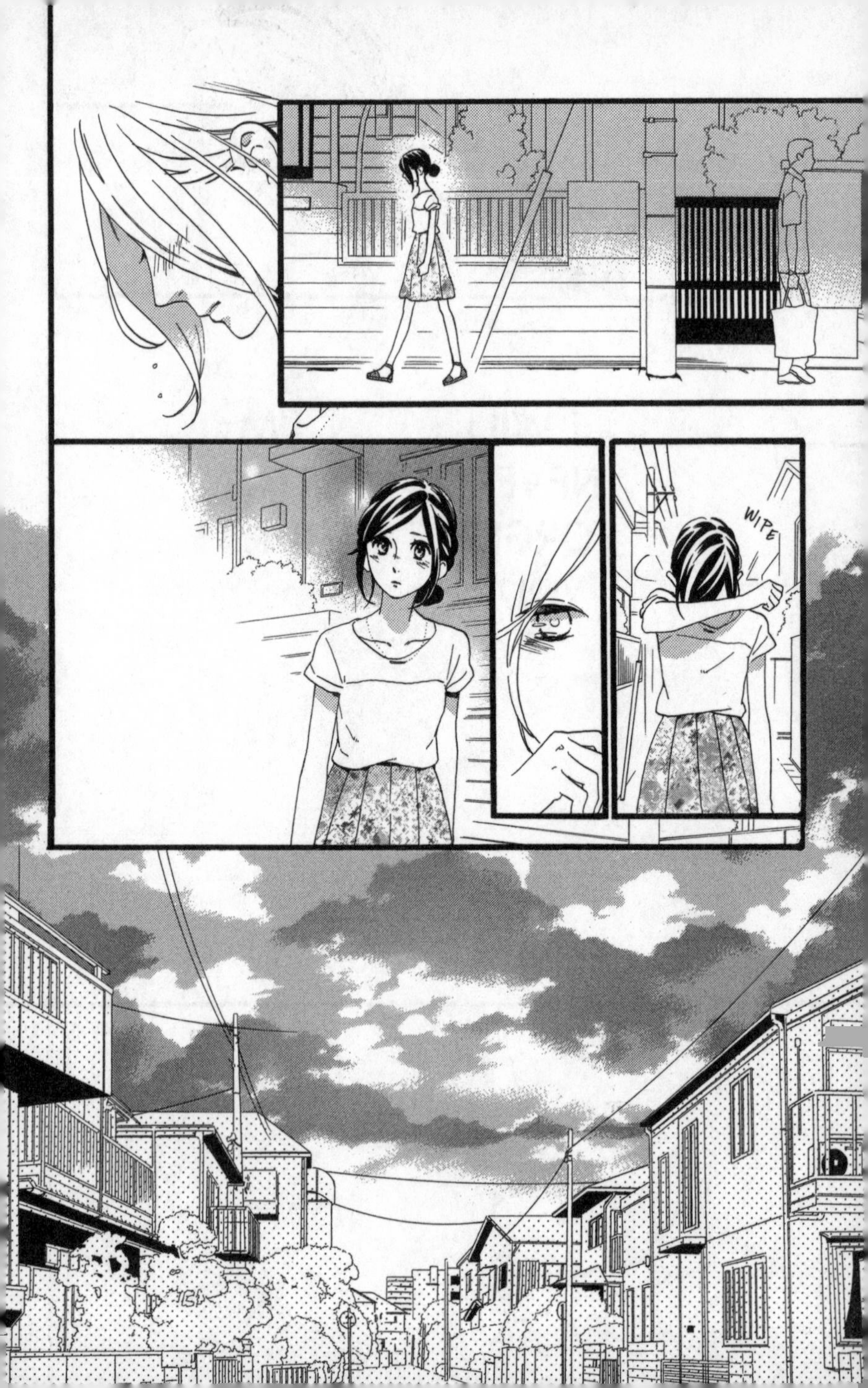
WIPE

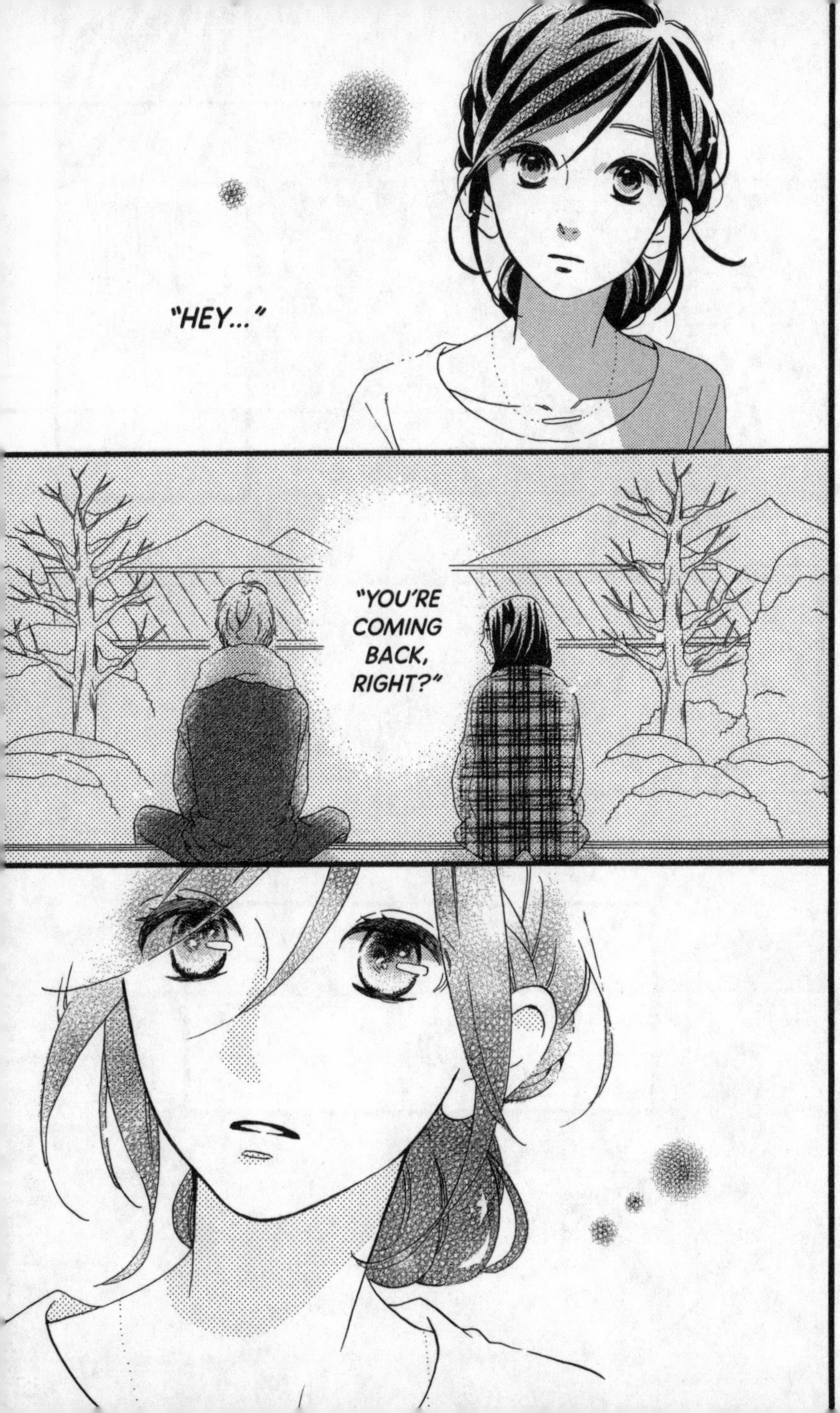
"HEY..."
"YOU'RE COMING BACK, RIGHT?"

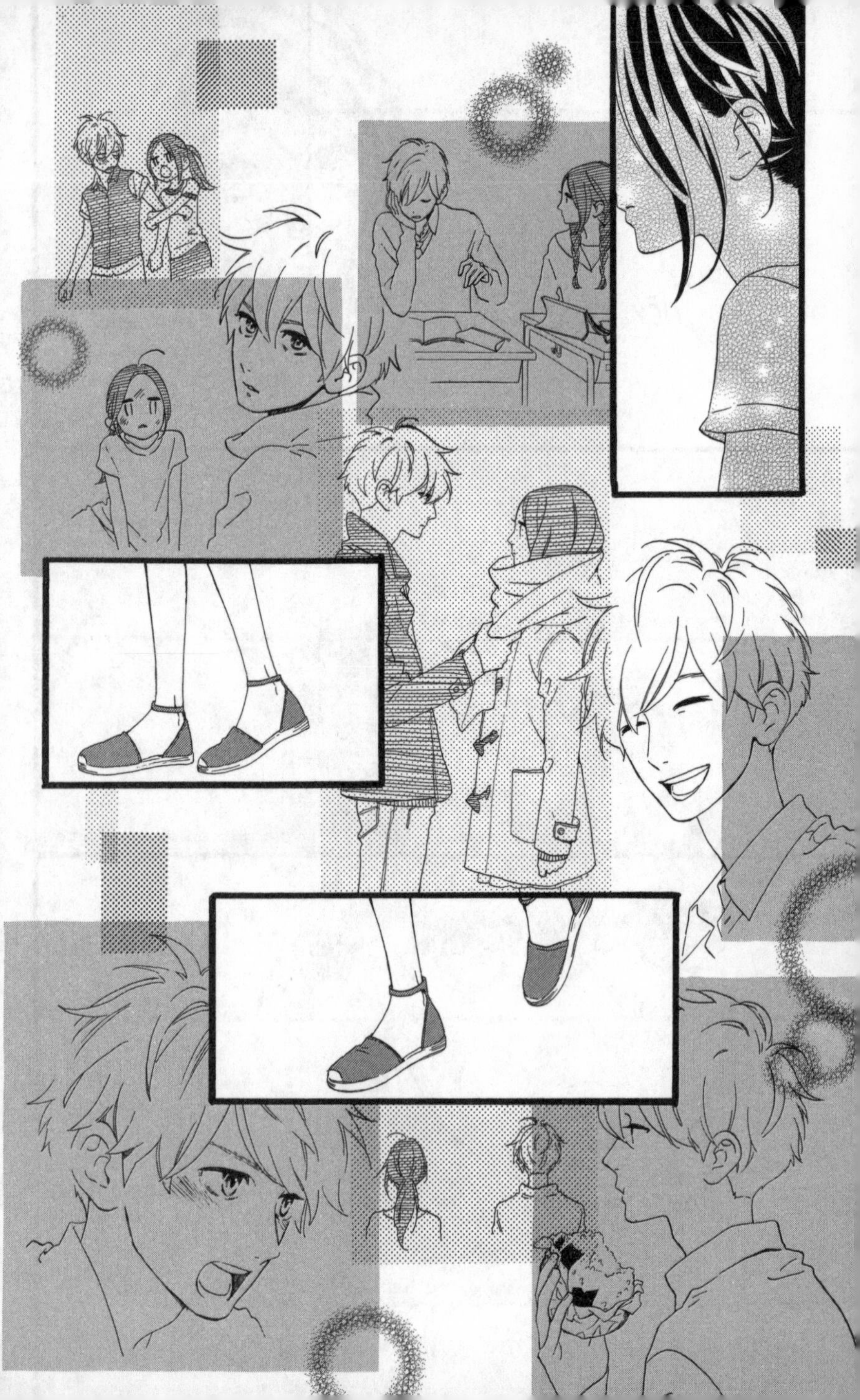

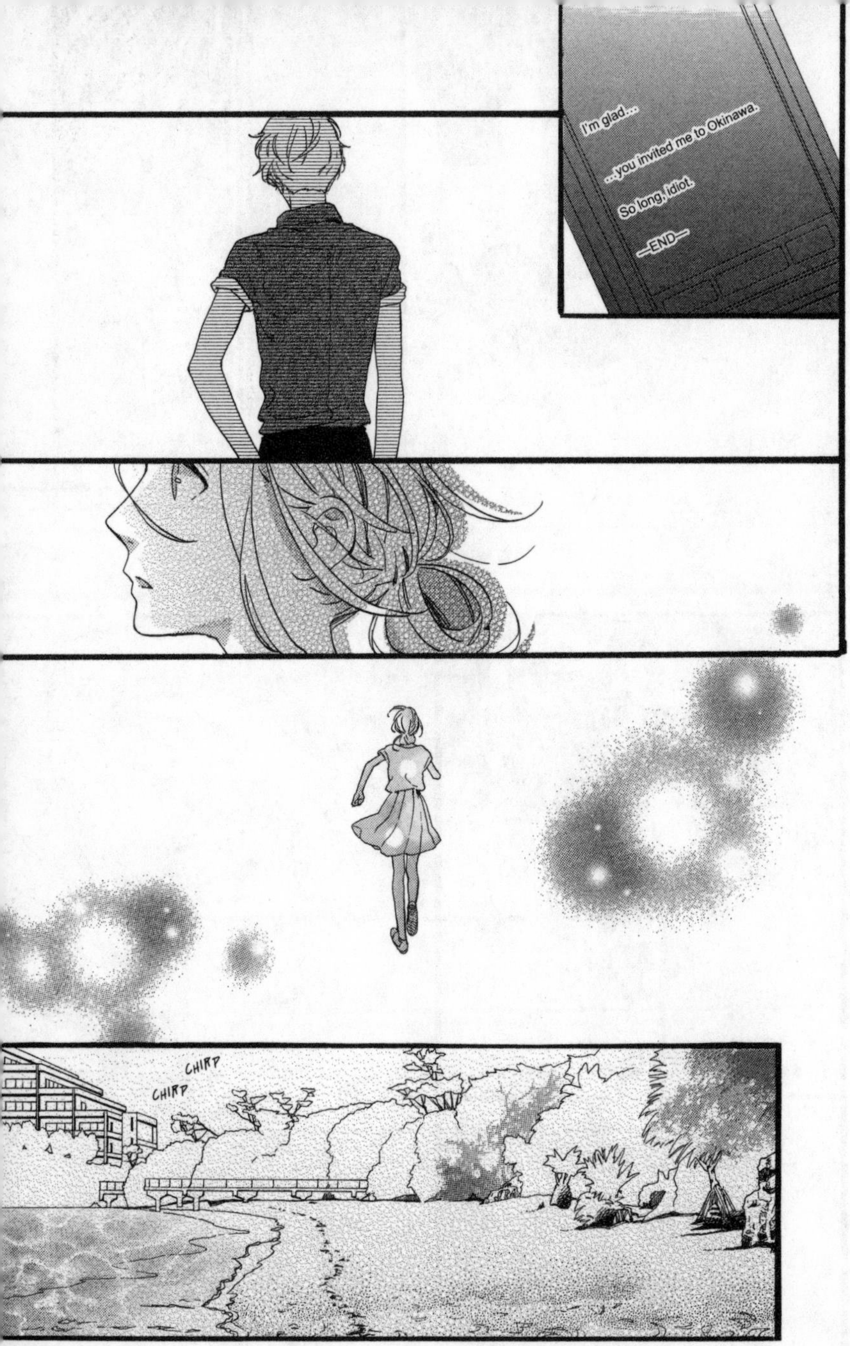
I'm glad...
...you invited me to Okinawa.
So long, idiot.
—END—
CHIRP
CHIRP

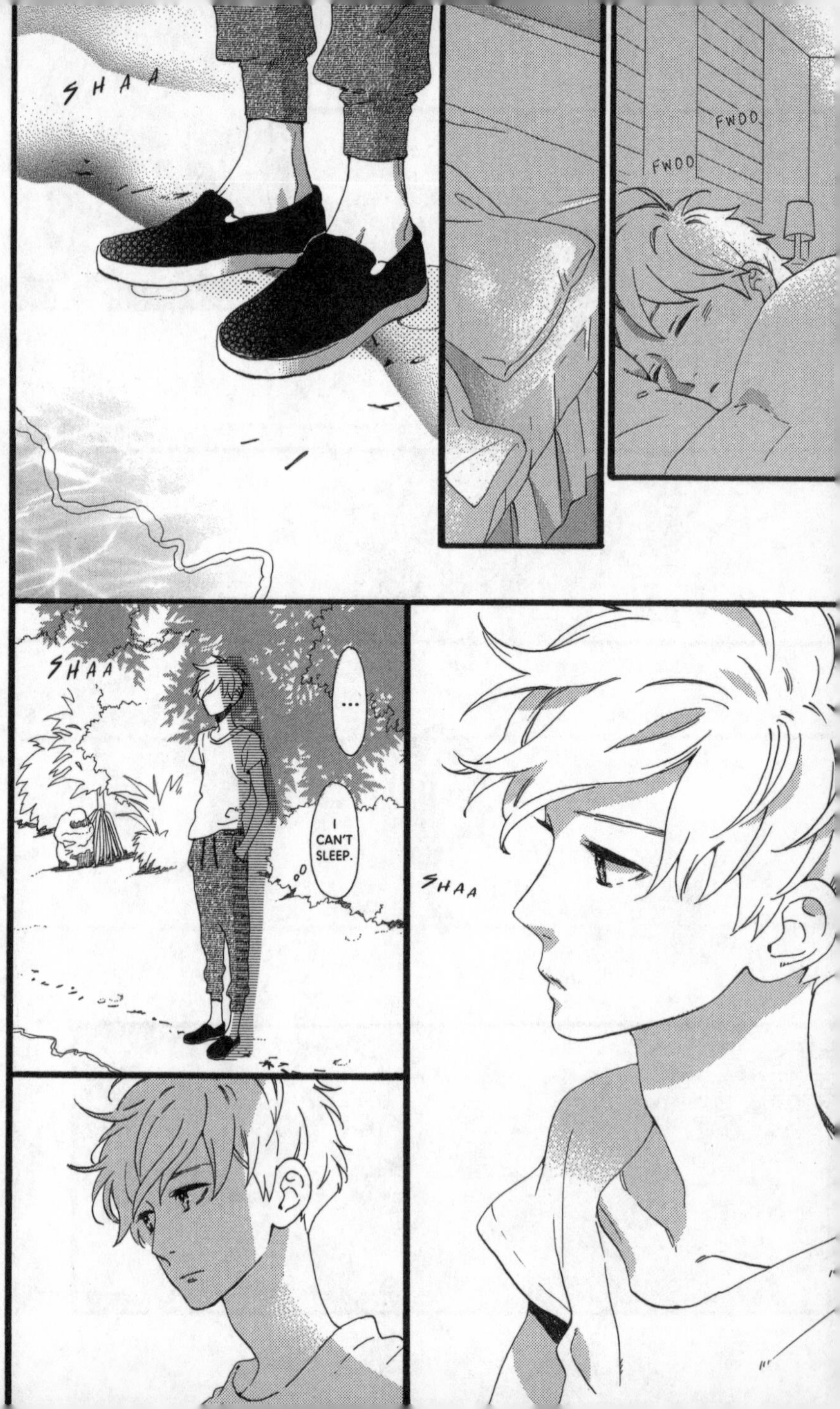
FWOO
FWOO
SHAA
SHAA
SHAA
...
I CAN'T SLEEP.

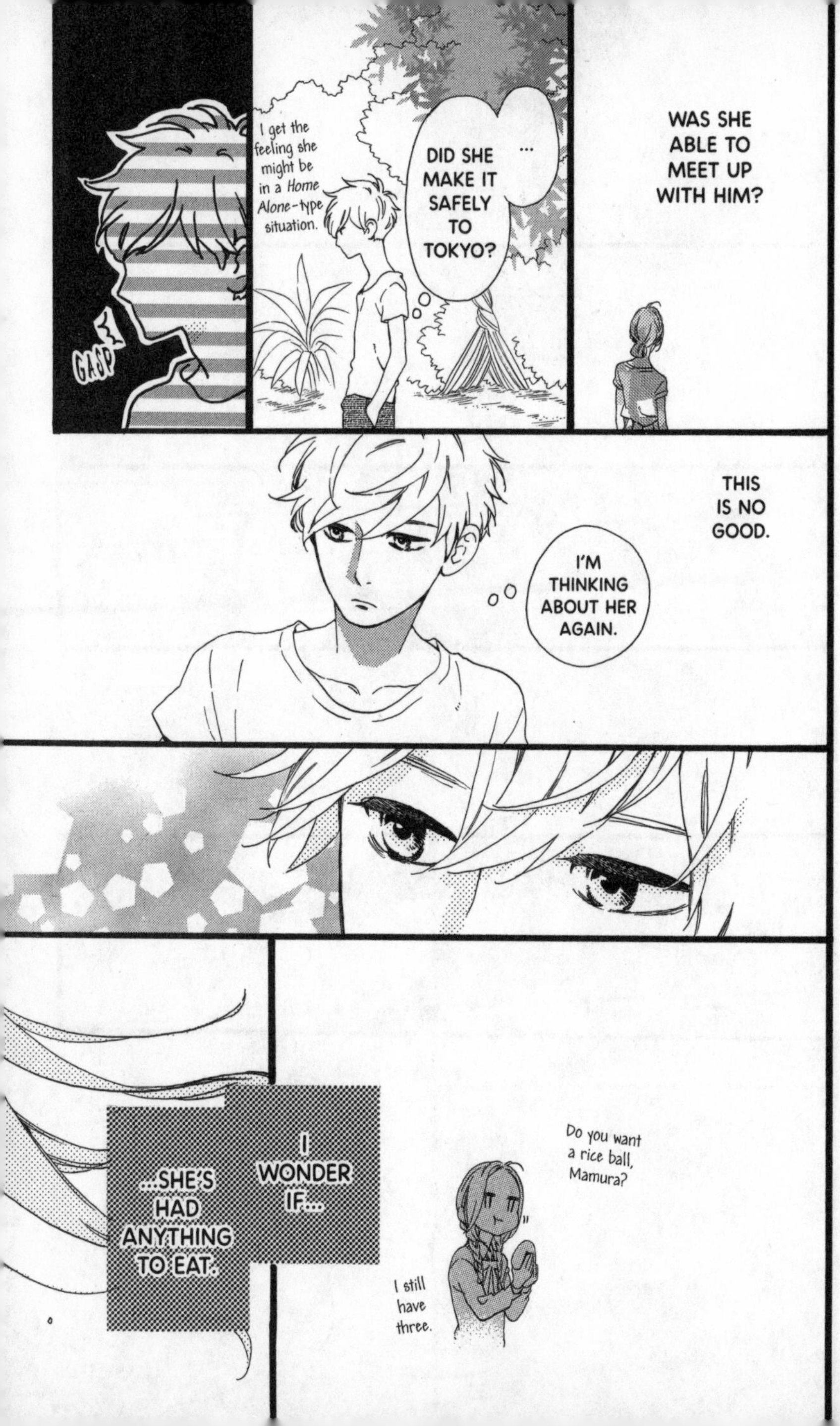

WAS SHE ABLE TO MEET UP WITH HIM?
...
DID SHE MAKE IT SAFELY TO TOKYO?
I get the feeling she might be in a *Home Alone*-type situation.
GASP
THIS IS NO GOOD.
I'M THINKING ABOUT HER AGAIN.
Do you want a rice ball, Mamura?
I still have three.
I WONDER IF...
...SHE'S HAD ANYTHING TO EAT.

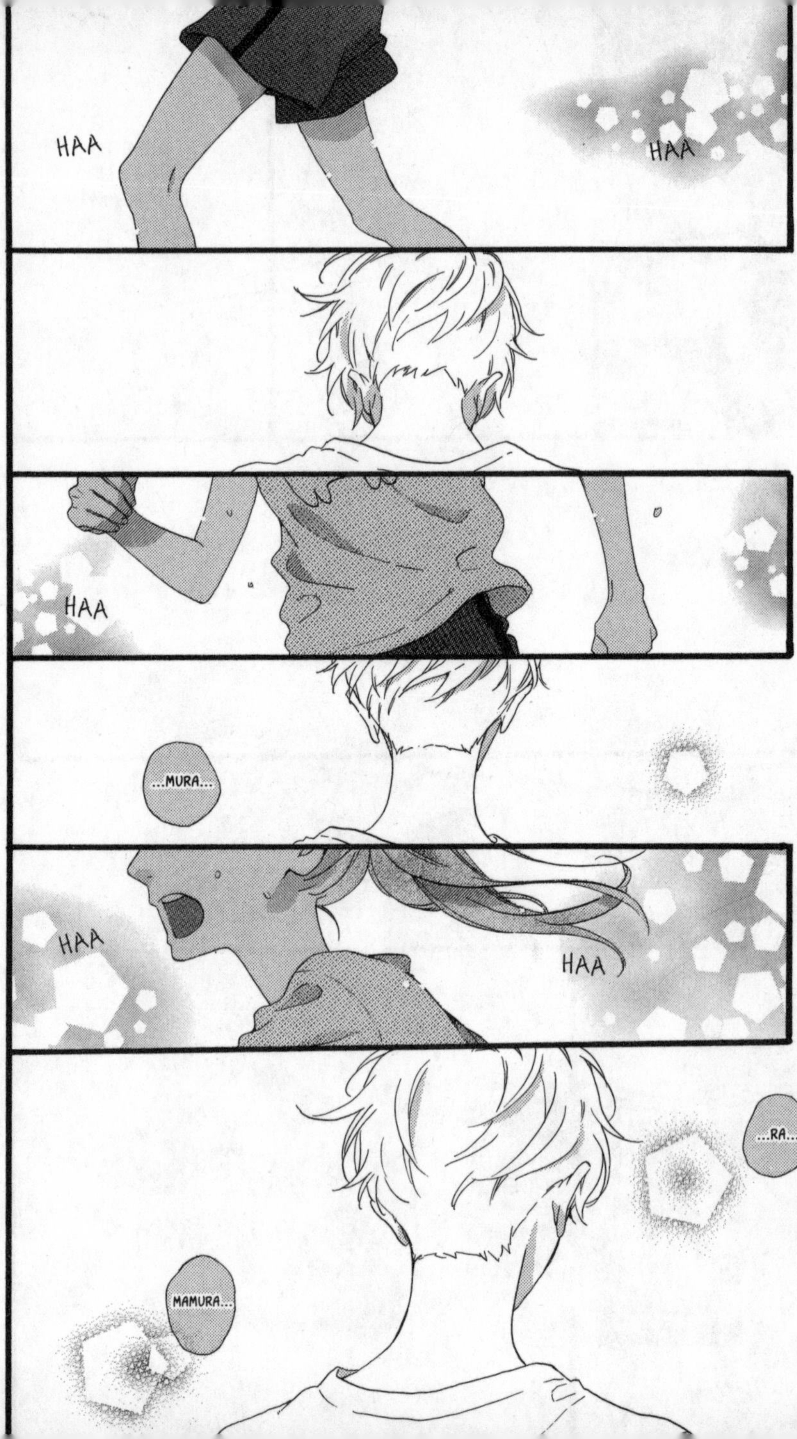
HAA
HAA
HAA
...MURA...
HAA
HAA
...RA...
MAMURA...

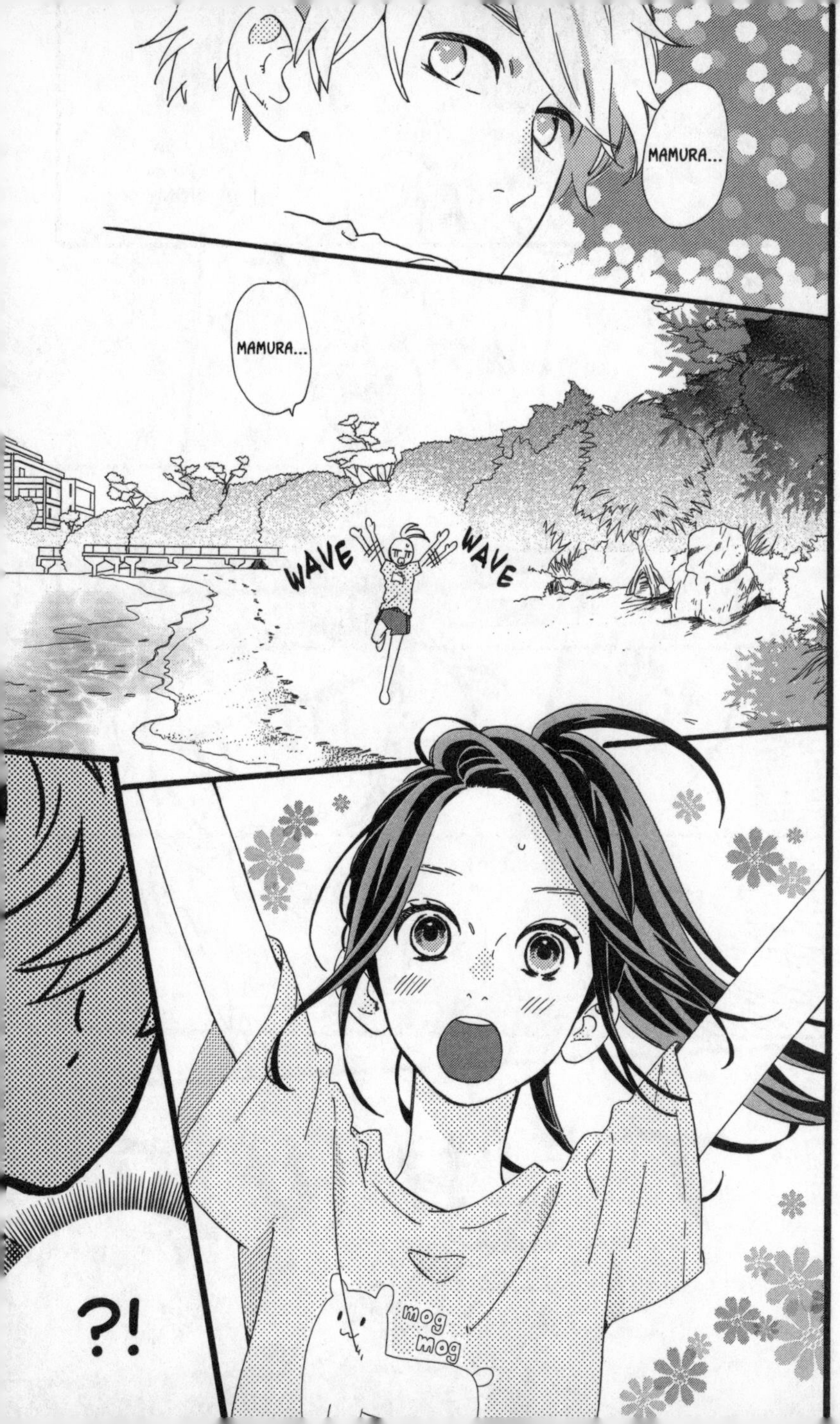
MAMURA...
MAMURA...
WAVE
WAVE
?!
mog
mog

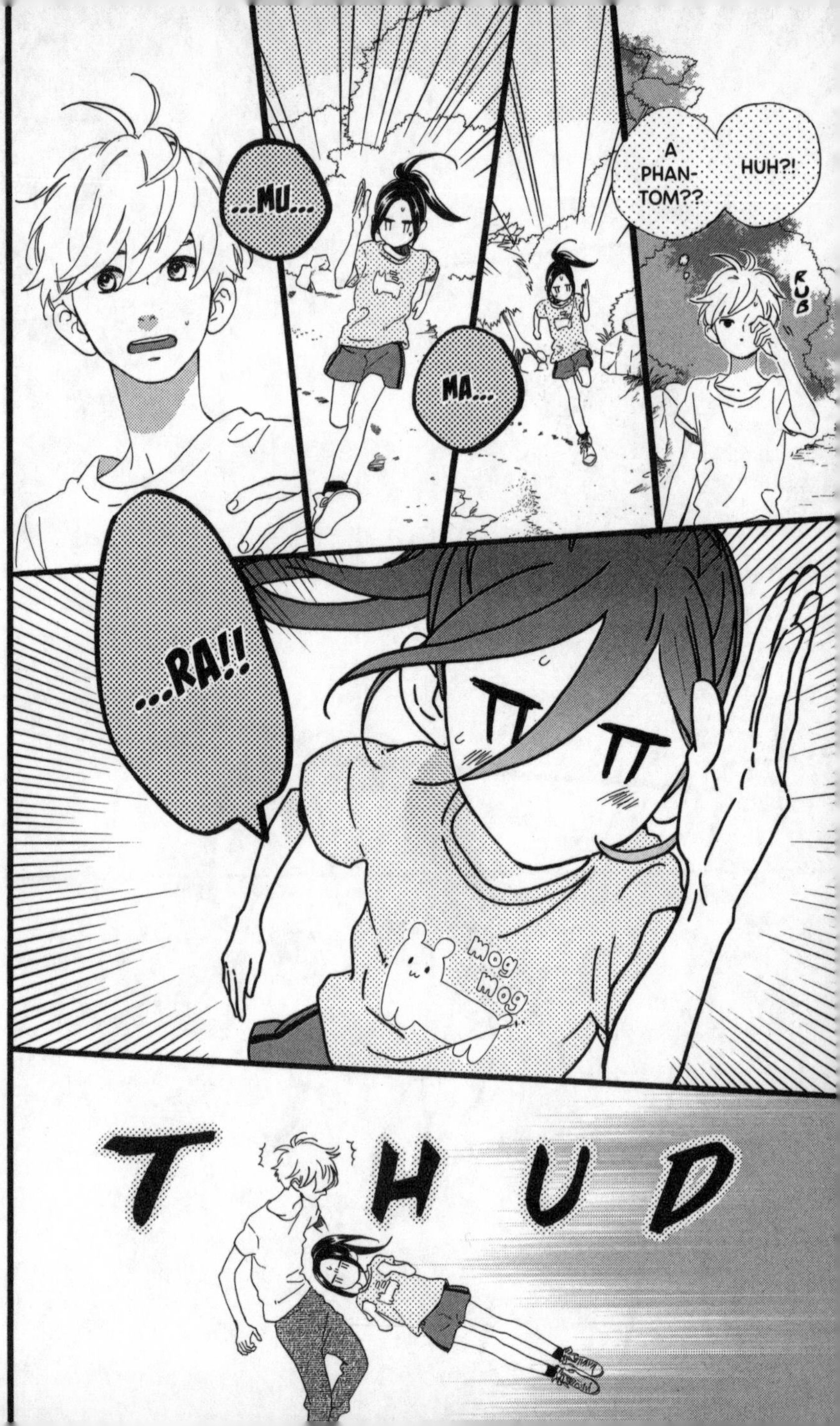
HUH?!
A PHANTOM??
RUB
MA...
...MU...
...RA!!
mog mog
THUD

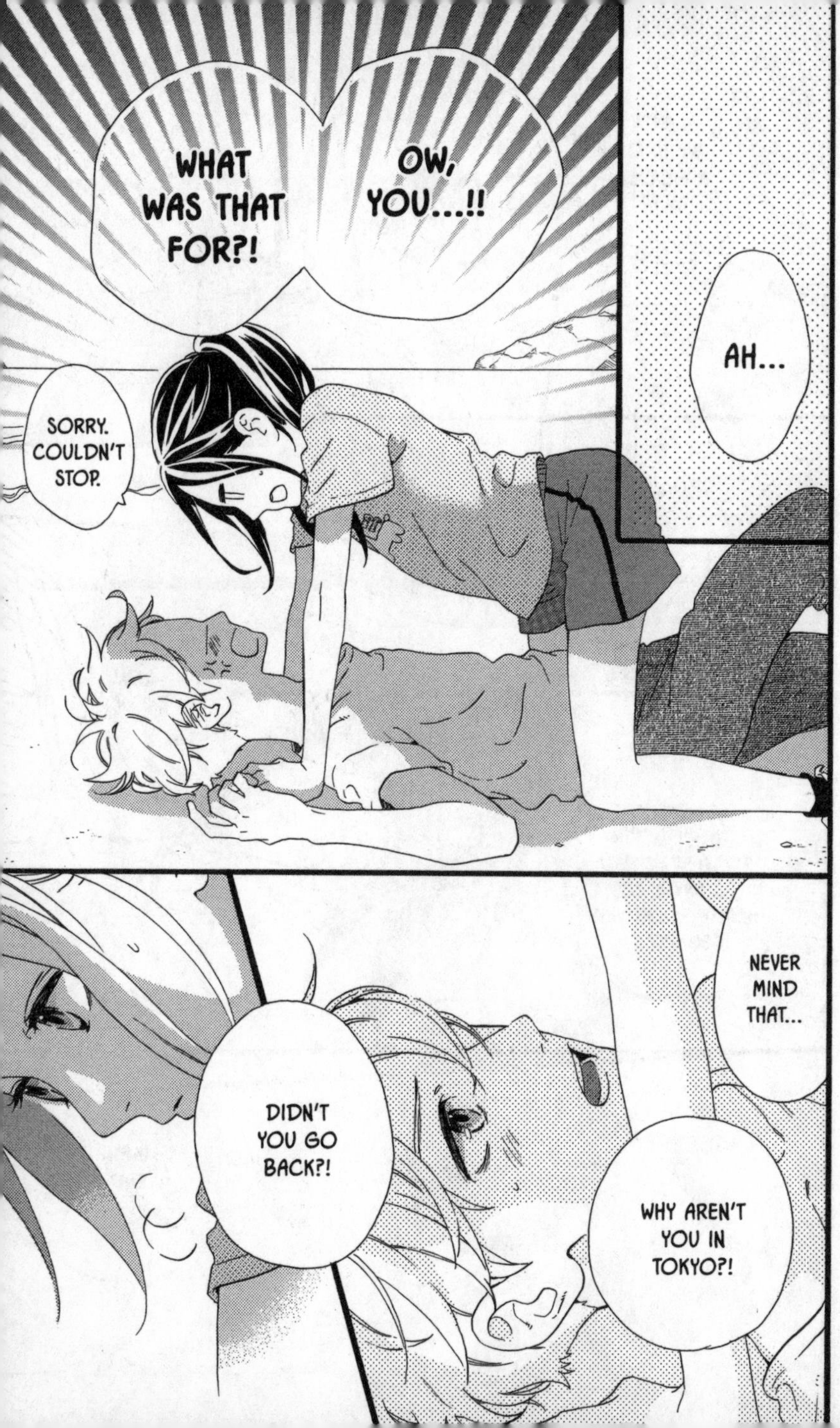
AH...
OW, YOU...!!
WHAT WAS THAT FOR?!
SORRY. COULDN'T STOP.
NEVER MIND THAT...
WHY AREN'T YOU IN TOKYO?!
DIDN'T YOU GO BACK?!

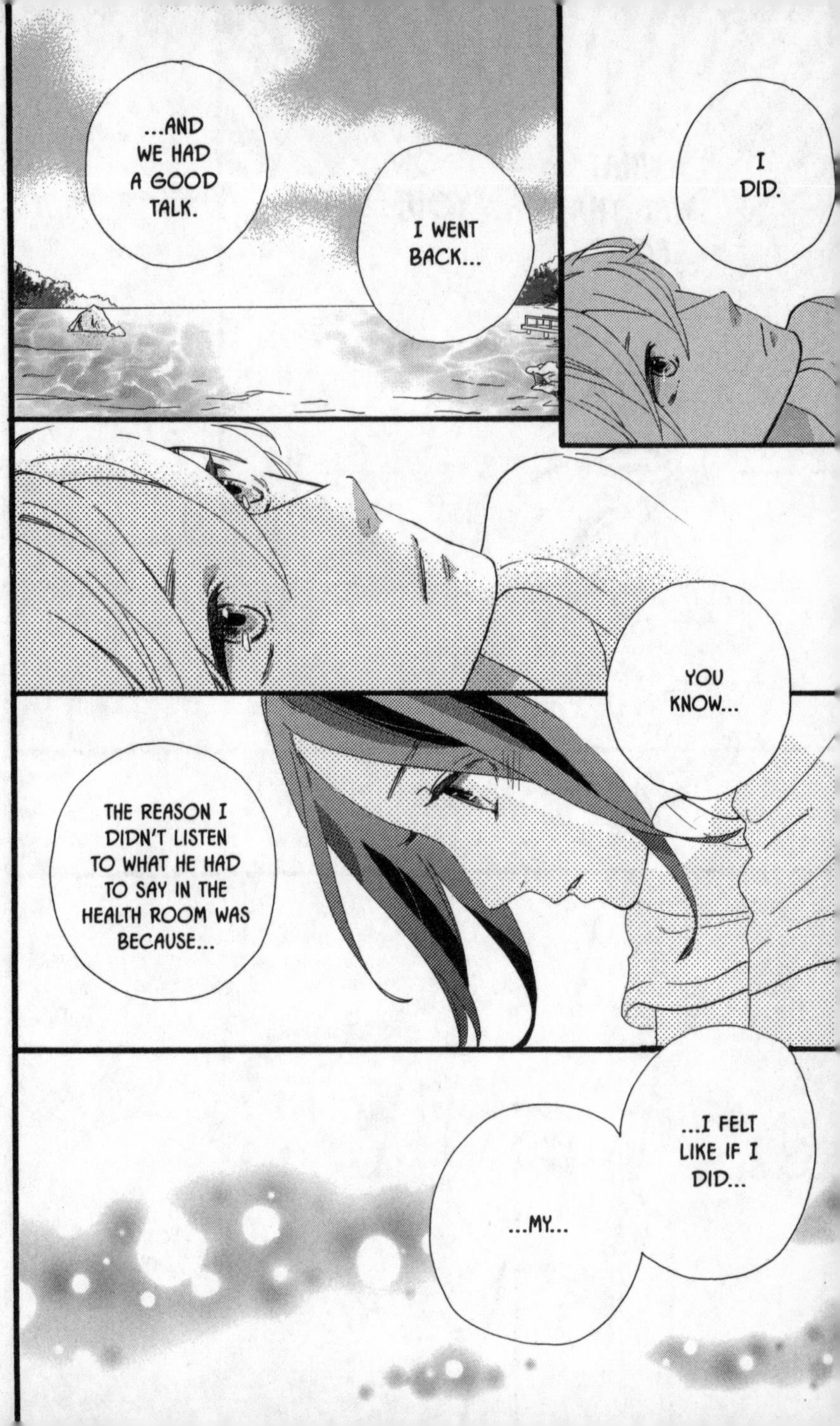
I DID.
I WENT BACK...
...AND WE HAD A GOOD TALK.
YOU KNOW...
THE REASON I DIDN'T LISTEN TO WHAT HE HAD TO SAY IN THE HEALTH ROOM WAS BECAUSE...
...I FELT LIKE IF I DID...
...MY...

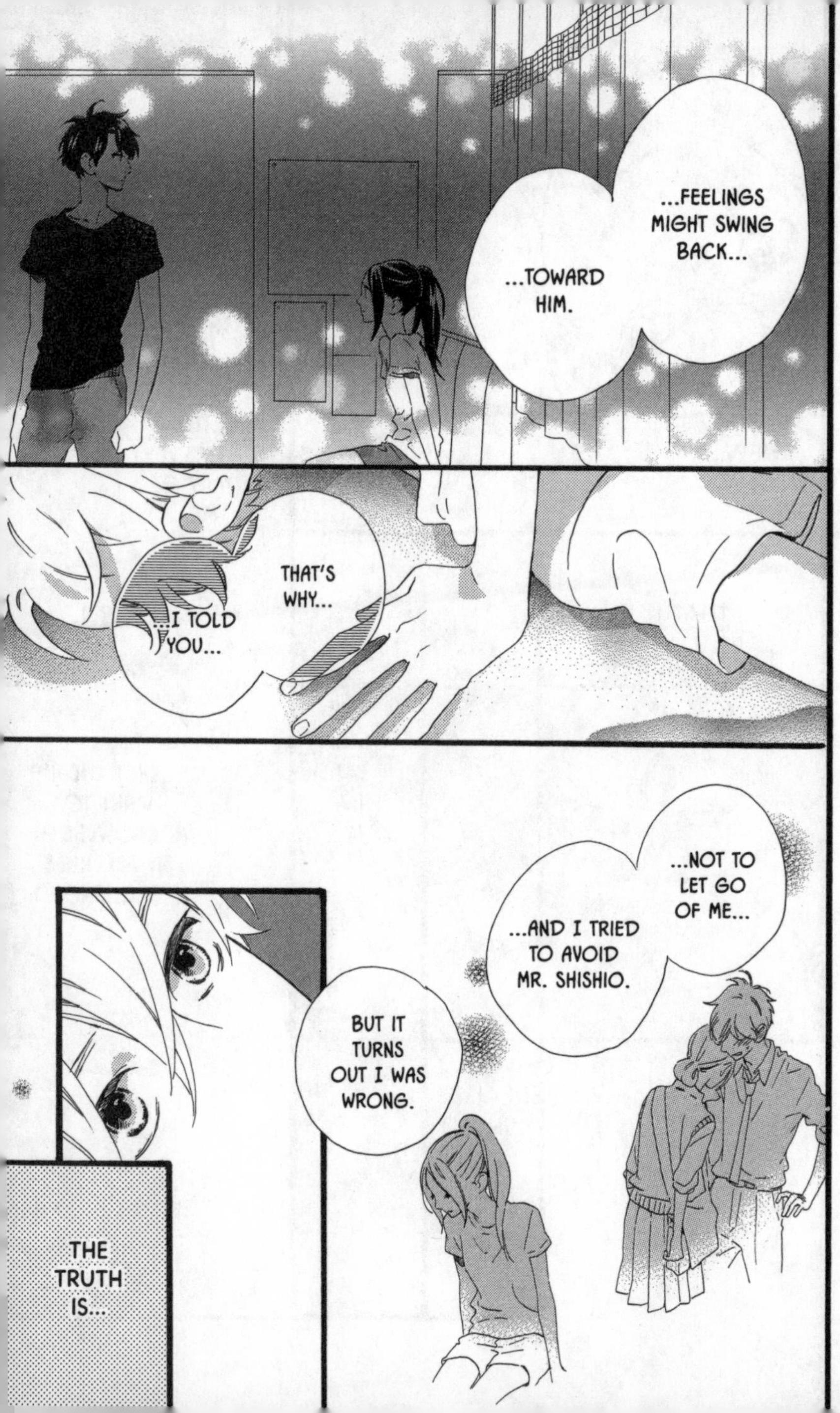
...FEELINGS MIGHT SWING BACK...
...TOWARD HIM.
THAT'S WHY...
...I TOLD YOU...
...NOT TO LET GO OF ME...
...AND I TRIED TO AVOID MR. SHISHIO.
BUT IT TURNS OUT I WAS WRONG.
THE TRUTH IS...

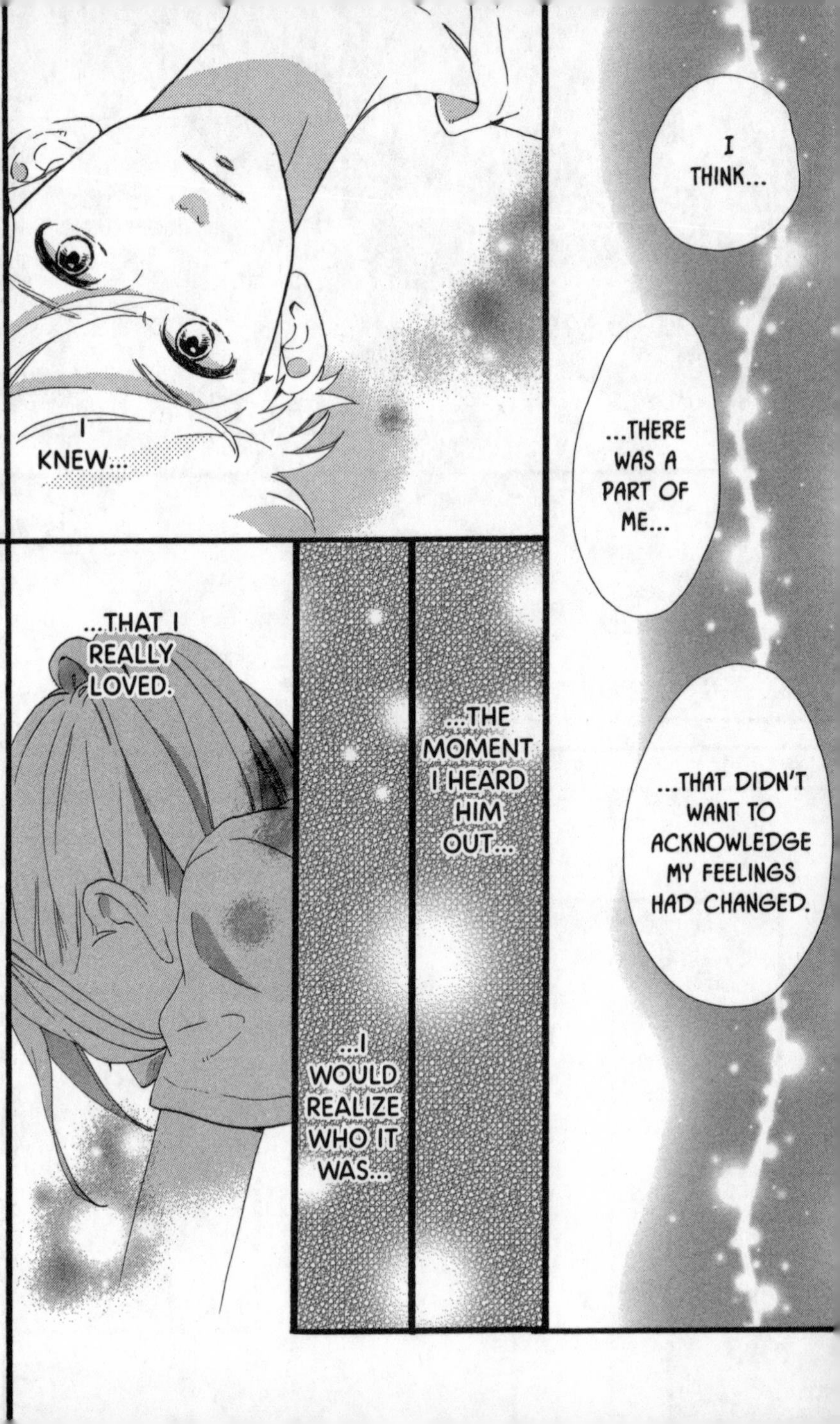
I THINK...
...THERE WAS A PART OF ME...
...THAT DIDN'T WANT TO ACKNOWLEDGE MY FEELINGS HAD CHANGED.
I KNEW...
...THE MOMENT I HEARD HIM OUT...
...I WOULD REALIZE WHO IT WAS...
...THAT I REALLY LOVED.

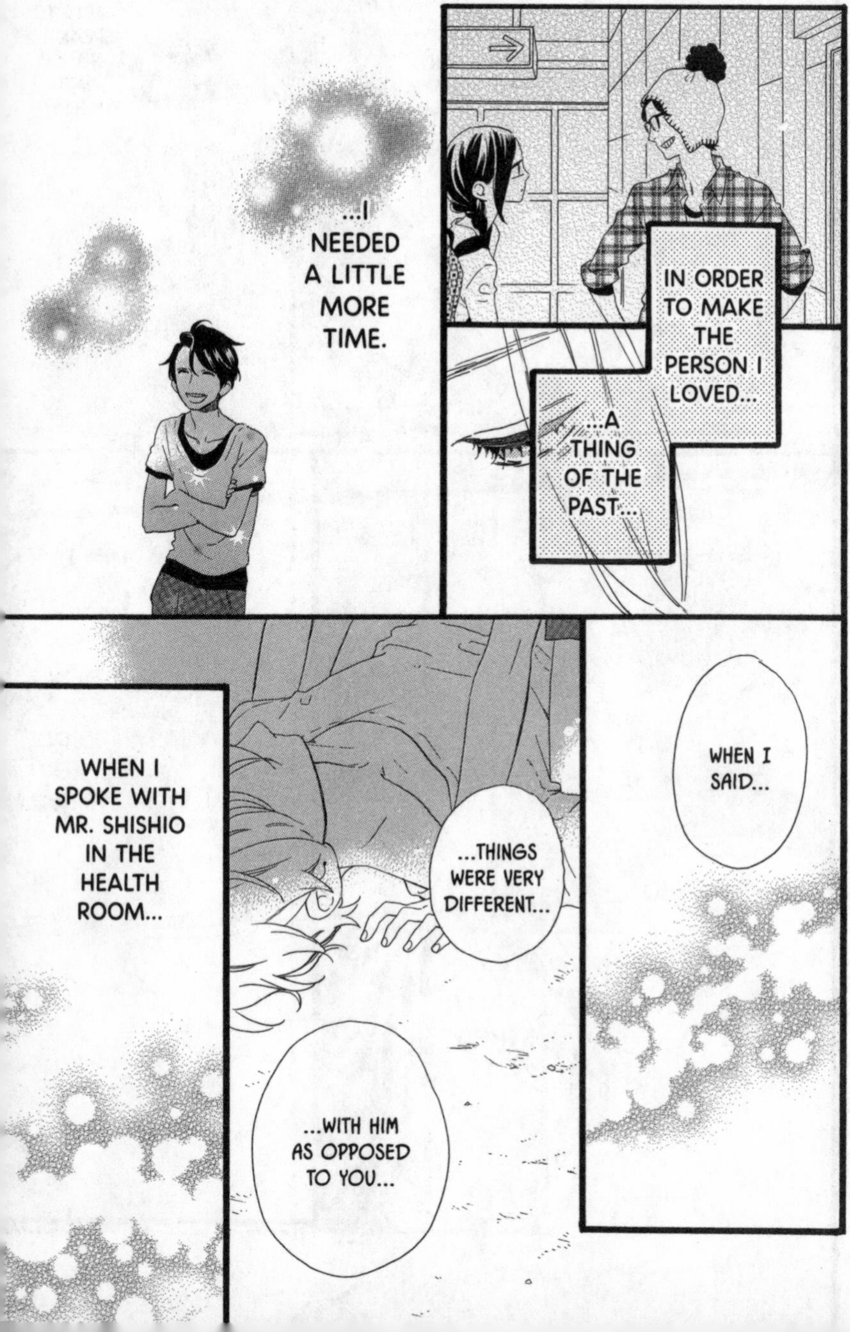

IN ORDER TO MAKE THE PERSON I LOVED...
...A THING OF THE PAST...
...I NEEDED A LITTLE MORE TIME.
WHEN I SAID...
...THINGS WERE VERY DIFFERENT...
...WITH HIM AS OPPOSED TO YOU...
WHEN I SPOKE WITH MR. SHISHIO IN THE HEALTH ROOM...

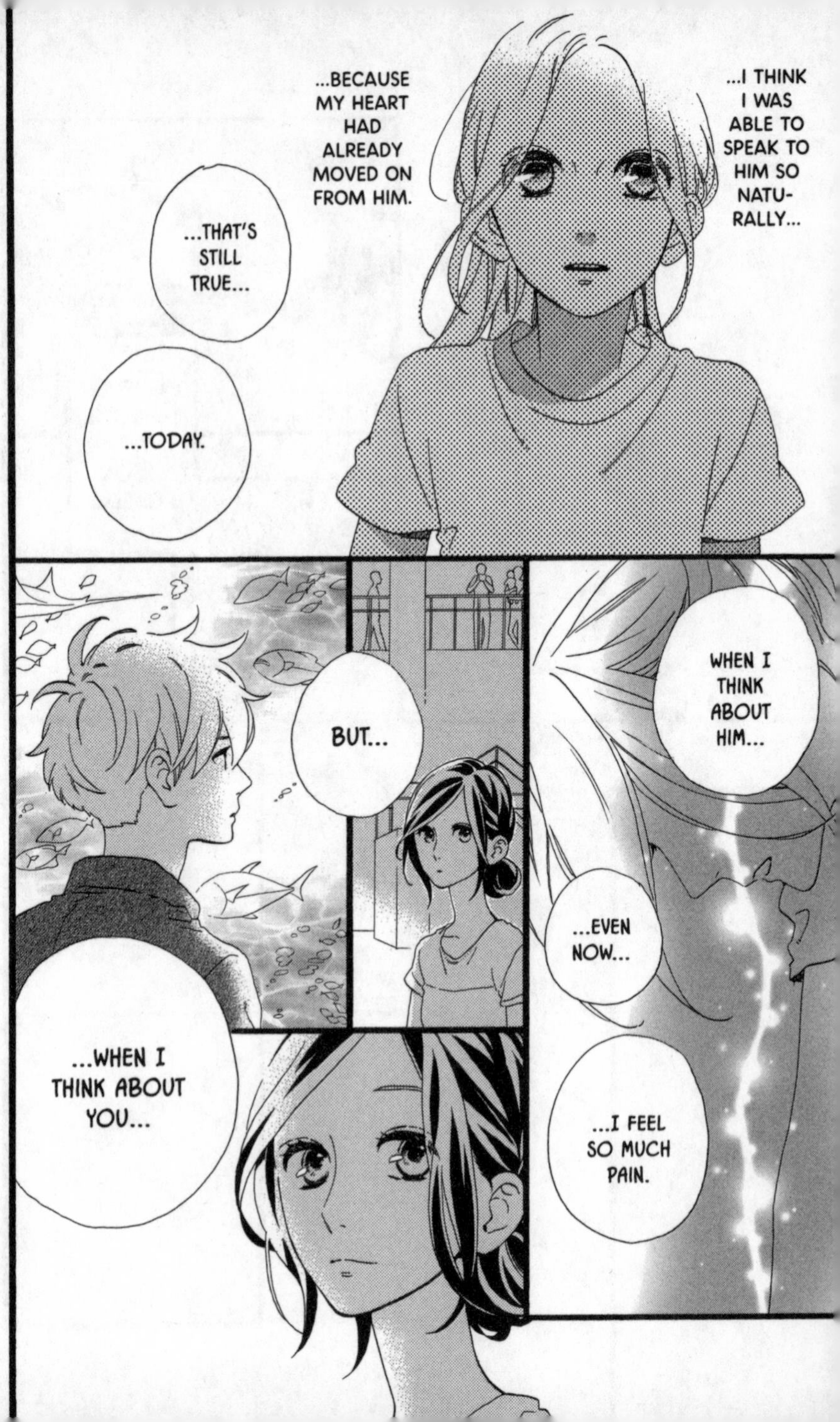
...I THINK I WAS ABLE TO SPEAK TO HIM SO NATURALLY...
...BECAUSE MY HEART HAD ALREADY MOVED ON FROM HIM.
...THAT'S STILL TRUE...
...TODAY.
WHEN I THINK ABOUT HIM...
...EVEN NOW...
...I FEEL SO MUCH PAIN.
BUT...
...WHEN I THINK ABOUT YOU...

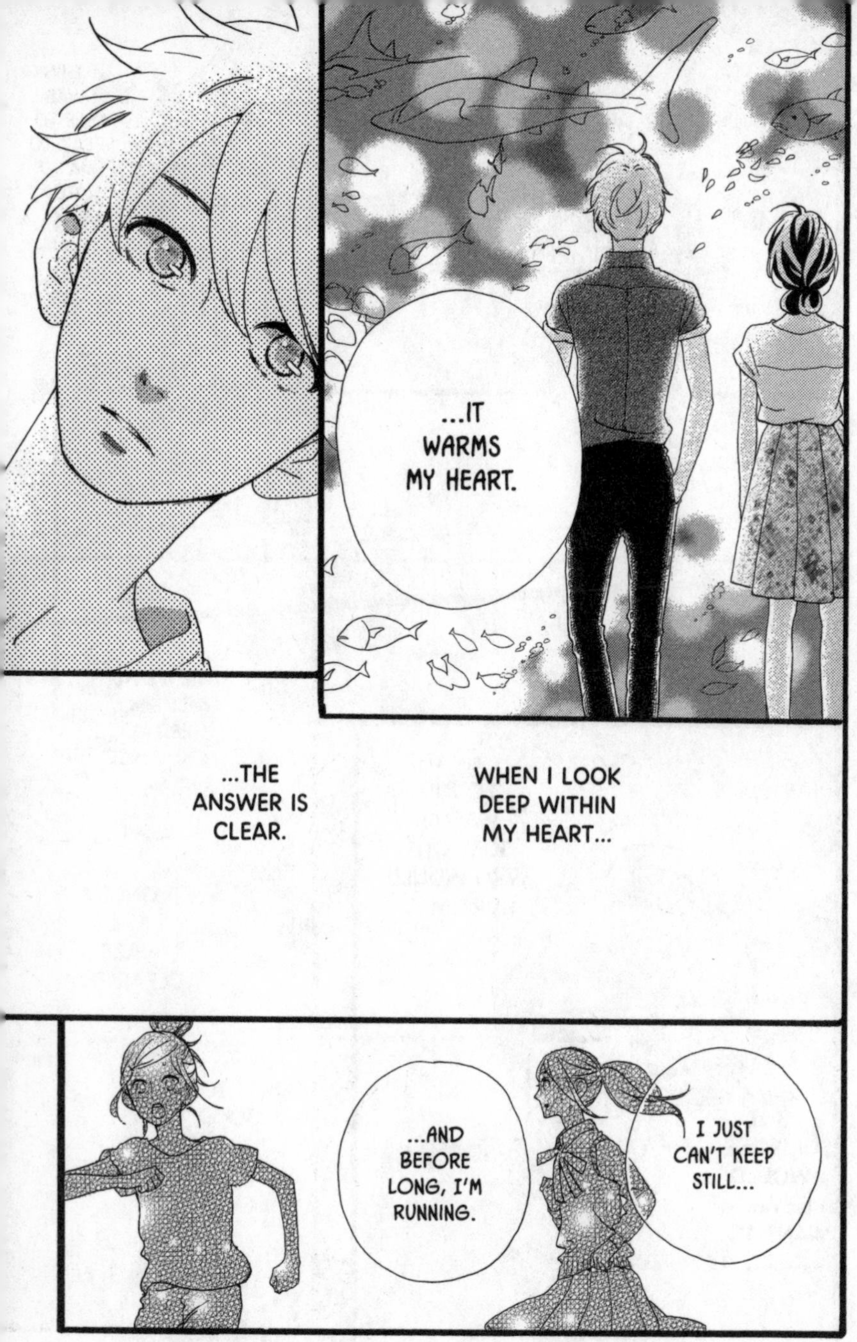
...IT WARMS MY HEART.
WHEN I LOOK DEEP WITHIN MY HEART...
...THE ANSWER IS CLEAR.
I JUST CAN'T KEEP STILL...
...AND BEFORE LONG, I'M RUNNING.

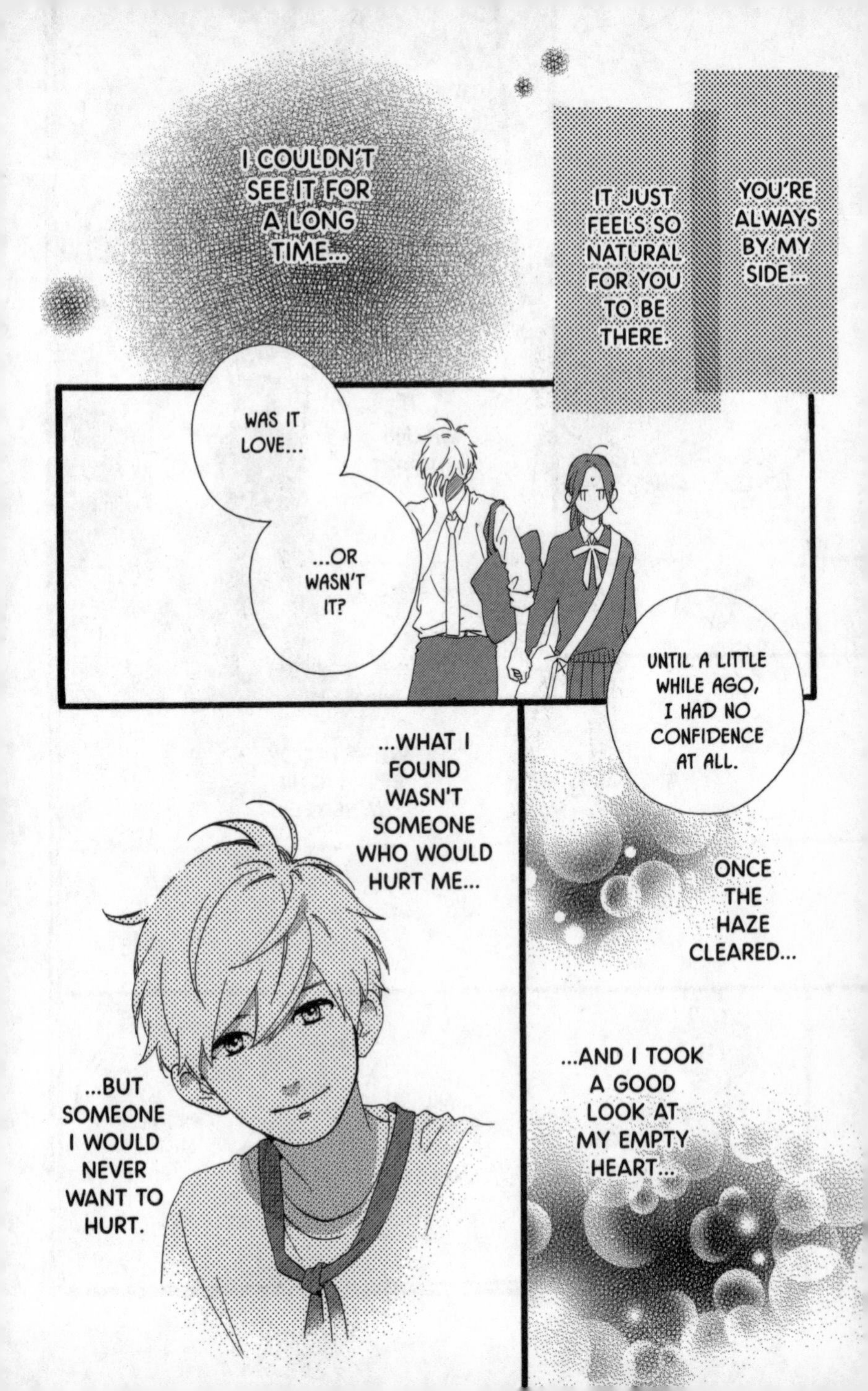

YOU'RE ALWAYS BY MY SIDE...
IT JUST FEELS SO NATURAL FOR YOU TO BE THERE.
I COULDN'T SEE IT FOR A LONG TIME...
WAS IT LOVE...
...OR WASN'T IT?
UNTIL A LITTLE WHILE AGO, I HAD NO CONFIDENCE AT ALL.
ONCE THE HAZE CLEARED...
...AND I TOOK A GOOD LOOK AT MY EMPTY HEART...
...WHAT I FOUND WASN'T SOMEONE WHO WOULD HURT ME...
...BUT SOMEONE I WOULD NEVER WANT TO HURT.

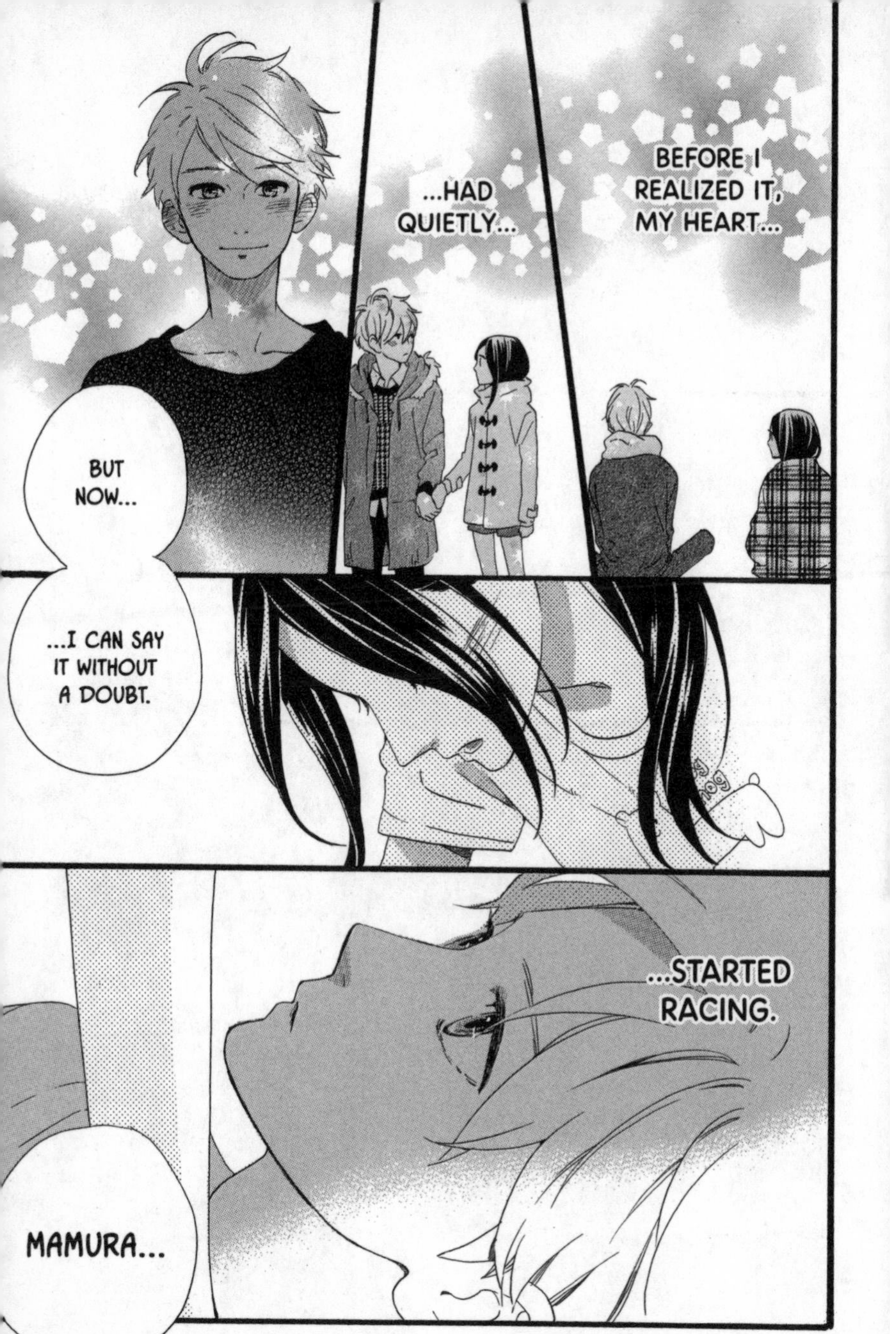
BEFORE I REALIZED IT, MY HEART...
...HAD QUIETLY...
BUT NOW...
...I CAN SAY IT WITHOUT A DOUBT.
...STARTED RACING.
MAMURA...

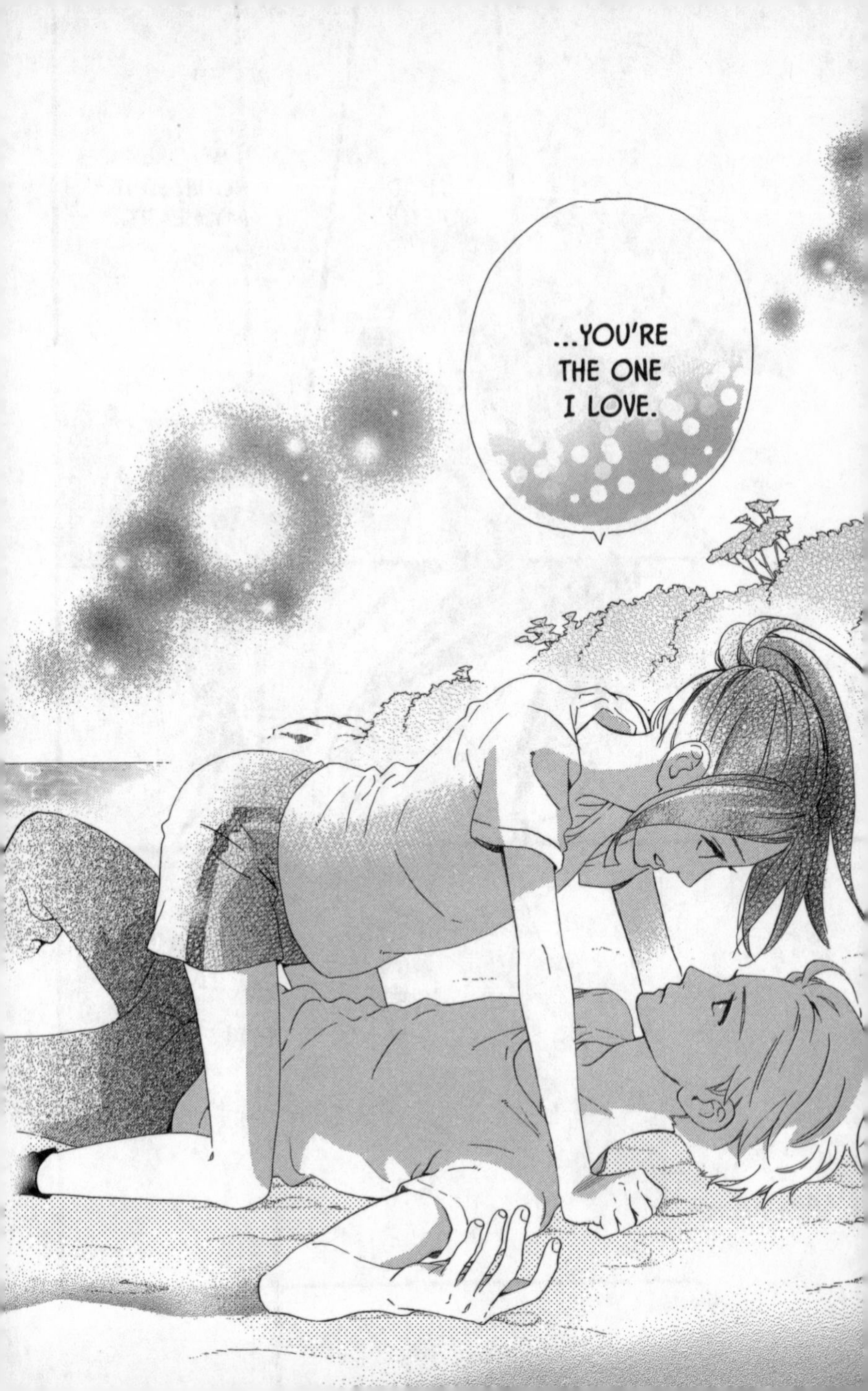
...YOU'RE THE ONE I LOVE.

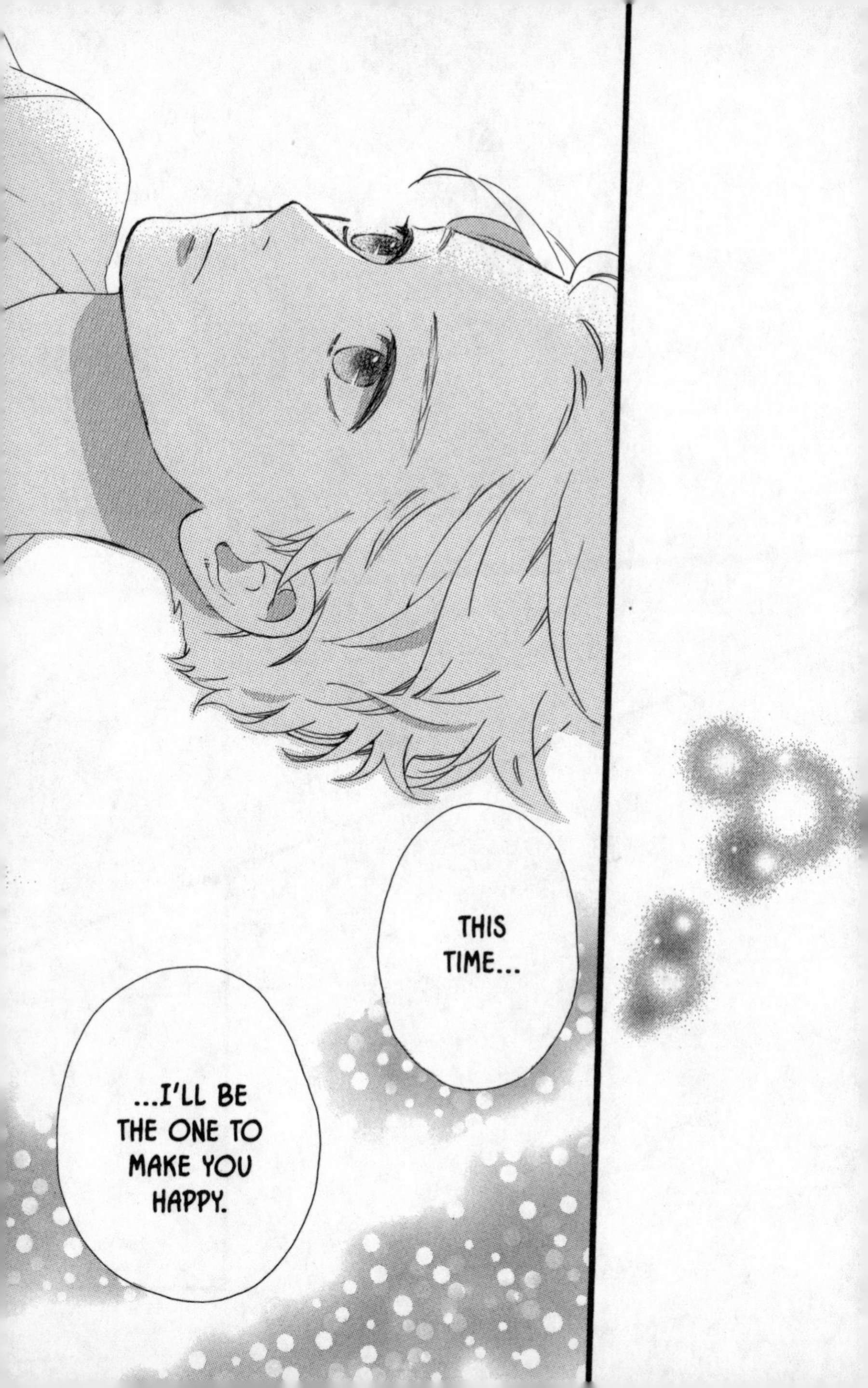
THIS TIME...
...I'LL BE THE ONE TO MAKE YOU HAPPY.

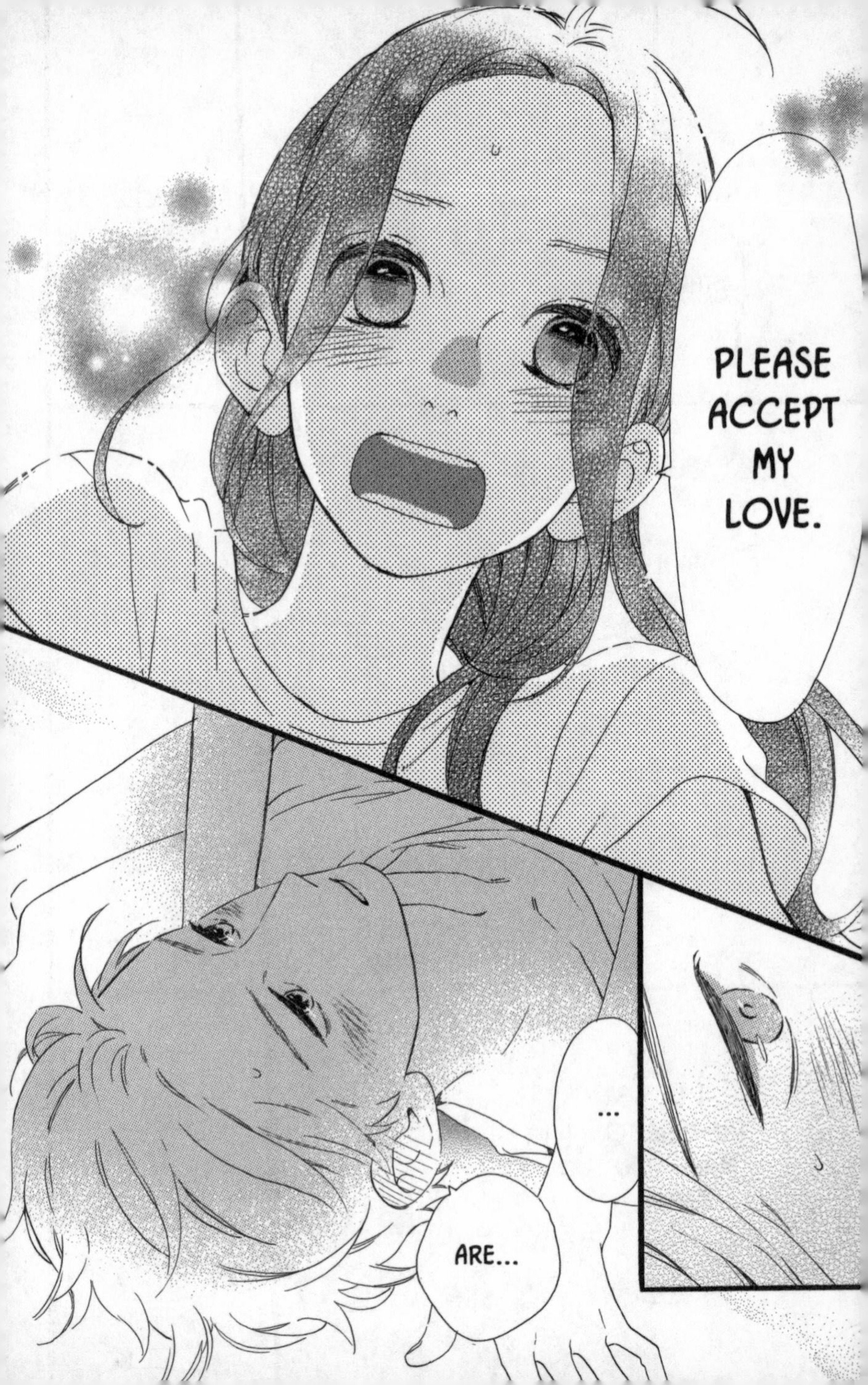
PLEASE ACCEPT MY LOVE.
...
ARE...

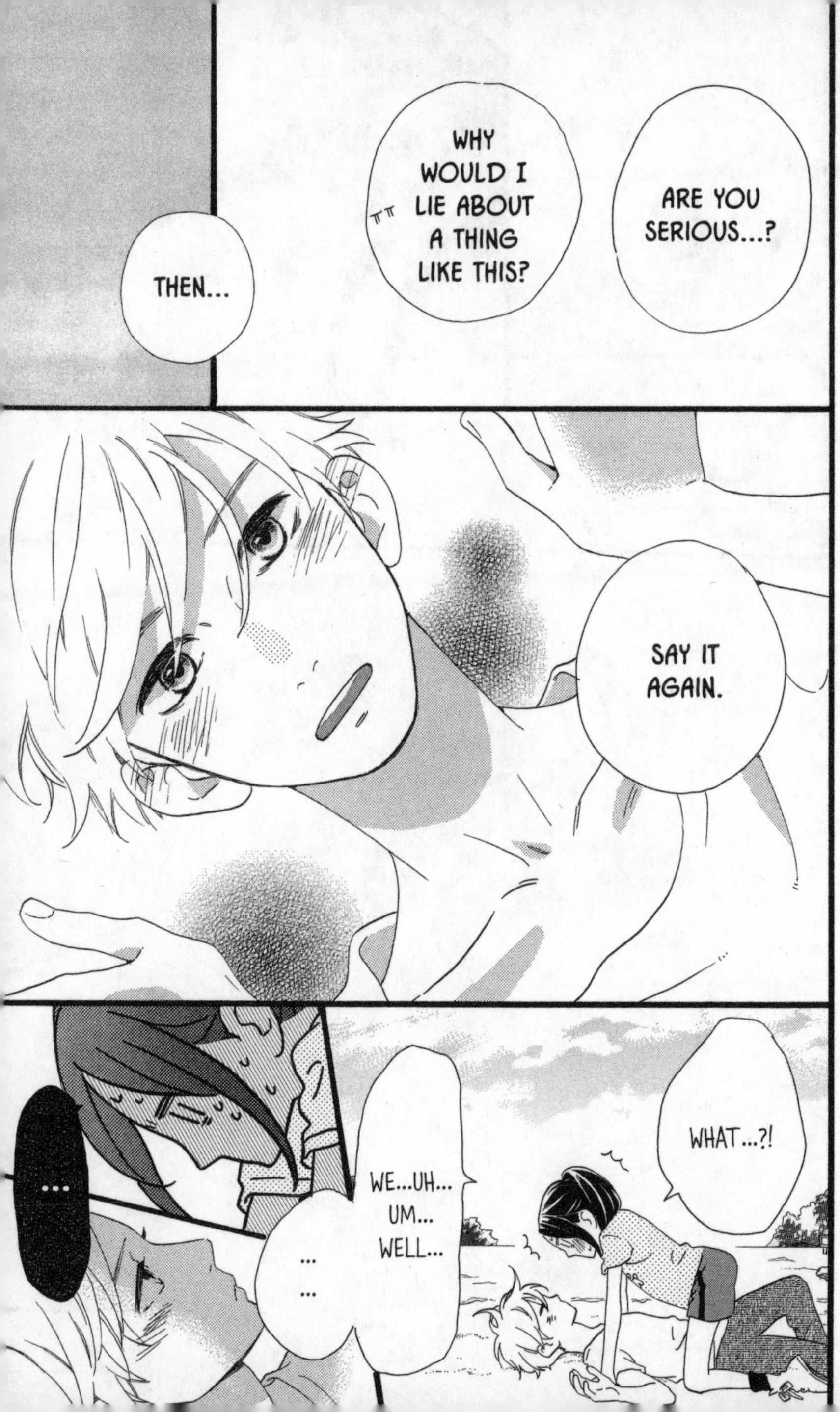
ARE YOU SERIOUS...?
WHY WOULD I LIE ABOUT A THING LIKE THIS?
THEN...
SAY IT AGAIN.
WHAT...?!
WE...UH... UM... WELL...
... ...
...

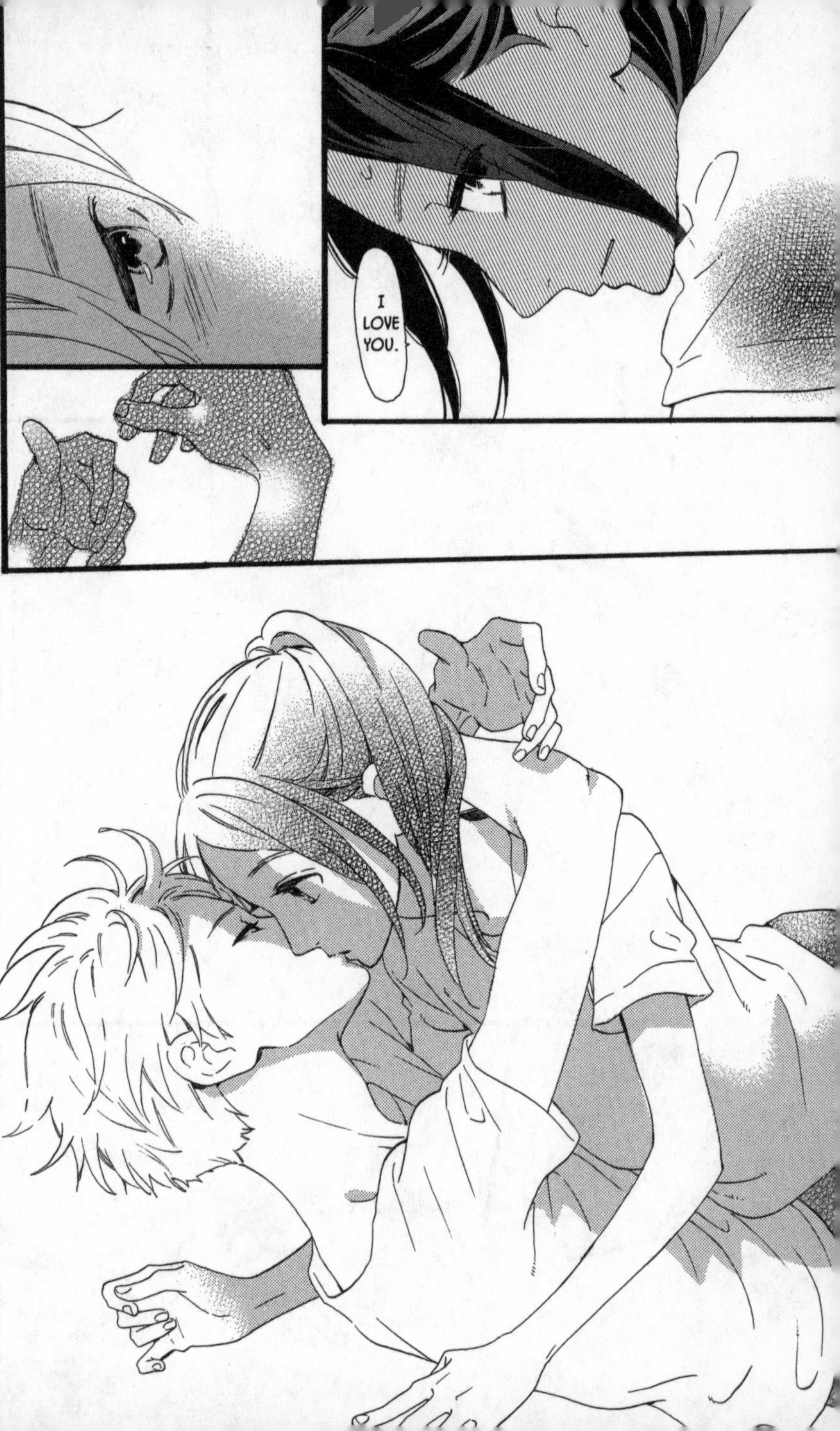
I LOVE YOU.

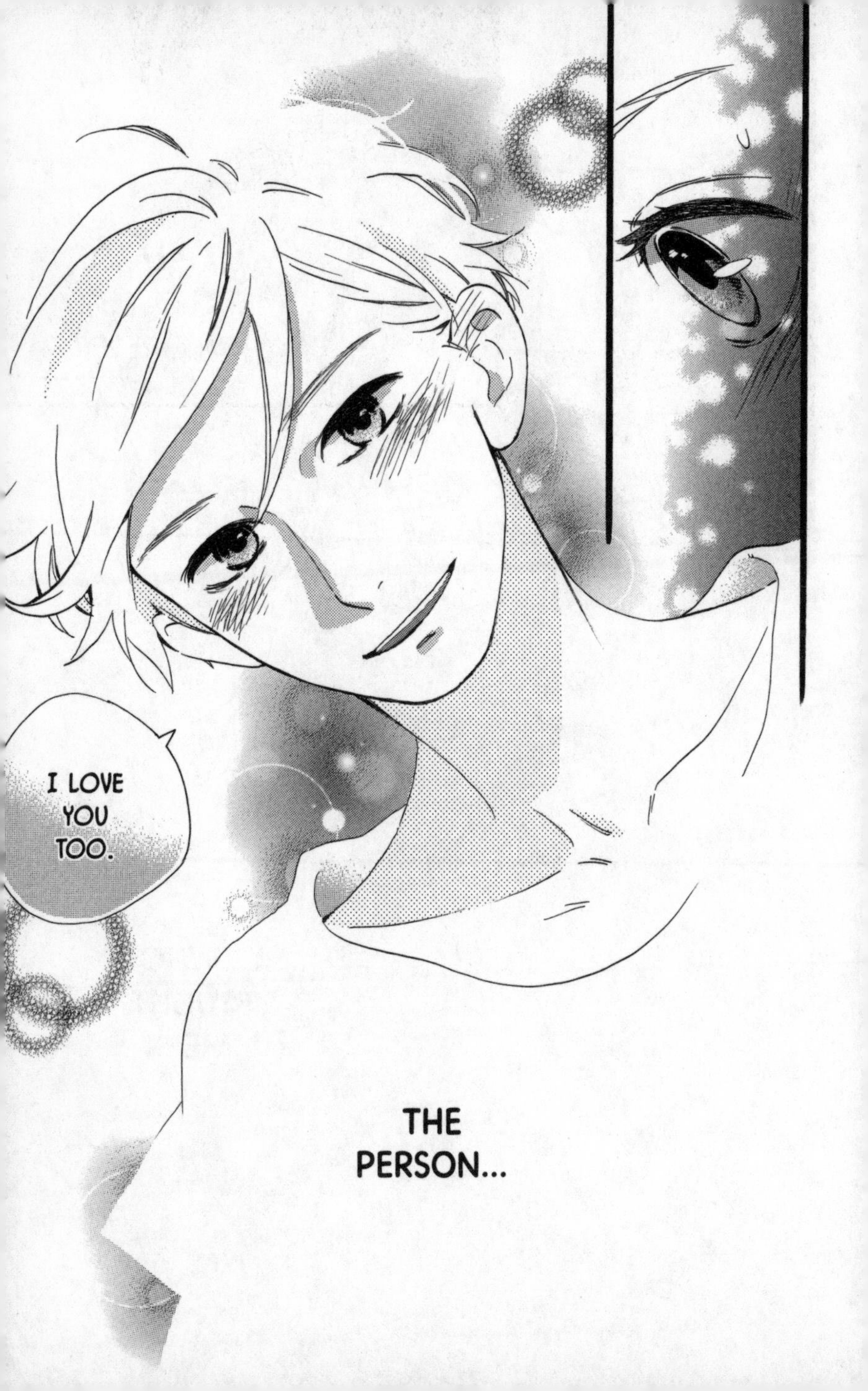
I LOVE YOU TOO.
THE PERSON...

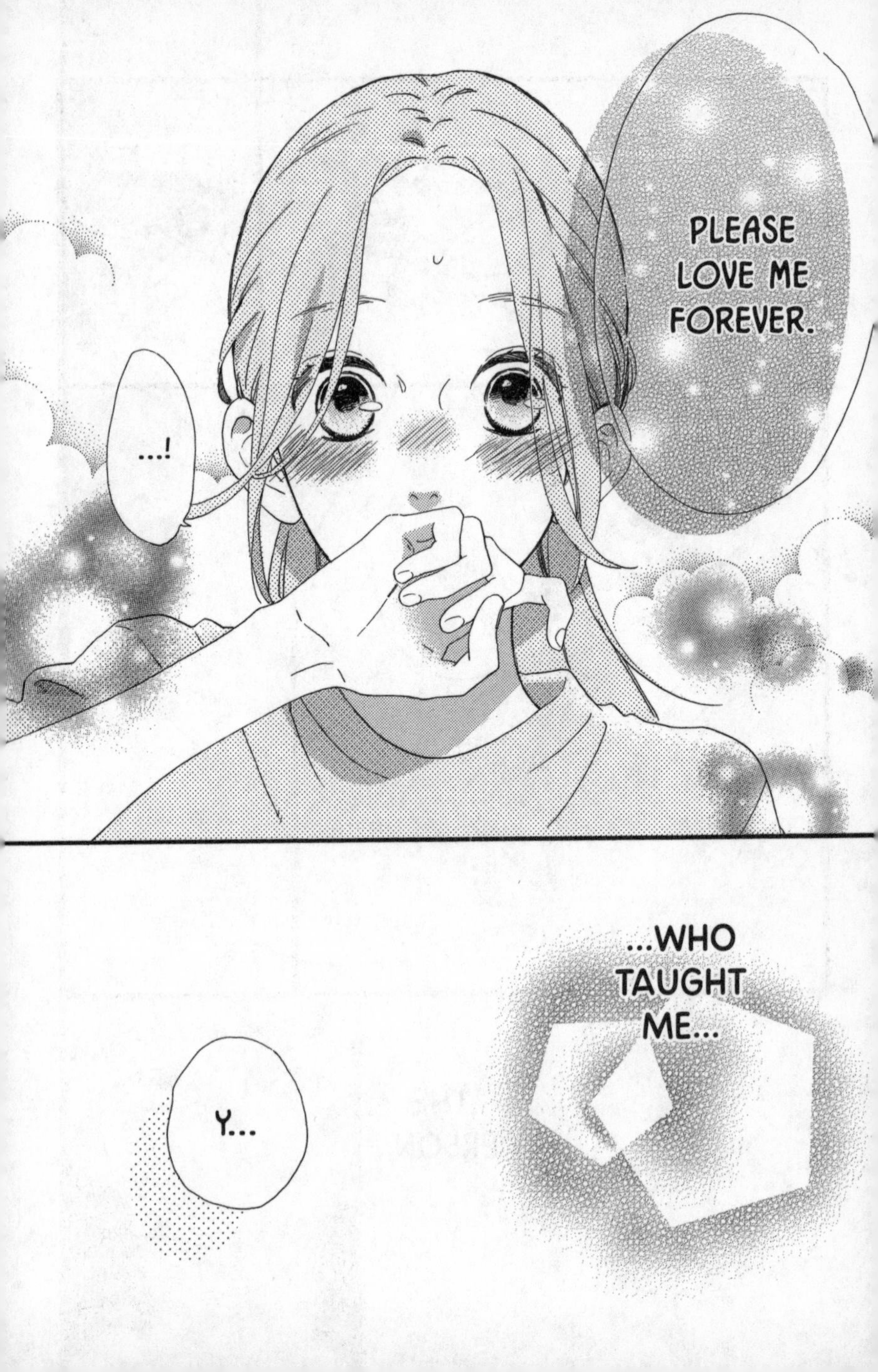
PLEASE LOVE ME FOREVER.
...!
...WHO TAUGHT ME...
Y...

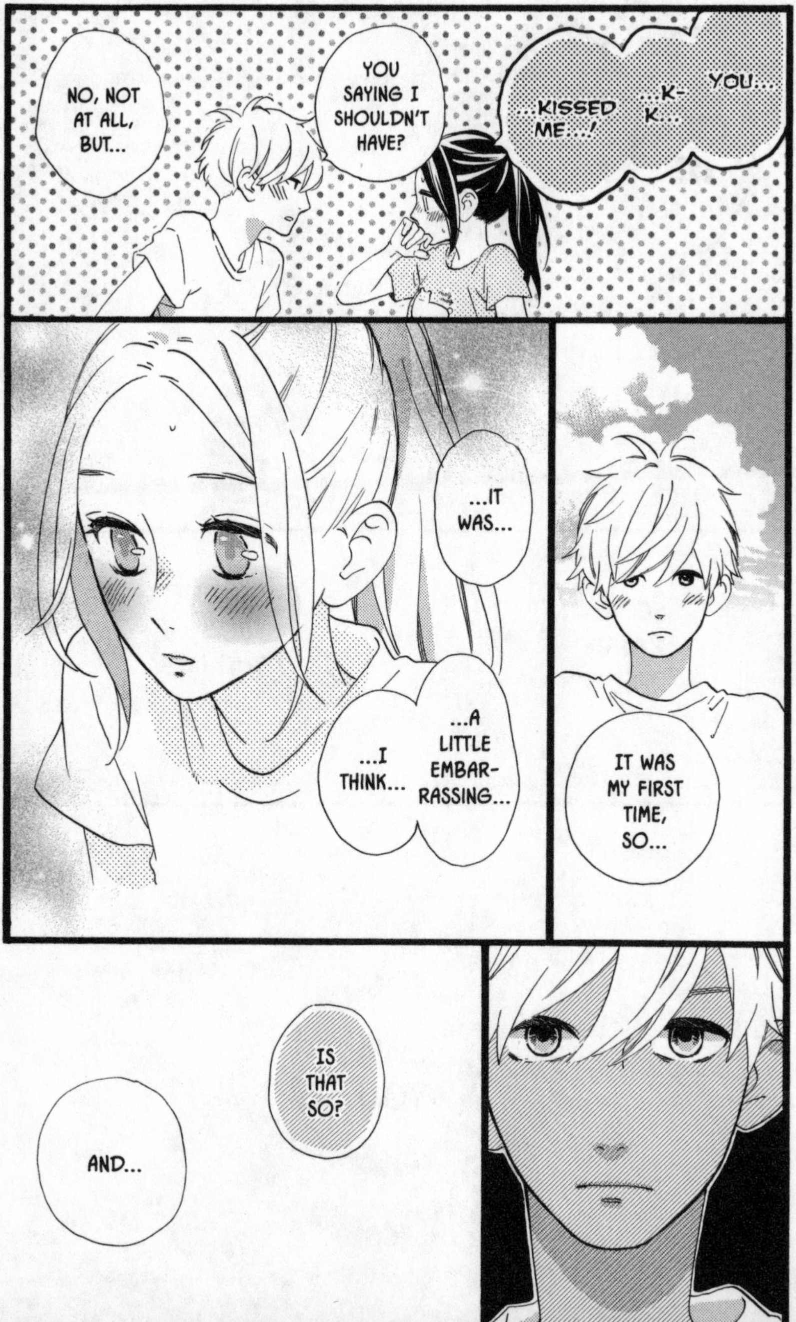
YOU...
...K- K...
...KISSED ME...!
YOU SAYING I SHOULDN'T HAVE?
NO, NOT AT ALL, BUT...
IT WAS MY FIRST TIME, SO...
...IT WAS...
...A LITTLE EMBARRASSING...
...I THINK...
IS THAT SO?
AND...

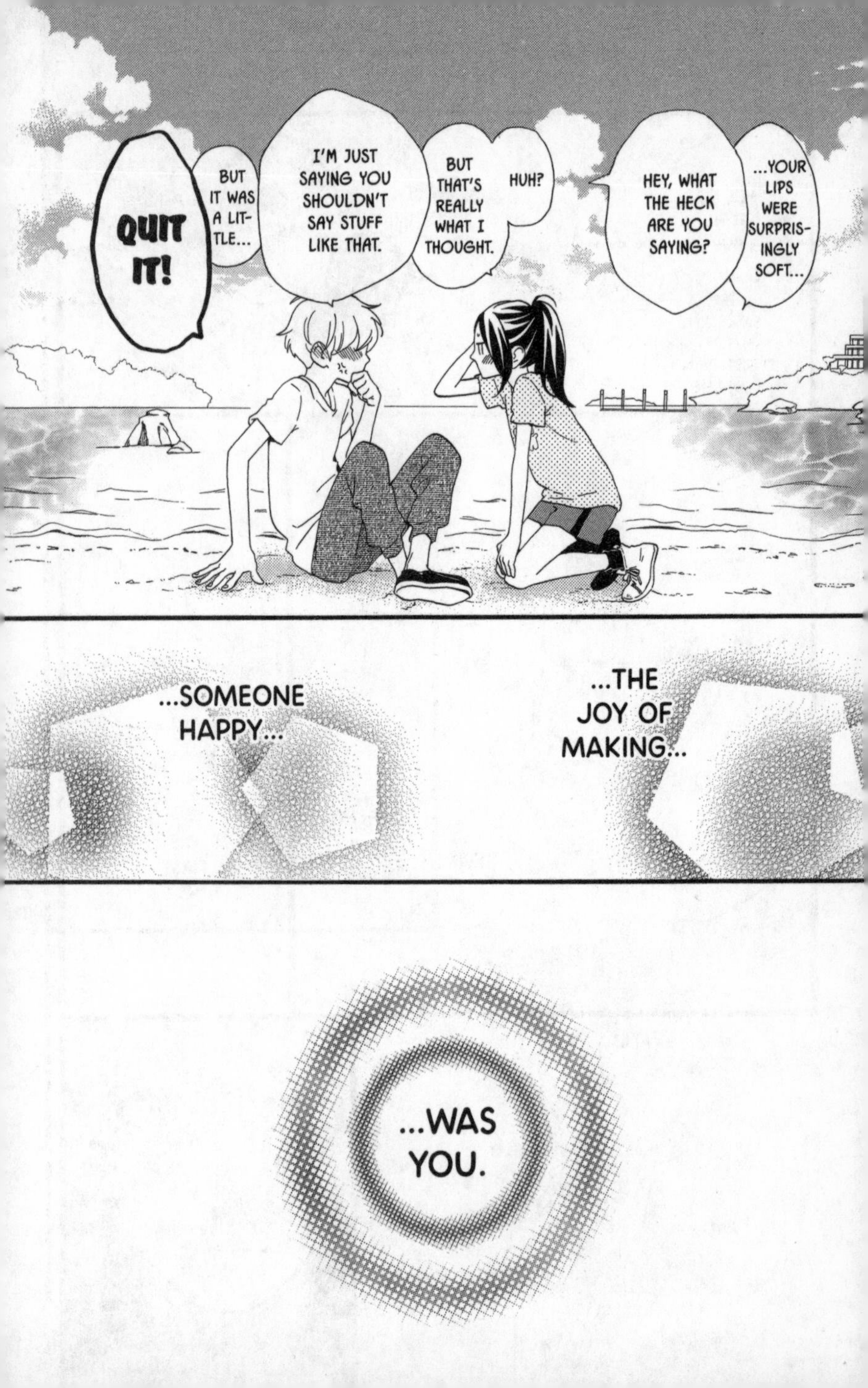
...YOUR LIPS WERE SURPRISINGLY SOFT...
HEY, WHAT THE HECK ARE YOU SAYING?
HUH?
BUT THAT'S REALLY WHAT I THOUGHT.
I'M JUST SAYING YOU SHOULDN'T SAY STUFF LIKE THAT.
BUT IT WAS A LITTLE...
QUIT IT!
...THE JOY OF MAKING...
...SOMEONE HAPPY...
...WAS YOU.

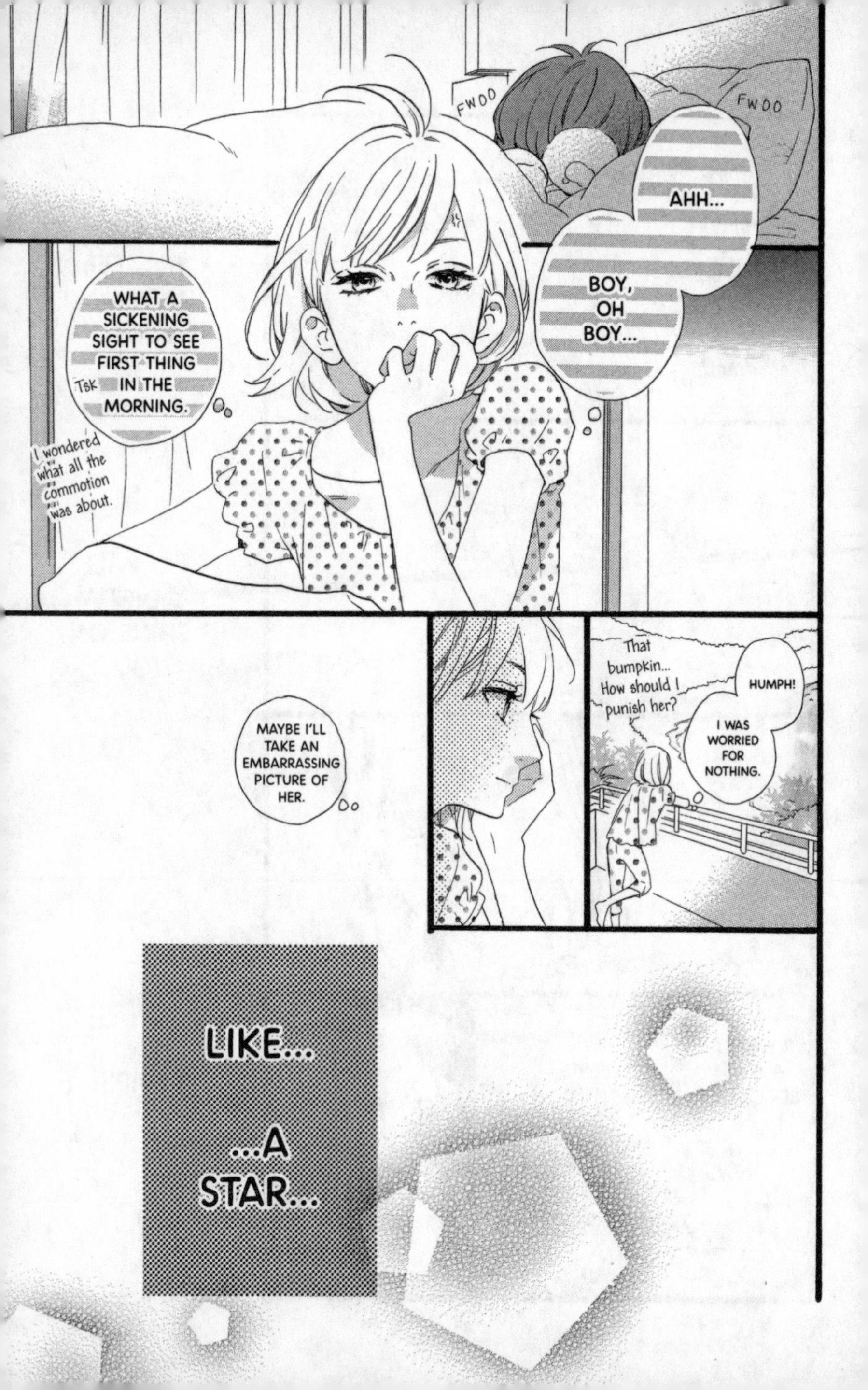
FWOO
FWOO
AHH...
BOY, OH BOY...
WHAT A SICKENING SIGHT TO SEE FIRST THING IN THE MORNING.
Tsk
I wondered what all the commotion was about.
HUMPH! I WAS WORRIED FOR NOTHING.
That bumpkin... How should I punish her?
MAYBE I'LL TAKE AN EMBARRASSING PICTURE OF HER.
LIKE...
...A STAR...

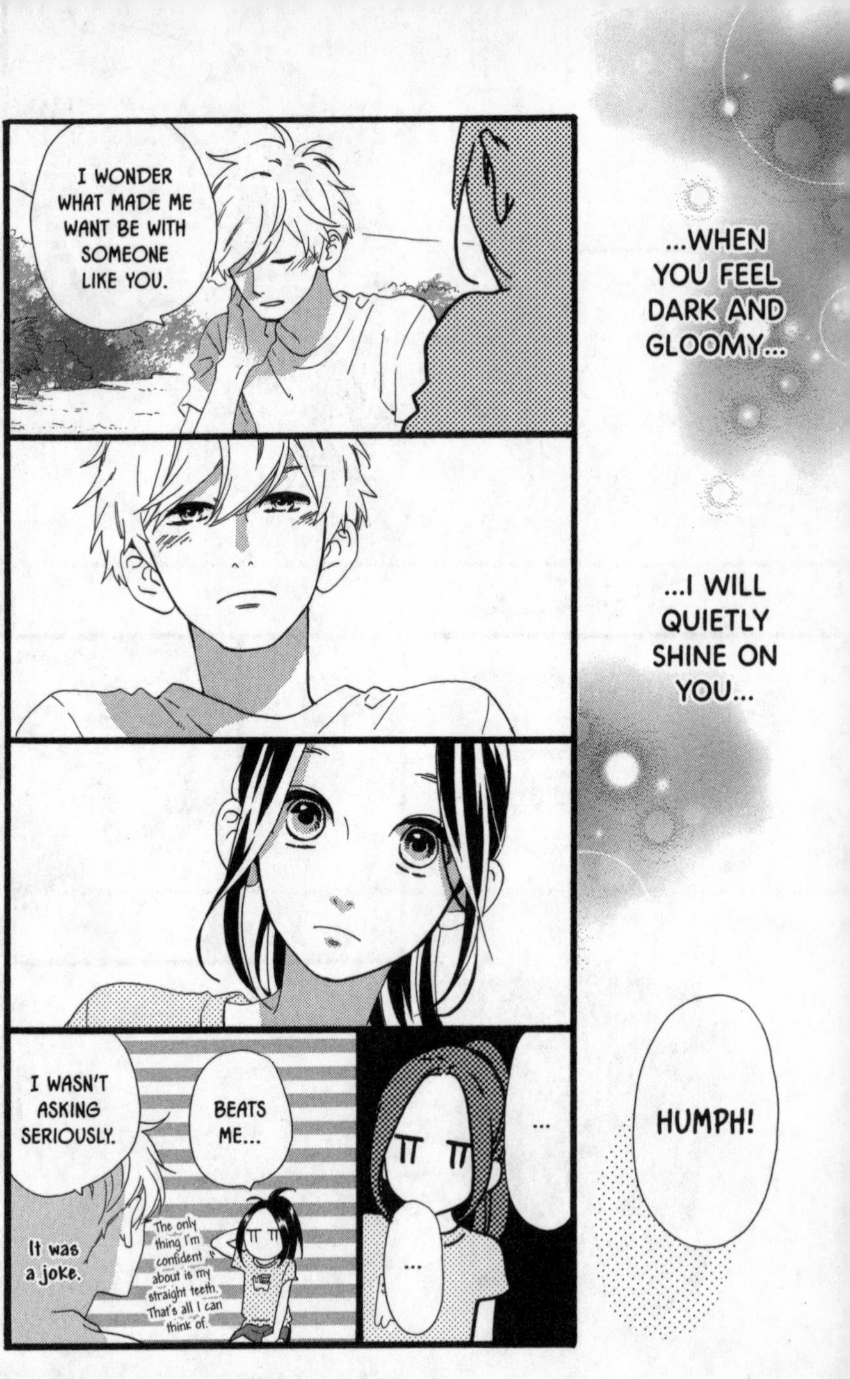
...WHEN YOU FEEL DARK AND GLOOMY...
I WONDER WHAT MADE ME WANT BE WITH SOMEONE LIKE YOU.
...I WILL QUIETLY SHINE ON YOU...
HUMPH!
...
...
BEATS ME...
The only thing I'm confident about is my straight teeth. That's all I can think of.
I WASN'T ASKING SERIOUSLY.
It was a joke.

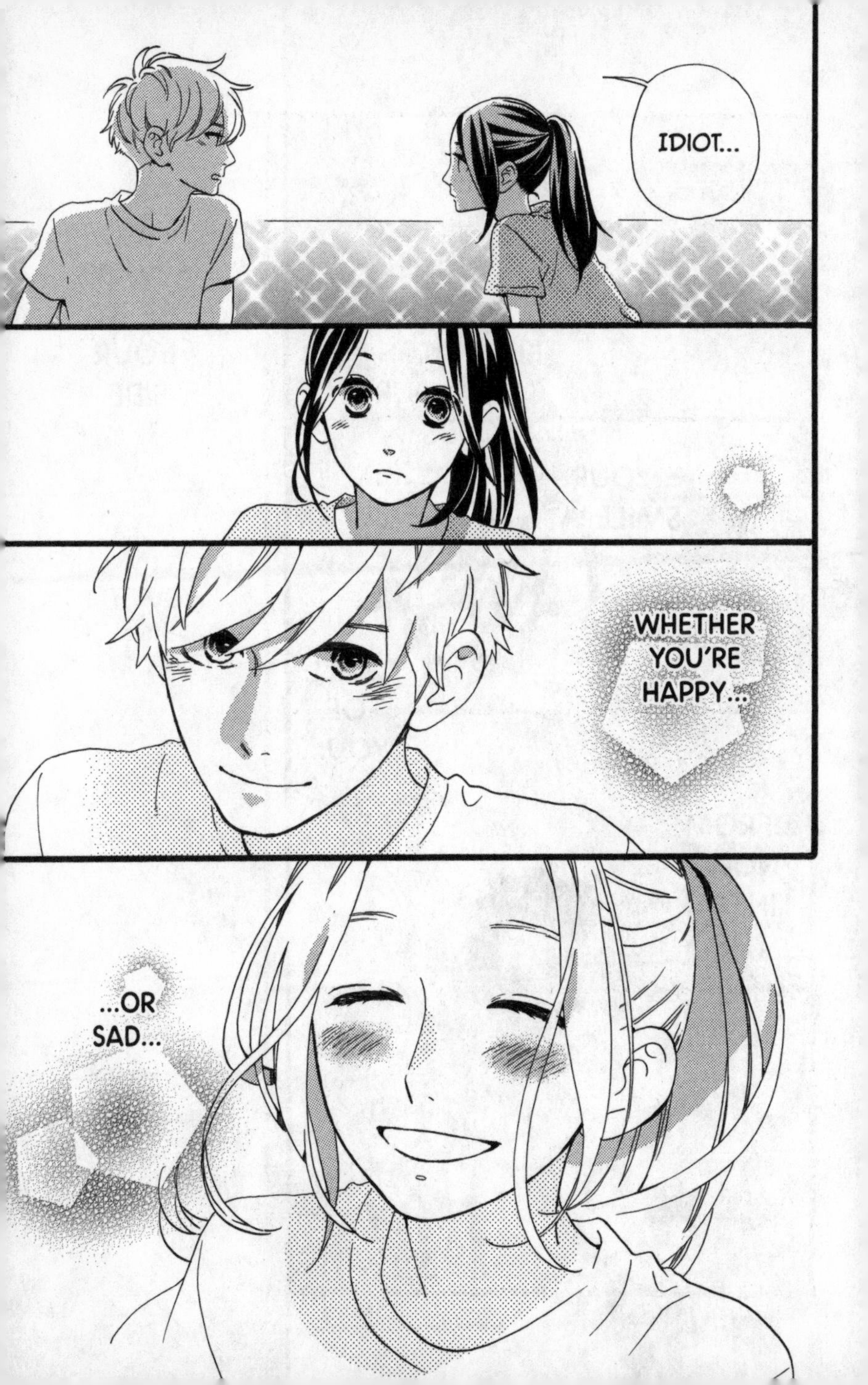
IDIOT...
WHETHER YOU'RE HAPPY...
...OR SAD...

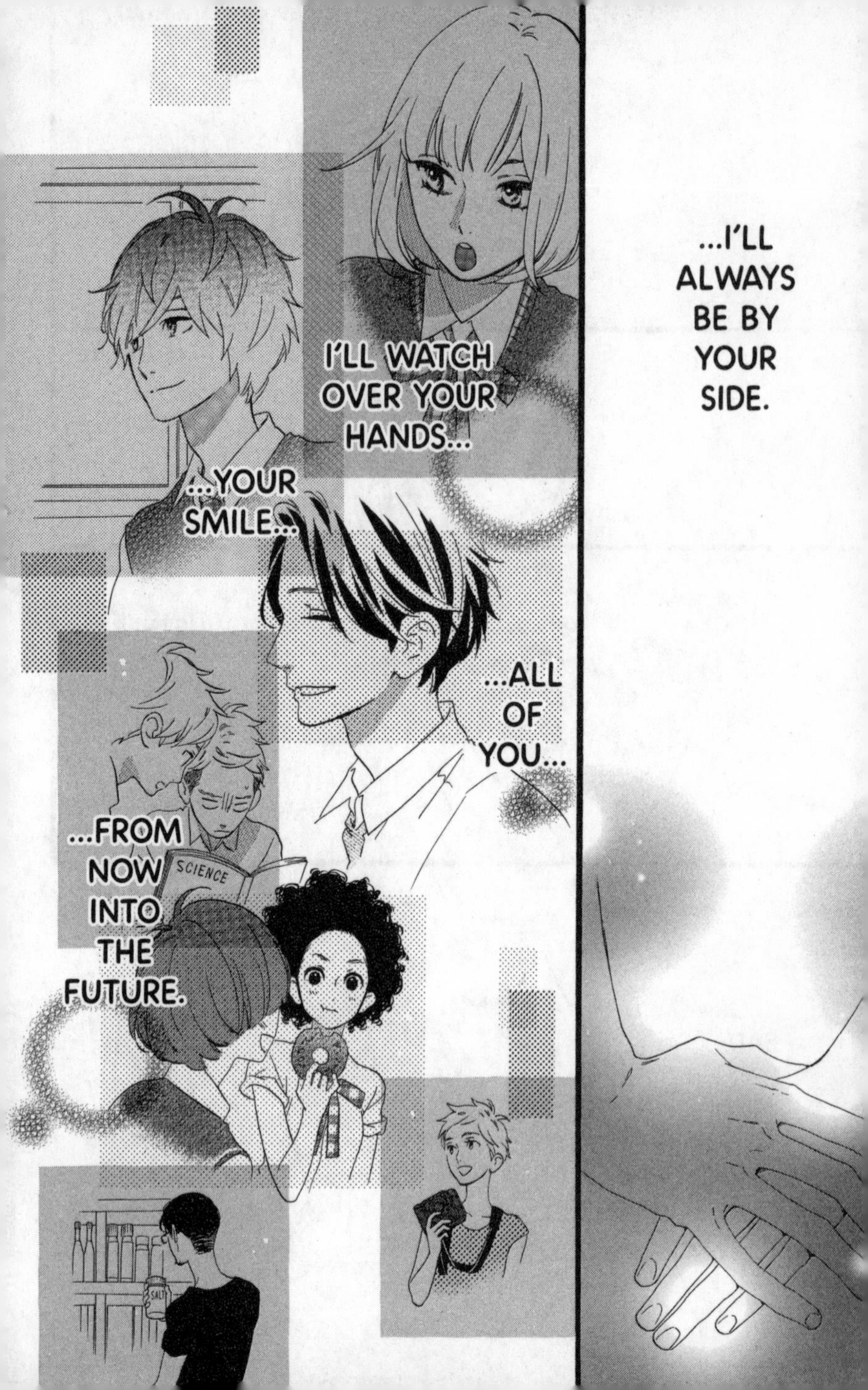
...I'LL ALWAYS BE BY YOUR SIDE.
I'LL WATCH OVER YOUR HANDS...
...YOUR SMILE...
...ALL OF YOU...
...FROM NOW INTO THE FUTURE.
SCIENCE

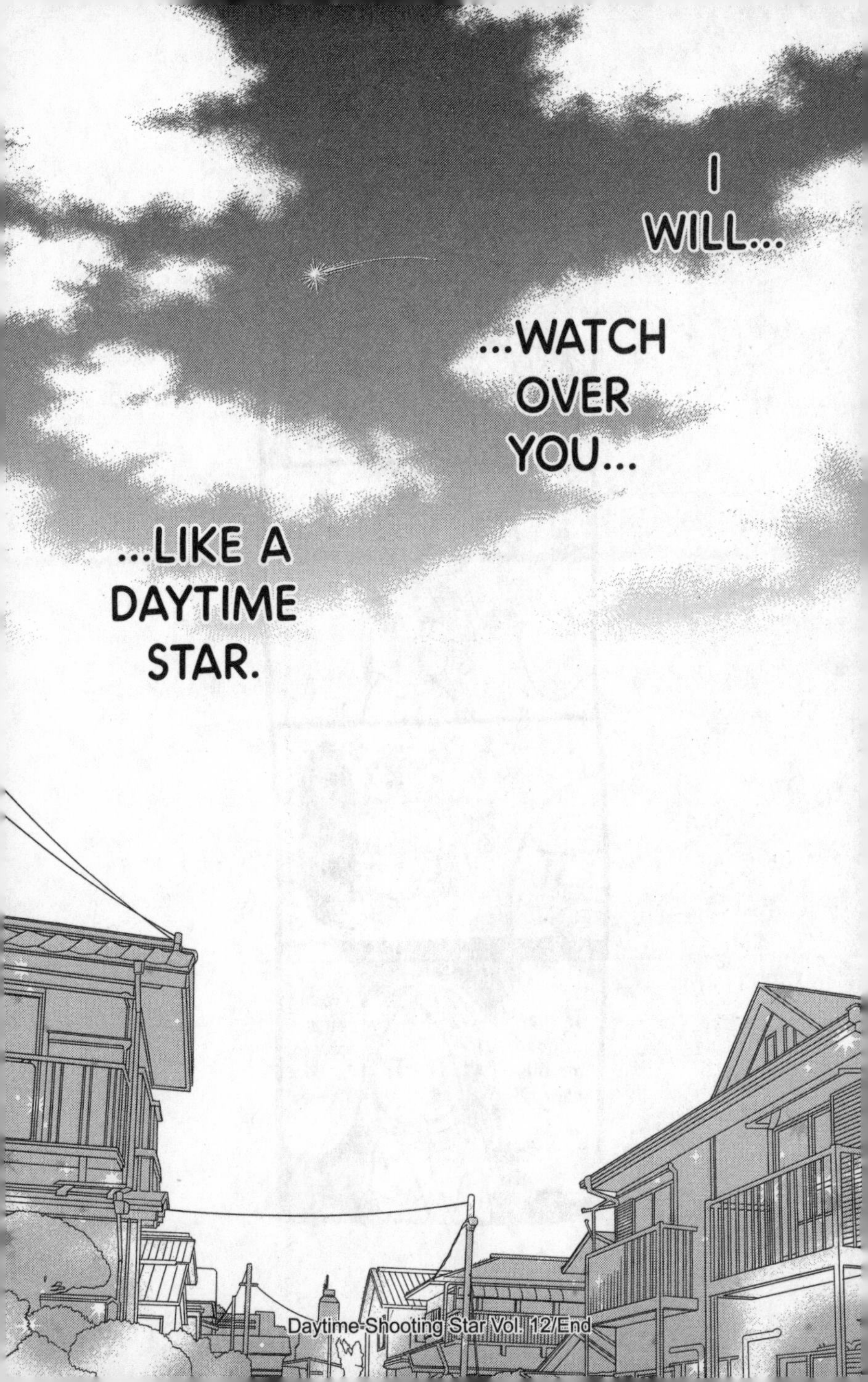
I WILL...
...WATCH OVER YOU...
...LIKE A DAYTIME STAR.
Daytime Shooting Star Vol. 12/End

By the way...

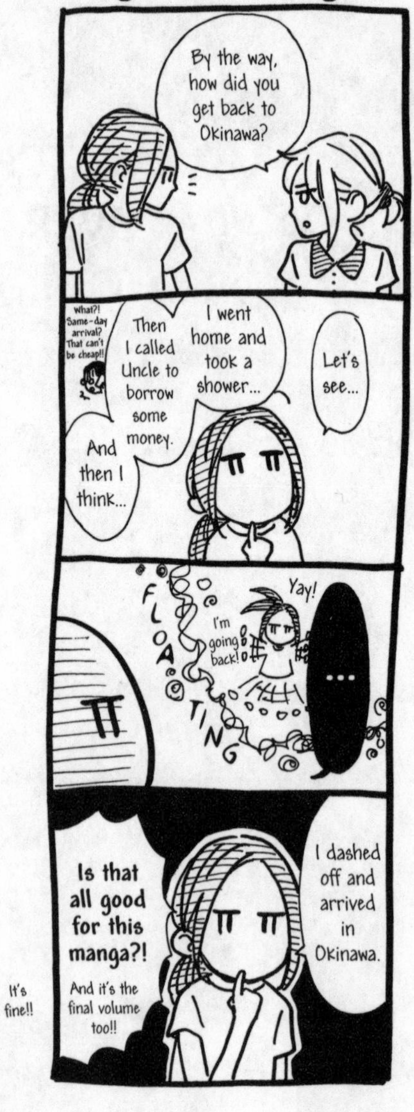

By the way, how did you get back to Okinawa?
Let's see...
I went home and took a shower...
Then I called Uncle to borrow some money.
And then I think...
What?! Same-day arrival? That can't be cheap!!
Yay!
...
I'm going back!
FLOATING
I dashed off and arrived in Okinawa.
Is that all good for this manga?!
And it's the final volume too!!
It's fine!!

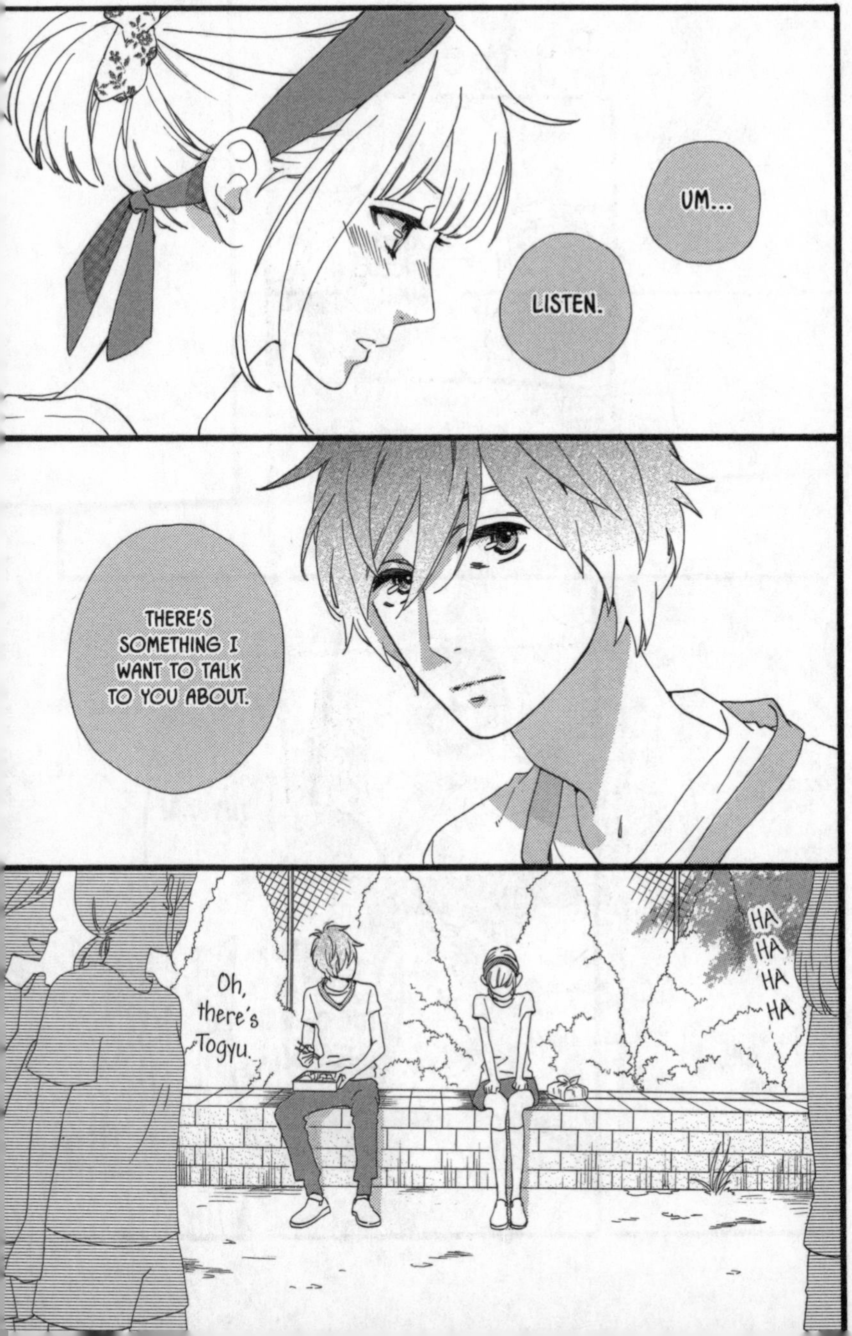
UM...
LISTEN.
THERE'S SOMETHING I WANT TO TALK TO YOU ABOUT.
HA HA HA HA
Oh, there's Togyu.

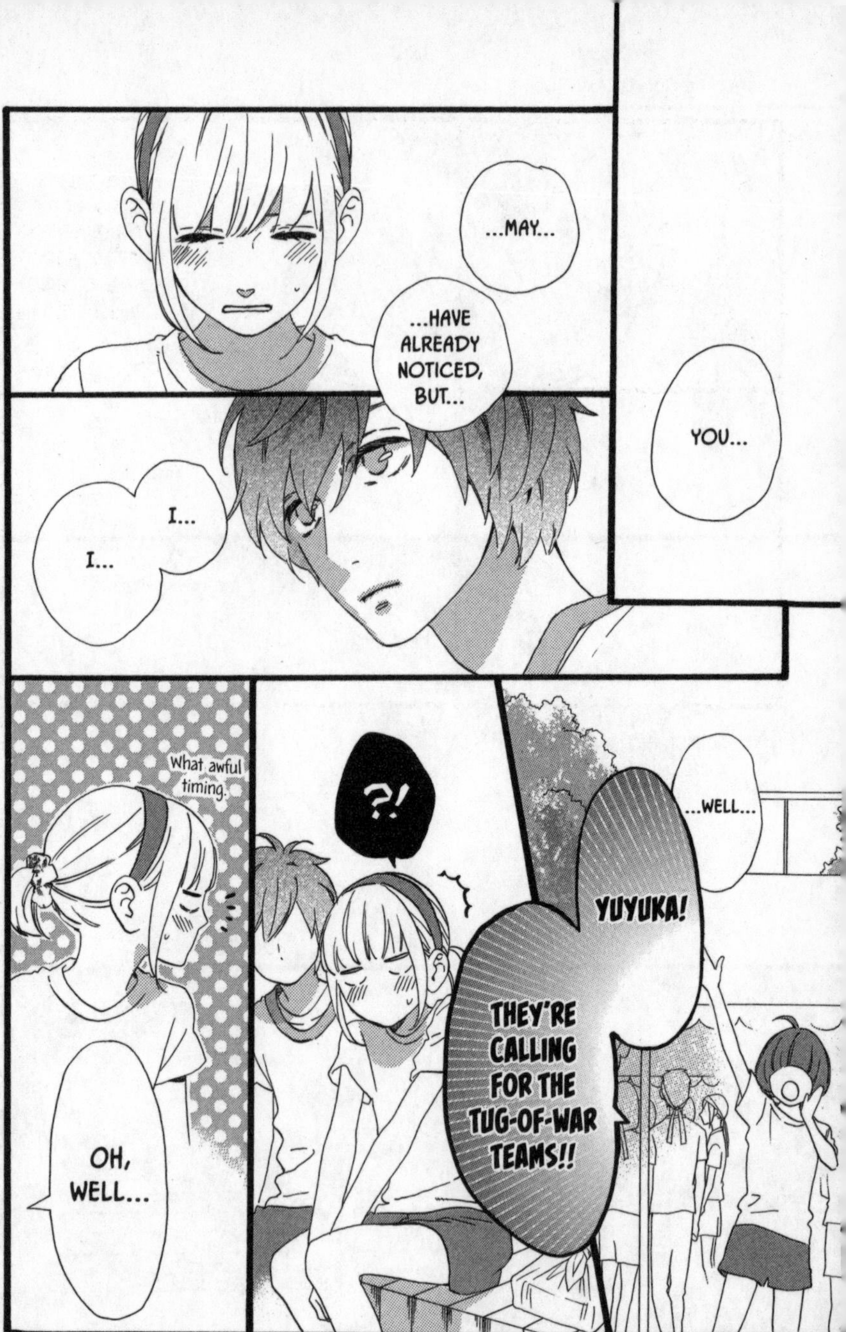
YOU...
...MAY...
...HAVE ALREADY NOTICED, BUT...
I...
I...
...WELL...
YUYUKA!
THEY'RE CALLING FOR THE TUG-OF-WAR TEAMS!!
?!
What awful timing.
OH, WELL...

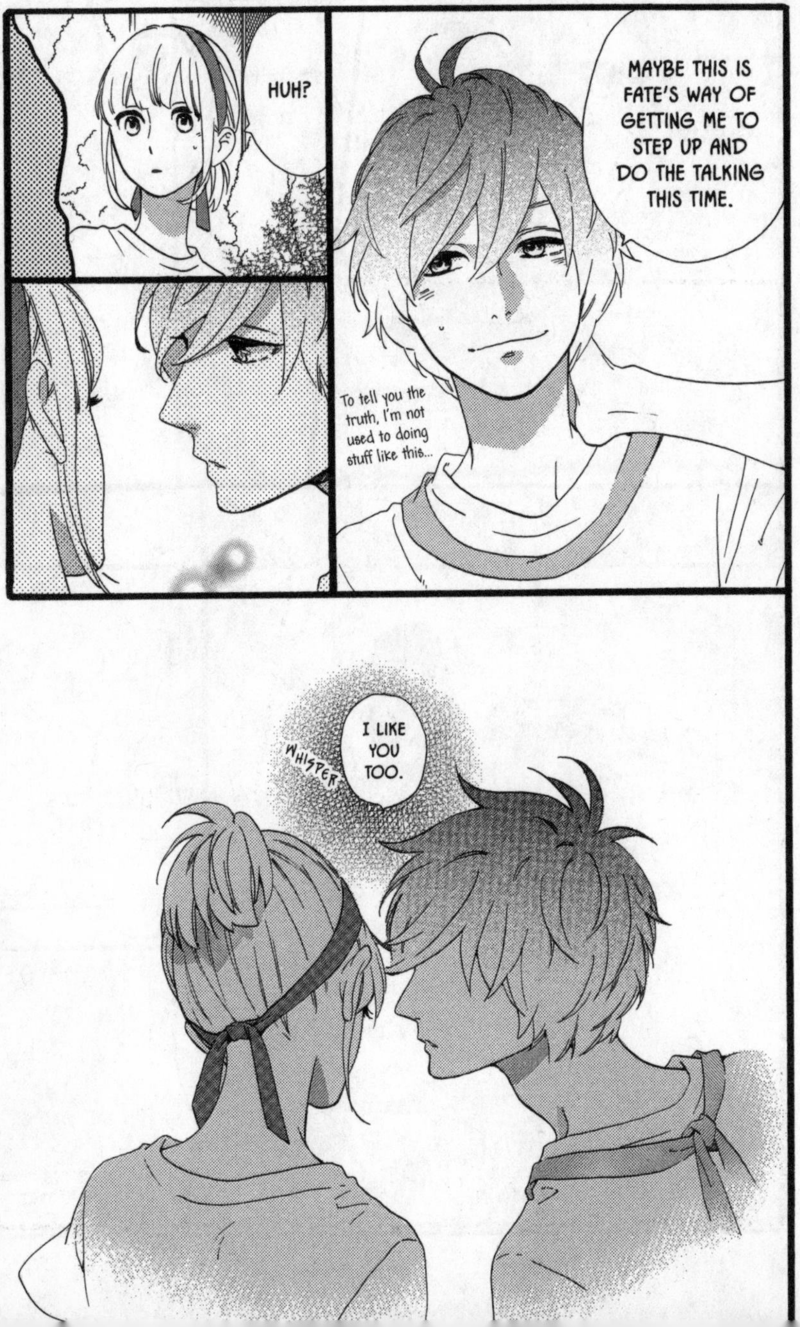
MAYBE THIS IS FATE'S WAY OF GETTING ME TO STEP UP AND DO THE TALKING THIS TIME.
To tell you the truth, I'm not used to doing stuff like this...
HUH?
I LIKE YOU TOO.
WHISPER

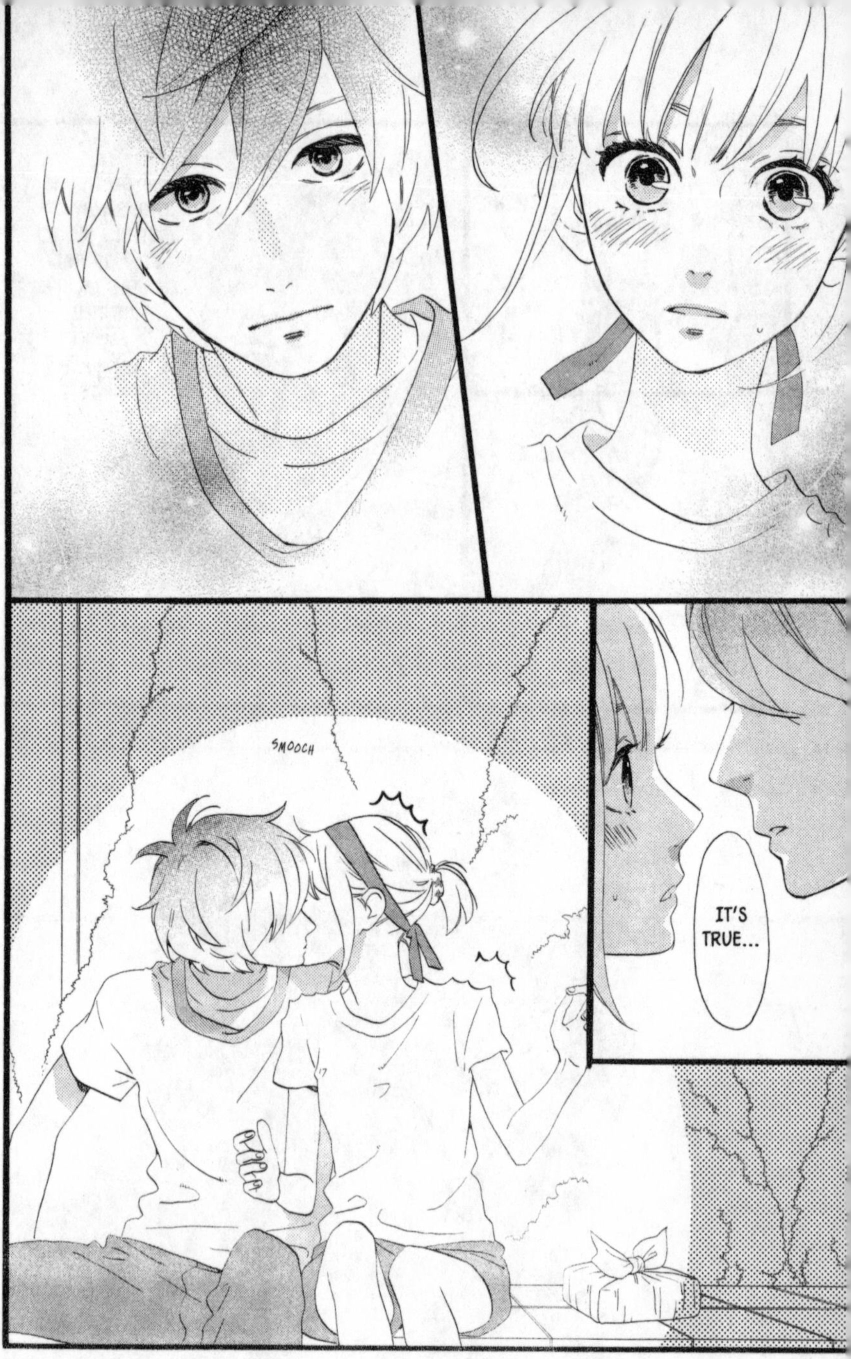
IT'S TRUE...
SMOOCH

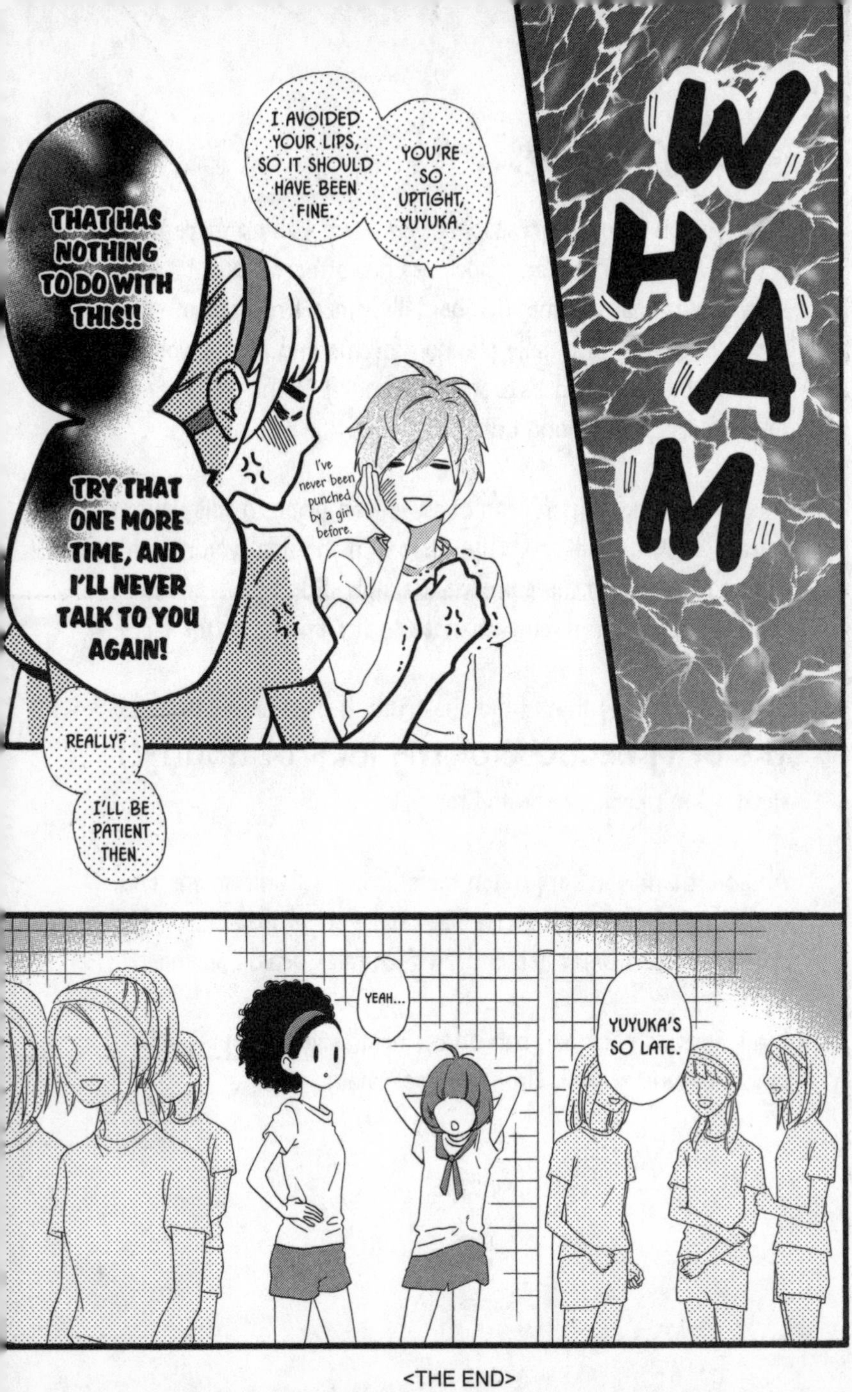
WHAM
YOU'RE SO UPTIGHT, YUYUKA.
I AVOIDED YOUR LIPS, SO IT SHOULD HAVE BEEN FINE.
THAT HAS NOTHING TO DO WITH THIS!!
I've never been punched by a girl before.
TRY THAT ONE MORE TIME, AND I'LL NEVER TALK TO YOU AGAIN!
REALLY?
I'LL BE PATIENT THEN.
YUYUKA'S SO LATE.
YEAH...

<THE END>

And so...

How did you enjoy *Daytime Shooting Star*? I think there may be a lot of you yelling, "Yamamori, get out of here," but it's true. This is our final volume. (Incidentally, since I ran out of space, the bonus story originally planned for the end of this volume will now be published as a separate book.) Thank you very much for reading along until the end.

By the way, the Twitter promotion we ran prior to this volume's release was done to drum up interest in the final volume. It has nothing to do with the storyline. I simply didn't have enough time to make last-minute changes to the ending of the story. TRULY

Some of you may think I hid the truth. If it came off that way, **it's only because of my lack of ability!!** Please don't criticize me too much.

And so, thank you very much for sticking with me to the end. I still can't believe the series has finally come to a close. I'm bummed that I won't get to draw Suzume's braids anymore.

I will work as hard as I can on my next series. I hope you'll read that one as well. Until we meet again...

February 2015